The Works of John Dryden

General Editors

EDWARD NILES HOOKER

H. T. SWEDENBERG, JR.

VOLUME ONE

EDITORS

Edward Niles Hooker   H. T. Swedenberg, Jr.

TEXTUAL EDITOR

Vinton A. Dearing

ASSOCIATE EDITORS

Frederick M. Carey   Godfrey Davies

Hugh G. Dick   Samuel H. Monk

John Harrington Smith

VOLUME I

The Works
of John Dryden

Poems 1649-1680

University of California Press

Berkeley and Los Angeles

1956

UNIVERSITY OF CALIFORNIA PRESS
Berkeley and Los Angeles, California

CAMBRIDGE UNIVERSITY PRESS
London, England

The copy texts of this edition have been drawn in the
main from the Dryden Collection of the
William Andrews Clark Memorial Library

To

Robert Gordon Sproul
on the
Twenty-fifth Anniversary
of His Inauguration
as President of the
University of California

Preface

Some years ago the idea of editing the works of Dryden took hold upon us with a certain insidious compulsion, an insistency which not even the long vista of eighteen volumes in the Scott-Saintsbury edition could entirely quell. We cannot say that we were not properly warned. One of our friends, herself a distinguished scholar who had survived a spell of editing, intimated that that way madness lies, and she left us no reason to suppose that she was alluding to lines 163–164 in Absalom and Achitophel. *Perhaps the charm could have been broken if the poems, essays, and plays had not yielded fresh enjoyment on each successive reading.*

But the decision to edit the works anew rests ultimately on two main considerations. First, no scholarly edition of the complete works has ever appeared; and, in fact, no full edition of any sort has been attempted since the Scott-Saintsbury printing was completed in 1893. Separate editions of poems, plays, and critical essays, as well as numerous selections from the poems, have been published in the past five decades and have served their readers well. But they have fallen short of the need in that they have offered faulty texts, or have provided an inadequate commentary, or have treated poems, plays, and essays in isolation. Partly as a result, the critical appreciation of Dryden as an artist lies in a somewhat deplorable state. This is not to deny that the admiration for his art, shared by Congreve, Pope, Gray, Dr. Johnson, Byron, Scott, and many another eminent man of letters, has been a living influence for two and a half centuries. In fact, our own time has seen a quickening of interest in his writings. In some measure Dryden has shared the acclaim given the "metaphysical" and ratiocinative poets of the seventeenth century. He has been admired for his strength of line, his firmness of control, his "logical structure," and his fine sense of language. T. S. Eliot has expressed the opinion that Dryden established standards for English verse "which it is desperate to ignore." And some of the more enthusiastic of Auden's critics have acknowledged his brilliance by calling him the Dryden of our age. Yet it has been possible for readers to think of Dryden as a journalist of extraordinary skill, strangely fascinating despite an alleged lack of sensibility and depth. Perhaps the greatest shortcoming in the criticism of Dryden has been its tendency to generalize about his life on the basis of a small acquaintance with his poems, and to deduce conclusions about his poems from a set of misapprehensions about his life.

The second consideration which seemed to justify a new edition was the growing concern with Dryden in the realm of scholarship, together with the wealth of learning now at hand, ready to be applied. To the noble work of Dr. Johnson, Malone, Scott, Saintsbury, Christie, Firth, Noyes, Raleigh, Verrall, Ker, and others, the past three decades have added handsomely with the contributions of such men as Bredvold, Macdonald, Osborn, Nichol Smith, Eliot, Van Doren, and Ward—to name only a few. As a result, the modern editor starts with a store of riches provided for him, almost enough to lull him into a false security.

In our edition we have gratefully availed ourselves of all the helps which the bounty of our predecessors and our contemporaries has laid up. But we have felt a challenge to do more, believing that a new edition should make its way by a fresh investigation of every work, of the intent behind it, of the art that formed it, and of its relations both to the thought and artistic development of the writer and to the culture in which he was nourished. That we have consistently succeeded in this aim, we shall be the last to pretend; and we are sufficiently conscious of how much remains to exercise the learning, taste, and ingenuity of Dryden's editors and critics in the future. Yet a good deal has emerged—enough, in fact, to confront us with a difficult problem of excision. Out of the mass of information which we have collected we have tried to select the materials and points of view that seemed most likely to increase the reader's understanding and enjoyment of Dryden's works. In a few instances we have even allowed a trace of our own enjoyment to intrude. Where we have erred through blindness or a faltering sense of proportion, we trust that our very frailties will serve as an in-

vitation for other students of Dryden to undertake comment and criticism more worthy of their subject.

Our edition will reprint all of Dryden's works—poems, plays, and prose—with the exception of the letters, which are available in Ward's edition. The critical essays which originally appeared as prefaces or dedications to poems or plays will be reprinted with those poems or plays to which they properly belong. Dramatic prologues and epilogues written for the plays of other writers will be printed with the poems, but grouped together at the end of the text in the volumes to which their date assigns them. Otherwise all works in each of the three categories will be arranged chronologically and printed in consecutively numbered volumes; the poems and prose pieces generally in the order of their original publication, the plays generally in order of their production in the theater.

We have aimed at a conservative, critical text, bringing us as close to what Dryden actually wrote as the techniques of modern textual criticism enable us to come; the principles on which the text of the poems is based are briefly stated in the introduction to the Textual Notes of Volume I. Our commentary is designed to help intelligent students and cultivated readers generally, but at the same time to provide for the needs of scholars. For each work the Commentary presents an introduction containing what impresses us as the salient relevant facts; but it stops short of drawing all possible inferences from the detailed notes on specific passages which follow. For certain poems we have supplied, at the end of the introduction, a discussion of the verse, in which we do not profess to give a complete or systematic analysis so much as to call attention to changing techniques or techniques of special interest to the poem in question—a treatment fragmentary and perhaps even tinged with willfulness. By a system of cross references we attempt to avoid repetitiousness in the notes. A topic that is woven into several works is given a more or less extensive treatment in the Commentary on that work where it may most appropriately be developed. For example, Dryden's attitude toward the Dutch *is dealt with in the Commentary on* Amboyna, *his use of technical terms and concepts drawn from the art of painting is discussed in the Commentary on the* Parallel of Poetry and Painting, *and his attitude toward the ideas of Hobbes is summarized in the Commentary on* The State of Innocence.

Though each volume is designed to be reasonably complete, the method of cross reference and of centering a topic for discussion in one place means a limited interdependence. In Volume I a certain incompleteness and disproportion have been almost inevitable. Because the poems required unusually heavy annotation, the notes on the two critical essays are not fully developed. But as the more important topics in them attracted Dryden's attention in later essays, we shall take the opportunity of discussing them in subsequent volumes. Again, the general discussion of the prologues and epilogues, so fascinatingly different in language and style from the other nondramatic poems, had to be deferred to a later volume.

A few peculiarities in our treatment of the notes should perhaps be mentioned. In the Commentary italics are generally omitted in all quotations; the ligatures æ and œ are printed as separate letters; and Latin sentences and verse lines are begun with lower case letters. All quotations from Dryden's critical essays, used in the Commentary, are taken from the first editions and will appear in subsequent volumes of this edition, but for temporary convenience we have given the reference to W. P. Ker's edition whenever the essays quoted are contained therein. Similarly our quotations from Dryden's plays are taken from the first editions, but we have given references to the Scott-Saintsbury edition of the Works, *which is widely available. Quotations from Johnson's* Life of Dryden *are taken from Volume VI of the* Works, *ed. Murphy (London, 1824), but for the convenience of the reader references are given to G. Birkbeck Hill's edition of the* Lives of the Poets. *In a few instances we have cited editions other than the standard ones, especially when the so-called standard edition proved inadequate.*

The General Editors are responsible for the plan of this edi-

tion of the poems, but they could not have ventured upon it without the assurance of help from other scholars here and elsewhere. Through the course of the work on Volume I we have been particularly indebted to six associates whose contributions have been extensive and invaluable. Vinton A. Dearing bore the responsibility of editing the text; and John Harrington Smith contributed the Commentary on the prologues and epilogues. Godfrey Davies prepared many of the notes on the historical and political background, and generously served as consultant in all matters related to this field of learning. In like manner Hugh G. Dick contributed notes on science and technology and acted as consultant on these and other lores. Samuel H. Monk supplied the notes on allusions to the art of painting, and some of the notes on optics. And Frederick M. Carey supervised all notes having to do with Dryden's knowledge and use of the ancient classics. The General Editors raised questions and themselves answered a great many of them; and they took the responsibility of synthesis and interpretation, of adding and subtracting to bring the materials to some semblance of balance and form. All oversights, inaccuracies, eccentricities, and downright blunders are to be laid solely to their charge.

In the editorial work on Volume I we have incurred a number of specific debts for which a specific acknowledgment is an inadequate return. Macdonald's bibliography has been an indispensable source of information. Sigurd Hustvedt has encouraged the undertaking from the start, and, in addition to collating texts in the early stages of the work and supervising the making of transcripts of the poems, has assisted in gathering illustrations for the notes. W. B. Gardner supplied us with typescripts of prologues and epilogues which he made from texts at the University of Texas, and allowed us to read his commentary on them before it was printed in his recent edition. Linda Van Norden placed at our disposal an exhaustive study of the relation of Dryden's translations in Ovid's Epistles to earlier English translations. William Eshelman first called attention to the common phrases in the many poems welcoming *the return of Charles in 1660. Alexander Chorney has with admirable resourcefulness turned up innumerable illustrations to clarify obscure or difficult passages. Summaries of all comments by scholars and former editors of Dryden on specific poems were prepared and arranged by Barbara M. Perkins.*

Among the many others who came to our aid as research assistants or voluntary workers are Jane Robinson, Gertrude Ruhnka, Maren-Sofie Rostvig, William Saunders, John Thygerson, Dorothy Mitchell, Maximillian Novak, Geneva Nibbe, Vada Pinnell, and Mildred Jordan.

For the considerable help given us by friends who have read the Commentary in manuscript we also wish to express our gratitude: to John Butt, Hallett Smith, and Slava Klima—and in extraordinary measure to James M. Osborn, who freely opened the remarkable stores of his learning for our use.

It is scarcely conceivable that we could have undertaken this work had it not been for the late William Andrews Clark, Jr., whose humane learning and public-spirited generosity prompted him to gather his superb collection of Dryden and then to pass it on to the University of California; and had it not been for Regent Edward A. Dickson and his associates, through whose good offices the William Andrews Clark Memorial Library became an important functioning part of the university.

Like all other scholars we are deeply in debt to library staffs, and we wish to convey our thanks particularly to those of the Huntington, Clark, Folger, and University of California, Los Angeles, libraries. Dr. Louis B. Wright, Director of the Folger Shakespeare Library, has for years interested himself in our edition and encouraged us in various ways; and Dr. Lawrence Clark Powell, Director of the Clark Library, has never failed to act when he could facilitate our labors.

The staff of the University of California Press, and in particular Mr. Glenn Gosling, have striven valiantly to rescue us from error and inconsistency.

Finally we must acknowledge our appreciation for financial aid: to Henry Allen Moe and the trustees of the John Simon

Guggenheim Memorial Foundation for fellowships granted to both of us; to the trustees of Amherst College for grants-in-aid which made it possible to work with the Dryden collection at the Folger Shakespeare Library; and to President Robert Gordon Sproul and the Research Committee of the University of California, Los Angeles, for research grants in support of the edition.

E. N. H.
H. T. S., JR.

Los Angeles
May 1953

Contents

Illustrations

POEMS 1649–1680

Upon the Death of the Lord Hastings

MUST Noble *Hastings* Immaturely die,
    (The Honour of his ancient Family?)
    Beauty and Learning thus together meet,
To bring a *Winding* for a *Wedding-sheet?*
Must *Vertue* prove *Death*'s Harbinger? Must She,
With him expiring, feel Mortality?
Is *Death* (Sin's wages) Grace's now? shall Art
Make us more Learned, onely to depart?
If Merit be Disease, if Vertue Death;
10 To be Good, Not to be; who'd then bequeath
Himself to Discipline? Who'd not esteem
Labour a Crime, Study Self-murther deem?
Our *Noble Youth* now have pretence to be
Dunces securely, Ign'rant healthfully.
Rare Linguist! whose Worth speaks it self, whose Praise,
Though not his Own, all Tongues Besides do raise:
Then Whom, Great *Alexander* may seem Less;
Who conquer'd Men, but not their Languages.
In his mouth Nations speak; his Tongue might be
20 Interpreter to *Greece, France, Italy.*
His native Soyl was the Four parts o' th' Earth;
All *Europe* was too narrow for his Birth.
A young Apostle; and (with rev'rence may
I speak'it) inspir'd with gift of Tongues, as They.
Nature gave him, a Childe, what Men in vain
Oft strive, by Art though further'd, to obtain.
His Body was an Orb, his sublime Soul
Did move on Vertue's and on Learning's Pole:
Whose Reg'lar Motions better to our view,
30 Then *Archimedes* Sphere, the Heavens did shew.
Graces and Vertues, Languages and Arts,

Beauty and Learning, fill'd up all the parts.
Heav'ns Gifts, which do, like falling Stars, appear
Scatter'd in Others; all, as in their Sphear,
Were fix'd and conglobate in 's Soul; and thence
Shone th'row his Body, with sweet Influence;
Letting their Glories so on each Limb fall,
The whole Frame render'd was Celestial.
Come, learned *Ptolomy,* and trial make,
40 If thou this Hero's Altitude canst take;
But that transcends thy skill; thrice happie all,
Could we but prove thus Astronomical.
Liv'd *Tycho* now, struck with this Ray, (which shone
More bright i' th' Morn, then others beam at Noon)
He'd take his *Astrolabe,* and seek out here
What new Star 't was did gild our Hemisphere.
Replenish'd then with such rare Gifts as these,
Where was room left for such a Foul Disease?
The Nations sin hath drawn that Veil, which shrouds
50 Our Day-spring in so sad benighting Clouds.
Heaven would no longer trust its Pledge; but thus
Recall'd it; rapt its *Ganymede* from us.
Was there no milder way but the Small Pox,
The very Filth'ness of *Pandora*'s Box?
So many Spots, like *næves,* our *Venus* soil?
One Jewel set off with so many a Foil?
Blisters with pride swell'd; which th'row 's flesh did sprout
Like Rose-buds, stuck i' th' Lily-skin about.
Each little Pimple had a Tear in it,
60 To wail the fault its rising did commit:
Who, Rebel-like, with their own Lord at strife,
Thus made an Insurrection 'gainst his Life.
Or were these Gems sent to adorn his Skin,
The Cab'net of a richer Soul within?
No Comet need foretel his Change drew on,
Whose Corps might seem a *Constellation.*
O had he di'd of old, how great a strife

Had been, who from his Death should draw their Life?
Who should, by one rich draught, become what ere
70 *Seneca, Cato, Numa, Cæsar,* were:
Learn'd, Vertuous, Pious, Great; and have by this
An universal *Metempsuchosis.*
Must all these ag'd Sires in one Funeral
Expire? All die in one so young, so small?
Who, had he liv'd his life out, his great Fame
Had swoln 'bove any *Greek* or *Romane* Name.
But hasty Winter, with one blast, hath brought
The hopes of Autumn, Summer, Spring, to nought.
Thus fades the Oak i' th' sprig, i' th' blade the Corn;
80 Thus, without Young, this *Phœnix* dies, new born.
Must then old three-legg'd gray-beards with their Gout,
Catarrhs, Rheums, Aches, live three Ages out?
Times Offal, onely fit for th' Hospital,
Or t' hang an Antiquaries room withal;
Must Drunkards, Lechers, spent with Sinning, live
With such helps as Broths, Possits, Physick give?
None live, but such as should die? Shall we meet
With none but Ghostly Fathers in the Street?
Grief makes me rail; Sorrow will force its way;
90 And, Show'rs of Tears, Tempestuous Sighs best lay.
The Tongue may fail; but over-flowing Eyes
Will weep out lasting streams of *Elegies.*

But thou, O *Virgin-Widow,* left alone,
Now thy belov'd, heaven-ravisht *Spouse* is gone,
(Whose skilful Sire in vain strove to apply
Med'cines, when thy Balm was no Remedy)
With greater then *Platonick* love, O wed
His Soul, though not his Body, to thy Bed:
Let that make thee a Mother; bring thou forth
100 Th' *Idea's* of his Vertue, Knowledge, Worth;
Transcribe th' Original in new Copies; give
Hastings o' th' better part: so shall he live

In 's Nobler Half; and the great Grandsire be
Of an Heroick Divine Progenie:
An Issue, which t' Eternity shall last,
Yet but th' Irradiations which he cast.
Erect no *Mausolæums:* for his best
Monument is his Spouses Marble brest.

To John Hoddesdon, on His Divine Epigrams

THOU hast inspir'd me with thy soul, and I
    Who ne're before could ken of **Poetry**
    Am grown so good proficient, I can lend
A line in commendation of my friend;
Yet 'tis but of the second hand, if ought
There be in this, 'tis from thy fancy brought.
Good thief who dar'st Prometheus-like aspire,
And fill thy poems with Celestiall fire:
Enliven'd by these sparks divine, their rayes
10 Adde a bright lustre to thy crown of bayes.
Young Eaglet who thy nest thus soon forsook,
So lofty and divine a course hast took
As all admire, before the down begin
To peep, as yet, upon thy smoother Chin;
And, making heaven thy aim, hast had the grace
To look the sunne of righteousnesse ith' face.
What may we hope, if thou go'st on thus fast!
Scriptures at first; Enthusiasmes at last!
Thou hast commenc'd, betimes, a saint: go on,
20 Mingling Diviner streams with Helicon:
That they who view what Epigrams here be
May learn to make like, in just praise of thee.
Reader, I've done, nor longer will withhold
Thy greedy eyes; looking on this pure gold
Thou'lt know adult'rate copper, which, like this,
Will onely serve to be a foil to his.

---

18 Enthusiasmes] Euthusiasmes O. [This and other sigla are identified in the Textual Notes.]

Letter to Honor Dryden

TO THE FAIRE HANDS OF MADAME HONOR DRYDEN THESE
CRAVE ADMITTANCE.

MADAME

If you have received the lines I sent by the reverend Levite, I doubt
not but they have exceedingly wrought vpon you; for beeing so longe
in a Clergy-mans pocket, assuredly they have acquired more Sanctity
then theire Authour meant them. Alasse Madame for ought I know
they may become a Sermon ere they could arrive at you; and believe
it haveing you for the text it could scarcely proove bad, if it light
vpon one that could handle it indifferently.   but I am so miserable a
preacher that though I have so sweet and copious a subject, I still
fall short in my expressions   And in stead of an vse of thanksgiveing
10 I am allways makeing one of comfort, that I may one day againe have
the happinesse to kisse your faire hand.   but that is a Message I
would not so willingly do by letter as by word of mouth. This is a
point I must confesse I could willingly dwell longer on, and in this
case what ever I say you may confidently take for gospell. But I must
hasten. And indeed Madame (Beloved I had almost sayd) hee had
need hasten who treats of you; for to speake fully to every part of
your excellencyes requires a longer houre then most persons have allotted them. But in a word your selfe hath been the best Expositor
vpon the text of your own worth, in that admirable Comment you
20 wrote vpon it, I meane your incomparable letter. By all thats good
(and you Madame are a great part of my Oath) it hath put mee so
farre besides my selfe that I have scarce patience to write prose.   and
my pen is stealing into verse every time I kisse your letter. I am sure
the poore paper smarts for my Idolatry, which by wearing it continually neere my brest will at last bee burnt and Martyrd in those flames
of adoration it hath kindled in mee. But I forgett Madame, what rarityes your letter came fraught with besides words; You are such a Deity

have scarce patience to write prose. and my
pen is stealing into verse every time I kisse
your letter. I am sure the poore paper smarts
for my Idolatry, which by wearing it continuall‑
neere my brest will at last bee burnt and Mar‑
tyr'd in those flames of adoration it hath kindled
in mee. But I forgett madame what rarityes
your letter came fraught with besides words.
You are such a Deity that commands worship
by providing the Sacrifice: you are pleas'd Ma‑
dam to force mee to write by sending mee Ma‑
terialls, and compell mee to my greatest happinesse.
yet though I highly vallue your magnificent
presents, pardon mee if I must tell the world
they are but imperfect Emblemes of your beauty,
For the while and red of waxe and paper are
but shaddowes of that vermillion and snowe
in your lips and forehead. And the silver of
the Inkehorne if it presume to vye whitenesse
with your purer skinne must confesse it selfe
blacker then the liquour it containes. what
then do I more then retrieve your own gaifts?
and present you that paper adulterated with
blotts which you gave spotlesse?

For since twas mine the white hath lost its hew
To show twas n'ere it selfe but whilst in you;
The Virgin Waxe hath blusht it selfe to red
Since it with mee hath lost its Maydenhead.

Letter to Honor Dryden (VERSO OF FIRST LEAF)

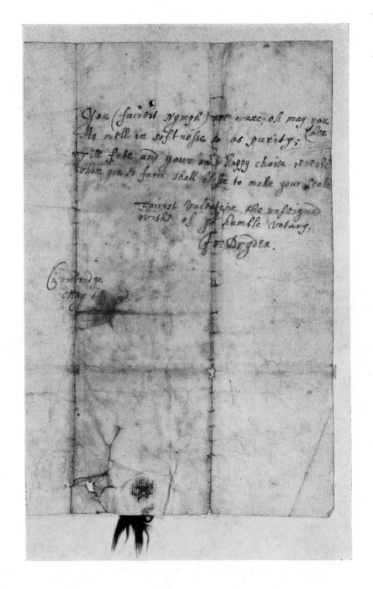

You (fairest Nymph) are waxe, oh may you
As well in softnesse be as purity;
Till fate and your owne happy choice revea
Whom you so farr shall blesse to make your selfe

Fairest Valentine the unfeigned
wish of yr humble Votary.

Jo: Dryden.

Cambridge
May the

Letter to Honor Dryden (RECTO OF SECOND LEAF)

Letter to Honor Dryden (VERSO OF SECOND LEAF)

Madame.

If you have received the lines I sent by the reverend Levite, I doubt not but they have exceedingly wrought vpon you; for being so long in a Clergy-mans pocket, assuredly they have acquired more Sanctity then theire Authour meant them. Alasse Madame, for ought I know they may become a Sermon ere they could arrive at you, and believe it having you for the text it could scarcely prove bad if it light vpon one that could handle it indifferently. but I am so miserable a preacher that though I have so sweet and copious a subject I still fall short in my expressions. And in stead of an vse of thanksgiving I am always makeing one of comfort, that I may one day againe have the happinesse to kisse your faire hand. but that is a message I would not so willingly doe by letter as by word of mouth. This is a point I must confesse I could willingly dwell longer on, and in this case what ever I say you may confidently take for gospell. But I must hasten. And indeed Madame (Beloved I had almost sayd) hee had need hasten who treats of you; for to speake fully to every part of your excellencyes requires a longer houre then most persons have allotted them. But in a word your selfe hath been the best Expositor vpon the text of your own worth, in that admirable Comment you wrote vpon it, I meane your incomparable letter. By all thats good (and you Madame are a great part of my oath) it hath put mee so farre besides my selfe that I

Letter to Honor Dryden (RECTO OF FIRST LEAF)

that commands worship by provideing the Sacrifice: you are pleasd
Madame to force mee to write by sending mee Materialls, and compell
mee to my greatest happinesse. Yet though I highly vallue your
Magnificent presents, pardon mee if I must tell the world they are
but imperfect Emblemes of your beauty; For the white and red of
waxe and paper are but shaddowes of that vermillion and Snowe in
your lips and forehead. And the Silver of the Inkehorne if it presume
to vye whitenesse with your purer skinne, must confesse it selfe
blacker then the liquour it containes. What then do I more then re-
10 trieve your own guifts? and present you that paper adulterated with
blotts which you gave spotlesse?

> For since t'was mine the white hath lost its hiew
> To show t'was n'ere it selfe but whilst in you;
> The Virgin Waxe hath blusht it selfe to red
> Since it with mee hath lost its Maydenhead.
> You (fairest Nymph) are waxe; oh may you bee
> As well in softnesse so as purity;
> Till fate and your ow[n] happy choise reveale
> Whom you so farre shall blesse to make your Seale.

Fairest Valentine the vnfeigned
wishe of yor humble Votary.
Jo: Dryden.

Cambridge
May the 23^d
16[53?]

THREE
POEMS

Upon the Death of his late

HIGHNESSE

OLIVER

LORD PROTECTOR

OF

England, Scotland, and
Ireland.

Written

By { Mr EDM. WALLER.
{ Mr JO. DRYDEN.
{ Mr SPRAT, of *Oxford.*

LONDON,
Printed by *william wilfon,* and are to be fold in
Well-yard neer Little St. *Bartholomew's*
Hoſpitall. 1659.

TITLE PAGE OF THE FIRST EDITION (MACDONALD 3A)

Heroique Stanzas to the Glorious Memory of Cromwell

AND now 'tis time; for their Officious haste,
  Who would before have born him to the sky,
  Like *eager Romans* ere all Rites were past
Did let too soon the *sacred Eagle* fly.
      2.
Though our best notes are treason to his fame
Joyn'd with the loud applause of publique voice;
Since Heav'n, what praise we offer to his name,
Hath render'd too authentick by its choice:
      3.
Though in his praise no Arts can liberall be,
10 Since they whose muses have the highest flown
Add not to his immortall Memorie,
But do an act of friendship to their own:
      4.
Yet 'tis our duty and our interest too
Such monuments as we can build to raise;
Lest all the World prevent what we should do
And claime a *Title* in him by their praise.
      5.
How shall I then begin, or where conclude
To draw a *Fame* so truly *Circular?*
For in a round what order can be shew'd,
20 Where all the parts so *equall perfect* are?
      6.
His *Grandeur* he deriv'd from Heav'n alone,
For he was great e're Fortune made him so;
And Warr's like mists that rise against the Sunne
Made him but greater seem, not greater grow.

---

12 own:] Q6–7; ~ . Q1, F, Q2–5, Q8, O1–3.

7.

No borrow'd Bay's his *Temples* did adorne,
But to our *Crown* he did fresh *Jewells* bring,
Nor was his Vertue poyson'd soon as born
With the too early thoughts of being King.

8.

Fortune (that easie Mistresse of the young
30 But to her auncient servants coy and hard)
Him at that age her favorites rank'd among
When she her best-lov'd *Pompey* did discard.

9.

He, private, mark'd the faults of others sway,
And set as *Sea-mark's* for himself to shun;
Not like rash *Monarch's* who their youth betray
By Acts their Age too late would wish undone.

10.

And yet *Dominion* was not his Designe,
We owe that blessing not to him but Heaven,
Which to faire Acts unsought rewards did joyn,
40 Rewards that lesse to him than us were given.

11.

Our former Cheifs like sticklers of the Warre
First sought t' inflame the Parties, then to poise;
The quarrell lov'd, but did the cause abhorre,
And did not strike to hurt but make a noise.

12.

Warre our consumption was their gainfull trade,
We inward bled whilst they prolong'd our pain:
He fought to end our fighting, and assaid
To stanch the blood by breathing of the vein.

13.

Swift and resistlesse through the Land he past
50 Like that bold *Greek* who did the East subdue;
And made to battails such Heroick haste
As if on wings of victory he flew.

14.

He fought secure of fortune as of fame,
Till by *new maps* the Island might be shown,
Of Conquests which he strew'd where e're he came
Thick as the *Galaxy* with starr's is sown.

15.

His *Palmes* though under weights they did not stand,
Still thriv'd; no *Winter* could his *Laurells* fade;
Heav'n in his Portraict shew'd a Workman's hand
60 And drew it perfect yet without a shade.

16.

Peace was the Prize of all his toyles and care,
Which Warre had banisht and did now restore;
Bolognia's walls thus mounted in the Ayre
To seat themselves more surely then before.

17.

Her safety rescu'd *Ireland* to him owes;
And Treacherous *Scotland* to no int'rest true,
Yet blest that fate which did his Armes dispose
Her Land to Civilize as to subdue.

18.

Nor was he like those *starr's* which only shine
70 When to pale *Mariners* they stormes portend,
He had his calmer influence; and his Mine
Did Love and Majesty together blend.

19.

'Tis true, his Count'nance did imprint an awe,
And naturally all souls to his did bow;
As *Wands of Divination* downward draw
And point to Beds where Sov'raign Gold doth grow.

20.

When past all Offerings to *Feretrian Jove*
He Mars depos'd, and Arms to Gowns made yield,

60   drew] F, Q2–8, O1–3; dtew Q1.
63   walls] Q6–8, O1–3; wall Q1, F, Q2–5.
65   owes;] Q8; ~∧ Q1; ~ , F, Q2–7, O1–3.
66   *Scotland*] F, Q2–8, O1–3; *Seotland* Q1.

Successefull Councells did him soon approve
80 As fit for close *Intrigues,* as open field.

      21.

To suppliant *Holland* he vouchsaf'd a peace,
Our once bold Rivall in the *British Main*
Now tamely glad her unjust claime to cease,
And buy our Friendship with her Idoll gaine.

      22.

Fame of th' asserted Sea through *Europe* blown
Made *France* and *Spaine* ambitious of his Love;
Each knew that side must conquer he would own
And for him fiercely as for Empire strove.

      23.

No sooner was the *French man*'s cause embrac'd
90 Than the light *Mounsire* the grave *Don* outwaigh'd,
His fortune turn'd the Scale where it was cast,
Though *Indian Mines* were in the other layd.

      24.

When absent, yet we conquer'd in his right;
For though some meaner Artist's skill were shown
In mingling colours, or in placing light,
Yet still the *faire Designment* was his own.

      25.

For from all tempers he could service draw;
The worth of each with its alloy he knew;
And as the *Confident* of *Nature* saw
100 How she Complexions did divide and brew.

      26.

Or he their single vertues did survay
By *intuition* in his own large brest,
Where all the rich *Idea's* of them lay,
That were the rule and measure to the rest.

      27.

When such *Heröique Vertue* Heav'n sets out,
The Starrs like *Commons* sullenly obey;

---

81 peace,] F, Q5–8, O1–3; ~ₐ Q1, Q3–4; ~ . Q2.
90 light] F, Q2–8, O1–3; leight Q1.

Because it draines them when it comes about,
And therefore is a taxe they seldome pay.
                    28.
From this high-spring our forraign-Conquests flow
110 Which yet more glorious triumphs do portend,
Since their Commencement to his Armes they owe,
If Springs as high as Fountaines may ascend.
                    29.
He made us *Freemen* of the *Continent*
Whom Nature did like Captives treat before,
To nobler prey's the *English Lyon* sent,
And taught him first in *Belgian walks* to rore.
                    30.
That old unquestion'd Pirate of the Land,
Proud *Rome,* with dread, the fate of *Dunkirk* har'd;
And trembling wish't behind more *Alpes* to stand,
120 Although an *Alexander* were her guard.
                    31.
By his command we boldly crost the Line
And bravely fought where *Southern Starrs* arise,
We trac'd the farre-fetchd Gold unto the mine
And that which brib'd our fathers made our prize.
                    32.
Such was our Prince; yet own'd a soul above
The highest Acts it could produce to show:
Thus poor *Mechanique Arts* in publique moove
Whilst the deep Secrets beyond practice goe.
                    33.
Nor dy'd he when his ebbing Fame went lesse,
130 But when fresh Lawrells courted him to live;
He seem'd but to prevent some new successe;
As if above what triumphs Earth could give.
                    34.
His latest Victories still thickest came
As, neer the *Center,* *Motion* does increase;

117 Land,] F, Q2–8, O1–3; ~ᴧ Q1.

Till he, pres'd down by his own weighty name,
Did, like the *Vestall,* under spoyles decease.

35.

But first the *Ocean* as a tribute sent
That Gyant *Prince* of all her watery Heard,
And th' *Isle* when her *Protecting Genius* went
140 Upon his *Obsequies* loud sighs confer'd.

36.

No Civill broyles have since his death arose,
But *Faction* now by *Habit* does obey:
And *Warrs* have that respect for his repose,
As *Winds* for *Halcyons* when they breed at Sea.

37.

His Ashes in a peacefull Urne shall rest,
His Name a great example stands to show
How strangely high endeavours may be blest,
Where *Piety* and *valour* joyntly goe.

---

138   Heard,] F, Q2; ∼ₐ Q1, Q3–5; ∼ ; Q6–8, O1–3.

To My Honored Friend, Sir Robert Howard

As there is Musick uninform'd by Art
  In those wild Notes, which with a merry heart
  The Birds in unfrequented shades expresse,
Who better taught at home, yet please us lesse:
So in your Verse, a native sweetnesse dwells,
Which shames Composure, and its Art excells.
Singing, no more can your soft numbers grace
Then Paint adds charms unto a beauteous Face.
Yet as when mighty Rivers gently creep,
10 Their even calmnesse does suppose them deep,
Such is your Muse: no Metaphor swell'd high
With dangerous boldnesse lifts her to the sky;
Those mounting Fancies when they fall again,
Shew sand and dirt at bottom do remain.
So firm a strength, and yet withall so sweet,
Did never but in *Sampson*'s Riddle meet.
'Tis strange each line so great a weight should bear,
And yet no signe of toil, no sweat appear.
Either your Art hides Art, as Stoicks feign
20 Then least to feel, when most they suffer pain;
And we, dull souls, admire, but cannot see
What hidden springs within the Engine be:
Or 'tis some happinesse that still pursues
Each act and motion of your gracefull muse.
Or is it Fortune's work, that in your head
The curious *Net that is for fancies spread,
Let's through its Meshes every meaner thought,
While rich Idea's there are onely caught?
Sure that's not all; this is a piece too fair
30 To be the child of Chance, and not of Care.

* *Rete Mirabile.* [Dryden's note.]

28   caught?] ~ . O1–4.

No Atoms casually together hurl'd
Could e're produce so beautifull a world.
Nor dare I such a doctrine here admit,
As would destroy the providence of wit.
'Tis your strong Genius then which does not feel
Those weights would make a weaker spirit reel:
To carry weight and run so lightly too
Is what alone your *Pegasus* can do.
Great *Hercules* himself could ne're do more
40 Than not to feel those Heav'ns and gods he bore.
Your easier Odes, which for delight were penn'd,
Yet our instruction make their second end,
We're both enrich'd and pleas'd, like them that woo
At once a Beauty and a Fortune too.
Of Morall Knowledge Poesie was Queen,
And still she might, had wanton wits not been;
Who like ill Guardians liv'd themselves at large,
And not content with that, debauch'd their charge:
Like some brave Captain, your successfull Pen
50 Restores the Exil'd to her Crown again;
And gives us hope, that having seen the days
When nothing flourish'd but Fanatique Bays,
All will at length in this opinion rest,
"A sober Prince's Government is best."
This is not all; your Art the way has found
To make improvement of the richest ground,
That soil which those immortall Lawrells bore,
That once the sacred *Maro*'s temples wore.
Elisa's griefs, are so exprest by you,
60 They are too eloquent to have been true.
Had she so spoke, *Æneas* had obey'd
What *Dido* rather then what *Jove* had said.
If funerall Rites can give a Ghost repose,
Your Muse so justly has discharged those,
Elisa's shade may now its wandring cease,

58 wore.] ~ˬ O1–4.   64 those,] ~ . O1–4.

And claim a title to the fields of peace.
But if *Æneas* be oblig'd, no lesse
Your kindnesse great *Achilles* doth confesse,
Who dress'd by *Statius* in too bold a look,
70 Did ill become those Virgin's Robes he took.
To understand how much we owe to you,
We must your Numbers with your Author's view;
Then we shall see his work was lamely rough,
Each figure stiffe as if design'd in buffe;
His colours laid so thick on every place,
As onely shew'd the paint, but hid the face:
But as in Perspective we Beauties see,
Which in the Glasse, not in the Picture be;
So here our sight obligeingly mistakes
80 That wealth which his your bounty onely makes.
Thus vulgar dishes are by Cooks disguis'd,
More for their dressing than their substance priz'd.
Your curious *Notes so search into that Age,
When all was fable but the sacred Page,
That since in that dark night we needs must stray,
We are at least misled in pleasant way.
But what we most admire, your Verse no lesse
The Prophet than the Poet doth confesse.
Ere our weak eyes discern'd the doubtfull streak
90 Of light, you saw great *Charls* his morning break.
So skilfull Sea-men ken the Land from far,
Which shews like mists to the dul Passenger.
To *Charls* your Muse first pays her dutious love,
As still the Antients did begin from *Jove*.
With *Monck* you end, whose name preserv'd shall be,
As *Rome* recorded † *Rufus* memory,
Who thought it greater honor to obey
His Countrey's interest than the world to sway.

---

* *Annotations on* Statius. [Dryden's note.]
† Hîc situs est *Rufus* qui pulso vindice quondam,
Imperium asseruit non sibi sed Patriæ. [Dryden's note.]

But to write worthy things of worthy men
100 Is the peculiar talent of your Pen:
Yet let me take your Mantle up, and I
Will venture in your right to prophesy.

"This Work by merit first of Fame secure
Is likewise happy in its Geniture:
For since 'tis born when *Charls* ascends the Throne,
It shares at once his Fortune and its own."

Astræa Redux.

A

P O E M

On the Happy

Reſtoration & Return

Of His Sacred Majeſty

Charles the Second.

By *JOHN DRIDEN.*

Jam Redit & Virgo, Redeunt Saturnia Regna. Virgil.

LONDON,

Printed by *J. M.* for *Henry Herringman*, and are to be ſold at his *Shop*, at the Blew-*Anchor*, in the lower Walk of the New-Exchange, 1 6 6 0.

TITLE PAGE OF THE FIRST EDITION (MACDONALD 5A)

Astraea Redux. A Poem on the Restoration of Charles the Second

Now with a general Peace the World was blest,
    While Ours, a World divided from the rest,
    A dreadful Quiet felt, and worser farre
Then Armes, a sullen Intervall of Warre:
Thus when black Clouds draw down the lab'ring Skies,
Ere yet abroad the winged Thunder flyes
An horrid Stillness first invades the ear,
And in that silence Wee the Tempest fear.
Th' Ambitious *Swede* like restless Billowes tost,
10 On this hand gaining what on that he lost,
Though in his life he Blood and Ruine breath'd,
To his now guideless Kingdome Peace bequeath'd.
And Heaven that seem'd regardless of our Fate,
For *France* and *Spain* did Miracles create,
Such mortal Quarrels to compose in Peace
As Nature bred and Int'rest did encrease.
We sigh'd to hear the fair *Iberian* Bride
Must grow a Lilie to the Lilies side,
While Our cross Stars deny'd us *Charles* his Bed
20 Whom Our first Flames and Virgin Love did wed.
For his long absence Church and State did groan;
Madness the Pulpit, Faction seiz'd the Throne:
Experienc'd Age in deep despair was lost
To see the Rebel thrive, the Loyal crost:
Youth that with Joys had unacquainted been
Envy'd gray hairs that once good days had seen:
We thought our Sires, not with their own content,
Had ere we came to age our Portion spent.
Nor could our Nobles hope their bold Attempt

---

11 breath'd,] Q; ~ₐ F1–2.

30 Who ruin'd Crowns would Coronets exempt:
For when by their designing Leaders taught
To strike at Pow'r which for themselves they sought,
The Vulgar gull'd into Rebellion, arm'd,
Their blood to action by the Prize was warm'd.
The Sacred Purple then and Scarlet Gown
Like sanguine Dye to Elephants was shown.
Thus when the bold *Typhoeus* scal'd the Sky,
And forc'd great *Jove* from his own Heaven to fly,
(What King, what Crown from Treasons reach is free,
40 If *Jove* and *Heaven* can violated be?)
The lesser Gods that shar'd his prosp'rous State
All suffer'd in the Exil'd Thund'rers Fate.
The Rabble now such Freedom did enjoy,
As Winds at Sea that use it to destroy:
Blind as the *Cyclops,* and as wild as he,
They own'd a lawless salvage Libertie,
Like that our painted Ancestours so priz'd
Ere Empires Arts their Breasts had Civiliz'd.
How Great were then Our *Charles* his Woes, who thus
50 Was forc'd to suffer for Himself and us!
He toss'd by Fate, and hurried up and down,
Heir to his Fathers Sorrows, with his Crown,
Could tast no sweets of youths desired Age,
But found his life too true a Pilgrimage.
Unconquer'd yet in that forlorne Estate
His Manly Courage overcame his Fate.
His wounds he took like *Romans* on his brest,
Which by his Vertue were with Lawrells drest.
As Souls reach Heav'n while yet in Bodies pent,
60 So did he live above his Banishment.
That Sun which we beheld with cous'ned eyes
Within the water, mov'd along the skies.
How easie 'tis when Destiny proves kind
With full spread Sails to run before the wind,
But those that 'gainst stiff gales laveering go

Must be at once resolv'd and skilful too.
He would not like soft *Otho* hope prevent
But stay'd and suffer'd Fortune to repent.
These Vertues *Galba* in a stranger sought;
70 And *Piso* to Adopted Empire brought.
How shall I then my doubtful thoughts express
That must his suff'rings both regret and bless!
For when his early Valour Heav'n had crost,
And all at *Worc'ster* but the honour lost,
Forc'd into exile from his rightful Throne
He made all Countries where he came his own.
And viewing Monarchs secret Arts of sway
A Royal Factor for their Kingdomes lay.
Thus banish'd *David* spent abroad his time,
80 When to be Gods Anointed was his Crime,
And when restor'd made his proud Neighbours rue
Those choise Remarques he from his Travels drew,
Nor is he onely by afflictions shown
To conquer others Realms but rule his own:
Recov'ring hardly what he lost before,
His right indears it much, his purchase more.
Inur'd to suffer ere he came to raigne
No rash procedure will his actions stain.
To bus'ness ripened by digestive thought
90 His future rule is into Method brought:
As they who first Proportion understand
With easie Practice reach a Masters hand.
Well might the Ancient Poets then confer
On Night the honour'd name of *Counseller,*
Since struck with rayes of prosp'rous fortune blind
We light alone in dark afflictions find.
In such adversities to Scepters train'd
The name of *Great* his famous Grandsire gain'd:
Who yet a King alone in Name and Right,
100 With hunger, cold and angry *Jove* did fight;

79 time,] Q; ∼ . F1–2.   80 Crime,] Q; ∼∧ F1–2.
85 before,] Q; ∼∧ F1–2.

Shock'd by a Covenanting Leagues vast Pow'rs
As holy and as Catholique as ours:
Till Fortunes fruitless spight had made it known
Her blowes not shook but riveted his Throne.
　　Some lazy Ages lost in sleep and ease
No action leave to busie Chronicles;
Such whose supine felicity but makes
In story *Chasmes,* in *Epoche's* mistakes;
O're whom *Time* gently shakes his wings of Down
110　Till with his silent sickle they are mown:
Such is not *Charles* his too too active age,
Which govern'd by the wild distemper'd rage
Of some black Star infecting all the Skies,
Made him at his own cost like *Adam* wise.
Tremble ye Nations who secure before
Laught at those Armes that 'gainst our selves we bore;
Rous'd by the lash of his own stubborn tail
Our Lyon now will forraign Foes assail.
With *Alga* who the sacred altar strowes?
120　To all the Sea-Gods *Charles* an Off'ring owes:
A Bull to thee *Portunus* shall be slain,
A Lamb to you the Tempests of the Main:
For those loud stormes that did against him rore
Have cast his shipwrack'd Vessel on the shore.
Yet as wise Artists mix their colours so
That by degrees they from each other go,
Black steals unheeded from the neighb'ring white
Without offending the well cous'ned sight:
So on us stole our blessed change; while we
130　Th' effect did feel but scarce the manner see.
Frosts that constrain the ground, and birth deny
To flow'rs, that in its womb expecting lye,
Do seldom their usurping Pow'r withdraw,
But raging floods pursue their hasty thaw:
Our thaw was mild, the cold not chas'd away
But lost in kindly heat of lengthned day.

121　slain,] Q; ~ˌ F1–2.

Heav'n would no bargain for its blessings drive
But what we could not pay for, freely give.
The Prince of Peace would like himself confer
140 A gift unhop'd without the price of war.
Yet as he knew his blessings worth, took care
That we should know it by repeated pray'r;
Which storm'd the skies and ravish'd *Charles* from thence
As Heav'n it self is took by violence.
Booth's forward Valour only serv'd to show
He durst that duty pay we all did owe:
Th' Attempt was fair; but Heav'ns prefixed hour
Not come; so like the watchful travellour
That by the Moons mistaken light did rise,
150 Lay down again, and clos'd his weary eyes.
'Twas M O N C K whom Providence design'd to loose
Those real bonds false freedom did impose.
The blessed Saints that watch'd this turning Scene
Did from their Stars with joyful wonder leane,
To see small clues draw vastest weights along,
Not in their bulk but in their order strong.
Thus Pencils can by one slight touch restore
Smiles to that changed face that wept before.
With ease such fond *Chymæra's* we pursue
160 As fancy frames for fancy to subdue,
But when our selves to action we betake
It shuns the Mint like gold that Chymists make:
How hard was then his task, at once to be
What in the body natural we see
Mans Architect distinctly did ordain
The charge of Muscles, Nerves, and of the Brain;
Through viewless Conduits Spirits to dispense,
The Springs of Motion from the Seat of Sense.
'Twas not the hasty product of a day,
170 But the well ripened fruit of wise delay.
He like a patient Angler, er'e he strooke
Would let them play a while upon the hook.

Our healthful food the Stomach labours thus
At first embracing what it strait doth crush.
Wise Leeches will not vain Receipts obtrude,
While growing pains pronounce the humours crude;
Deaf to complaints they wait upon the ill
Till some safe *Crisis* authorise their skill.
Nor could his Acts too close a vizard wear
180 To scape their eyes whom guilt had taught to fear,
And guard with caution that polluted nest
Whence Legion twice before was dispossest,
Once sacred house which when they enter'd in
They thought the place could sanctifie a sin;
Like those that vainly hop'd kind Heav'n would wink
While to excess on Martyrs tombs they drink.
And as devouter *Turks* first warn their souls
To part, before they tast forbidden bowls,
So these when their black crimes they went about
190 First timely charm'd their useless conscience out.
Religions name against it self was made;
The shadow serv'd the substance to invade:
Like Zealous Missions they did care pretend
Of souls in shew, but made the Gold their end.
Th' incensed Powr's beheld with scorn from high
An Heaven so far distant from the sky,
Which durst with horses hoofs that beat the ground
And Martial brass bely the thunders sound.
'Twas hence at length just Vengeance thought it fit
200 To speed their ruine by their impious wit.
Thus *Sforza,* curs'd with a too fertile brain,
Lost by his wiles the Pow'r his wit did gain.
Henceforth their Fogue must spend at lesser rate
Then in its flames to wrap a Nations Fate.
Suffer'd to live, they are like *Helots* set
A vertuous shame within us to beget.

---

182   dispossest,] ~ . F1–2, Q.
201   *Sforza,* . . . brain,] Q; ~∧ . . . ~∧ F1–2.

For by example most we sinn'd before,
And, glass-like, clearness mixt with frailty bore.
But since reform'd by what we did amiss,
210 We by our suff'rings learn to prize our bliss:
Like early Lovers whose unpractis'd hearts
Were long the May-game of malicious arts,
When once they find their Jealousies were vain
With double heat renew their fires again.
'Twas this produc'd the joy that hurried o're
Such swarmes of English to the Neighb'ring shore,
To fetch that prize, by which *Batavia* made
So rich amends for our impoverish'd Trade.
Oh had you seen from *Schevelines* barren shore
220 (Crowded with troops, and barren now no more,)
Afflicted *Holland* to his farewell bring
True Sorrow, *Holland* to regret a King;
While waiting him his Royal Fleet did ride
And willing winds to their low'rd sayles deny'd.
The wavering Streamers, Flags, and Standart out,
The merry Seamens rude but chearful shout,
And last the Cannons voice that shook the skies ⎤
And, as it fares in sudden Extasies   ⎬
At once bereft us both of ears and eyes.   ⎦
230 The *Naseby* now no longer *Englands* shame
But better to be lost in *Charles* his name
(Like some unequal Bride in nobler sheets)
Receives her Lord: the joyful *London* meets
The Princely *York,* himself alone a freight;
The *Swift-sure* groans beneath Great *Gloc'sters* weight.
Secure as when the *Halcyon* breeds, with these
He that was born to drown might cross the Seas.
Heav'n could not own a Providence and take
The wealth three Nations ventur'd at a stake.
240 The same indulgence *Charles* his Voyage bless'd

Which in his right had Miracles confess'd.
The winds that never Moderation knew
Afraid to blow too much, too faintly blew;
Or out of breath with joy could not enlarge
Their straightned lungs, or conscious of their Charge.
The British *Amphitryte* smooth and clear
In richer Azure never did appear;
Proud her returning Prince to entertain
With the submitted Fasces of the Main.

250   And welcome now (*Great Monarch*) to your own;
Behold th' approaching cliffes of *Albion;*
It is no longer Motion cheats your view,
As you meet it, the Land approacheth you.
The Land returns, and in the white it wears
The marks of penitence and sorrow bears.
But you, whose goodness your discent doth show,
Your Heav'nly Parentage and earthly too;
By that same mildness which your Fathers Crown
Before did ravish, shall secure your own.
260 Not ty'd to rules of Policy, you find
Revenge less sweet then a forgiving mind.
Thus when th' Almighty would to *Moses* give
A sight of all he could behold and live;
A voice before his entry did proclaim
Long-Suff'ring, Goodness, Mercy in his Name.
Your Pow'r to Justice doth submit your Cause,
Your Goodness only is above the Laws;
Whose rigid letter while pronounc'd by you
Is softer made. So winds that tempests brew
270 When through Arabian Groves they take their flight
Made wanton with rich Odours, lose their spight.
And as those Lees that trouble it, refine
The agitated Soul of Generous Wine,
So tears of joy for your returning spilt,
Work out and expiate our former guilt.

Methinks I see those Crowds on *Dovers* Strand
Who in their hast to welcome you to Land
Choak'd up the Beach with their still growing store,
And made a wilder Torrent on the shore,
280 While spurr'd with eager thoughts of past delight
Those who had seen you, court a second sight;
Preventing still your steps, and making hast
To meet you often where so e're you past.
How shall I speak of that triumphant Day
When you renew'd the expiring Pomp of *May!*
(A Month that owns an Intrest in your Name:
You and the Flow'rs are its peculiar Claim.)
That Star that at your Birth shone out so bright
It stain'd the duller Suns Meridian light,
290 Did once again its potent Fires renew
Guiding our eyes to find and worship you.
    And now times whiter Series is begun
Which in soft Centuries shall smoothly run;
Those Clouds that overcast your Morne shall fly
Dispell'd to farthest corners of the sky.
Our Nation with united Int'rest blest
Not now content to poize, shall sway the rest.
Abroad your Empire shall no Limits know,
But like the Sea in boundless Circles flow.
300 Your much lov'd Fleet shall with a wide Command
Besiege the petty Monarchs of the Land:
And as Old Time his Off-spring swallow'd down
Our Ocean in its depths all Seas shall drown.
Their wealthy Trade from Pyrates Rapine free
Our Merchants shall no more Advent'rers be:
Nor in the farthest East those Dangers fear
Which humble *Holland* must dissemble here.
Spain to your Gift alone her Indies owes;
For what the Pow'rful takes not he bestowes.
310 And *France* that did an Exiles presence fear

279 shore,] ~ . F1–2, Q.

May justly apprehend you still too near.
At home the hateful names of Parties cease
And factious Souls are weary'd into peace.
The discontented now are only they
Whose Crimes before did your Just Cause betray:
Of those your Edicts some reclaim from sins,
But most your Life and Blest Example wins.
Oh happy Prince whom Heav'n hath taught the way
By paying Vowes, to have more Vowes to pay!
320 Oh Happy Age! Oh times like those alone
By Fate reserv'd for Great *Augustus* Throne!
When the joint growth of Armes and Arts foreshew
The World a Monarch, and that Monarch *You*.

TO HIS SACRED
MAIESTY,
A
PANEGYRICK
ON HIS
CORONATION.

BY JOHN DRYDEN.

LONDON,

Printed for *Henry Herringman* , at the *Anchor* on the Lower walk in the New Exchange. 1 6 6 1.

TITLE PAGE OF THE FIRST EDITION (MACDONALD 6A)

To His Sacred Majesty, A Panegyrick on His Coronation

In that wild Deluge where the World was drownd,
  When life and sin one common tombe had found,
  The first small prospect of a rising hill
With various notes of Joy the Ark did fill:
Yet when that flood in its own depths was drownd
It left behind it false and slipp'ry ground;
And the more solemn pomp was still deferr'd
Till new-born Nature in fresh looks appeard:
Thus (Royall Sir) to see you landed here
10 Was cause enough of triumph for a year:
Nor would your care those glorious Joyes repeat
Till they at once might be secure and great:
Till your kind beams by their continu'd stay
Had warm'd the ground, and call'd the Damps away.
Such vapours while your pow'rfull influence dryes
Then soonest vanish when they highest rise.
Had greater hast these sacred rights prepar'd
Some guilty Moneths had in your triumphs shar'd:
But this untainted year is all your own,
20 Your glory's may without our crimes be shown.
We had not yet exhausted all our store
When you refresh'd our joyes by adding more:
As Heav'n of old dispenc'd Cælestial dew,
You give us Manna and still give us new.
   Now our sad ruines are remov'd from sight,
The Season too comes fraught with new delight;
Time seems not now beneath his years to stoop
Nor do his wings with sickly feathers droop:
Soft western winds waft ore the gaudy spring
30 And opend Scenes of flow'rs and blossoms bring

To grace this happy day, while you appear
Not King of us alone but of the year.
All eyes you draw, and with the eyes the heart,
Of your own pomp your self the greatest part:
Loud shouts the Nations happiness proclaim
And Heav'n this day is feasted with your name.
Your Cavalcade the fair Spectators view
From their high standings, yet look up to you.
From your brave train each singles out a prey,
40   And longs to date a Conquest from your day.
Now charg'd with blessings while you seek repose,
Officious slumbers hast your eyes to close:
And glorious dreams stand ready to restore
The pleasing shapes of all you saw before.
Next, to the sacred Temple you are led,
Where waites a Crown for your more sacred Head:
How justly from the Church that Crown is due,
Preserv'd from ruine and restor'd by you!
The gratefull quire their harmony employ
50   Not to make greater but more solemn joy.
Wrapt soft and warm your Name is sent on high,
As flames do on the wings of Incense fly:
Musique her self is lost, in vain she brings
Her choisest notes to praise the best of Kings:
Her melting strains in you a tombe have found,
And lye like Bees in their own sweetnesse drown'd.
He that brought peace and discord could attone,
His Name is Musick of it self alone.
Now while the sacred Oyl annoints your head,
60   And fragrant scents, begun from you, are spread
Through the large Dome, the peoples joyful sound
Sent back, is still preserv'd in hallow'd ground:
Which in one blessing mixt descends on you,
As heightned spirits fall in richer dew.
Not that our wishes do increase your store,
Full of your self you can admit no more:

45   Next,] Q; ~ᴧ F1-2, O1-2.

We add not to your glory, but employ
Our time like Angels in expressing joy.
Nor is it duty or our hopes alone
70 Create that joy, but full fruition;
We know those blessings which we must possesse,
And judge of future by past happinesse.
No promise can oblige a Prince so much
Still to be good as long to have been such.
A noble Emulation heats your breast,
And your own fame now robbs you of your rest:
Good actions still must be maintain'd with good,
As bodies nourish'd with resembling food.
You have already quench'd seditions brand;
80 And zeal (which burnt it) only warms the Land.
The jealous Sects that dare not trust their cause
So farre from their own will as to the Laws,
You for their Umpire and their Synod take,
And their appeal alone to *Cæsar* make.
Kind Heav'n so rare a temper did provide
That guilt repenting might in it confide.
Among our crimes oblivion may be set,
But 'tis our Kings perfection to forget.
Virtues unknown to these rough Northern climes
90 From milder heav'ns you bring, without their crimes:
Your calmnesse does no after storms provide,
Nor seeming patience mortal anger hide.
When Empire first from families did spring,
Then every Father govern'd as a King;
But you that are a Soveraign Prince, allay
Imperial pow'r with your paternal sway.
From those great cares when ease your soul unbends
Your pleasures are design'd to noble ends:
Born to command the Mistress of the Seas,
100 Your thoughts themselves in that blue Empire please.
Hither in Summer ev'nings you repair
To take the fraischeur of the purer air:
Vndaunted here you ride when Winter raves,

With *Cæsars* heart that rose above the waves.
More I could sing but fear my Numbers stayes;
No Loyal Subject dares that courage praise.
In stately Frigats most delight you find,
Where well-drawn Battels fire your martial mind.
What to your cares we owe is learnt from hence,
110 When ev'n your pleasures serve for our defence.
Beyond your Court flows in th' admitted tide,
Where in new depths the wondring fishes glide:
Here in a Royal bed the waters sleep,
When tir'd at Sea within this bay they creep.
Here the mistrustfull foul no harm suspects,
So safe are all things which our King protects.
From your lov'd *Thames* a blessing yet is due,
Second alone to that it brought in you;
A Queen, from whose chast womb, ordain'd by Fate,
120 The souls of Kings unborn for bodies wait.
It was your Love before made discord cease:
Your love is destin'd to your Countries peace.
Both *Indies* (Rivalls in your bed) provide
With Gold or Jewels to adorn your Bride.
This to a mighty King presents rich ore,
While that with Incense does a God implore.
Two Kingdomes wait your doom, and as you choose,
This must receive a Crown, or that must loose.
Thus from your Royal Oke, like *Jove*'s of old,
130 Are answers sought, and destinies fore-told:
Propitious Oracles are beg'd with vows,
And Crowns that grow upon the sacred boughs.
Your Subjects, while you weigh the Nations fate,
Suspend to both their doubtfull love or hate:
Choose only, (Sir,) that so they may possesse
With their own peace their Childrens happinesse.

---

122   Your love] O1, Q; Your your love F1–2 (*in most copies the second* "your" *is blocked out with ink*); *passage omitted from* O2.
136   own] O1, Q; ovn F1–2; *passage omitted from* O2.

TO

MY LORD

CHANCELLOR,

Prefented on

New-years-day,

By *J. Driden.*

L O N D O N,

Printed for *Henry Herringman* at the
Anchor in the Lower-walk in the *New*
Exchange. 1 6 6 2.

To My Lord Chancellor

MY LORD,
While flattering crouds officiously appear
To give themselves, not you, an happy year;
And by the greatness of their Presents prove
How much they hope, but not how well they love;
The Muses (who your early courtship boast,
Though now your flames are with their beauty lost)
Yet watch their time, that if you have forgot
They were your Mistresses, the World may not:
Decay'd by time and wars, they only prove
10 Their former beauty by your former love;
And now present, as antient Ladies do
That courted long at length are forc'd to woo.
For still they look on you with such kind eyes
As those that see the Churches Soveraign rise
From their own Order chose, in whose high State
They think themselves the second choice of Fate.
When our Great Monarch into Exile went
Wit and Religion suffer'd banishment:
Thus once when *Troy* was wrapt in fire and smoak
20 The helpless Gods their burning shrines forsook;
They with the vanquisht Prince and party go,
And leave their Temples empty to the fo:
At length the Muses stand restor'd again
To that great charge which Nature did ordain;
And their lov'd Druyds seem reviv'd by Fate
While you dispence the Laws and guide the State.
The Nations soul (our Monarch) does dispence
Through you to us his vital influence;
You are the Chanel where those spirits flow
30 And work them higher as to us they go.

In open prospect nothing bounds our eye
Until the Earth seems joyn'd unto the Sky:
So in this Hemisphær our utmost view
Is only bounded by our King and you:
Our sight is limited where you are joyn'd
And beyond that no farther Heav'n can find.
So well your Vertues do with his agree
That though your Orbs of different greatness be,
Yet both are for each others use dispos'd,
40 His to inclose, and yours to be inclos'd.
Nor could another in your room have been
Except an Emptinesse had come between.
Well may he then to you his Cares impart
And share his burden where he shares his heart.
In you his sleep still wakes; his pleasures find
Their share of bus'nesse in your labr'ing mind:
So when the weary Sun his place resigns
He leaves his light and by reflection shines.
  Justice that sits and frowns where publick **Laws**
50 Exclude soft mercy from a private cause,
In your Tribunal most her self does please;
There only smiles because she lives at ease;
And like young *David* finds her strength the more
When disincumberd from those arms she wore:
Heav'n would your Royal Master should exceed
Most in that Vertue which we most did need,
And his mild Father (who too late did find
All mercy vain but what with pow'r was joyn'd,)
His fatal goodnesse left to fitter times,
60 Not to increase but to absolve our Crimes:
But when the Heir of this vast treasure knew
How large a Legacy was left to you,
(Too great for any Subject to retain)
He wisely ti'd it to the Crown again:
Yet passing through your hands it gathers more,
As streams through Mines bear tincture of their Ore.

While Emp'rique politicians use deceipt,
Hide what they give, and cure but by a cheat;
You boldly show that skill which they pretend,
70 And work by means as noble as your end:
Which, should you veil, we might unwind the clue
As men do Nature, till we came to you.
And as the *Indies* were not found before
Those rich perfumes which from the happy shore
The winds upon their balmy wings convay'd,
Whose guilty sweetnesse first their World betray'd;
So by your Counsels we are brought to view
A rich and undiscover'd World in you.
By you our Monarch does that fame assure
80 Which Kings must have or cannot live secure:
For prosp'rous Princes gain the Subjects heart,
Who love that praise in which themselves have part:
By you he fits those Subjects to obey,
As Heavens Eternal Monarch does convey
His pow'r unseen, and man to his designs,
By his bright Ministers the Stars, inclines.
    Our setting Sun from his declining seat
Shot beams of kindnesse on you, not of heat:
And when his love was bounded in a few,
90 That were unhappy that they might be true;
Made you the favo'rite of his last sad times,
That is a suff'rer in his Subjects crimes:
Thus those first favours you receiv'd were sent
Like Heav'ns rewards, in earthly punishment.
Yet Fortune conscious of your destiny
Ev'n then took care to lay you softly by:
And wrapt your fate among her precious things,
Kept fresh to be unfolded with your Kings.
Shown all at once you dazled so our eyes,
100 As new-born *Pallas* did the Gods surprise;
When springing forth from *Jove*'s new-closing wound
She struck the Warlick Spear into the ground;

Which sprouting leaves did suddenly inclose,
And peaceful Olives shaded as they rose.
    How strangely active are the arts of Peace,
Whose restlesse motions lesse than Wars do cease!
Peace is not freed from labour but from noise;
And War more force but not more pains employs;
Such is the mighty swiftnesse of your mind
110 That (like the earth's) it leaves our sence behind;
While you so smoothly turn and roul our Sphear,
That rapid motion does but rest appear.
For as in Natures swiftnesse, with the throng
Of flying Orbs while ours is born along,
All seems at rest to the deluded eye:
(Mov'd by the Soul of the same harmony)
So carry'd on by your unwearied care
We rest in Peace and yet in motion share.
Let Envy then those Crimes within you see
120 From which the Happy never must be free;
(Envy that does with misery reside,
The joy and the revenge of ruin'd Pride;)
Think it not hard if at so cheap a rate
You can secure the constancy of Fate,
Whose kindnesse sent, what does their malice seem,
By lesser ills the greater to redeem.
Nor can we this weak show'r a tempest call
But drops of heat that in the Sun-shine fall.
You have already weary'd Fortune so
130 She can not farther be your friend or fo;
But sits all breathlesse, and admires to feel
A Fate so weighty that it stops her wheel.
In all things else above our humble fate
Your equal mind yet swells not into state,
But like some mountain in those happy Isles
Where in perpetual Spring young Nature smiles,
Your greatnesse shows: no horrour to afright
But Trees for shade, and Flow'rs to court the sight;

Sometimes the Hill submits itself a while
140 In small descents, which do its height beguile;
And sometimes mounts, but so as billows play
Whose rise not hinders but makes short our way.
Your brow which does no fear of thunder know
Sees rouling tempests vainly beat below;
And (like *Olympus* top,) th' impression wears
Of Love and Friendship writ in former years.
Yet unimpair'd with labours or with time
Your age but seems to a new youth to climb.
Thus Heav'nly bodies do our time begct;
150 And measure Change, but share no part of it.
And still it shall without a weight increase,
Like this New-year, whose motions never cease;
For since the glorious Course you have begun
Is led by *C H A R L S,* as that is by the Sun,
It must both weightlesse and immortal prove,
Because the Center of it is above.

To My Honored Friend, Dr. Charleton

THE longest Tyranny that ever sway'd,
   Was that wherein our Ancestors betray'd
   Their free-born *Reason* to the *Stagirite,*
And made his Torch their universal Light.
So *Truth,* while onely one suppli'd the State,
Grew scarce, and dear, and yet sophisticate,
Until 'twas bought, like Emp'rique Wares, or Charms,
Hard words seal'd up with *Aristotle*'s Armes.
Columbus was the first that shook his Throne;
10 And found a *Temp'rate* in a *Torrid* Zone:
The fevrish aire fann'd by a cooling breez,
The fruitful Vales set round with shady Trees;
And guiltless *Men,* who danc'd away their time,
Fresh as their *Groves,* and *Happy* as their *Clime.*
Had we still paid that homage to a *Name,*
Which onely *God* and *Nature* justly claim;
The *Western* Seas had been our utmost bound,
Where *Poets* still might dream the *Sun* was drown'd:
And all the *Starrs,* that shine in *Southern* Skies,
20 Had been admir'd by none but *Salvage* Eyes.

   Among th' *Assertors* of free Reason's claim,
Th' *English* are not the least in Worth, or Fame.
The World to *Bacon* does not onely owe
Its *present* Knowledge, but its *future* too.
Gilbert shall live, till *Load-stones* cease to draw,
Or *British* Fleets the boundless Ocean awe;
And noble *Boyle,* not less in *Nature* seen,
Than his great *Brother* read in *States* and *Men.*
The *Circling* streams, once thought but pools, of blood

---

6 sophisticate,] ∼ . Q1–2.   26 awe;] ∼ . Q1–2.

30 (Whether Life's fewel, or the Bodie's food)
From dark Oblivion *Harvey*'s name shall save;
While *Ent* keeps all the honour that he gave.
Nor are *You,* Learned Friend, the least renown'd;
Whose Fame, not circumscrib'd with *English* ground,
Flies like the nimble journeys of the Light;
And is, like that, unspent too in its flight.
What ever *Truths* have been, by *Art,* or *Chance,*
Redeem'd from *Error,* or from *Ignorance,*
Thin in their *Authors,* (like rich veins of Ore)
40 Your Works unite, and still discover more.
Such is the healing virtue of Your Pen,
To perfect Cures on *Books,* as well as *Men.*
Nor is This Work the least: You well may give
To *Men* new vigour, who make *Stones* to live.
Through You, the *D A N E S* (their short Dominion lost)
A longer Conquest than the *Saxons* boast.
STONE-HENG, once thought a *Temple,* You have found
A *Throne,* where Kings, our Earthly Gods, were Crown'd,
Where by their wondring Subjects They were seen,
50 Joy'd with their Stature, and their Princely meen.
Our *Soveraign* here above the rest might stand;
And here be chose again to rule the Land.

    These Ruines sheltred once *His* Sacred Head,
Then when from *Wor'sters* fatal Field *He* fled;
Watch'd by the Genius of this Royal place,
And mighty Visions of the Danish Race.
His *Refuge* then was for a *Temple* shown:
But, *He* Restor'd, 'tis now become a *Throne.*

———

48 Crown'd,] ~. Q1-2.

To the Lady Castlemaine, upon Her Incouraging His First Play

As Sea-men shipwrackt on some happy shore,
      Discover Wealth in Lands unknown before;
      And what their Art had labour'd long in vain,
By their misfortunes happily obtain:
So my much-envy'd Muse by Storms long tost,
Is thrown upon your Hospitable Coast;
And finds more favour by her ill success,
Than she could hope for by her happiness.
Once *Cato*'s Virtue did the Gods oppose;
10 While they the Victor, he the Vanquish'd chose:
But you have done what *Cato* could not do,
To chuse the Vanquish'd, and restore him too.
Let others still triumph, and gain their cause
By their deserts, or by the Worlds applause;
Let Merit Crowns, and Justice Laurels give,
But let me Happy by your Pity live.
True Poets empty Fame and Praise despise;
Fame is the Trumpet, but your Smile the Prize.
You sit above, and see vain men below
20 Contend for what you only can bestow:
But those great Actions others do by chance,
Are, like your Beauty, your Inheritance.
So great a Soul, such sweetness joyn'd in One,
Could only spring from Noble *Grandison;*
You, like the Stars, not by reflexion bright,
Are born to your own Heav'n, and your own Light:
Like them are good, but from a Nobler Cause,
From your own Knowledg, not from Natures Laws.

3   long] O2, M; for O1.   6   thrown] O2; cast O1, M.
9   Virtue] O2, M; Virtues O1.   9   oppose;] O2; ~ , O1, M.
10   While] O2; When O1, M.
17   Fame and Praise] O2, M; Praise and Fame O1.
18   Smile] O2, M; Smiles O1.

Your pow'r you never use but for defence,
30 To guard your own, or others Innocence.
Your Foes are such as they, not you, have made;
And Virtue may repel, though not invade.
Such courage did the Ancient *Hero's* show,
Who, when they might prevent, would wait the blow;
With such assurance, as they meant to say,
We will o'recome, but scorn the safest way.
    [Well may I rest secure in your great Fate,
And dare my Stars to be unfortunate.]
What further fear of danger can there be?
40 Beauty, which captives all things, sets me free.
Posterity will judge by my success,
I had the Grecian Poets happiness,
Who waving Plots, found out a better way;
Some God descended and preserv'd the Play.
    When first the Triumphs of your Sex were sung
By those old Poets, Beauty was but young;
And few admir'd the native red and white,
Till Poets drest them up to charm the sight.
So Beauty took on trust, and did engage
50 For sums of praises, till she came to age:
But this long growing Debt to Poetry,
You justly (Madam) have discharg'd to me,
When your applause and favour did infuse
New life to my condemn'd and dying Muse;
[Which, that the World as well as you may see,
Let these rude Verses your Acquittance be.
    Receiv'd in full this present day and year,
    One soveraign smile from Beauties general Heir.]

---

29   never use but for] O2, M; use but for your own O1.
34   would] O2, M; did O1.   35   such] O2; that O1, M.
37–38   *Omitted from O2.*   40   which] O2; that O1, M.
40   captives] O2, M; castives O1.   41   will] O2, M; would O1.
47   the] O2; her O1; their M.   48   them] O2, M; her O1.
50   to age] O2, M; of age O1.
51   this long growing] O2; this vast growing O1; your vast wondrous M.
51   to Poetry] O2, M; of Poesie O1.
52   You justly (Madam)] O2; You, Madam, justly O1, M.
55–58   *Omitted from O2.*

ANNUS MIRABILIS:

The Year of

WONDERS,
1 6 6 6.

AN HISTORICAL

POEM:

CONTAINING

The Progress and various Successes of our Naval
War with *Holland*, under the Conduct of His
Highness Prince RUPERT, and His Grace the
Duke of ALBEMARL.

And describing

THE FIRE
OF
LONDON.

By JOHN DRYDEN, Esq;

Multium interest res poscat, an homines latius imperare velint.
Trajan. Imperator. ad Plin.

u bs antiqua ruit, multos dominata per annos. Virg.

London, Printed for *Henry Herringman*, at the *Anchor* in the Lower Walk of the *New Exchange*. 1667.

TITLE PAGE OF THE FIRST EDITION (MACDONALD 9A)

Annus Mirabilis: The Year of Wonders, 1666

TO THE METROPOLIS OF GREAT BRITAIN, THE MOST RENOWNED AND
LATE FLOURISHING CITY OF LONDON, IN ITS REPRESENTATIVES
THE LORD MAYOR AND COURT OF ALDERMEN, THE SHERIFS
AND COMMON COUNCIL OF IT.

As perhaps I am the first who ever presented a work of this nature
to the Metropolis of any Nation, so is it likewise consonant to
Justice, that he who was to give the first Example of such a
Dedication should begin it with that City, which has set a pattern
to all others of true Loyalty, invincible Courage and unshaken Constancy. Other Cities have been prais'd for the same Virtues, but I am
much deceiv'd if any have so dearly purchas'd their reputation; their
fame has been won them by cheaper trials then an expensive, though
necessary, War, a consuming Pestilence, and a more consuming Fire.
10 To submit your selves with that humility to the Judgments of Heaven,
and at the same time to raise your selves with that vigour above all
humane Enemies; to be combated at once from above and from below, to be struck down and to triumph; I know not whether such
trials have been ever parallel'd in any Nation, the resolution and
successes of them never can be. Never had Prince or People more
mutual reason to love each other, if suffering for each other can in-
dear affection. You have come together a pair of matchless Lovers,
through many difficulties; He, through a long Exile, various traverses
of Fortune, and the interposition of many Rivals, who violently
20 ravish'd and with-held You from Him: And certainly you have had
your share in sufferings. But Providence has cast upon you want of
Trade, that you might appear bountiful to your Country's necessities;
and the rest of your afflictions are not more the effects of God's displeasure, (frequent examples of them having been in the Reign of the
most excellent Princes) then occasions for the manifesting of your

Christian and Civil virtues. To you therefore this Year of Wonders is justly dedicated, because you have made it so. You who are to stand a wonder to all Years and Ages, and who have built your selves an immortal Monument on your own ruines. You are now a *Phœnix* in her ashes, and, as far as Humanity can approach, a great Emblem of the suffering Deity. But Heaven never made so much Piety and Vertue to leave it miserable. I have heard indeed of some vertuous persons who have ended unfortunately, but never of any vertuous Nation: Providence is engag'd too deeply, when the cause becomes so general.

10 And I cannot imagine it has resolv'd the ruine of that people at home, which it has blessed abroad with such successes. I am therefore to conclude, that your sufferings are at an end; and that one part of my Poem has not been more an History of your destruction, then the other a Prophecy of your restoration. The accomplishment of which happiness, as it is the wish of all true *English-men,* so is by none more passionately desired then by

> *The greatest of your Admirers, and*
> *most humble of your Servants,*
> JOHN DRYDEN.

An account of the ensuing Poem, in a Letter to the Honorable, Sir Robert Howard

SIR,

I am so many ways oblig'd to you, and so little able to return your favours, that, like those who owe too much, I can onely live by getting farther into your debt. You have not onely been careful of my Fortune, which was the effect of your Nobleness, but you have been sollicitous of my Reputation, which is that of your Kindness. It is not long since I gave you the trouble of perusing a Play for me, and now, instead of an acknowledgment, I have given you a greater, in the correction of a Poem. But since you are to bear this persecution, I will at least give you the encouragement of a Martyr, you could never suffer in a nobler cause. For I have chosen the most heroick Subject which any Poet could desire: I have taken upon me to describe the motives, the beginning, progress and successes of a most just and necessary War; in it, the care, management and prudence of our King; the conduct and valour of a Royal Admiral, and of two incomparable Generals; the invincible courage of our Captains and Sea-

10　men, and three glorious Victories, the result of all. After this I have, in the Fire, the most deplorable, but withall the greatest Argument that can be imagin'd: the destruction being so swift, so sudden, so vast and miserable, as nothing can parallel in Story. The former part of this Poem, relating to the War, is but a due expiation for my not serving my King and Country in it. All Gentlemen are almost oblig'd to it: And I know no reason we should give that advantage to the Commonalty of *England* to be formost in brave actions, which the Noblesse of *France* would never suffer in their Peasants. I should not have written this but to a Person, who has been ever forward to ap-

20　pear in all employments, whither his Honour and Generosity have call'd him. The latter part of my Poem, which describes the Fire, I owe first to the Piety and Fatherly Affection of our Monarch to his suffering Subjects; and, in the second place, to the courage, loyalty and magnanimity of the City: both which were so conspicuous, that I have wanted words to celebrate them as they deserve. I have call'd my Poem *Historical,* not *Epick,* though both the Actions and Actors are as much Heroick, as any Poem can contain. But since the Action is not properly one, nor that accomplish'd in the last successes, I have judg'd it too bold a Title for a few *Stanza's,* which are little more in

30　number then a single *Iliad,* or the longest of the *Æneids.* For this reason, (I mean not of length, but broken action, ti'd too severely to the Laws of History) I am apt to agree with those who rank *Lucan* rather among Historians in Verse, then Epique Poets: In whose room, if I am not deceiv'd, *Silius Italicus,* though a worse Writer, may more

---

17　formost] Q; *for most* O1–5.　　　33　Historians] O5, Q; *Historiaus* O1–4.

justly be admitted. I have chosen to write my Poem in *Quatrains* or
Stanza's of four in alternate rhyme, because I have ever judg'd them
more noble, and of greater dignity, both for the sound and number,
then any other Verse in use amongst us; in which I am sure I have
your approbation. The learned Languages have, certainly, a great
advantage of us, in not being tied to the slavery of any Rhyme; and
were less constrain'd in the quantity of every syllable, which they
might vary with *Spondæes* or *Dactiles,* besides so many other helps
of Grammatical Figures, for the lengthning or abbreviation of them,
10 then the Modern are in the close of that one Syllable, which often
confines, and more often corrupts the sense of all the rest. But in this
necessity of our Rhymes, I have always found the couplet Verse most
easie, (though not so proper for this occasion) for there the work is
sooner at an end, every two lines concluding the labour of the Poet:
but in Quattrains he is to carry it farther on; and not onely so, but
to bear along in his head the troublesome sense of four lines together.
For those who write correctly in this kind must needs acknowledge,
that the last line of the Stanza is to be consider'd in the composition
of the first. Neither can we give our selves the liberty of making any
20 part of a Verse for the sake of Rhyme, or concluding with a word
which is not currant *English,* or using the variety of Female Rhymes,
all which our Fathers practis'd; and for the Female Rhymes, they are
still in use amongst other Nations: with the *Italian* in every line, with
the *Spaniard* promiscuously, with the *French* alternately, as those who
have read the *Alarique,* the *Pucelle,* or any of their latter Poems, will
agree with me. And besides this, they write in *Alexandrins,* or Verses
of six feet, such as amongst us is the old Translation of *Homer,* by
Chapman; all which, by lengthning of their Chain, makes the sphere
of their activity the larger. I have dwelt too long upon the choice of
30 my Stanza, which you may remember is much better defended in the
Preface to *Gondibert,* and therefore I will hasten to acquaint you
with my endeavours in the writing. In general I will onely say, I have
never yet seen the description of any Naval Fight in the proper terms
which are us'd at Sea; and if there be any such in another Language,

3 for] Q; *fro* O1–4; *from* O5.

as that of *Lucan* in the third of his *Pharsalia,* yet I could not prevail my self of it in the *English;* the terms of Arts in every Tongue bearing more of the Idiom of it then any other words. We hear, indeed, among our Poets, of the thundring of Guns, the smoke, the disorder and the slaughter; but all these are common notions. And certainly as those who, in a Logical dispute, keep in general terms, would hide a fallacy, so those who do it in any Poetical description would vail their ignorance.

> *Descriptas servare vices operumque colores*
> 10   *Cur ego, si nequeo ignoroque, poeta salutor?*

For my own part, if I had little knowledge of the Sea, yet I have thought it no shame to learn: and if I have made some few mistakes, 'tis onely, as you can bear me witness, because I have wanted opportunity to correct them, the whole Poem being first written, and now sent you from a place, where I have not so much as the converse of any Sea-man. Yet, though the trouble I had in writing it was great, it was more then recompens'd by the pleasure; I found my self so warm in celebrating the praises of military men, two such especially as the *Prince* and *General,* that it is no wonder if they inspir'd me with 20 thoughts above my ordinary level. And I am well satisfi'd, that as they are incomparably the best subject I have ever had, excepting onely the *Royal Family;* so also, that this I have written of them is much better then what I have perform'd on any other. I have been forc'd to help out other Arguments, but this has been bountiful to me; they have been low and barren of praise, and I have exalted them, and made them fruitful: but here—*Omnia sponte suâ reddit justissima tellus.* I have had a large, a fair and a pleasant field, so fertile, that, without my cultivating, it has given me two Harvests in a Summer, and in both oppress'd the Reaper. All other greatness in subjects is onely 30 counterfeit, it will not endure the test of danger; the greatness of Arms is onely real: other greatness burdens a Nation with its weight, this supports it with its strength. And as it is the happiness of the Age, so is it the peculiar goodness of the best of Kings, that we may praise his Subjects without offending him: doubtless it proceeds from a just confidence of his own vertue, which the lustre of no other can be so

great as to darken in him: for the Good or the Valiant are never safely
prais'd under a bad or a degenerate Prince. But to return from this
digression to a farther account of my Poem, I must crave leave to
tell you, that as I have endeavour'd to adorn it with noble thoughts, so
much more to express those thoughts with elocution. The composition of all Poems is or ought to be of wit, and wit in the Poet, or wit
writing, (if you will give me leave to use a School distinction) is no
other then the faculty of imagination in the writer, which, like a
nimble Spaniel, beats over and ranges through the field of Memory,
till it springs the Quarry it hunted after; or, without metaphor, which
searches over all the memory for the species or Idea's of those things
which it designs to represent. Wit written, is that which is well defin'd,
the happy result of thought, or product of that imagination. But to
proceed from wit in the general notion of it, to the proper wit of an
Heroick or Historical Poem, I judge it chiefly to consist in the delightful imaging of persons, actions, passions, or things. 'Tis not the
jerk or sting of an Epigram, nor the seeming contradiction of a poor
Antithesis, (the delight of an ill judging Audience in a Play of Rhyme)
nor the gingle of a more poor *Paranomasia:* neither is it so much the
morality of a grave sentence, affected by *Lucan,* but more sparingly
used by *Virgil;* but it is some lively and apt description, dress'd in
such colours of speech, that it sets before your eyes the absent object,
as perfectly and more delightfully then nature. So then, the first
happiness of the Poet's imagination is properly Invention, or finding
of the thought; the second is Fancy, or the variation, deriving or
moulding of that thought, as the judgment represents it proper to
the subject; the third is Elocution, or the Art of clothing and adorn-
ing that thought so found and varied, in apt, significant and sounding words: the quickness of the Imagination is seen in the Invention,
the fertility in the Fancy, and the accuracy in the Expression. For the
two first of these *Ovid* is famous amongst the Poets, for the latter
Virgil. Ovid images more often the movements and affections of the
mind, either combating between two contrary passions, or extremely
discompos'd by one: his words therefore are the least part of his care,
for he pictures Nature in disorder, with which the study and choice

25 deriving] Q; *driving* O1–5.

of words is inconsistent. This is the proper wit of Dialogue or Discourse, and, consequently, of the *Drama,* where all that is said is to be suppos'd the effect of sudden thought; which, though it excludes not the quickness of wit in repartees, yet admits not a too curious election of words, too frequent allusions, or use of Tropes, or, in fine, any thing that showes remoteness of thought, or labour in the Writer. On the other side, *Virgil* speaks not so often to us in the person of another, like *Ovid,* but in his own, he relates almost all things as from himself, and thereby gains more liberty then the other, to express his
10 thoughts with all the graces of elocution, to write more figuratively, and to confess, as well the labour as the force of his imagination. Though he describes his *Dido* well and naturally, in the violence of her passions, yet he must yield in that to the *Myrrha,* the *Biblis,* the *Althæa,* of *Ovid;* for, as great an admirer of him as I am, I must acknowledge, that, if I see not more of their Souls then I see of *Dido's,* at least I have a greater concernment for them: and that convinces me that *Ovid* has touch'd those tender strokes more delicately then *Virgil* could. But when Action or Persons are to be describ'd, when any such Image is to be set before us, how bold, how masterly are
20 the strokes of *Virgil!* we see the objects he represents us with in their native figures, in their proper motions; but we so see them, as our own eyes could never have beheld them so beautiful in themselves. We see the Soul of the Poet, like that universal one of which he speaks, informing and moving through all his Pictures, *Totamque infusa per artus mens agitat molem, & magno se corpore miscet;* we behold him embellishing his Images, as he makes *Venus* breathing beauty upon her son *Æneas.*

　　　　　　　——*lumenque juventæ*
Purpureum, & lætos oculis afflârat honores:
30 *Quale manus addunt Ebori decus, aut ubi flavo*
Argentum, Pariusve lapis circundatur auro.

　　See his Tempest, his Funeral Sports, his Combat of *Turnus* and *Æneas,* and in his *Georgicks,* which I esteem the Divinest part of

---

19　be set] O5, Q; *beset* O1–4.　　　25　*molem*] Q; motem O1–5.
31　*Pariusve*] Q; pariusve O1–5.

all his writings, the Plague, the Country, the Battel of Bulls, the labour of the Bees, and those many other excellent Images of Nature, most of which are neither great in themselves, nor have any natural ornament to bear them up: but the words wherewith he describes them are so excellent, that it might be well appli'd to him which was said by *Ovid, Materiam superabat opus:* the very sound of his words has often somewhat that is connatural to the subject, and while we read him, we sit, as in a Play, beholding the Scenes of what he represents. To perform this, he made frequent use of Tropes, which you
10 know change the nature of a known word, by applying it to some other signification; and this is it which *Horace* means in his Epistle to the *Pisos.*

> *Dixeris egregie notum si callida verbum*
> *Reddiderit junctura novum*————

But I am sensible I have presum'd too far, to entertain you with a rude discourse of that Art, which you both know so well, and put into practise with so much happiness. Yet before I leave *Virgil,* I must own the vanity to tell you, and by you the world, that he has been my Master in this Poem: I have followed him every where, I
20 know not with what success, but I am sure with diligence enough: my Images are many of them copied from him, and the rest are imitations of him. My expressions also are as near as the Idioms of the two Languages would admit of in translation. And this, Sir, I have done with that boldness, for which I will stand accomptable to any of our little Criticks, who, perhaps, are not better acquainted with him then I am. Upon your first perusal of this Poem, you have taken notice of some words which I have innovated (if it be too bold for me to say refin'd) upon his *Latin;* which, as I offer not to introduce into *English* prose, so I hope they are neither improper, nor altogether unelegant
30 in Verse; and, in this, *Horace* will again defend me.

> *Et nova, fictaque nuper habebunt verba fidem, si*
> *Græco fonte cadant, parcè detorta*————

The inference is exceeding plain; for if a *Roman* Poet might have

---

5 excellent] O4–5, Q; *excellent* O1–3.

liberty to coin a word, supposing onely that it was derived from the *Greek,* was put into a *Latin* termination, and that he us'd this liberty but seldom, and with modesty: How much more justly may I challenge that privilege to do it with the same præwrequisits, from the best and most judicious of *Latin* Writers? In some places, where either the fancy, or the words, were his, or any others, I have noted it in the Margin, that I might not seem a Plagiary: in others I have neglected it, to avoid as well the tediousness, as the affectation of doing it too often. Such descriptions or images, well wrought, which I promise not

10 for mine, are, as I have said, the adequate delight of heroick Poesie, for they beget admiration, which is its proper object; as the images of the Burlesque, which is contrary to this, by the same reason beget laughter; for the one shows Nature beautified, as in the picture of a fair Woman, which we all admire; the other shows her deformed, as in that of a Lazar, or of a fool with distorted face and antique gestures, at which we cannot forbear to laugh, because it is a deviation from Nature. But though the same images serve equally for the Epique Poesie, and for the Historique and Panegyrique, which are branches of it, yet a several sort of Sculpture is to be used in them:

20 if some of them are to be like those of *Juvenal, Stantes in curribus Æmiliani,* Heroes drawn in their triumphal Chariots, and in their full proportion; others are to be like that of *Virgil, Spirantia mollius æra:* there is somewhat more of softness and tenderness to be shown in them. You will soon find I write not this without concern. Some who have seen a paper of Verses which I wrote last year to her Highness the *Dutchess,* have accus'd them of that onely thing I could defend in them; they have said I did *humi serpere,* that I wanted not onely height of fancy, but dignity of words to set it off; I might well answer with that of *Horace, Nunc non erat hic locus,* I knew I

30 address'd them to a Lady, and accordingly I affected the softness of expression, and the smoothness of measure, rather then the height of thought; and in what I did endeavour, it is no vanity to say, I have succeeded. I detest arrogance, but there is some difference betwixt that and a just defence. But I will not farther bribe your candour, or the Readers. I leave them to speak for me, and, if they can, to make out that character, not pretending to a greater, which I have given them.

VERSES TO HER HIGHNESS THE DUTCHESS, ON THE MEMORABLE
VICTORY GAIN'D BY THE DUKE AGAINST THE HOLLANDERS,
JUNE THE 3. 1665. AND ON HER JOURNEY AFTERWARDS
INTO THE NORTH.

MADAM,

When, for our sakes, your *Heroe* you resign'd
To swelling Seas, and every faithless wind;
When you releas'd his courage, and set free
A valour fatal to the Enemy,
You lodg'd your Countries cares within your breast;
(The mansion where soft Love should onely rest:)
And ere our foes abroad were overcome,
The noblest conquest you had gain'd at home.
Ah, what concerns did both your Souls divide!
10 Your Honour gave us what your Love deni'd:
And 'twas for him much easier to subdue
Those foes he fought with, then to part from you.
That glorious day, which two such Navies saw,
As each, unmatch'd, might to the world give Law,
Neptune, yet doubtful whom he should obey,
Held to them both the Trident of the Sea:
The winds were hush'd, the waves in ranks were cast,
As awfully as when God's people past:
Those, yet uncertain on whose sails to blow,
20 These, where the wealth of Nations ought to flow.
Then with the Duke your Highness rul'd the day:⎤
While all the brave did his command obey, ⎬
The fair and pious under you did pray. ⎦
How pow'rful are chast vows! the wind and tyde
You brib'd to combat on the *English* side.
Thus to your much lov'd Lord you did convey
An unknown succour, sent the nearest way.

14 Law,] ∼. O1–5, Q.   22 obey,] Q; ∼. O1–5.

New vigour to his wearied arms you brought;
(So *Moses* was upheld while *Israel* fought.)
While, from afar, we heard the Canon play,
Like distant Thunder on a shiny day,
For absent friends we were asham'd to fear,
When we consider'd what you ventur'd there.
Ships, Men and Arms our Country might restore,
But such a Leader could supply no more.
With generous thoughts of conquest he did burn,
10 Yet fought not more to vanquish then return.
Fortune and victory he did pursue,
To bring them, as his Slaves, to wait on you.
Thus Beauty ravish'd the rewards of Fame,
And the Fair triumph'd when the Brave o'rcame.
Then, as you meant to spread another way
By Land your Conquests far as his by Sea,
Leaving our Southern Clime, you march'd along
The stubborn North, ten thousand *Cupid's* strong.
Like Commons the Nobility resort
20 In crowding heaps, to fill your moving Court:
To welcome your approach the Vulgar run,
Like some new Envoy from the distant Sun.
And Country Beauties by their Lovers go,
Blessing themselves, and wondring at the show.
So when the new-born *Phœnix* first is seen,
Her feather'd Subjects all adore their Queen.
And, while she makes her progress through the East,
From every grove her numerous train's increast:
Each Poet of the air her glory sings,
30 And round him the pleas'd Audience clap their wings.

And now, Sir, 'tis time I should relieve you from the tedious length
of this account. You have better and more profitable employment for
your hours, and I wrong the Publick to detain you longer. In conclusion, I must leave my Poem to you with all its faults, which I hope
to find fewer in the printing by your emendations. I know you are

---

22 Envoy] O5, Q; Envoy' O1–4.

not of the number of those, of whom the younger *Pliny* speaks, *Nec sunt parum multi qui carpere amicos suos judicium vocant;* I am rather too secure of you on that side. Your candour in pardoning my errors may make you more remiss in correcting them; if you will not withall consider that they come into the world with your approbation, and through your hands. I beg from you the greatest favor you can confer upon an absent person, since I repose upon your management what is dearest to me, my Fame and Reputation; & therefore I hope it will stir you up to make my Poem fairer by many of your blots; if not, you know the story of the Gamester who married the rich man's daughter, and when her father denyed the portion, christned all the children by his sirname, that if, in conclusion, they must beg, they should do so by one name, as well as by the other. But since the reproach of my faults will light on you, 'tis but reason I should do you that justice to the Readers, to let them know that if there be any thing tolerable in this Poem, they owe the Argument to your choice, the writing to your encouragement, the correction to your judgment, and the care of it to your friendship, to which he must ever acknowledge himself to owe all things, who is,

SIR,

From *Charleton* in
Wiltshire, Novem.
10. 1666.

*The most obedient and most
faithful of your Servants,*
J O H N   D R Y D E N.

Annus Mirabilis: The Year of Wonders, 1666

IN thriving Arts long time had *Holland* grown,
  Crouching at home, and cruel when abroad:
  Scarce leaving us the means to claim our own.
Our King they courted, & our Merchants aw'd.
        2.
Trade, which like bloud should circularly flow,
  Stop'd in their Channels, found its freedom lost:

Thither the wealth of all the world did go,
    And seem'd but shipwrack'd on so base a Coast.

3.

For them alone the Heav'ns had kindly heat,
10   ᵃIn Eastern Quarries ripening precious Dew:
For them the *Idumæan* Balm did sweat,
    And in hot *Ceilon* Spicy Forrests grew.

4.

The Sun but seem'd the Lab'rer of their Year;
    ᵇEach wexing Moon suppli'd her watry store,
To swell those Tides, which from the Line did bear
    Their brim-full Vessels to the *Belg'an* shore.

5.

Thus mighty in her Ships, stood *Carthage* long,
    And swept the riches of the world from far;
Yet stoop'd to *Rome,* less wealthy, but more strong:
20   And this may prove our second Punick War.

6.

What peace can be where both to one pretend?
    (But they more diligent, and we more strong)
Or if a peace, it soon must have an end
    For they would grow too pow'rful were it long.

7.

Behold two Nations then, ingag'd so far,
    That each seav'n years the fit must shake each Land:
Where *France* will side to weaken us by War,
    Who onely can his vast designs withstand.

8.

See how he feeds th' ᶜ*Iberian* with delays,
30   To render us his timely friendship vain;

    ᵃ *In Eastern Quarries, &c. Precious Stones at first are Dew, condens'd and harden'd by the warmth of the Sun, or subterranean Fires.* [All notes to this poem marked by reference letters or asterisks are Dryden's.]

    ᵇ *Each wexing, &c. according to their opinion, who think that great heap of waters under the Line is depressed into Tydes by the Moon, towards the Poles.*

    ᶜ *Th' Iberian, the* Spaniard.

And, while his secret Soul on *Flanders* preys,
    He rocks the Cradle of the Babe of *Spain*.
9.

Such deep designs of Empire does he lay
    O're them whose cause he seems to take in hand:
And, prudently, would make them Lords at Sea,
    To whom with ease he can give Laws by Land.
10.

This saw our King; and long within his breast
    His pensive counsels ballanc'd too and fro;
He griev'd the Land he freed should be oppress'd,
40   And he less for it then Usurpers do.
11.

His gen'rous mind the fair Idea's drew
    Of Fame and Honour which in dangers lay;
Where wealth, like fruit on precipices, grew,
    Not to be gather'd but by Birds of prey.
12.

The loss and gain each fatally were great;
    And still his Subjects call'd aloud for war:
But peaceful Kings o'r martial people set,
    Each others poize and counter-ballance are.
13.

He, first, survey'd the charge with careful eyes,
50   Which none but mighty Monarchs could maintain;
Yet judg'd, like vapours that from Limbecks rise,
    It would in richer showers descend again.
14.

At length resolv'd t' assert the watry Ball,
    He in himself did whole Armado's bring:
Him, aged Sea-men might their Master call,
    And choose for General were he not their King.
15.

It seems as every Ship their Sovereign knows,
    His awful summons they so soon obey;

---

43 on] O1–4 *errata,* O5, Q; an O1–4 *text.*

So hear the skaly Herd when [d]*Proteus* blows,
60　　And so to pasture follow through the Sea.
　　　　　16.
To see this Fleet upon the Ocean move
　　Angels drew wide the Curtains of the skies:
And Heav'n, as if their wanted Lights above,
　　For Tapers made two glareing Comets rise.
　　　　　17.
Whether they unctuous Exhalations are,
　　Fir'd by the Sun, or seeming so alone,
Or each some more remote and slippery Star,
　　Which looses footing when to Mortals shown.
　　　　　18.
Or one that bright companion of the Sun,
70　　Whose glorious aspect seal'd our new-born King;
And now a round of greater years begun,
　　New influence from his walks of light did bring.
　　　　　19.
Victorious *York* did, first, with fam'd success,
　　To his known valour make the *Dutch* give place:
Thus Heav'n our Monarch's fortune did confess,
　　Beginning conquest from his Royal Race.
　　　　　20.
But since it was decreed, Auspicious King,
　　In *Britain*'s right that thou should'st wed the Main,
Heav'n, as a gage, would cast some precious thing
80　　And therefore doom'd that *Lawson* should be slain.
　　　　　21.
Lawson amongst the formost met his fate,
　　Whom Sea-green *Syrens* from the Rocks lament:
Thus as an off'ring for the *Grecian* State,
　　He first was kill'd who first to Battel went.

---

d *When* Proteus *blows, or* Cæruleus Proteus immania ponti armenta & magnas pascit sub gurgite Phocas. *Virg.*

59　hear] here O1–5, Q.
Note *d*　ponti armenta & magnas pascit] O1–4 *errata,* O5; . . . poscit Q; pouti armenta, & magnas poscit O1–4 *text.*

22.

*Their Chief blown up, in air, not waves expir'd,
  To which his pride presum'd to give the Law:
The *Dutch* confess'd Heav'n present, and retir'd,
  And all was *Britain* the wide Ocean saw.
        23.
To nearest Ports their shatter'd Ships repair,
90 Where by our dreadful Canon they lay aw'd:
So reverently men quit the open air
  When thunder speaks the angry Gods abroad.

THE ATTEMPT AT BERGHEN
        24.
And now approach'd their Fleet from *India,* fraught
  With all the riches of the rising Sun:
And precious Sand from ᵉSouthern Climates brought,
  (The fatal Regions where the War begun.)
        25.
Like hunted *Castors,* conscious of their store,
  Their way-laid wealth to *Norway*'s coasts they bring:
There first the North's cold bosome Spices bore,
100 And Winter brooded on the Eastern Spring.
        26.
By the rich scent we found our perfum'd prey,
  Which flanck'd with Rocks did close in covert lie:
And round about their murdering Canon lay,
  At once to threaten and invite the eye.
        27.
Fiercer then Canon, and then Rocks more hard,
  The *English* undertake th' unequal War:
Seven Ships alone, by which the Port is barr'd,
  Besiege the *Indies,* and all *Denmark* dare.

---

  * *The Admiral of* Holland.
  ᵉ *Southern Climates,* Guinny.

---

106 undertake] O1–4 *errata,* O5, Q; undertook O1–4 *text.*

28.

These fight like Husbands, but like Lovers those:
110   These fain would keep, and those more fain enjoy:
And to such height their frantick passion grows,
    That what both love, both hazard to destroy.

29.

Amidst whole heaps of Spices lights a Ball,
    And now their Odours arm'd against them flie:
Some preciously by shatter'd Porc'lain fall,
    And some by Aromatick splinters die.

30.

And though by Tempests of the prize bereft,
    In Heavens inclemency some ease we find:
Our foes we vanquish'd by our valour left,
120   And onely yielded to the Seas and Wind.

31.

Nor wholly lost we so deserv'd a prey;
    For storms, repenting, part of it restor'd:
Which, as a tribute from the Balthick Sea,
    The British Ocean sent her mighty Lord.

32.

Go, Mortals, now, and vex your selves in vain
    For wealth, which so uncertainly must come:
When what was brought so far, and with such pain,
    Was onely kept to lose it neerer home.

33.

The Son, who, twice three month's on th' Ocean tost,
130   Prepar'd to tell what he had pass'd before,
Now sees, in *English* Ships the *Holland* Coast,
    And Parents arms in vain stretch'd from the shore.

34.

This carefull Husband had been long away,
    Whom his chast wife and little children mourn;
Who on their fingers learn'd to tell the day
    On which their Father promis'd to return.

35.
ᶠSuch are the proud designs of human kind,
　And so we suffer Shipwrack every where!
Alas, what Port can such a Pilot find,
140　　Who in the night of Fate must blindly steer!
36.
The undistinguish'd seeds of good and ill
　Heav'n, in his bosom, from our knowledge hides;
And draws them in contempt of human skill,
　　Which oft, for friends, mistaken foes provides.

37.
Let *Munsters* Prelate ever be accurst,
　In whom we seek the ᵍ*German* faith in vain:
Alas, that he should teach the *English* first
　　That fraud and avarice in the Church could reign!
38.
Happy who never trust a Strangers will,
150　　Whose friendship's in his interest understood!
Since money giv'n but tempts him to be ill
　　When pow'r is too remote to make him good.

WAR DECLAR'D BY FRANCE
39.
Till now, alone the Mighty Nations strove:
　The rest, at gaze, without the Lists did stand:
And threatning *France,* plac'd like a painted *Jove,*
　　Kept idle thunder in his lifted hand.
40.
That Eunuch Guardian of rich *Hollands* trade,
　Who envies us what he wants pow'r t' enjoy!
Whose noisefull valour does no foe invade,
160　　And weak assistance will his friends destroy.

ᶠ *Such are,* &c. *from* Petronius. Si, bene calculum ponas ubique fit naufragium.
ᵍ *The* German *faith.* Tacitus *saith of them,* Nullos mortalium fide aut armis ante Germanos esse.

Note *f*　fit naufragium] O1–4 errata, O5, Q; naufragiunt est O1–4 *text.*
Note *g*　them,] O5; ∼ . O1–4, Q.

41.

Offended that we fought without his leave,
   He takes this time his secret hate to show:
Which *Charles* does with a mind so calm receive
   As one that neither seeks, nor shuns his foe.

42.

With *France,* to aid the *Dutch,* the *Danes* unite:
   France as their Tyrant, *Denmark* as their Slave.
But when with one three Nations joyn to fight,
   They silently confess that one more brave.

43.

Lewis had chas'd the *English* from his shore;
170   But *Charles* the *French* as Subjects does invite.
Would Heav'n for each some *Salomon* restore,
   Who, by their mercy, may decide their right.

44.

Were Subjects so but onely by their choice,
   And not from Birth did forc'd Dominion take,
Our Prince alone would have the publique voice;
   And all his Neighbours Realms would desarts make.

45.

He without fear a dangerous War pursues,
   Which without rashness he began before.
As Honour made him first the danger choose,
180   So still he makes it good on virtues score.

46.

The doubled charge his Subjects love supplies,
   Who, in that bounty, to themselves are kind:
So glad Egyptians see their *Nilus* rise,
   And in his plenty their abundance find.

PRINCE RUPERT AND DUKE ALBEMARL SENT TO SEA

47.

With equal pow'r he does two Chiefs create,
   Two such, as each seem'd worthiest when alone:

Each able to sustain a Nations fate,
    Since both had found a greater in their own.
        48.
Both great in courage, Conduct and in Fame,
190   Yet neither envious of the others praise;
Their duty, faith, and int'rest too the same,
    Like mighty Partners equally they raise.
        49.
The Prince long time had courted Fortune's love,
    But once possess'd did absolutely reign;
Thus with their *Amazons* the *Heroes* strove,
    And conquer'd first those Beauties they would gain.
        50.
The Duke beheld, like *Scipio,* with disdain
    That *Carthage,* which he ruin'd, rise once more:
And shook aloft the Fasces of the Main,
200   To fright those Slaves with what they felt before.
        51.
Together to the watry Camp they haste,
    Whom Matrons passing, to their children show:
Infants first vows for them to Heav'n are cast,
    And [h]future people bless them as they go.
        52.
With them no riotous pomp, nor *Asian* train,
    T' infect a Navy with their gawdy fears:
To make slow fights, and victories but vain;
    But war, severely, like it self, appears.
        53.
Diffusive of themselves, where e'r they pass,
210   They make that warmth in others they expect:
Their valour works like bodies on a glass,
    And does its Image on their men project.

---

[h] *Future people,* Examina infantium futurusque populus. Plin. Jun. in pan. ad Traj.

---

190 praise;] Q; ~ . O1–5.   191 same,] O5, Q; ~ . O1–4.
197 Duke] Q; ~ , O1–5.

DUKE OF ALBEMARL'S BATTEL, FIRST DAY

54.

Our Fleet divides, and straight the *Dutch* appear,
  In number, and a fam'd Commander, bold:
The Narrow Seas can scarce their Navy bear,
  Or crowded Vessels can their Soldiers hold.

55.

The Duke, less numerous, but in courage more,
  On wings of all the winds to combat flies:
His murdering Guns a loud defiance roar,
220   And bloudy Crosses on his Flag-staffs rise.

56.

Both furl their sails, and strip them for the fight,
  Their folded sheets dismiss the useless air:
ᶦTh' *Elean* Plains could boast no nobler sight,
  When strugling Champions did their bodies bare.

57.

Born each by other in a distant Line,
  The Sea-built Forts in dreadful order move:
So vast the noise, as if not Fleets did joyn,
  ᵏBut Lands unfix'd, and floating Nations, strove.

58.

Now pass'd, on either side they nimbly tack,
230   Both strive to intercept and guide the wind:
And, in its eye, more closely they come back
  To finish all the deaths they left behind.

59.

On high-rais'd Decks the haughty *Belgians* ride,
  Beneath whose shade our humble Fregats go:
Such port the Elephant bears, and so defi'd
  By the *Rhinocero's* her unequal foe.

ᶦ *Th' Elean, &c. Where the Olimpick Games were celebrated.*
ᵏ *Lands unfix'd, from* Virgil: *Credas innare revulsas Cycladas, &c.*

---

219   a loud] O1–4 *errata*, O5, Q; aloud O1–4 *text.*
226   dreadful] O1–4 *errata*, O5, Q; distant O1–4 *text.*
Note k   *revulsas*] Q; *revultas* O1–5.

60.

And as the built, so different is the fight;
   Their mounting shot is on our sails design'd:
Deep in their hulls our deadly bullets light,
240   And through the yielding planks a passage find.

61.

Our dreaded Admiral from far they threat,
   Whose batter'd rigging their whole war receives.
All bare, like some old Oak which tempests beat,
   He stands, and sees below his scatter'd leaves.

62.

Heroes of old, when wounded, shelter sought,
   But he, who meets all danger with disdain,
Ev'n in their face his ship to Anchor brought,
   And Steeple high stood propt upon the Main.

63.

At this excess of courage, all amaz'd,
250   The foremost of his foes a while withdraw.
With such respect in enter'd *Rome* they gaz'd,
   Who on high Chairs the God-like Fathers saw.

64.

And now, as where *Patroclus* body lay,
   Here *Trojan* Chiefs advanc'd, & there the *Greek:*
Ours o'r the Duke their pious wings display,
   And theirs the noblest spoils of *Britain* seek.

65.

Mean time, his busie Marriners he hasts,
   His shatter'd sails with rigging to restore:
And willing Pines ascend his broken Masts,
260   Whose lofty heads rise higher then before.

66.

Straight to the *Dutch* he turns his dreadful prow,
   More fierce th' important quarrel to decide.
Like Swans, in long array his Vessels show,
   Whose creasts, advancing, do the waves divide.

67.

They charge, re-charge, and all along the Sea
    They drive, and squander the huge *Belgian* Fleet.
Berkley alone, who neerest Danger lay,
    Did a like fate with lost *Creüsa* meet.

68.

The night comes on, we, eager to pursue
270   The Combat still, and they asham'd to leave:
Till the last streaks of dying day withdrew,
    And doubtful Moon-light did our rage deceive.

69.

In th' *English* Fleet each ship resounds with joy,
    And loud applause of their great Leader's fame.
In fiery dreams the *Dutch* they still destroy,
    And, slumbring, smile at the imagin'd flame.

70.

Not so the *Holland* Fleet, who tir'd and done,
    Stretch'd on their decks like weary Oxen lie:
Faint sweats all down their mighty members run,
280   (Vast bulks which little souls but ill supply.)

71.

In dreams they fearful precipices tread,
    Or, shipwrack'd, labour to some distant shore:
Or in dark Churches walk among the dead:
    They wake with horrour, & dare sleep no more.

SECOND DAYS BATTEL

72.

The morn they look on with unwilling eyes,
    Till, from their Main-top, joyful news they hear
Of ships, which by their mould bring new supplies,
    And in their colours *Belgian* Lions bear.

73.

Our watchful General had discern'd, from far,
290   This mighty succour which made glad the foe.

---

267   who neerest Danger lay] O3–4, Q; not making equal way O1–2, O5.

He sigh'd, but, like a Father of the War,
  [1]His face spake hope, while deep his sorrows flow.
     74.
His wounded men he first sends off to shore:
  (Never, till now, unwilling to obey.)
They, not their wounds but want of strength deplore,
  And think them happy who with him can stay.
     75.
Then, to the rest, Rejoyce, (said he) to day
  In you the fortune of *Great Britain* lies:
Among so brave a people you are they
300   Whom Heav'n has chose to fight for such a Prize.
     76.
If number *English* courages could quell,
  We should at first have shun'd, not met our foes;
Whose numerous sails the fearful onely tell:
  Courage from hearts, and not from numbers grows.
     77.
He said; nor needed more to say: with hast
  To their known stations chearfully they go:
And all at once, disdaining to be last,
  Sollicite every gale to meet the foe.
     78.
Nor did th' incourag'd *Belgians* long delay,
310   But, bold in others, not themselves, they stood:
So thick, our Navy scarce could sheer their way,
  But seem'd to wander in a moving wood.
     79.
Our little Fleet was now ingag'd so far,
  That, like the Sword-fish in the Whale, they fought.
The Combat onely seem'd a Civil War,
  Till through their bowels we our passage wrought.
     80.
Never had valour, no not ours before,
  Done ought like this upon the Land or Main:

---

[1]*His face, &c.* Spem vultu simulat premit alto corde dolorem. *Virg.*

Where not to be o'rcome was to do more
320   Then all the Conquests former Kings did gain.
          81.
The mighty Ghosts of our great *Harries* rose,
    And armed *Edwards* look'd, with anxious eyes,
To see this Fleet among unequal foes,
    By which fate promis'd them their *Charls* should rise.
          82.
Mean time the *Belgians* tack upon our Reer,
    And raking Chace-guns through our sterns they send:
Close by, their Fire-ships, like *Jackals,* appear,
    Who on their Lions for the prey attend.
          83.
Silent in smoke of Canons they come on:
330   (Such vapours once did fiery *Cacus* hide.)
In these the height of pleas'd revenge is shown,
    Who burn contented by another's side.
          84.
Sometimes, from fighting Squadrons of each Fleet,
    (Deceiv'd themselves, or to preserve some friend)
Two grapling *Ætna's* on the Ocean meet,
    And *English* fires with *Belgian* flames contend.
          85.
Now, at each Tack, our little Fleet grows less;
    And, like maim'd fowl, swim lagging on the Main.
Their greater loss their numbers scarce confess
340   While they lose cheaper then the *English* gain.
          86.
Have you not seen when, whistled from the fist,
    Some Falcon stoops at what her eye design'd,
And, with her eagerness, the quarry miss'd,
    Straight flies at check, and clips it down the wind,
          87.
The dastard Crow, that to the wood made wing,
    And sees the Groves no shelter can afford,

---

344   wind,] ∼ . O1-5, Q.

With her loud Kaws her Craven kind does bring,
  Who, safe in numbers cuff the noble Bird?
        88.
Among the *Dutch* thus *Albemarl* did fare:
350 He could not conquer, and disdain'd to flie.
Past hope of safety, 'twas his latest care,
  Like falling *Cesar,* decently to die.
        89.
Yet pity did his manly spirit move
  To see those perish who so well had fought:
And, generously, with his dispair he strove,
  Resolv'd to live till he their safety wrought.
        90.
Let other Muses write his prosp'rous fate,
  Of conquer'd Nations tell, and Kings restor'd:
But mine shall sing of his eclips'd estate,
360 Which, like the Sun's, more wonders does afford.
        91.
He drew his mighty Fregates all before,
  On which the foe his fruitless force employes:
His weak ones deep into his Reer he bore,
  Remote from Guns as sick men are from noise.
        92.
His fiery Canon did their passage guide,
  And foll'wing smoke obscur'd them from the foe.
Thus *Israel* safe from the *Egyptian*'s pride,
  By flaming pillars, and by clouds did go.
        93.
Elsewhere the *Belgian* force we did defeat,
370 But here our courages did theirs subdue:
So *Xenophon* once led that fam'd retreat,
  Which first the *Asian* Empire overthrew.
        94.
The foe approach'd: and one, for his bold sin,
  Was sunk, (as he that touch'd the Ark was slain;)

---

348 Bird?] ~ . O1–5, Q.

The wild waves master'd him, and suck'd him in,
  And smiling Eddies dimpled on the Main.
            95.
This seen, the rest at awful distance stood;
  As if they had been there as servants set,
To stay, or to go on, as he thought good,
380   And not persue, but wait on his retreat.
            96.
So *Lybian* Huntsmen, on some sandy plain,
  From shady coverts rouz'd, the Lion chace:
The Kingly beast roars out with loud disdain,
  mAnd slowly moves, unknowing to give place.
            97.
But if some one approach to dare his force,
  He swings his tail, and swiftly turns him round:
With one paw seizes on his trembling Horse,
  And with the other tears him to the ground.
            98.
Amidst these toils succeeds the balmy night,
390   Now hissing waters the quench'd guns restore;
nAnd weary waves, withdrawing from the fight,
  Lie lull'd and panting on the silent shore.
            99.
The Moon shone clear on the becalmed floud,
  Where, while her beams like glittering silver play,
Upon the Deck our careful General stood,
  And deeply mus'd on the osucceeding day.
            100.
That happy Sun, said he, will rise again,
  Who twice victorious did our Navy see:
And I alone must view him rise in vain,
400   Without one ray of all his Star for me.

---

m *The simile is* Virgil's, Vestigia retro improperata refert, &c.
n *Weary waves, from* Statius Sylv. Nec trucibus fluviis idem sonus: occidit horror
æquoris, ac terris maria acclinata quiescunt.
o *The third of* June, *famous for two former Victories.*

Note *n* ac terris] ac tenis O1–5; antennis Q.

101.

Yet, like an *English* Gen'ral will I die,
    And all the Ocean make my spatious grave.
Women and Cowards on the Land may lie,
    The Sea's a Tomb that's proper for the brave.

102.

Restless he pass'd the remnants of the night,
    Till the fresh air proclaim'd the morning nigh,
And burning ships, the Martyrs of the fight,
    With paler fires beheld the Eastern sky.

THIRD DAY

103.

But now, his stores of Ammunition spent,
410   His naked valour is his onely guard:
Rare thunders are from his dumb Canon sent,
    And solitary Guns are scarcely heard.

104.

Thus far had Fortune pow'r, here forc'd to stay,
    Nor longer durst with vertue be at strife:
This, as a ransome *Albemarl* did pay
    For all the glories of so great a life.

105.

For now brave *Rupert* from afar appears,
    Whose waving streamers the glad General knows:
With full spread Sails his eager Navy steers,
420   And every Ship in swift proportion grows.

106.

The anxious Prince had heard the Canon long,
    And from that length of time dire *Omens* drew
Of *English* over-match'd, and *Dutch* too strong,
    Who never fought three days but to pursue.

417–420 O2–4, Q; O1 *and* O5 *read:*
            For now brave *Rupert*'s Navy did appear,
                Whose waving streamers from afar he knows:
            As in his fate something divine there were,
                Who dead and buried the third day arose.

107.

Then, as an Eagle, (who, with pious care,
  Was beating widely on the wing for prey)
To her now silent Eiry does repair,
  And finds her callow Infants forc'd away;
          108.

Stung with her love she stoops upon the plain,
430   The broken air loud whistling as she flies:
She stops, and listens, and shoots forth again,
  And guides her pinions by her young ones cries:
          109.

With such kind passion hastes the Prince to fight,
  And spreads his flying canvass to the sound:
Him, whom no danger, were he there could fright,
  Now, absent, every little noise can wound.
          110.

As, in a drought, the thirsty creatures cry,
  And gape upon the gather'd clowds for rain,
And first the Martlet meets it in the sky,
440   And, with wet wings, joys all the feather'd train,
          111.

With such glad hearts did our dispairing men
  Salute th' appearance of the Princes Fleet:
And each ambitiously would claim the Ken
  That with first eyes did distant safety meet.
          112.

The *Dutch,* who came like greedy Hinds before,
  To reap the harvest their ripe ears did yield,
Now look like those, when rowling thunders roar,
  And sheets of Lightning blast the standing field.
          113.

Full in the Princes passage, hills of sand
450   And dang'rous flats in secret ambush lay,
Where the false tides skim o'r the cover'd Land,
  And Sea-men with dissembled depths betray:

---

428 away;] ~ . O1–5, Q.   432 cries:] ~ . O1–5, Q.
440 train,] ~ . O1–5, Q.

114.

The wily *Dutch,* who, like fall'n Angels, fear'd
    This new *Messiah*'s coming, there did wait,
And round the verge their braving Vessels steer'd,
    To tempt his courage with so fair a bait.

115.

But he, unmov'd, contemns their idle threat,
    Secure of fame when ere he please to fight:
His cold experience tempers all his heat,
460   And inbred worth does boasting valour slight.

116.

Heroique virtue did his actions guide,
    And he the substance not th' appearance chose:
To rescue one such friend he took more pride
    Than to destroy whole thousands of such foes.

117.

But, when approach'd, in strict embraces bound,
    Rupert and *Albemarl* together grow:
He joys to have his friend in safety found,
    Which he to none but to that friend would owe.

118.

The chearful Souldiers, with new stores suppli'd,
470   Now long to execute their spleenfull will;
And, in revenge for those three days they tri'd,
    Wish one, like *Joshuah*'s, when the Sun stood still.

FOURTH DAYS BATTEL

119.

Thus re-inforc'd, against the adverse Fleet
    Still doubling ours, brave *Rupert* leads the way.
With the first blushes of the Morn they meet,
    And bring night back upon the new-born day.

120.

His presence soon blows up the kindling fight,
    And his loud Guns speak thick like angry men:
It seem'd as slaughter had been breath'd all night,
480   And death new pointed his dull dart agen.

121.

The *Dutch,* too well his mighty Conduct knew,
    And matchless Courage since the former fight:
Whose Navy like a stiff stretch'd cord did show
    Till he bore in, and bent them into flight.

122.

The wind he shares while half their Fleet offends
    His open side, and high above him shows,
Upon the rest at pleasure he descends,
    And, doubly harm'd, he double harms bestows.

123.

Behind, the Gen'ral mends his weary pace,
490   And sullenly to his revenge he sails:
ᵖSo glides some trodden Serpent on the grass,
    And long behind his wounded vollume trails.

124.

Th' increasing sound is born to either shore,
    And for their stakes the throwing Nations fear.
Their passions double with the Cannons roar,
    And with warm wishes each man combats there.

125.

Pli'd thick and close as when the fight begun,
    Their huge unwieldy Navy wasts away:
So sicken waning Moons too neer the Sun,
500   And blunt their crescents on the edge of day.

126.

And now reduc'd on equal terms to fight,
    Their Ships like wasted Patrimonies show:
Where the thin scatt'ring Trees admit the light,
    And shun each others shadows as they grow.

127.

The warlike Prince had sever'd from the rest
    Two giant ships, the pride of all the Main;

ᵖ *So glides, &c. from* Virgil. Quum medii nexus, extremæque agmina caudæ solvuntur; tardosque trahit sinus ultimus orbes, &c.

---

495 passions] passion, O1–5, Q.
Note *p* extremæque] O5; extremœque O1–4, Q.

Which, with his one, so vigorously he press'd,
    And flew so home they could not rise again.
        128.
Already batter'd, by his Lee they lay,
510   In vain upon the passing winds they call:
The passing winds through their torn canvass play,
    And flagging sails on heartless Sailors fall.
        129.
Their open'd sides receive a gloomy light,
    Dreadful as day let in to shades below:
Without, grim death rides bare-fac'd in their sight,
    And urges ent'ring billows as they flow.
        130.
When one dire shot, the last they could supply,
    Close by the board the Prince's Main-mast bore:
All three now, helpless, by each other lie,
520   And this offends not, and those fear no more.
        131.
So have I seen some fearful Hare maintain
    A Course, till tir'd before the Dog she lay:
Who, stretch'd behind her, pants upon the plain,
    Past pow'r to kill as she to get away.
        132.
With his loll'd tongue he faintly licks his prey,
    His warm breath blows her flix up as she lies:
She, trembling, creeps upon the ground away,
    And looks back to him with beseeching eyes.
        133.
The Prince unjustly does his Stars accuse,
530   Which hinder'd him to push his fortune on:
For what they to his courage did refuse,
    By mortal valour never must be done.
        134.
This lucky hour the wise *Batavian* takes,
    And warns his tatter'd Fleet to follow home:

---

507 one] O1–4 *errata,* O5, Q; own O1–4 *text.*
518 board] Q; boar'd O1–5.

Proud to have so got off with equal stakes,
 qWhere 'twas a triumph not to be o'r-come.
   135.
The General's force, as kept alive by fight,
 Now, not oppos'd, no longer can persue:
Lasting till Heav'n had done his courage right,
540 When he had conquer'd he his weakness knew.
   136.
He casts a frown on the departing foe,
 And sighs to see him quit the watry field:
His stern fix'd eyes no satisfaction show,
 For all the glories which the Fight did yield.
   137.
Though, as when Fiends did Miracles avow,
 He stands confess'd ev'n by the boastful *Dutch,*
He onely does his conquest disavow,
 And thinks too little what they found too much.
   138.
Return'd, he with the Fleet resolv'd to stay,
550 No tender thoughts of home his heart divide:
Domestick joys and cares he puts away,
 For Realms are housholds which the Great must guide.
   139.
As those who unripe veins in Mines explore,
 On the rich bed again the warm turf lay,
Till time digests the yet imperfect Ore,
 And know it will be Gold another day:
   140.
So looks our Monarch on this early fight,
 Th' essay, and rudiments of great success,
Which all-maturing time must bring to light,
560 While he, like Heav'n, does each days labour bless.

 q *From* Horace: Quos opimus fallere & effugere est triumphus.

556 day:] ∼. O1–5, Q.
Note *q* opimus] opinius O1–5, Q.

141.

Heav'n ended not the first or second day,
　　Yet each was perfect to the work design'd:
God and Kings work, when they their work survey,
　　And passive aptness in all subjects find.

HIS MAJESTY REPAIRS THE FLEET

142.

In burden'd Vessels, first, with speedy care,
　　His plenteous Stores do season'd timber send:
Thither the brawny Carpenters repair,
　　And as the Surgeons of maim'd ships attend.

143.

With Cord and Canvass from rich *Hamburgh* sent,
570　　His Navies molted wings he imps once more:
Tall *Norway* Fir, their Masts in Battel spent,
　　And *English* Oak sprung leaks and planks restore.

144.

All hands employ'd, ʳthe Royal work grows warm,
　　Like labouring Bees on a long Summers day,
Some sound the Trumpet for the rest to swarm,
　　And some on bells of tasted Lillies play:

145.

With glewy wax some new foundation lay
　　Of Virgin combs, which from the roof are hung:
Some arm'd within doors, upon duty stay,
580　　Or tend the sick, or educate the young.

146.

So here, some pick out bullets from the sides,
　　Some drive old Okum through each seam & rift:
Their left-hand does the Calking-iron guide,
　　The ratling Mallet with the right they lift.

ʳ Fervet opus: *the same similitude in* Virgil.

568　Surgeons] O1–4 *errata*, O5, Q; Chyrurg'ons O1–4 *text.*

147.

With boiling Pitch another near at hand
  (From friendly *Sweden* brought) the seams instops:
Which well paid o'r the salt-Sea waves withstand,
  And shakes them from the rising beak in drops.

148.

Some the gall'd ropes with dawby Marling bind,
590 Or sear-cloth Masts with strong Tarpawling coats:
To try new shrouds one mounts into the wind,
  And one, below, their ease or stifness notes.

149.

Our careful Monarch stands in Person by,
  His new-cast Canons firmness to explore:
The strength of big-corn'd powder loves to try,
  And Ball and Cartrage sorts for every bore.

150.

Each day brings fresh supplies of Arms and Men,
  And Ships which all last Winter were abrode:
And such as fitted since the Fight had been,
600 Or new from Stocks were fall'n into the Road.

LOYAL LONDON DESCRIB'D

151.

The goodly *London* in her gallant trim,
  (The *Phœnix* daughter of the vanish'd old:)
Like a rich Bride does to the Ocean swim,
  And on her shadow rides in floating gold.

152.

Her Flag aloft spread ruffling to the wind,
  And sanguine Streamers seem the floud to fire:
The Weaver charm'd with what his Loom design'd,
  Goes on to Sea, and knows not to retire.

153.

With roomy decks, her Guns of mighty strength,
610 (Whose low-laid mouthes each mounting billow laves:)
Deep in her draught, and warlike in her length,
  She seems a Sea-wasp flying on the waves.

154.

This martial Present, piously design'd,
  The Loyal City give their best-lov'd King:
And with a bounty ample as the wind,
  Built, fitted and maintain'd to aid him bring.

DIGRESSION CONCERNING SHIPPING AND NAVIGATION

155.

By viewing Nature, Natures Hand-maid, Art,
  Makes mighty things from small beginnings grow:
Thus fishes first to shipping did impart
620   Their tail the Rudder, and their head the Prow.

156.

Some Log, perhaps, upon the waters swam
  An useless drift, which, rudely cut within,
And hollow'd, first a floating trough became,
  And cross some Riv'let passage did begin.

157.

In shipping such as this the *Irish Kern,*
  And untaught *Indian,* on the stream did glide:
Ere sharp-keel'd Boats to stem the floud did learn,
  Or fin-like Oars did spread from either side.

158.

Adde but a Sail, and *Saturn* so appear'd,
630   When, from lost Empire, he to Exile went,
And with the Golden age to *Tyber* steer'd,
  Where Coin & first Commerce he did invent.

159.

Rude as their Ships was Navigation, then;
  No useful Compass or Meridian known:
Coasting, they kept the Land within their ken,
  And knew no North but when the Pole-star shone.

160.

Of all who since have us'd the open Sea,
  Then the bold *English* none more fame have won:

ˢBeyond the Year, and out of Heav'ns high-way,
640 They make discoveries where they see no Sun.
   161.
But what so long in vain, and yet unknown,
 By poor man-kinds benighted wit is sought,
Shall in this Age to *Britain* first be shown,
 And hence be to admiring Nations taught.
   162.
The Ebbs of Tydes, and their mysterious flow,
 We, as Arts Elements shall understand:
And as by Line upon the Ocean go,
 Whose paths shall be familiar as the Land.
   163.
ᵗInstructed ships shall sail to quick Commerce;
650 By which remotest Regions are alli'd:
Which makes one City of the Universe,
 Where some may gain, and all may be suppli'd.
   164.
Then, we upon our Globes last verge shall go,
 And view the Ocean leaning on the sky:
From thence our rolling Neighbours we shall know,
 And on the Lunar world securely pry.

  APOSTROPHE TO THE ROYAL SOCIETY
   165.
This I fore-tel, from your auspicious care,
 Who great in search of God and Nature grow:
Who best your wise Creator's praise declare,
660 Since best to praise his works is best to know.
   166.
O truly Royal! who behold the Law,
 And rule of beings in your Makers mind,

---

s Extra anni solisque vias. *Virg.*
t *By a more exact knowledge of Longitudes.*

---

655 know,] O5, Q; ~ . O1–4.
Note *s* vias] O1–4 *errata,* O5, Q; vicis O1–4 *text.*

And thence, like Limbecks, rich Idea's draw,
 To fit the levell'd use of humane kind.
   167.
But first the toils of war we must endure,
 And, from th' Injurious *Dutch* redeem the Seas.
War makes the valiant of his right secure,
 And gives up fraud to be chastis'd with ease.
   168.
Already were the *Belgians* on our coast,
670 Whose Fleet more mighty every day became,
By late success, which they did falsly boast,
 And now, by first appearing seem'd to claim.
   169.
Designing, subtil, diligent, and close,
 They knew to manage War with wise delay:
Yet all those arts their vanity did cross,
 And, by their pride, their prudence did betray.
   170.
Nor staid the *English* long: but, well suppli'd,
 Appear as numerous as th' insulting foe.
The Combat now by courage must be tri'd,
680 And the success the braver Nation show.
   171.
There was the *Plimouth* Squadron new come in,
 Which in the *Straights* last Winter was abroad:
Which twice on *Biscay*'s working Bay had been,
 And on the Mid-land Sea the *French* had aw'd.
   172.
Old expert *Allen,* loyal all along,
 Fam'd for his action on the *Smirna* Fleet,
And *Holmes,* whose name shal live in Epique Song,
 While Musick Numbers, or while Verse has Feet.
   173.
Holmes, the *Achates* of the Gen'rals fight,
690 Who first bewitch'd our eyes with *Guinny* Gold:
As once old *Cato* in the *Roman's* sight
 The tempting fruits of *Africk* did unfold.

174.

With him went *Sprag,* as bountiful as brave,
   Whom his high courage to command had brought:
Harman, who did the twice fir'd *Harry* save,
   And in his burning ship undaunted fought.

175.

Young *Hollis,* on a *Muse* by *Mars* begot,
   Born, *Cesar*-like, to write and act great deeds:
Impatient to revenge his fatal shot,
700   His right hand doubly to his left succeeds.

176.

Thousands were there in darker fame that dwell,
   Whose deeds some nobler Poem shall adorn:
And, though to me unknown, they, sure, fought well,
   Whom *Rupert* led, and who were *British* born.

177.

Of every size an hundred fighting Sail,
   So vast the Navy now at Anchor rides,
That underneath it the press'd waters fail,
   And, with its weight, it shoulders off the Tydes.

178.

Now Anchors weigh'd, the Sea-men shout so shrill,
710   That Heav'n & Earth and the wide Ocean rings:
A breeze from Westward waits their sails to fill,
   And rests, in those high beds, his downy wings.

179.

The wary *Dutch* this gathering storm foresaw,
   And durst not bide it on the *English* coast:
Behind their treach'rous shallows they withdraw,
   And their lay snares to catch the *British* Hoast.

180.

So the false Spider, when her Nets are spread,
   Deep ambush'd in her silent den does lie:
And feels, far off, the trembling of her thread,
720   Whose filmy cord should bind the strugling Fly.

181.

Then, if at last, she find him fast beset,
    She issues forth, and runs along her Loom:
She joys to touch the Captive in her Net,
    And drags the little wretch in triumph home.

182.

The *Belgians* hop'd that, with disorder'd haste,
    Our deep-cut keels upon the sands might run:
Or, if with caution leisurely were past,
    Their numerous gross might charge us one by one.

183.

But, with a fore-wind pushing them above,
730   And swelling tyde that heav'd them from below,
O'r the blind flats our warlike Squadrons move,
    And, with spread sails, to welcome Battel go.

184.

It seem'd as there the *British Neptune* stood,
    With all his host of waters at command,
Beneath them to submit th' officious floud:
    [u]And, with his Trident, shov'd them off the sand.

185.

To the pale foes they suddenly draw near,
    And summon them to unexpected fight:
They start like Murderers when Ghosts appear,
740   And draw their Curtains in the dead of night.

SECOND BATTEL

186.

Now Van to Van the formost Squadrons meet,
    The midmost Battels hasting up behind,
Who view, far off, the storm of falling Sleet,
    And hear their thunder ratling in the wind.

---

[u] Levat ipse Tridenti, & vastas aperit Syrtes, &c. *Virg.*

---

731 flats] O1–4 *errata,* O5, Q; flots O1–4 *text.*

187.

At length the adverse Admirals appear:
(The two bold Champions of each Countries right)
Their eyes describe the lists as they come near,
    And draw the lines of death before they fight.

188.

The distance judg'd for shot of every size,
750   The Linstocks touch, the pond'rous ball expires:
The vig'rous Sea-man every port-hole plies,
    And adds his heart to every Gun he fires.

189.

Fierce was the fight on the proud *Belgians* side,
    For honour, which they seldome sought before:
But now they by their own vain boasts were ti'd,
    And forc'd, at least in show, to prize it more.

190.

But sharp remembrance on the *English* part,
    And shame of being match'd by such a foe:
Rouze conscious vertue up in every heart,
760   ʷAnd seeming to be stronger makes them so.

191.

Nor long the *Belgians* could that Fleet sustain,
    Which did two Gen'rals fates, and *Cesar's* bear.
Each several Ship a victory did gain,
    As *Rupert* or as *Albemarl* were there.

192.

Their batter'd Admiral too soon withdrew,
    Unthank'd by ours for his unfinish'd fight:
But he the minds of his *Dutch* Masters knew,
    Who call'd that providence which we call'd flight.

193.

Never did men more joyfully obey,
770   Or sooner understood the sign to flie:
With such alacrity they bore away,
    As if to praise them all the States stood by.

w Possunt quia posse videntur. *Virg.*

194.

O famous Leader of the *Belgian* Fleet,
   Thy Monument inscrib'd such praise shall wear
As *Varro,* timely flying, once did meet,
   Because he did not of his *Rome* despair.

195.

Behold that Navy which a while before
   Provok'd the tardy *English* to the fight,
Now draw their beaten vessels close to shore,
780   As Larks lie dar'd to shun the Hobbies flight.

196.

Who ere would *English* Monuments survey,
   In other records may our courage know:
But let them hide the story of this day,
   Whose fame was blemish'd by too base a foe.

197.

Or if too busily they will enquire
   Into a victory which we disdain:
Then let them know, the *Belgians* did retire
   ˣBefore the Patron Saint of injur'd *Spain.*

198.

Repenting *England* this revengeful day
790   ʸTo *Philip*'s Manes did an off'ring bring:
England, which first, by leading them astray,
   Hatch'd up Rebellion to destroy her King.

199.

Our Fathers bent their baneful industry
   To check a Monarchy that slowly grew:
But did not *France* or *Holland*'s fate foresee,
   Whose rising pow'r to swift Dominion flew.

200.

In fortunes Empire blindly thus we go,
   And wander after pathless destiny:

ˣ *Patron Saint:* St. James, *on whose day this victory was gain'd.*
ʸ *Philip's Manes:* Philip *the second, of* Spain, *against whom the* Hollanders *rebelling, were aided by Queen* Elizabeth.

775 *Varro*] O1-4 *errata,* O5, Q; *Verro* O1-4 *text.*
790 bring:] Q; ∼ . O1-5.

Whose dark resorts since prudence cannot know,
800   In vain it would provide for what shall be.
                201.
But what ere *English* to the bless'd shall go,
    And the fourth *Harry* or first *Orange* meet:
Find him disowning of a *Burbon* foe,
    And him detesting a *Batavian* Fleet.
                202.
Now on their coasts our conquering Navy rides,
    Way-lays their Merchants, and their Land besets:
Each day new wealth without their care provides,
    They lie asleep with prizes in their nets.
                203.
So, close behind some Promontory lie
810   The huge Leviathans t' attend their prey:
And give no chace, but swallow in the frie,
    Which through their gaping jaws mistake the way.

BURNING OF THE FLEET IN THE VLY BY SIR ROBERT HOLMES
                204.
Nor was this all: in Ports and Roads remote,
    Destructive Fires among whole Fleets we send:
Triumphant flames upon the water flote,
    And out-bound ships at home their voyage end.
                205.
Those various Squadrons, variously design'd,
    Each vessel fraighted with a several load:
Each Squadron waiting for a several wind,
820   All find but one, to burn them in the Road.
                206.
Some bound for *Guinny,* golden sand to find,
    Bore all the gawds the simple Natives wear:
Some for the pride of *Turkish* Courts design'd,
    For folded *Turbans* finest *Holland* bear.
                207.
Some *English* Wool, vex'd in a *Belgian* Loom,
    And into Cloth of spungy softness made:

799   know,] O5; ~ . O1–4; ~ ; Q.

Did into *France* or colder *Denmark* doom,
　　To ruine with worse ware our staple Trade.
　　　　208.
Our greedy Sea-men rummage every hold,
830　　Smile on the booty of each wealthier Chest:
And, as the Priests who with their gods make bold,
　　Take what they like, and sacrifice the rest.

　　　TRANSITUM TO THE FIRE OF LONDON
　　　　209.
But ah! how unsincere are all our joys!
　　Which, sent from Heav'n, like Lightning make no stay:
Their palling taste the journeys length destroys,
　　Or grief, sent post, o'r-takes them on the way.
　　　　210.
Swell'd with our late successes on the Foe,
　　Which *France* and *Holland* wanted power to cross:
We urge an unseen Fate to lay us low,
840　　And feed their envious eyes with *English* loss.
　　　　211.
Each Element his dread command obeys,
　　Who makes or ruines with a smile or frown;
Who as by one he did our Nation raise,
　　So now he with another pulls us down.
　　　　212.
Yet, *London,* Empress of the Northern Clime,
　　By an high fate thou greatly didst expire;
[z]Great as the worlds, which at the death of time
　　Must fall, and rise a nobler frame by fire.
　　　　213.
As when some dire Usurper Heav'n provides,
850　　To scourge his Country with a lawless sway:
His birth, perhaps, some petty Village hides,
　　And sets his Cradle out of Fortune's way:

---

[z] Quum mare quum tellus correptaque regia Cœli, ardeat, &c. *Ovid.*

830　Smile] O1–4 *errata,* O5, Q; Smiles O1–4 *text.*
835　palling] O1–4 *errata,* O5, Q; falling O1–4 *text.*

214.

Till fully ripe his swelling fate breaks out,
    And hurries him to mighty mischiefs on:
His Prince surpriz'd at first, no ill could doubt,
    And wants the pow'r to meet it when 'tis known:

215.

Such was the rise of this prodigious fire,
    Which in mean buildings first obscurely bred,
From thence did soon to open streets aspire,
860   And straight to Palaces and Temples spread.

216.

The diligence of Trades and noiseful gain,
    And luxury, more late, asleep were laid:
All was the nights, and in her silent reign,
    No sound the rest of Nature did invade.

217.

In this deep quiet, from what source unknown,
    Those seeds of fire their fatal birth disclose:
And first, few scatt'ring sparks about were blown,
    Big with the flames that to our ruine rose.

218.

Then, in some close-pent room it crept along,
    And, smouldring as it went, in silence fed:
870 Till th' infant monster, with devouring strong,
    Walk'd boldly upright with exalted head.

219.

Now, like some rich or mighty Murderer,
    Too great for prison, which he breaks with gold:
Who fresher for new mischiefs does appear,
    And dares the world to tax him with the old:

220.

So scapes th' insulting fire his narrow Jail,
    And makes small out-lets into open air:
There the fierce winds his tender force assail,
880   And beat him down-ward to his first repair.

---

856 known:] ∼ . O1–5, Q.   865 source] scource O1–5, Q.
874 Too] O5, Q; To O1–4.   876 old:] ∼ . O1–5, Q.
879 tender] O1–4 *errata,* O5, Q; open O1–4 *text.*

221.

ᵃThe winds, like crafty Courtezans, with-held
   His flames from burning, but to blow them more:
And, every fresh attempt, he is repell'd
   With faint denials, weaker then before.

222.

And now, no longer letted of his prey,
   He leaps up at it with inrag'd desire:
O'r-looks the neighbours with a wide survey,
   And nods at every house his threatning fire.

223.

The Ghosts of Traitors, from the *Bridge* descend,
890   With bold Fanatick Spectres to rejoyce:
About the fire into a Dance they bend,
   And sing their Sabbath Notes with feeble voice.

224.

Our Guardian Angel saw them where he sate
   Above the Palace of our slumbring King,
He sigh'd, abandoning his charge to Fate,
   And, drooping, oft lookt back upon the wing.

225.

At length the crackling noise and dreadful blaze,
   Call'd up some waking Lover to the sight:
And long it was ere he the rest could raise,
900   Whose heavy eye-lids yet were full of night.

226.

The next to danger, hot pursu'd by fate,
   Half cloth'd, half naked, hastily retire:
And frighted Mothers strike their breasts, too late,
   For helpless Infants left amidst the fire.

227.

Their cries soon waken all the dwellers near:
   Now murmuring noises rise in every street:
The more remote run stumbling with their fear,
   And, in the dark, men justle as they meet.

a *Like crafty, &c.* Hæc arte tractabat cupidum virum, ut illius animum inopia accenderet.

896 lookt] Q; look O1–5.   903 Mothers] Q; Mother O1–5.
Note *a* accenderet] O1–4 *errata*, O5, Q; accruderet O1–4 *text.*

228.

So weary Bees in little Cells repose:
910   But if night-robbers lift the well-stor'd Hive,
An humming through their waxen City grows,
     And out upon each others wings they drive.

229.

Now streets grow throng'd and busie as by day:
     Some run for Buckets to the hallow'd Quire:
Some cut the Pipes, and some the Engines play,
     And some more bold mount Ladders to the fire.

230.

In vain: for, from the East, a *Belgian* wind,
     His hostile breath through the dry rafters sent:
The flames impell'd, soon left their foes behind,
920   And forward, with a wanton fury went.

231.

A Key of fire ran all along the shore,
     ᵇAnd lighten'd all the River with the blaze:
The waken'd Tydes began again to roar,
     And wond'ring Fish in shining waters gaze.

232.

Old Father *Thames* rais'd up his reverend head,
     But fear'd the fate of *Simoeis* would return:
Deep in his *Ooze* he sought his sedgy bed,
     And shrunk his waters back into his Urn.

233.

The fire, mean time, walks in a broader gross,
930   To either hand his wings he opens wide:
He wades the streets, & straight he reaches cross,
     And plays his longing flames on th' other side.

234.

At first they warm, then scorch, and then they take:
     Now with long necks from side to side they feed:
At length, grown strong, their Mother fire forsake,
     And a new Collony of flames succeed.

---

b Sigæa igni freta lata relucent. *Virg.*

235.

To every nobler portion of the Town,
 The curling billows roul their restless Tyde:
In parties now they straggle up and down,
940 As Armies, unoppos'd, for prey divide.

236.

One mighty Squadron, with a side wind sped,
 Through narrow lanes his cumber'd fire does haste:
By pow'rful charms of gold and silver led,
 The *Lombard* Banquers and the *Change* to waste.

237.

Another backward to the *Tow'r* would go,
 And slowly eats his way against the wind:
But the main body of the marching foe
 Against th' Imperial Palace is design'd.

238.

Now day appears, and with the day the King,
950 Whose early care had robb'd him of his rest:
Far off the cracks of falling houses ring,
 And shrieks of subjects pierce his tender breast.

239.

Near as he draws, thick harbingers of smoke,
 With gloomy pillars, cover all the place:
Whose little intervals of night are broke
 By sparks that drive against his Sacred Face.

240.

More then his Guards his sorrows made him known,
 And pious tears which down his cheeks did show'r:
The wretched in his grief forgot their own:
960 (So much the pity of a King has pow'r.)

241.

He wept the flames of what he lov'd so well,
 And what so well had merited his love.
For never Prince in grace did more excel,
 Or Royal City more in duty strove.

242.

Nor with an idle care did he behold:
  (Subjects may grieve, but Monarchs must redress.)
He chears the fearful, and commends the bold,
  And makes despairers hope for good success.

243.

Himself directs what first is to be done,
970 And orders all the succours which they bring.
The helpful and the good about him run,
  And form an Army worthy such a King.

244.

He sees the dire contagion spread so fast,
  That where it seizes, all relief is vain:
And therefore must unwillingly lay waste
  That Country which would, else, the foe maintain.

245.

The powder blows up all before the fire:
  Th' amazed flames stand gather'd on a heap;
And from the precipices brinck retire,
980 Afraid to venture on so large a leap.

246.

Thus fighting fires a while themselves consume,
  But straight, like *Turks,* forc'd on to win or die,
They first lay tender bridges of their fume,
  And o'r the breach in unctuous vapours flie.

247.

Part stays for passage till a gust of wind
  Ships o'r their forces in a shining sheet:
Part, creeping under ground, their journey blind,
  And, climbing from below, their fellows meet.

248.

Thus, to some desart plain, or old wood side,
990 Dire night-hags come from far to dance their round:
And o'r brode Rivers on their fiends they ride,
  Or sweep in clowds above the blasted ground.

990 night-hags] O1–4 *errata,* O5, Q; night has O1–4 *text.*

249.

No help avails: for, *Hydra*-like, the fire,
    Lifts up his hundred heads to aim his way.
And scarce the wealthy can one half retire,
    Before he rushes in to share the prey.

250.

The rich grow suppliant, & the poor grow proud:
    Those offer mighty gain, and these ask more.
So void of pity is th' ignoble crowd,
1000   When others ruine may increase their store.

251.

As those who live by shores with joy behold
    Some wealthy vessel split or stranded nigh;
And, from the Rocks, leap down for shipwrack'd Gold,
    And seek the Tempest which the others flie:

252.

So these but wait the Owners last despair,
    And what's permitted to the flames invade:
Ev'n from their jaws they hungry morsels tear,
    And, on their backs, the spoils of *Vulcan* lade.

253.

The days were all in this lost labour spent;
1010   And when the weary King gave place to night,
His Beams he to his Royal Brother lent,
    And so shone still in his reflective light.

254.

Night came, but without darkness or repose,
    A dismal picture of the gen'ral doom:
Where Souls distracted when the Trumpet blows,
    And half unready with their bodies come.

255.

Those who have homes, when home they do repair
    To a last lodging call their wand'ring friends.
Their short uneasie sleeps are broke with care,
1020   To look how near their own destruction tends.

1004 flie:] ~ . O1–5, Q.   1015 blows,] O5, Q; ~ . O1–4.

256.

Those who have none sit round where once it was,
      And with full eyes each wonted room require:
Haunting the yet warm ashes of the place,
      As murder'd men walk where they did expire.

257.

Some stir up coals and watch the Vestal fire,
      Others in vain from sight of ruine run:
And, while through burning Lab'rinths they retire,
      With loathing eyes repeat what they would shun.

258.

The most, in fields, like herded beasts lie down;
1030   To dews obnoxious on the grassie floor:
And while their Babes in sleep their sorrows drown,
      Sad Parents watch the remnants of their store.

259.

While by the motion of the flames they ghess
      What streets are burning now, & what are near:
An Infant, waking, to the paps would press,
      And meets, instead of milk, a falling tear.

260.

No thought can ease them but their Sovereign's care,
      Whose praise th' afflicted as their comfort sing:
Ev'n those whom want might drive to just despair,
1040   Think life a blessing under such a King.

261.

Mean time he sadly suffers in their grief,
      Out-weeps an Hermite, and out-prays a Saint:
All the long night he studies their relief,
      How they may be suppli'd, and he may want.

KING'S PRAYER
262.

O God, said he, thou Patron of my days,
      Guide of my youth in exile and distress!

Who me unfriended, brought'st by wondrous ways
   The Kingdom of my Fathers to possess:
        263.
Be thou my Judge, with what unwearied care
1050   I since have labour'd for my People's good:
To bind the bruises of a Civil War,
   And stop the issues of their wasting bloud.
        264.
Thou, who hast taught me to forgive the ill,
   And recompense, as friends, the good misled;
If mercy be a Precept of thy will,
   Return that mercy on thy Servant's head.
        265.
Or, if my heedless Youth has stept astray,
   Too soon forgetful of thy gracious hand:
On me alone thy just displeasure lay,
1060   But take thy judgments from this mourning Land.
        266.
We all have sinn'd, and thou hast laid us low,
   As humble Earth from whence at first we came:
Like flying shades before the clowds we show,
   And shrink like Parchment in consuming flame.
        267.
O let it be enough what thou hast done,
   When spotted deaths ran arm'd through every street,
With poison'd darts, which not the good could shun,
   The speedy could out-fly, or valiant meet.
        268.
The living few, and frequent funerals then,
1070   Proclam'd thy wrath on this forsaken place:
And now those few who are return'd agen
   Thy searching judgments to their dwellings trace.

1048   possess:] ∼ . O1–5, Q.
1054   friends, the good] Q; friends the good, O1–5.
1067   shun,] Q; ∼ . O1–5.

269.

O pass not, Lord, an absolute decree,
    Or bind thy sentence unconditional:
But in thy sentence our remorce foresee,
    And, in that foresight, this thy doom recall.

270.

Thy threatnings, Lord, as thine, thou maist revoke:
    But, if immutable and fix'd they stand,
Continue still thy self to give the stroke,
1080   And let not foreign foes oppress thy Land.

271.

Th' Eternal heard, and from the Heav'nly Quire,
    Chose out the Cherub with the flaming sword:
And bad him swiftly drive th' approaching fire
    From where our Naval Magazins were stor'd.

272.

The blessed Minister his wings displai'd,
    And like a shooting Star he cleft the night:
He charg'd the flames, and those that disobey'd,
    He lash'd to duty with his sword of light.

273.

The fugitive flames, chastis'd, went forth to prey
1090   On pious Structures, by our Fathers rear'd:
By which to Heav'n they did affect the way,
    Ere Faith in Church-men without Works was heard.

274.

The wanting Orphans saw, with watry eyes,
    Their Founders charity in dust laid low:
And sent to God their ever-answer'd cries,
    (For he protects the poor who made them so.)

275.

Nor could thy Fabrick, *Paul*'s, defend thee long,
    Though thou wert Sacred to thy Makers praise:
Though made immortal by a Poet's Song;
1100   And Poets Songs the *Theban* walls could raise.

276.

The dareing flames peep't in and saw from far,
  The awful beauties of the Sacred Quire:
But, since it was prophan'd by Civil War,
  Heav'n thought it fit to have it purg'd by fire.

277.

Now down the narrow streets it swiftly came,
  And, widely opening, did on both sides prey.
This benefit we sadly owe the flame,
  If onely ruine must enlarge our way.

278.

And now four days the Sun had seen our woes,
1110 Four nights the Moon beheld th' incessant fire:
It seem'd as if the Stars more sickly rose,
  And farther from the feav'rish North retire.

279.

In th' Empyrean Heaven, (the bless'd abode)
  The Thrones and the Dominions prostrate lie,
Not daring to behold their angry God:
  And an hush'd silence damps the tuneful sky.

280.

At length th' Almighty cast a pitying eye,
  And mercy softly touch'd his melting breast:
He saw the Town's one half in rubbish lie,
1120 And eager flames give on to storm the rest.

281.

An hollow chrystal Pyramid he takes,
  In firmamental waters dipt above;
Of it a brode Extinguisher he makes,
  And hoods the flames that to their quarry strove.

282.

The vanquish'd fires withdraw from every place,
  Or full with feeding, sink into a sleep:
Each houshold Genius shows again his face,
  And, from the hearths, the little Lares creep.

1115 Not] Nor O1–5, Q.

283.

Our King this more then natural change beholds;
1130   With sober joy his heart and eyes abound:
To the All-good his lifted hands he folds,
    And thanks him low on his redeemed ground.

284.

As when sharp frosts had long constrain'd the earth,
    A kindly thaw unlocks it with mild rain:
And first the tender blade peeps up to birth,
    And straight the green fields laugh with promis'd grain:

285.

By such degrees, the spreading gladness grew
    In every heart, which fear had froze before:
The standing streets with so much joy they view,
1140   That with less grief the perish'd they deplore.

286.

The Father of the people open'd wide
    His stores, and all the poor with plenty fed:
Thus God's Annointed God's own place suppli'd,
    And fill'd the empty with his daily bread.

287.

This Royal bounty brought its own reward,
    And, in their minds, so deep did print the sense:
That if their ruines sadly they regard,
    'Tis but with fear the sight might drive him thence.

CITIES REQUEST TO THE KING NOT TO LEAVE THEM
288.

But so may he live long, that Town to sway,
1150   Which by his Auspice they will nobler make,
As he will hatch their ashes by his stay,
    And not their humble ruines now forsake.

289.

They have not lost their Loyalty by fire;
    Nor is their courage or their wealth so low,
That from his Wars they poorly would retire,
    Or beg the pity of a vanquish'd foe.

290.

Not with more constancy the *Jews* of old,
  By *Cyrus* from rewarded Exile sent:
Their Royal City did in dust behold,
1160 Or with more vigour to rebuild it went.

291.

The utmost malice of their Stars is past,
  And two dire Comets which have scourg'd the Town,
In their own Plague and Fire have breath'd their last,
  Or, dimly, in their sinking sockets frown.

292.

Now frequent Trines the happier lights among,
  And high-rais'd *Jove* from his dark prison freed:
(Those weights took off that on his Planet hung)
  Will gloriously the new laid work succeed.

293.

Me-thinks already, from this Chymick flame,
1170 I see a City of more precious mold:
Rich as the Town which gives the ᶜ*Indies* name,
  With Silver pav'd, and all divine with Gold.

294.

Already, Labouring with a mighty fate,
  She shakes the rubbish from her mounting brow,
And seems to have renew'd her Charters date,
  Which Heav'n will to the death of time allow.

295.

More great then humane, now, and more ᵈ*August*,
  New deifi'd she from her fires does rise:
Her widening streets on new foundations trust,
1180 And, opening, into larger parts she flies.

296.

Before, she like some Shepherdess did show,
  Who sate to bathe her by a River's side:
Not answering to her fame, but rude and low,
  Nor taught the beauteous Arts of Modern pride.

ᶜ *Mexico.*
ᵈ Augusta, *the old name of* London.

297.

Now, like a Maiden Queen, she will behold,
    From her high Turrets, hourly Sutors come:
The East with Incense, and the West with Gold,
    Will stand, like Suppliants, to receive her doom.

298.

The silver *Thames,* her own domestick Floud,
1190   Shall bear her Vessels, like a sweeping Train;
And often wind (as of his Mistress proud)
    With longing eyes to meet her face again.

299.

The wealthy *Tagus,* and the wealthier *Rhine,*
    The glory of their Towns no more shall boast:
And *Sein,* That would with *Belgian* Rivers joyn,
    Shall find her lustre stain'd, and Traffick lost.

300.

The vent'rous Merchant, who design'd more far,
    And touches on our hospitable shore:
Charm'd with the splendour of this Northern Star,
1200   Shall here unlade him, and depart no more.

301.

Our pow'rful Navy shall no longer meet,
    The wealth of *France* or *Holland* to invade:
The beauty of this Town, without a Fleet,
    From all the world shall vindicate her Trade.

302.

And, while this fam'd Emporium we prepare,
    The *British* Ocean shall such triumphs boast,
That those who now disdain our Trade to share,
    Shall rob like Pyrats on our wealthy Coast.

303.

Already we have conquer'd half the War,
1210   And the less dang'rous part is left behind:
Our trouble now is but to make them dare,
    And not so great to vanquish as to find.

304.
Thus to the Eastern wealth through storms we go;
But now, the Cape once doubled, fear no more:
A constant Trade-wind will securely blow,
And gently lay us on the Spicy shore.

To Mr. Lee, on His Alexander

THE Blast of common Censure cou'd I fear,
 Before your Play my Name shou'd not appear;
 For 'twill be thought, and with some colour too,
I pay the Bribe I first receiv'd from You:
That mutual Vouchers for our Fame we stand,
To play the Game into each others Hand;
And as cheap Pen'orths to our selves afford
As *Bessus,* and the Brothers of the Sword.
Such Libels private Men may well endure,
10 When States, and Kings themselves are not secure:
For ill Men, conscious of their inward guilt,
Think the best Actions on By-ends are built.
And yet my silence had not scap'd their spight,
Then envy had not suffer'd me to write:
For, since I cou'd not Ignorance pretend,
Such worth I must or envy or commend.
So many Candidates there stand for Wit,
A place in Court is scarce so hard to get;
In vain they croud each other at the Door;
20 For ev'n Reversions are all beg'd before:
Desert, how known so e're, is long delay'd;
And, then too, Fools and Knaves are better pay'd.
Yet, as some Actions bear so great a Name,
That Courts themselves are just, for fear of shame:
So has the mighty Merit of your Play
Extorted praise, and forc'd it self a Way.
'Tis here, as 'tis at Sea; who farthest goes,
Or dares the most, makes all the rest his Foes;
Yet, when some Virtue much out-grows the rest,
30 It shoots too fast, and high, to be opprest;
As his Heroic worth struck Envy dumb

Who took the *Dutchman,* and who cut the Boom:
Such praise is yours, while you the Passions move,
That 'tis no longer feign'd; 'tis real Love:
Where Nature Triumphs over wretched Art;
We only warm the Head, but you the Heart.
Alwayes you warm! and if the rising Year,
As in hot Regions, bring the Sun too near,
Tis but to make your Fragrant Spices blow,
40 Which in our colder Climates will not grow.
They only think you animate your Theme
With too much Fire, who are themselves all Phle'me:
Prizes wou'd be for Lags of slowest pace,
Were Cripples made the Judges of the Race.
Despise those Drones, who praise while they accuse
The too much vigour of your youthful Muse:
That humble Stile which they their Virtue make
Is in your pow'r; you need but stoop and take.
Your beauteous Images must be allow'd
50 By all, but some vile Poets of the Crowd;
But how shou'd any Sign-post-dawber know
The worth of *Titian,* or of *Angelo?*
Hard Features every Bungler can command;
To draw true Beauty shews a Masters Hand.

OVID's
EPISTLES,
TRANSLATED
BY
SEVERAL HANDS.

Vel tibi compositâ cantetur Epistola voce :
Ignotum hoc aliis ille novavit opus. Ovid.

LONDON,

Printed for *Jacob Tonson* at the Sign of the
Judges Head in *Chancery Lane*, near
Fleet-Street. 1680.

TITLE PAGE OF THE FIRST EDITION (MACDONALD 11A)

Contributions to Ovid's Epistles

PREFACE

THE Life of *Ovid* being already writen in our Language before the Translation of his *Metamorphoses,* I will not presume so far upon my self, to think I can add any thing to Mr. *Sandys* his undertaking. The *English* Reader may there be satisfied, that he flourish'd in the Reign of *Augustus Cæsar,* that he was Extracted from an Antient Family of *Roman* Knights; that he was born to the Inheritance of a Splendid Fortune, that he was design'd to the Study of the Law; and had made considerable progress in it, before he quitted that Profession, for this of *Poetry,* to which he was more naturally form'd. The Cause of his Banishment is unknown; because he was himself unwilling further to provoke the Emperour, by ascribing it to any other reason, than what was pretended by *Augustus,* which was the Lasciviousness of his Elegies, and his Art of Love. 'Tis true they are not to be Excus'd in the severity of Manners, as being able to Corrupt a larger Empire, if there were any, than that of *Rome;* yet this may be said in behalf of *Ovid,* that no man has ever treated the Passion of Love with so much Delicacy of Thought, and of Expression, or search'd into the nature of it more Philosophically than he. And the Emperour who Condemn'd him, had as little reason as another man to punish that fault with so much severity, if at least he were the Authour of a certain *Epigram,* which is ascrib'd to him, relating to the Cause of the first Civil War betwixt himself and *Mark Anthony* the Triumvir, which is more fulsome than any passage I have met with in our Poet. To pass by the naked Familiarity of his Expressions to *Horace,* which are cited in that Authours Life, I need only mention one notorious Act of his in taking *Livia* to his Bed, when she was not only Married, but with Child by her Husband, then living. But Deeds, it seems, may be Justified by Arbitrary Power, when words are question'd in a Poet. There is another ghess of the *Grammarians,* as far from truth as the first from Reason; they will have him Ban-

───────

23 passage] O2–5; *paslage* O1.

ish'd for some favours, which they say he receiv'd from *Julia,* the
Daughter of *Augustus,* whom they think he Celebrates under the
Name of *Corinna* in his *Elegies:* but he who will observe the Verses
which are made to that Mistress, may gather from the whole Con-
texture of them, that *Corinna* was not a Woman of the highest Quality: If *Julia* were then Married to *Agrippa,* why should our Poet make
his Petition to *Isis,* for her safe Delivery, and afterwards, Condole her
Miscarriage; which for ought he knew might be by her own Husband?
Or indeed how durst he be so bold to make the least discovery of such
10 a Crime, which was no less than Capital, especially Committed against
a Person of *Agrippa*'s Rank? Or if it were before her Marriage, he
would surely have been more discreet, than to have publish'd an
Accident, which must have been fatal to them both. But what most
Confirms me against this Opinion is, that *Ovid* himself complains that
the true Person of *Corinna* was found out by the Fame of his Verses
to her: which if it had been *Julia,* he durst not have own'd; and besides, an immediate punishment must have follow'd. He seems himself more truly to have touch'd at the Cause of his Exile in those
obscure Verses,

20   *Cur aliquid vidi, cur noxia Lumina feci?* &c.

Namely, that he had either seen, or was Conscious to somewhat, which
had procur'd him his disgrace. But neither am I satisfyed that this
was the Incest of the Emperour with his own Daughter: For *Augustus*
was of a Nature too vindicative to have contented himself with so
small a Revenge, or so unsafe to himself, as that of simple Banishment, and would certainly have secur'd his Crimes from publick notice by the death of him who was witness to them. Neither have
Histories given us any sight into such an Action of this Emperour:
nor would he (the greatest Polititian of his time,) in all probability,
30 have manag'd his Crimes with so little secresie, as not to shun the
Observation of any man. It seems more probable that *Ovid* was either
the Confident of some other passion, or that he had stumbled by some
inadvertency upon the privacies of *Livia,* and seen her in a Bath: For
the words

---

1 some] O2–5; *ome* O1.

Nudam sine veste Dianam,

agree better with *Livia,* who had the Fame of Chastity, than with
either of the *Julias,* who were both noted of Incontinency. The first
Verses which were made by him in his Youth, and recited publickly,
according to the Custom were, as he himself assures us to *Corinna:*
his Banishment happen'd not till the Age of fifty; from which it may
be deduc'd, with probability enough, that the love of *Corinna,* did
not occasion it: Nay he tells us plainly, that his offence was that of
Errour only, not of wickedness: and in the same paper of Verses also,
10 that the cause was notoriously known at *Rome,* though it be left so
obscure to after Ages.

But to leave Conjectures on a Subject so incertain, and to write
somewhat more Authentick of this Poet: That he frequented the
Court of *Augustus,* and was well receiv'd in it, is most undoubted: all
his Poems bear the Character of a Court, and appear to be written as
the *French* call it *Cavalierement:* Add to this, that the Titles of many
of his Elegies, and more of his Letters in his Banishment, are address'd
to persons well known to us, even at this distance, to have been considerable in that Court.

20 Nor was his acquaintance less with the famous Poets of his Age,
than with the Noblemen and Ladies; he tells you himself, in a particular Account of his own Life, that *Macer, Horace, Tibullus, Propertius,* and many others of them were his familiar Friends, and that
some of them communicated their Writings to him: but that he had
only seen *Virgil.*

If the Imitation of Nature be the business of a Poet, I know no
Authour who can justly be compar'd with ours, especially in the
Description of the Passions. And to prove this, I shall need no other
Judges than the generality of his Readers: for all Passions being in-
30 born with us, we are almost equally Judges when we are concern'd
in the representation of them: Now I will appeal to any man who
has read this Poet, whether he find not the natural Emotion of the
same Passion in himself, which the Poet describes in his feign'd
Persons? His thoughts which are the Pictures and results of those
Passions, are generally such as naturally arise from those disorderly

Motions of our Spirits. Yet, not to speak too partially in his behalf, I
will confess that the Copiousness of his Wit was such, that he often
writ too pointedly for his Subject, and made his persons speak more
Eloquently than the violence of their Passion would admit: so that
he is frequently witty out of season: leaving the Imitation of Nature,
and the cooler dictates of his Judgment, for the false applause of
Fancy. Yet he seems to have found out this Imperfection in his riper
age: for why else should he complain that his *Metamorphoses* was
left unfinish'd? Nothing sure can be added to the Wit of that Poem,
10   or of the rest: but many things ought to have been retrench'd; which
I suppose would have been the business of his Age, if his Misfortunes
had not come too fast upon him. But take him uncorrected as he is
transmitted to us, and it must be acknowledg'd in spight of his *Dutch*
Friends, the Commentators, even of *Julius Scaliger* himself, that
Seneca's Censure will stand good against him;

Nescivit quod bene cessit relinquere:

he never knew how to give over, when he had done well: but continually varying the same sence an hundred waies, and taking up in
another place, what he had more than enough inculcated before, he
20   sometimes cloys his Readers instead of satisfying them: and gives
occasion to his Translators, who dare not Cover him, to blush at the
nakedness of their Father. This then is the Allay of *Ovids* writing,
which is sufficiently recompenc'd by his other Excellencys; nay this
very fault is not without it's Beauties: for the most severe Censor
cannot but be pleas'd with the prodigality of his Wit, though at the
same time he could have wish'd, that the Master of it had been a
better Menager. Every thing which he does, becomes him, and if sometimes he appear too gay, yet there is a secret gracefulness of youth,
which accompanies his Writings, though the staydness and sobriety of
30   Age be wanting. In the most material part, which is the Conduct, 'tis
certain that he seldom has miscarried: for if his Elegies be compar'd
with those of *Tibullus,* and *Propertius* his Contemporaries, it will be
found that those Poets seldom design'd before they writ; And though
the Language of *Tibullus* be more polish'd, and the Learning of
Propertius, especially in his Fourth Book, more set out to ostenta-

---

8   *Metamorphoses*] O4–5; Metamorphosis O1–3.

tion: Yet their common practice, was to look no further before them than the next Line: whence it will inevitably follow, that they can drive to no certain point, but ramble from one Subject to another, and conclude with somewhat which is not of a piece with their beginning:

> *Purpureus late qui splendeat, unus & alter*
> *Assuitur pannus:*

As *Horace* says, though the Verses are golden, they are but patch'd into the Garment. But our Poet has always the Goal in his Eye, which directs him in his Race; some Beautiful design, which he first estab-
10 lishes, and then contrives the means, which will naturally conduct it to his end. This will be Evident to Judicious Readers in this work of his Epistles, of which somewhat, at least in general, will be expected.

The Title of them in our late Editions is *Epistolæ Heroidum,* The Letters of the *Heroines.* But *Heinsius* has Judg'd more truly, that the *Inscription* of our Authour was barely, *Epistles;* which he concludes from his cited Verses, where *Ovid* asserts this work as his own Invention, and not borrow'd from the *Greeks,* whom (as the Masters of their Learning,) the *Romans* usually did imitate. But it appears not from their writers, that any of the *Grecians* ever touch'd upon this
20 way, which our Poet therefore justly has vindicated to himself. I quarrel not at the word *Heroidum,* because 'tis us'd by *Ovid* in his Art of Love:

> *Jupiter ad veteres supplex* Heroidas *ibat.*

But sure he cou'd not be guilty of such an Oversight, to call his Work by the Name of *Heroines,* when there are divers men or *Heroes,* as Namely *Paris, Leander,* and *Acontius,* joyn'd in it. Except *Sabinus,* who writ some Answers to *Ovids* Letters,

> *(Quam celer è toto rediit meus orbe Sabinus,)*

I remember not any of the *Romans* who have treated this Subject,
30 save only *Propertius,* and that but once, in his Epistle of *Arethusa* to *Lycotas,* which is written so near the Style of *Ovid,* that it seems to be but an Imitation, and therefore ought not to defraud our Poet of the Glory of his Invention.

---

4 somewhat] O2–5; *some what* O1.

Concerning this work of the Epistles, I shall content my self to observe these few particulars. First, that they are generally granted to be the most perfect piece of *Ovid,* and that the Style of them is tenderly passionate and Courtly; two properties well agreeing with the Persons which were *Heroines,* and *Lovers.* Yet where the Characters were lower, as in *Oenone,* and *Hero,* he has kept close to Nature in drawing his Images after a Country Life, though perhaps he has Romaniz'd his *Grecian* Dames too much, and made them speak sometimes as if they had been born in the City of *Rome,* and under the Empire of
10 *Augustus.* There seems to be no great variety in the particular Subjects which he has chosen: most of the Epistles being written from Ladies who were forsaken by their Lovers: which is the reason that many of the same thoughts come back upon us in divers Letters: But of the general Character of Women which is Modesty, he has taken a most becoming care; for his amorous Expressions go no further than virtue may allow, and therefore may be read, as he intended them, by Matrons without a blush.

Thus much concerning the Poet: whom you find translated by divers hands, that you may at least have that variety in the *English,*
20 which the Subject denyed to the Authour of the *Latine.* It remains that I should say somewhat of Poetical Translations in general, and give my Opinion (with submission to better Judgments) which way of Version seems to me most proper.

All Translation I suppose may be reduced to these three heads:

First, that of Metaphrase, or turning an Authour word by word, and Line by Line, from one Language into another. Thus, or near this manner, was *Horace* his Art of Poetry translated by *Ben. Johnson.* The second way is that of Paraphrase, or Translation with Latitude, where the Authour is kept in view by the Translator, so as never to be
30 lost, but his words are not so strictly follow'd as his sense, and that too is admitted to be amplyfied, but not alter'd. Such is Mr. *Wallers* Translation of *Virgils* Fourth *Æneid.* The Third way is that of Imitation, where the Translator (if now he has not lost that Name) assumes the liberty not only to vary from the words and sence, but to forsake them both as he sees occasion: and taking only some general hints

---

24 heads:] O3–5; ~ . O1–2.

from the Original, to run division on the ground-work, as he pleases. Such is Mr. *Cowleys* practice in turning two Odes of *Pindar,* and one of *Horace* into *English.*

Concerning the first of these Methods, our Master *Horace* has given us this Caution,

> *Nec verbum verbo curabis reddere, fidus*
> *Interpres*————

Nor word for word too faithfully translate, as the *Earl* of *Roscommon* has excellently render'd it. Too faithfully is indeed pedantically: 'tis
10 a faith like that which proceeds from Superstition, blind and zealous: Take it in the Expression of Sir *John Denham,* to Sir *Rich. Fanshaw,* on his Version of the *Pastor Fido.*

> *That servile path, thou nobly do'st decline,*
> *Of tracing word by word and Line by Line;*
> *A new and nobler way thou do'st pursue,*
> *To make Translations, and Translators too:*
> *They but preserve the Ashes, thou the Flame,*
> *True to his Sence, but truer to his Fame.*

'Tis almost impossible to Translate verbally, and well, at the same
20 time; For the Latin, (a most severe and Compendious Language) often expresses that in one word, which either the Barbarity, or the narrowness of modern Tongues cannot supply in more. 'Tis frequent also that the Conceit is couch'd in some Expression, which will be lost in *English.*

> *Atque ijdem Venti vela fidemq; ferent.*

What Poet of our Nation is so happy as to express this thought Literally in *English,* and to strike Wit or almost Sense out of it?

In short the Verbal Copyer is incumber'd with so many difficulties at once, that he can never disentangle himself from all. He is to con-
30 sider at the same time the thought of his Authour, and his words, and to find out the Counterpart to each in another Language: and be-

---

8   *translate,* as] translate. As O1–5.   11   *Rich.*] O2–5; ~ ∧ O1.
12   *Pastor*] *italics of copy text not changed to romans.*
22   in] O2–5; it O1.   26   What] O3–5; *what* O1–2.

sides this he is to confine himself to the compass of Numbers, and the Slavery of Rhime. 'Tis much like dancing on Ropes with fetter'd Leggs: A man may shun a fall by using Caution, but the gracefulness of Motion is not to be expected: and when we have said the best of it, 'tis but a foolish Task; for no sober man would put himself into a danger for the Applause of scaping without breaking his Neck. We see *Ben. Johnson* could not avoid obscurity in his literal Translation of *Horace,* attempted in the same compass of Lines: nay *Horace* himself could scarce have done it to a *Greek* Poet.

10   *Brevis esse laboro, obscurus fio.*

Either perspicuity or gracefulness will frequently be wanting. *Horace* has indeed avoided both these Rocks in his Translation of the three first Lines of *Homers Odysses,* which he has Contracted into two.

> *Dic mihi Musa Virum captæ post tempora Trojæ*
> *Qui mores hominum multorum vidit & urbes.*
> *Muse, speak the man, who since the Siege of Troy,* ⎱ Earl of
> *So many Towns, such Change of Manners saw.* ⎰ Rosc.

But then the sufferings of *Ulysses,* which are a Considerable part of that Sentence are omitted.

20   [Ὃς μάλα πολλὰ πλάγχθη.]

The Consideration of these difficulties, in a servile, literal Translation, not long since made two of our famous Wits, *Sir John Denham,* and *Mr. Cowley* to contrive another way of turning Authours into our Tongue, call'd by the latter of them, *Imitation.* As they were Friends, I suppose they Communicated their thoughts on this Subject to each other, and therefore their reasons for it are little different: though the practice of one is much more moderate. I take Imitation of an Authour in their sense to be an Endeavour of a later Poet to write like one who has written before him on the same Subject: that is, not to

30 Translate his words, or to be Confin'd to his Sense, but only to set him as a Patern, and to write, as he supposes, that Authour would have done, had he liv'd in our Age, and in our Country. Yet I dare

---

11 Either] *either* O1–5.   20   ῾Ος] O2–5; ῾Ος O1.
24 *Imitation.*] O2–5; ~ₐ O1.

not say that either of them have carried this libertine way of rendring Authours (as Mr. *Cowley* calls it) so far as my Definition reaches. For in the *Pindarick Odes*, the Customs and Ceremonies of Ancient *Greece* are still preserv'd: but I know not what mischief may arise hereafter from the Example of such an Innovation, when writers of unequal parts to him, shall imitate so bold an undertaking. To add and to diminish what we please, which is the way avow'd by him, ought only to be granted to Mr. *Cowley,* and that too only in his Translation of *Pindar,* because he alone was able to make him
10 amends, by giving him better of his own, when ever he refus'd his Authours thoughts. *Pindar* is generally known to be a dark writer, to want Connexion, (I mean as to our understanding) to soar out of sight, and leave his Reader at a Gaze: So wild and ungovernable a Poet cannot be Translated litterally, his Genius is too strong to bear a Chain, and *Sampson* like he shakes it off: A Genius so Elevated and unconfin'd as Mr. *Cowley*'s, was but necessary to make *Pindar* speak *English,* and that was to be perform'd by no other way than Imitation. But if *Virgil* or *Ovid,* or any regular intelligible Authours be thus us'd, 'tis no longer to be call'd their work, when neither the
20 thoughts nor words are drawn from the Original: but instead of them there is something new produc'd, which is almost the creation of another hand. By this way 'tis true, somewhat that is Excellent may be invented perhaps more Excellent than the first design, though *Virgil* must be still excepted, when that perhaps takes place: Yet he who is inquisitive to know an Authours thoughts will be disappointed in his expectation. And 'tis not always that a man will be contented to have a Present made him, when he expects the payment of a Debt. To state it fairly, Imitation of an Authour is the most advantagious way for a Translator to shew himself, but the greatest wrong
30 which can be done to the Memory and Reputation of the dead. Sir *John Denham* (who advis'd more Liberty than he took himself,) gives this Reason for his Innovation, in his admirable Preface before the Translation of the second *Æneid:* "Poetry is of so subtil a Spirit, that in pouring out of one Language into another, it will all Evaporate; and if a new Spirit be not added in the transfusion, there will remain

---

6 undertaking. To] O2; *undertaking, to* O1; *undertaking; to* O3–5.
25–26 disappointed] O2–5; *disapointed* O1.

nothing but a *Caput Mortuum.*" I confess this Argument holds good
against a litteral Translation, but who defends it? Imitation and
verbal Version are in my Opinion the two Extreams, which ought to
be avoided: and therefore when I have propos'd the mean betwixt
them, it will be seen how far his Argument will reach.

No man is capable of Translating Poetry, who besides a Genius to
that Art, is not a Master both of his Authours Language, and of his
own: Nor must we understand the Language only of the Poet, but his
particular turn of Thoughts, and of Expression, which are the Characters that distinguish, and as it were individuate him from all other
writers. When we are come thus far, 'tis time to look into our selves,
to conform our Genius to his, to give his thought either the same turn
if our tongue will bear it, or if not, to vary but the dress, not to alter
or destroy the substance. The like Care must be taken of the more
outward Ornaments, the Words: when they appear (which is but
seldom) litterally graceful, it were an injury to the Authour that they
should be chang'd: But since every Language is so full of its own
proprieties, that what is Beautiful in one, is often Barbarous, nay
sometimes Nonsense in another, it would be unreasonable to limit a
Translator to the narrow compass of his Authours words: 'tis enough
if he choose out some Expression which does not vitiate the Sense. I
suppose he may stretch his Chain to such a Latitude, but by innovation of thoughts, methinks he breaks it. By this means the Spirit of
an Authour may be transfus'd, and yet not lost: and thus 'tis plain
that the reason alledg'd by Sir *John Denham,* has no farther force
than to Expression: for thought, if it be Translated truly, cannot be
lost in another Language, but the words that convey it to our apprehension (which are the Image and Ornament of that thought) may
be so ill chosen as to make it appear in an unhandsome dress, and
rob it of its native Lustre. There is therefore a Liberty to be allow'd
for the Expression, neither is it necessary that Words and Lines
should be confin'd to the measure of their Original. The sence of an
Authour, generally speaking, is to be Sacred and inviolable. If the
Fancy of *Ovid* be luxuriant, 'tis his Character to be so, and if I retrench it, he is no longer *Ovid.* It will be replyed that he receives advantage by this lopping of his superfluous branches, but I rejoyn

19 unreasonable] O2–5; *unreasonahle* O1.   32 Original.] O2–5; ∼ , O1.

that a Translator has no such Right: when a *Painter* Copies from the life, I suppose he has no priviledge to alter Features, and Lineaments, under pretence that his Picture will look better: perhaps the Face which he has drawn would be more Exact, if the Eyes, or Nose were alter'd, but 'tis his business to make it resemble the Original. In two Cases only there may a seeming difficulty arise, that is, if the thought be notoriously trivial or dishonest; But the same Answer will serve for both, that then they ought not to be Translated.

————*Et quæ*
Desperes tractata nitescere posse, relinquas.

Thus I have ventur'd to give my Opinion on this Subject against the Authority of two great men, but I hope without offence to either of their Memories, for I both lov'd them living, and reverence them now they are dead. But if after what I have urg'd, it be thought by better Judges that the praise of a Translation Consists in adding new Beauties to the piece, thereby to recompence the loss which it sustains by change of Language, I shall be willing to be taught better, and to recant. In the mean time it seems to me, that the true reason why we have so few Versions which are tolerable, is not from the too close persuing of the Authours Sence: but because there are so few who have all the Talents which are requisite for Translation: and that there is so little praise and so small Encouragement for so considerable a part of Learning.

To apply in short, what has been said, to this present work, the Reader will here find most of the Translations, with some little Latitude or variation from the Authours Sence: That of *Oenone* to *Paris,* is in Mr. *Cowleys* way of Imitation only. I was desir'd to say that the Authour who is of the *Fair Sex,* understood not *Latine.* But if she does not, I am afraid she has given us occasion to be asham'd who do.

For my own part I am ready to acknowledge that I have transgress'd the Rules which I have given; and taken more liberty than a just Translation will allow. But so many Gentlemen whose Wit and Learning are well known, being Joyn'd in it, I doubt not but that their Excellencies will make you ample Satisfaction for my Errours.

9 ————*Et quæ*] O2–5; Et quæ———— O1.

Canace to Macareus

Macareus and Canace *Son and Daughter to* Æolus, *God of the Winds, lov'd each other Incestuously:* Canace *was delivered of a Son, and committed him to her Nurse, to be secretly convey'd away. The Infant crying out, by that means was discover'd to* Æolus, *who inrag'd at the wickedness of his Children, commanded the Babe to be expos'd to Wild Beasts on the Mountains: and, withal, sent a Sword to* Canace, *with this Message, That her Crimes would instruct her how to use it. With this Sword she slew her self: but before she died, she writ the following Letter to her Brother* Macareus, *who had taken Sanctuary in the Temple of* Apollo.

IF streaming blood my fatal Letter stain,
   Imagine, er'e you read, the Writer slain:
   One hand the Sword, and one the Pen employs,
And in my lap the ready paper lyes.
Think in this posture thou behold'st me Write:
In this my cruel Father wou'd delight.
O were he present, that his eyes and hands
Might see & urge the death which he commands,
Than all his raging Winds more dreadful, he
10 Unmov'd, without a tear, my wounds wou'd see.
Jove justly plac'd him on a stormy Throne,
His Peoples temper is so like his own.
The *North* and *South,* and each contending blast
Are underneath his wide Dominion cast:
Those he can rule; but his tempestuous mind
Is, like his airy Kingdom, unconfin'd.
Ah! what avail my Kindred Gods above,
That in their number I can reckon *Jove!*
What help will all my heav'nly friends afford,
20 When to my breast I lift the pointed Sword?

That hour which joyn'd us came before its time,
In death we had been one without a crime:
Why did thy flames beyond a *Brothers* move?
Why lov'd I thee with more than *Sisters* love?
For I lov'd too; and knowing not my wound,
A secret pleasure in thy Kisses found:
My Cheeks no longer did their colour boast,
My Food grew loathsom, and my strength I lost:
Still er'e I spoke, a sigh wou'd stop my tongue;
30 Short were my slumbers, & my nights were long.
I knew not from my love these griefs did grow,
Yet was, alas, the thing I did not know.
My wily Nurse by long experience found,
And first discover'd to my Soul its wound.
'Tis Love, said she; and then my down-cast eyes,
And guilty dumbness, witness'd my surprize.
Forc'd at the last, my shameful pain I tell:
And, oh, what follow'd we both know too well!
'When half denying, more than half content,
40 'Embraces warm'd me to a full consent:
'Then with Tumultuous Joyes my Heart did beat,
'And guilt that made them anxious, made them great.
But now my swelling womb heav'd up my breast,
And rising weight my sinking Limbs opprest.
What Herbs, what Plants, did not my Nurse produce
To make Abortion by their pow'rful Juice?
What Medicines try'd we not, to thee unknown?
Our first crime common; this was mine alone.
But the strong Child, secure in his dark Cell,
50 With Natures vigour did our arts repell.
And now the pale-fac'd Empress of the Night
Nine times had fill'd her Orb with borrow'd light:
Not knowing 'twas my Labour, I complain
Of sudden shootings, and of grinding pain:
My throws came thicker, and my cryes increast,
Which with her hand the conscious Nurse supprest:

47   not,] O3–5; ~ₐ O1–2.

To that unhappy fortune was I come,
Pain urg'd my clamours; but fear kept me dumb.
With inward struggling I restrain'd my cries;
60 And drunk the tears that trickled from my eyes.
Death was in sight, *Lucina* gave no aid;
And ev'n my dying had my guilt betray'd.
Thou cam'st; and in thy Count'nance sate Despair:
Rent were thy Garments all, and torn thy Hair:
Yet, feigning comfort which thou cou'dst not give,
(Prest in thy Arms, and whisp'ring me to live)
For both our sakes, (said'st thou) preserve thy life;
Live, my dear Sister, and my dearer Wife.
Rais'd by that name, with my last pangs I strove:
70 Such pow'r have words, when spoke by those we love.
The *Babe,* as if he heard what thou hadst sworn,
With hasty joy sprung forward to be born.
What helps it to have weather'd out one Storm?
Fear of our *Father* does another form.
High in his Hall, rock'd in a Chair of State,
The King with his tempestuous Council sate:
Through this large Room our only passage lay,
By which we cou'd the new-born *Babe* convey.
Swath'd, in her lap, the bold Nurse bore him out;
80 With Olive branches cover'd round about:
And, mutt'ring pray'rs, as holy Rites she meant,
Through the divided Crowd, unquestion'd, went.
Just at the door th' unhappy Infant cry'd:
The Grandsire heard him, and the theft he spy'd.
Swift as a Whirl-wind to the Nurse he flyes;
And deafs his stormy Subjects with his cries.
With one fierce puff, he blows the leaves away:
Expos'd, the self-discover'd Infant lay.
The noise reach'd me, and my presaging mind
90 Too soon its own approaching woes divin'd.
Not Ships at Sea with winds are shaken more,
Nor Seas themselves, when angry Tempests roar,
Than I, when my loud Fathers voice I hear:

88 Expos'd,] O3–5; ~∧ O1–2.

The *Bed* beneath me trembled with my fear.
He rush'd upon me, and divulg'd my stain;
Scarce from my Murther cou'd his hands refrain.
I only answer'd him with silent tears;
They flow'd; my tongue was frozen up with fears.
His little Grandchild he commands away,
100 To Mountain Wolves, and every Bird of prey.
The Babe cry'd out, as if he understood,
And beg'd his pardon with what voice he cou'd.
By what expressions can my grief be shown?
(Yet you may guess my anguish by your own)
To see my bowels, and what yet was worse,
Your bowels too, condemn'd to such a Curse!
Out went the King; my voice its freedom found,
My breasts I beat, my blubber'd Cheeks I wound.
And now appear'd the Messenger of death,
110 Sad were his Looks, and scarce he drew his Breath,
To say, *Your Father sends you*———(with that word
His trembling hands presented me a Sword:)
Your Father sends you this: and lets you know
That your own Crimes the use of it will show.
Too well I know the sence those words impart:
His *Present* shall be treasur'd in my heart.
Are these the Nuptial Gifts a Bride receives?
And this the fatal Dow'r a Father gives?
Thou God of Marriage shun thy own disgrace;
120 And take thy Torch from this detested place:
Instead of that, let Furies light their brands;
And Fire my pile with their infernal hands.
With happier fortune may my Sisters wed;
Warn'd by the dire Example of the dead.
For thee, poor Babe, what Crime cou'd they pretend?
How cou'd thy Infant innocence offend?
A guilt there was; but oh that guilt was mine!
Thou suffer'st for a sin that was not thine.
Thy Mothers grief and Crime! but just enjoy'd,
130 Shown to my sight, and born to be destroy'd!
Unhappy Off-spring of my teeming Womb!

Drag'd head-long from thy Cradle to thy Tomb!
Thy unoffending life I could not save,
Nor weeping cou'd I follow to thy Grave!
Nor on thy Tomb cou'd offer my shorn Hair;
Nor show the grief which tender Mothers bear.
Yet long thou shalt not from my Arms be lost,
For soon I will o're-take thy Infant Ghost.
But thou, my Love, and now my Love's Despair,
140 Perform his Funerals with paternal care.
His scatter'd Limbs with my dead body burn;
And once more joyn us in the pious Urn.
If on my wounded breast thou drop'st a tear,
Think for whose sake my breast that wound did bear;
And faithfully my last desires fulfill,
As I perform my cruel Fathers will.

Helen to Paris

THE ARGUMENT

Helen, *having received the foregoing Epistle from* Paris, *returns the
following Answer: wherein she seems at first to chide him for his
Presumption in Writing, as he had done, which could only proceed
from his low Opinion of her Vertue; then owns her self to be sensible
of the Passion, which he had expressed for her, tho she much suspect
his Constancy; and at last discovers her Inclinations to be favourable
to him. The whole Letter shewing the extream artifice of Woman-
kind.*

WHEN loose Epistles violate Chast Eyes,
   She half Consents, who silently denies:
   How dares a Stranger with designs so vain,
Marriage and Hospitable Rights Prophane?
Was it for this, your Fate did shelter find

From swelling Seas and every faithless wind?
(For tho a distant Country brought you forth,
Your usage here was equal to your worth.)
Does this deserve to be rewarded so?
10 Did you come here a Stranger, or a Foe?
Your partial Judgment may perhaps complain;
And think me barbarous for my just disdain;
Ill-bred then let me be, but not unchast,
Nor my clear fame with any spot defac'd:
Tho in my face there's no affected Frown,
Nor in my Carriage a feign'd niceness shown,
I keep my Honor still without a stain,
Nor has my Love made any Coxcomb vain.
Your Boldness I with admiration see;
20 What hope had you to gain a Queen like me?
Because a Hero forc'd me once away,
Am I thought fit to be a second prey?
Had I been won, I had deserv'd your blame,
But sure my part was nothing but the shame:
Yet the base theft to him no fruit did bear,
I scap'd unhurt by any thing but fear.
Rude force might some unwilling Kisses gain,
But that was all he ever cou'd obtain.
You on such terms would nere have let me go,
30 Were he like you, we had not parted so.
Untouch'd the Youth restor'd me to my Friends,
And modest usage made me some amends;
'Tis vertue to repent a vicious deed;
Did he repent that *Paris* might succeed?
Sure 'tis some Fate that sets me above wrongs,
Yet still exposes me to busie tongues.
Il'e not complain, for who's displeas'd with Love,
If it sincere, discreet, and Constant prove?
But that I fear; not that I think you base,
40 Or doubt the blooming beauties of my face,

37 who's] O2–5; whose's O1.   40 face,] O2–5; ~ ? O1.

But all your Sex is subject to deceive,
And ours alas, too willing to believe.
Yet others yield: and Love o'recomes the best,
But why should I not shine above the rest?
Fair *Leda*'s Story seems at first to be
A fit example ready found for me;
But she was Cousen'd by a borrow'd shape,
And under harmless Feathers felt a Rape:
If I should yield, what Reason could I use?
50 By what mistake the Loving Crime excuse?
Her fault was in her pow'rful Lover lost,
But of what *Jupiter* have I to boast?
Tho you to Heroes, and to Kings succeed,
Our Famous Race does no addition need,
And great Alliances but useless prove
To one that's come her self from mighty *Jove*.
Go then and boast in some less haughty place,
Your *Phrygian* Blood, and *Priam*'s Ancient race,
Which I wou'd shew I valu'd, if I durst;
60 You are the fifth from *Jove,* but I the first.
The Crown of *Troy* is pow'rful I confess,
But I have reason to think ours no less.
Your Letter fill'd with promises of all,
That Men can good, or Women pleasant call,
Gives expectation such an ample field,
As wou'd move Goddesses themselves to yield.
But if I e're offend great *Juno*'s Laws,
Your self shall be the Dear, the only Cause;
Either my Honour I'll to death maintain,
70 Or follow you, without mean thoughts of Gain.
Not that so fair a Present I despise,
We like the Gift, when we the giver prize.
But 'tis your Love moves me, which made you take,
Such pains, & run such hazards for my sake;
I have perceiv'd (though I dissembled too)
A Thousand things that Love has made you do;
Your eager Eyes would almost dazle mine,
In which (wild man) your wanton thoughts wou'd shine.

Sometimes you'd sigh, sometimes disorder'd stand,
80 And with unusual ardor, press my hand;
Contrive just after me to take the Glass,
Nor wou'd you let the least occasion pass,
Which oft I fear'd I did not mind alone,
And blushing sate for things which you have done;
Then murmur'd to my self, he'll for my sake
Do any thing; I hope 'twas no mistake:
Oft have I read within this pleasing Grove,
Under my Name those Charming words, *I Love,*
I frowning, seem'd not to believe your Flame,
90 But now, alas, am come to write the same.
If I were capable to do amiss,
I could not but be sensible of this.
For oh! your Face has such peculiar charms,
That who can hold from flying to your arms?
But what I ner'e can have without offence,
May some blest Maid possess with innocence.
Pleasure may tempt, but vertue more should move,
O Learn of me to want the thing you Love.
What you desire is sought by all mankind:
100 As you have eyes, so others are not blind.
Like you they see, like you my charms adore,
They wish not less, but you dare venture more:
Oh! had you then upon our Coasts been brought,
My Virgin Love when thousand Rivals sought,
You had I seen, you should have had my voice;
Nor could my Husband justly blame my Choice.
For both our hopes, alas you come too late!
Another now is Master of my Fate.
More to my wish I cou'd have liv'd with you,
110 And yet my present lot can undergo.
Cease to solicit a weak Woman's will,
And urge not her you Love, to so much ill.
But let me live contented as I may,

83 fear'd] ∼ , O1–5.   86 thing;] O3–5; ∼ , O1–2.
88 *I*] O2–5; I O1.   104 Love] ∼ , O1–5.
107 too] O2–5; to O1.

And make not my unspotted fame your prey.
Some Right you claim, since naked to your eyes
Three Goddesses disputed Beauties prize;
One offer'd Valour, t' other Crowns, but she
Obtain'd her Cause, who smiling promis'd me.
But first I am not of belief so light,
120 To think such Nymphs wou'd shew you such a sight.
Yet granting this, the other part is feign'd:
A Bribe so mean, your sentence had not gain'd.
With partial eyes I shou'd my self regard,
To think that *Venus* made me her reward:
I humbly am content with human praise;
A Goddesse's applause wou'd envy raise:
But be it as you say, for 'tis confest,
The Men who flatter highest, please us best.
That I suspect it, ought not to displease;
130 For Miracles are not believ'd with ease.
One joy I have, that I had *Venus* voice;
A greater yet, that you confirm'd her Choice;
That proffer'd Laurels, promis'd Sov'raignty,
Juno and *Pallas* you contemn'd for me.
Am I your Empire then, and your renown?
What heart of Rock but must by this be won?
And yet bear witness, O you Powr's above,
How rude I am in all the Arts of Love!
My hand is yet untaught to write to men;
140 This is th' Essay of my unpractis'd pen:
Happy those Nymphs, whom use has perfect made;
I think all Crime, and tremble at a shade.
Ev'n while I write, my fearful conscious eyes
Look often back, misdoubting a surprize.
For now the Rumour spreads among the Croud,
At Court in whispers, but in Town aloud:
Dissemble you, what er'e you hear 'em say:
To leave off Loving were your better way,
Yet if you will dissemble it, you may.

117 t' other] O2–5; to' ther O1.   147 'em] O2–5; e'm O1.

150 Love secretly: the absence of my Lord,
    More freedom gives, but does not all afford:
    Long is his Journey, long will be his stay;
    Call'd by affairs of Consequence away.
    To go or not when unresolv'd he stood,
    I bid him make what swift return he cou'd:
    Then Kissing me, he said I recommend
    All to thy Care, but most my *Trojan* Friend.
    I smil'd at what he innocently said,
    And only answer'd, you shall be obey'd.
160 Propitious winds have born him far from hence,
    But let not this secure your confidence.
    Absent he is, yet absent he Commands,
    You know the Proverb, Princes have long hands.
    My Fame's my burden, for the more I'm prais'd;
    A juster ground of jealousie is rais'd.
    Were I less fair, I might have been more blest:
    Great Beauty through great danger is possest.
    To leave me here his venture was not hard,
    Because he thought my vertue was my Guard.
170 He fear'd my Face, but trusted to my Life,
    The Beauty doubted, but believ'd the Wife:
    You bid me use th' occasion while I can,
    Put in our hands by the good easie man.
    I wou'd, and yet I doubt, 'twixt Love and fear;
    One draws me from you, and one brings me near.
    Our flames are mutual: and my Husband's gone,
    The nights are long; I fear to lie alone.
    One House contains us, and weak Walls divide,
    And you're too pressing to be long denied:
180 Let me not live, but every thing conspires,
    To joyn our Loves, and yet my fear retires.
    You Court with words, when you shou'd force employ,
    A Rape is requisite to shamefac'd joy.
    Indulgent to the wrongs which we receive,
    Our Sex can suffer what we dare not give.
    What have I said! for both of us 'twere best,

Our kindling fires, if each of us supprest.
The Faith of Strangers is too prone to change,
And like themselves their wandring Passions range.
190 *Hipsypile,* and the fond *Minoian* Maid,
Were both by trusting of their Ghests betray'd.
How can I doubt that other men deceive,
When you your self did fair *Oenone* leave?
But lest I shou'd upbraid your treachery,
You make a merit of that Crime to me:
Yet grant you were to faithful Love inclin'd,
Your weary *Trojans* wait but for a wind.
Shou'd you prevail while I assign the night,
Your Sails are hoysted, and you take your flight:
200 Some bawling Mariner our Love destroys,
And breaks asunder our unfinish'd joys.
But I with you may leave the *Spartan* Port,
To view the *Trojan* Wealth, and *Priam*'s Court.
Shown while I see, I shall expose my Fame:
And fill a foreign Country with my shame.
In *Asia* what reception shall I find?
And what dishonour leave in *Greece* behind?
What will your Brothers, *Priam, Hecuba,*
And what will all your modest Matrons say?
210 Ev'n you, when on this action you reflect,
My future Conduct justly may suspect:
And what er'e Stranger Lands upon your Coast,
Conclude me, by your own example, lost.
I from your rage, a Strumpet's Name shall hear,
While you forget, what part in it you bear.
You my Crimes Authour, will my Crime upbraid:
Deep under ground, Oh let me first be laid!
You boast the Pomp and Plenty of your Land,
And promise all shall be at my Command;
220 Your *Trojan* Wealth, believe me, I despise;
My own poor Native Land has dearer ties.
Shou'd I be injur'd on your *Phrygian* Shore,

What help of Kindred cou'd I there implore?
Medea was by *Jasons* flatt'ry won:
I may like her believe and be undon.
Plain honest hearts, like mine, suspect no cheat;
And Love contributes to its own deceit.
The Ships about whose sides loud Tempests roar,
With gentle Winds were wafted from the Shore.
230 Your teeming Mother dreamt a flaming Brand
Sprung from her Womb consum'd the *Trojan* Land.
To second this, old Prophecies conspire,
That *Ilium* shall be burnt with *Grecian* fire:
Both give me fear, nor is it much allai'd,
That *Venus* is oblig'd our Loves to aid.
For they who lost their Cause, revenge will take,
And for one Friend two Enemies you make.
Nor can I doubt, but shou'd I follow you,
The Sword wou'd soon our fatal Crime pursue:
240 A wrong so great my Husband's rage wou'd rouze,
And my Relations wou'd his Cause espouse.
You boast your Strength and Courage, but alas!
Your words receive small credit from your Face.
Let Heroes in the Dusty field delight,
Those Limbs were fashion'd for another fight.
Bid *Hector* sally from the Walls of *Troy,*
A sweeter quarrel shou'd your arms employ.
Yet fears like these, shou'd not my mind perplex,
Were I as wise as many of my Sex.
250 But time and you, may bolder thoughts inspire;
And I perhaps may yield to your desire.
You last demand a private Conference,
These are your words, but I can ghess your sense.
Your unripe hopes their harvest must attend:
Be Rul'd by me, and time may be your friend.
This is enough to let you understand,
For now my Pen has tir'd my tender hand:

---

247 sweeter] O2–5; sweter O1.

My Woman Knows the secret of my heart,
And may hereafter better news impart.

Dido to Aeneas

THE ARGUMENT

Æneas, *the Son of* Venus *and* Anchises, *having at the Destruction of*
Troy, *saved his Gods, his Father and Son* Ascanius *from the Fire, put
to Sea with twenty Sail of Ships, and having bin long tost with Tempests, was at last cast upon the Shore of* Lybia, *where Queen* Dido,
(flying from the Cruelty of Pigmalion *her Brother, who had Killed
her Husband* Sichæus,) *had lately built* Carthage. *She entertained*
Æneas *and his Fleet with great civility, fell passionately in Love with
him, and in the end denyed him not the last Favours. But* Mercury
admonishing Æneas *to go in search of* Italy, *(a Kingdom promised to
him by the Gods,) he readily prepared to Obey him.* Dido *soon perceived it, and having in vain try'd all other means to engage him to
stay, at last in Despair, writes to him as follows.*

So, on *Mæander's* banks, when death is nigh,
   The mournful *Swan* sings her own Elegie.
   Not that I hope, (for oh, that hope were vain!)
By words your lost affection to regain;
But having lost what ere was worth my care,
Why shou'd I fear to loose a dying pray'r?
'Tis then resolv'd poor *Dido* must be left,
Of Life, of Honour, and of Love bereft!
While you, with loosen'd Sails & Vows, prepare
10 To seek a Land that flies the Searchers care.
Nor can my rising Tow'rs your flight restrain,
Nor my new Empire, offer'd you in vain.
Built Walls you shun, unbuilt you seek; that Land
Is yet to Conquer; but you this Command.

Suppose you Landed where your wish design'd,
Think what Reception Forreiners would find.
What People is so void of common sence,
To Vote Succession from a Native Prince?
Yet there new Scepters and new Loves you seek;
20 New Vows to plight, and plighted Vows to break.
When will your Tow'rs the height of *Carthage* know?
Or when, your eyes discern such crowds below?
If such a Town and Subjects you cou'd see,
Still wou'd you want a Wife who lov'd like me.
For, oh, I burn, like fires with incense bright;
Not holy Tapers flame with purer light:
Æneas is my thoughts perpetual Theme:
Their daily longing, and their nightly dream.
Yet he ungrateful and obdurate still:
30 Fool that I am to place my heart so ill!
My self I cannot to my self restore:
Still I complain, and still I love him more.
Have pity, *Cupid,* on my bleeding heart;
And pierce thy Brothers with an equal dart.
I rave: nor canst thou *Venus'* offspring be,
Love's Mother cou'd not bear a Son like Thee.
From harden'd Oak, or from a Rocks cold womb,
At least thou art from some fierce *Tygress* come,
Or, on rough Seas, from their foundation torn,
40 Got by the winds, and in a Tempest born:
Like that which now thy trembling Sailors fear:
Like that, whose rage should still detain thee here.
Behold how high the Foamy Billows ride!
The winds and waves are on the juster side.
To Winter weather, and a stormy Sea,
I'll owe what rather I wou'd owe to thee.
Death thou deserv'st from Heav'ns avenging Laws;
But I'm unwilling to become the cause.
To shun my Love, if thou wilt seek thy Fate,

18 Prince?] O2–5; ~ . O1.

50 'Tis a dear purchase, and a costly hate.
Stay but a little, till the Tempest cease;
And the loud winds are lull'd into a peace.
May all thy rage, like theirs, unconstant prove!
And so it will, if there be pow'r in Love.
Know'st thou not yet what dangers Ships sustain,
So often wrack'd, how darst thou tempt the Main?
Which, were it smooth; were every wave asleep,
Ten thousand forms of death are in the deep.
In that abyss the Gods their vengance store,
60 For broken Vows of those who falsely swore.
There winged storms on Sea-born *Venus* wait,
To vindicate the Justice of her State.
Thus, I to Thee the means of safety show:
And lost my self, would still preserve my Foe.
False as thou art, I not thy death design:
O rather live to be the cause of mine!
Shou'd some avenging storm thy Vessel tear,
(But Heav'n forbid my words shou'd Omen bear,)
Then, in thy face thy perjur'd Vows would fly;
70 And my wrong'd Ghost be present to thy eye.
With threatning looks, think thou beholdst me stare,
Gasping my mouth, and clotted all my hair.
Then shou'd fork'd Lightning and red Thunder fall,
What coud'st thou say, but I deserv'd 'em all?
Lest this shou'd happen, make not hast away:
To shun the danger will be worth thy stay.
Have pity on thy Son, if not on me:
My death alone is guilt enough for thee.
What has his Youth, what have thy Gods deserv'd,
80 To sink in Seas, who were from fires preserv'd?
But neither Gods nor Parent didst thou bear,
(Smooth stories all, to please a Womans ear.)
False was the tale of thy Romantick life;
Nor yet am I thy first deluded wife.

75 away:] ~ . O1–3; ~ , O4–5.

Left to pursuing Foes *Creüsa* stai'd,
By thee, base man, forsaken and betray'd.
This, when thou told'st me, struck my tender heart,
That such requital follow'd such desert.
Nor doubt I but the Gods, for crimes like these,
90 Sev'n Winters kept thee wandring on the Seas.
Thy starv'd Companions, cast a Shore, I fed,
Thy self admitted to my Crown and Bed.
To harbour Strangers, succour the distrest,
Was kind enough; but oh too kind the rest!
Curst be the Cave which first my ruin brought:
Where, from the storm, we common shelter sought!
A dreadful howling eccho'd round the place,
The Mountain Nymphs, thought I, my Nuptials grace.
I thought so then, but now too late I know
100 The Furies yell'd my Funerals from below.
O Chastity and violated Fame,
Exact your dues to my dead Husbands name!
By Death redeem my reputation lost;
And to his Arms restore my guilty Ghost.
Close by my Palace, in a Gloomy Grove,
Is rais'd a Chappel to my murder'd Love.
There, wreath'd with boughs and wool his Statue stands,
The pious Monument of Artful hands:
Last night, methought, he call'd me from the dome,
110 And thrice with hollow voice, cry'd, *Dido,* come.
She comes: thy Wife thy lawful summons hears:
But comes more slowly, clogg'd with conscious fears.
Forgive the wrong I offer'd to thy bed,
Strong were his charms, who my weak faith misled.
His Goddess Mother, and his aged Sire,
Born on his back, did to my Fall conspire.
O such he was, and is, that were he true,
Without a blush I might his Love pursue.
But cruel Stars my birth day did attend:

85 *Creüsa*] *Crëusa* O1; *Creusa* O2–5.

120 And as my Fortune open'd, it must end.
　　My plighted Lord was at the Altar slain,
　　Whose wealth was made my bloody Brothers gain:
　　Friendless, and follow'd by the Murd'rers hate,
　　To forein Countrey's I remov'd my Fate;
　　And here, a suppliant, from the Natives hands,
　　I bought the ground on which my City stands,
　　With all the Coast that stretches to the Sea;
　　Ev'n to the friendly Port that sheltred Thee:
　　Then rais'd these Walls, which mount into the Air,
130 At once my Neighbours wonder, and their fear.
　　For now they Arm; and round me Leagues are made
　　My scarce Establisht Empire to invade.
　　To Man my new built Walls I must prepare,
　　An helpless Woman and unskill'd in War.
　　Yet thousand Rivals to my Love pretend;
　　And for my Person, would my Crown Defend:
　　Whose jarring Votes in one complaint agree,
　　That each unjustly is disdain'd for Thee.
　　To proud *Hyarbas* give me up a prey;
140 (For that must follow, if thou go'st away.)
　　Or to my Husbands Murd'rer leave my life;
　　That to the Husband he may add the Wife.
　　Go then; since no complaints can move thy mind:
　　Go perjur'd man, but leave thy Gods behind.
　　Touch not those Gods by whom thou art forsworn;
　　Who will in impious hands no more be born.
　　Thy Sacrilegious worship they disdain,
　　And rather wou'd the *Grecian* fires sustain.
　　Perhaps my greatest shame is still to come;
150 And part of thee lies hid within my womb.
　　The Babe unborn must perish by thy hate,
　　And perish guiltless in his Mothers Fate.
　　Some God, thou say'st, thy Voyage does command:
　　Wou'd the same God had barr'd thee from my Land.

_____
126 stands,] ∼ . O1–5.

The same, I doubt not, thy departure Steers,
Who kept thee out at Sea so many years,
Where thy long labours were a price so great,
As thou to purchase *Troy* wouldst not repeat.
But *Tyber* now thou seek'st; to be at best
160 When there arriv'd, a poor precarious Ghest.
Yet it deludes thy search: perhaps it will
To thy Old Age lie undiscover'd still.
A ready Crown and Wealth in Dow'r I bring;
And without Conqu'ring here thou art a King.
Here thou to *Carthage* may'st transfer thy *Troy;*
Here young *Ascanius* may his Arms employ:
And, while we live secure in soft repose,
Bring many Laurells home from Conquer'd Foes.
By Cupids Arrows, I adjure thee, stay;
170 By all the Gods, Companions of thy way.
So may thy *Trojans,* who are yet alive
Live still, and with no future Fortune strive:
So may thy Youthful Son old age attain,
And thy dead Fathers Bones in peace remain,
As thou hast pity on unhappy me,
Who know no Crime but too much Love of thee.
I am not born from fierce *Achilles'* Line:
Nor did my Parents against *Troy* combine.
To be thy Wife, if I unworthy prove,
180 By some inferiour name admit my Love.
To be secur'd of still possessing thee,
What wou'd I do, and what wou'd I not be!
Our *Lybian* Coasts their certain seasons know,
When free from Tempests Passengers may go.
But now with Northern Blasts the Billows roar,
And drive the floating Sea-weed to the Shore.
Leave to my care the time to Sail away;
When safe, I will not suffer thee to stay.
Thy weary Men wou'd be with ease content;

156 years,] ∼ . O1–5.

190 Their Sails are tatter'd, and their Masts are spent:
    If by no merit I thy mind can move,
    What thou deny'st my merit, give my Love.
    Stay, till I learn my loss to undergo;
    And give me time to struggle with my woe.
    If not; know this, I will not suffer long;
    My life's too loathsome, and my love too strong.
    Death holds my pen, and dictates what I say,
    While cross my lap thy *Trojan* Sword I lay.
    My tears flow down; the sharp edge cuts their flood,
200 And drinks my sorrows, that must drink my blood.
    How well thy gift does with my Fate agree!
    My Funeral pomp is cheaply made by thee.
    To no new wounds my bosom I display:
    The Sword but enters where Love made the way.
    But thou, dear Sister, and yet dearer friend,
    Shalt my cold Ashes to their Urn attend.
    Sichæus Wife let not the Marble boast,
    I lost that Title when my Fame I lost.
    This short Inscription only let it bear,
210 "Unhappy *Dido* lies in quiet here.
    The cause of death, & Sword by which she dy'd,
    Æneas gave: the rest her arm supply'd."

PROLOGUES AND EPILOGUES 1668–1680

Prologue to Albumazar

To say this Commedy pleas'd long a go,
 Is not enough, to make it pass you now:
 Yet gentlemen, your Ancestors had witt,
When few men censurd, and when fewer writ.
And *Iohnson* (of those few the best) chose this,
As the best modell of his master-piece;
Subtle was got by our *Albumazar,*
That *Alchamist* by this Astrologer.
Here he was fashion'd, and we may suppose,
He lik'd the fashion well, who wore the Cloaths.
But *Ben* made nobly his, what he did mould,
What was anothere's Lead, becomes his Gold;
Like an unrighteous Conquerer he raigns,
Yet rules that well, which he unjustly gains.
But this our age such Authors does afford,
As make whole Playes, and yet scarce write one word:
Who in this Anarchy of witt, rob all,
And what's their Plunder, their Possession call;
Who like bold Padders scorn by night to prey,
But Rob by Sun-shine, in the face of day;
Nay scarce the common Ceremony use,
Of stand, Sir, and deliver up your Muse;
But knock the Poet down; and, with a grace,
Mount *Pegasus* before the owners Face.

---

4 and when] O3–4, M; and O1–2.
5 *Iohnson* (of those few the best)] O3–4; Johnson of those few the best, M; *Iohn-son,* of those few, the best O1; *Iohnson* of those few, the best O2.
6 As . . . master-piece] O3–4, M; And . . . master piece O1–2.
9 we may] O3–4, M; I should O1–2.
10 lik'd the . . . who wore the] O3–4, M; likes my . . . that wears my O1–2.
12 becomes] O3–4, M; became O1–2. 16 one] O3–4, M; a O1–2.
18 call;] ∼ . O1–4, M. 21 Nay] O3–4, M; Who O1–2.
22 Muse;] O3–4, M; ∼ . O1–2.

Faith if you have such Country *Toms,* abroad,
Tis time for all true men to leave that Road.
Yet it were modest, could it but be sed,
They strip the living, but these rob the dead:
Dare with the mummeys of the Muses Play,
30 And make love to 'em, the *Ægyptian,* way:
Or as a Rhyming Authour would have sed,
Joyn the dead living, to the living dead.
Such men in Poetry may claim some part,
They have the Licence, though they want the Art,
And might, where Theft was prais'd, for Laureats stand,
Poets, not of the head, but of the hand;
They make the benefits of others studying,
Much like the meales of Politick, *Jack Pudding:*
Whose Dish to challenge, no man has the courage,
40 Tis all his own, when once h' has spit i' th' Porredge.
But Gentlemen, y' are all concernd in this,
You are in fault for what they do amiss:
For they their thefts still undiscover'd think,
And durst not steal unless you please to winck.
Perhaps, you may award by your Decree,
They shou'd refund, but that can never be.
For should you Letters of reprizall seal,
These men write that, which no man else would steale.

---

28 strip . . . these] O3–4, M; stript . . . they O1–2.
29 Dare . . . mummeys] O3–4, M; 'Twill . . . mummey O1–2.
30 way:] O3–4; ~ . O1–2; ~ ; M.   33 Such men] O3–4, M; Yet such O1–2.
34 Art,] M; ~ . O1–4.
35 And might, where Theft was prais'd, for Laureats] O3–4, M; Such as in *Sparta* weight for Laurels O1; . . . might for Laurels O2.
37 the] O3–4, M; their O1–2.   37 benefits] O3–4; benefit O1–2, M.
38 *Jack Pudding*] O3–4; *Jack* Pudding O1–2; Jack Pudding M.
39 Whose Dish to challenge, no man] O3–4, M; Where Broth to claim, there's no one O1–2.
40 when once h'] O3–4, M; after he O1–2.
42 amiss] O3–4, M; a miss O1–2.   43 still] O3–4, M; will O1–2.
45–46 *These lines are not in O1–2.*
47 For . . . you] O3–4, M; Now . . . we O1–2.

Prologue to Witt without Money

So shipwrackt Passengers escape to land,
    So look they, when on the bare Beach they stand,
    Dropping and cold; and their first feare scarce o're,
Expecting famine on a desert shore;
From that hard Climate we must wait for bread
Whence even the Natives forc't by hunger fled.
Our stage does humane chance present to view,
But ne're before was seen so sadly true,
You are chang'd too, and your pretence to see
10 Is but a nobler name for charitie.
Your own provisions furnish out our feasts
While you the founders make your selves the guests.
Of all mankind besides Fate had some care,
But for poore Witt no portion did prepare,
'Tis left a rent-charge to the brave and faire.
You cherisht it, & now its fall you mourne,
Which blind unmannerd Zealots make their scorne,
Who think that fire a Judgment on the stage,
Which spar'd not Temples in its furious rage.
20 *But as our new-built City rises higher,*
So from old Theaters *may new aspire,*
Since Fate contrives magnificence by fire.
Our great Metropolis does farr surpasse,
What ere is now, & equals all that was;
Our Witt as far does forrein wit excell,

2 on the] O5–6, M1–2; on O1–4.   4 on] O5–6, M1–2; from O1–4.
9 too] O4–6, M1–2; to O1–3.   10 for] O5–6, M1–2; of O1–4.
12 While] O5–6; Whilst O1–4, M1–2.
12 the guests] O5–6, M1–2; our guests O1–4.
18 that fire] O4–6, M1–2; the fire O1–3.
23 does] O4–6, M1; doth O1–2, M2; *passage omitted from O3.*
24 equals] O2, O4–6, M1–2; equald O1; *passage omitted from O3.*
25 does] O4–6, M1; doth O1–2, M2; *passage omitted from O3.*

And like a king should in a Pallace dwell.
But we with golden hopes are vainely fed,
Talk high, and entertaine you in a shed:
Your presence here, for which we humbly sue,
30 Will grace old *Theaters,* and build up new.

Prologue for the Women

WERE none of you Gallants e're driven so hard,
As when the poor kind Soul was under guard
And could not do 't at home, in some by-street,
To take a Lodging, and in private meet?
Such is our Case, We can't appoint our House,
The Lovers old and wonted Rendezvouz.
But hither to this trusty Nook remove,
The worse the Lodging is, the more the Love.
For much good Pastime, many a dear sweet hug
10 Is stoln in Garrets on the humble Rugg.
Here's good Accommodation in the Pit,
The Grave demurely in the midst may Sit.
And so the hot *Burgundian* on the Side,
Ply Vizard Masque, and o're the Benches stride:
Here are convenient upper Boxes too,
For those that make the most triumphant show,
All that keep Coaches must not Sit below.
There Gallants, You betwixt the Acts retire,
And at dull Plays have something to admire:
20 We who look up, can Your Addresses mark;
And see the Creatures Coupled in the Ark:
So we expect the *Lovers, Braves,* and *Wits,*
The Gaudy House with Scenes, will serve for *Citts.*

---

1 Were] Where O1–2.
6 wonted] wanted O1–2.

Prologue to Arviragus *Reviv'd*

W ITH sickly Actors and an old House too,
  We're match'd with Glorious Theatres and New
  And with our Alehouse Scenes, and Cloaths bare worn,
Can neither raise Old Plays, nor New adorn.
If all these ills could not undo us quite,
A Brisk *French* Troop is grown your dear delight,
Who with broad bloody Bills call you each day,
To laugh, and break your Buttons at their Play,
Or see some serious Piece, which we presume
10 Is fal'n from some incomparable Plume;
And therefore, *Messieurs,* if you'l do us grace,
Send Lacquies early to preserve your Place.
We dare not on your Priviledge intrench,
Or ask you why you like 'em? They are *French.*
Therefore some go with Courtesie exceeding,
Neither to Hear nor See, but show their Breeding,
Each Lady striving to out-laugh the rest,
To make it seem they understood the Jest:
Their Countrymen come in, and nothing pay,
20 To teach Us *English* where to Clap the Play:
Civil *Igad:* Our Hospitable Land,
Bears all the charge for them to understand:
Mean time we Languish, and neglected lye,
Like Wives, while You keep better Company;
And wish for our own sakes, without a Satyr,
You'd less good Breeding, or had more good Nature.

---

6 delight,] ~ . O1–2. 8 Play,] ~ . O1–2.
16 Breeding,] ~ . O1–2.

Prologue and Epilogue to the
University of Oxon. [1673]

WHAT *Greece,* when Learning flourish'd, onely Knew,
　　(*Athenian* Judges,) you this day Renew.
　　Here too are Annual Rites to *Pallas* done,
And here Poetique prizes lost or won.
Methinks I see you, Crown'd with Olives sit,
And strike a sacred Horrour from the Pit.
A Day of Doom is this of your Decree,
Where even the Best are but by Mercy free:
A Day which none but *Johnson* durst have wish'd to see.

10　Here they who long have known the usefull Stage,
Come to be taught themselves to teach the Age.
As your Commissioners our Poets goe,
To Cultivate the Virtue which you sow:
In your *Lycæum,* first themselves refind,
And Delegated thence to Humane kind.
But as Embassadours, when long from home,
For new Instructions to their Princes come;
So Poets who your Precepts have forgot,
Return, and beg they may be better taught:
20　Follies and Faults elsewhere by them are shown,
But by your Manners they Correct their Own.
Th' illiterate Writer, Emperique like, applies
To minds diseas'd, unsafe, chance Remedies:
The Learn'd in Schools, where Knowledge first began,
Studies with Care th' Anatomy of Man;
Sees Vertue, Vice, and Passions in their Cause,
And Fame from Science, not from Fortune draws.
So Poetry, which is in *Oxford* made
An Art, in *London* onely is a Trade.
30　There Haughty Dunces whose unlearned Pen

Could ne'er Spell Grammar, would be reading Men.
Such build their Poems the *Lucretian* way,
So many Huddled Atoms make a Play,
And if they hit in Order by some Chance,
They call that Nature, which is Ignorance.
To such a Fame let mere Town-Wits aspire,
And their Gay Nonsense their own Citts admire.
Our Poet, could he find Forgiveness here
Would wish it rather than a *Plaudit* there.
40 He owns no Crown from those *Prætorian* bands,
But knows *that* Right is in this Senates hands.
Not Impudent enough to hope your Praise, ⎫
Low at the Muses feet, his Wreath he lays, ⎬
And where he took it up Resigns his Bays. ⎭
Kings make their Poets whom themselves think fit,
But 'tis your Suffrage makes Authentique Wit.

EPILOGUE

No poor *Dutch* Peasant, wing'd with all his Fear,
 Flies with more haste, when the *French* arms draw near,
 Than We with our Poetique train come down
For refuge hither, from th' infected Town;
Heaven for our Sins this Summer has thought fit
To visit us with all the Plagues of Wit.
 A *French* Troop first swept all things in its way,
But those Hot *Monsieurs* were too quick to stay;
Yet, to our Cost in that short time, we find
10 They left their Itch of Novelty behind.
 Th' *Italian* Merry-Andrews took their place,
And quite Debauch'd the Stage with lewd Grimace;
Instead of Wit, and Humours, your Delight

---

40 *Prætorian*] O2, M; *Prætorian* O1.

Was there to see two Hobby-horses Fight,
Stout *Scaramoucha* with Rush Lance rode in,
And ran a Tilt at Centaure *Arlequin*.
For Love you heard how amorous Asses bray'd,
And Cats in Gutters gave their Serenade.
Nature was out of Countenance, and each Day
20 Some new born Monster shewn you for a Play.
  But when all fail'd, to strike the Stage quite Dumb,
Those wicked Engines call'd Machines are come.
Thunder and Lightning now for Wit are Play'd,
And shortly Scenes in *Lapland* will be Lay'd:
Art Magique is for Poetry profest,
And Cats and Dogs, and each obscener Beast
To which *Ægyptian* Dotards once did Bow,
Upon our *English* stage are worship'd now.
Witchcraft reigns there, and raises to Renown
30 *Macbeth*, the *Simon Magus* of the Town.
Fletcher's despis'd, your *Johnson* out of Fashion,
And Wit the onely Drug in all the Nation.
In this low Ebb our Wares to you are shown, ⎤
By you those Staple Authours worth is known, ⎬
For Wit's a Manufacture of your Own. ⎦
When you, who onely can, their Scenes have prais'd,
We'll boldly back, and say their Price is rais'd.

Prologue and Epilogue Spoken at the Opening of the New House

A Plain Built House after so long a stay,
  Will send you half unsatisfy'd away;
  When, fal'n from your expected Pomp, you find
A bare convenience only is design'd.
You who each day can Theatres behold,

Like *Nero*'s Palace, shining all with Gold,
Our mean ungilded Stage will scorn, we fear,
And for the homely Room, disdain the Chear.
Yet now cheap Druggets to a Mode are grown, ⎤
10 And a plain Sute (since we can make but one) ⎬
Is better than to be by tarnisht gawdry known. ⎦
They who are by Your Favours wealthy made,
With mighty Sums may carry on the Trade:
We, broken Banquers, half destroy'd by Fire, ⎤
With our small Stock to humble Roofs retire, ⎬
Pity our Loss, while you their Pomp admire. ⎦
For Fame and Honour we no longer strive,
We yield in both, and only beg to Live:
Unable to support their vast Expence,
20 Who Build, and Treat with such Magnificence;
That like th' Ambitious Monarchs of the Age,
They give the Law to our Provincial Stage:
Great Neighbours enviously promote Excess,
While they impose their Splendor on the less.
But only Fools, and they of vast Estate, ⎤
Th' extremity of Modes will imitate, ⎬
The dangling Knee-fringe, and the Bib-Cravat. ⎦
Yet if some Pride with want may be allow'd,
We in our plainness may be justly proud:
30 Our Royal Master will'd it should be so,
What e're He's pleas'd to own, can need no show:
That Sacred Name gives Ornament and Grace,
And, like his stamp, makes basest Mettals pass.
'Twere Folly now a stately Pile to raise,
To build a Play-House while You throw down Plays,
Whilst Scenes, Machines, and empty *Opera's* reign,
And for the Pencil You the Pen disdain.
While Troops of famisht *Frenchmen* hither drive,
And laugh at those upon whose Alms they live:
40 Old *English* Authors vanish, and give place

18 Live:] M; ~ . O1–2.   35 Plays,] M; ~ . O1–2.

To these new Conqu'rors of the *Norman* Race;
More tamely, than your Fathers You submit,
You'r now grown Vassals to 'em in your wit:
Mark, when they Play, how our fine Fops advance ⎤
The mighty Merits of these Men of *France,*   ⎬
Keep Time, cry *Ben,* and humour the Cadence: ⎦
Well please your selves, but sure 'tis understood,
That *French* Machines have ne'r done *England* good:
I wou'd not prophesie our Houses Fate:
50 But while vain Shows and Scenes you over-rate,
'Tis to be fear'd————
That as a Fire the former House o'rethrew,
Machines and Tempests will destroy the new.

EPILOGUE

T HOUGH what our Prologue said was sadly true, ⎤
  Yet, Gentlemen, our homely House is new,   ⎬
  A Charm that seldom fails with, wicked, You. ⎦
A Country Lip may have the Velvet touch, ⎤
Tho' She's no Lady, you may think her such, ⎬
A strong imagination may do much.   ⎦
But you, loud Sirs, who thro' your Curls look big,
Criticks in Plume and white vallancy Wig,
Who lolling on our foremost Benches sit,
10 And still charge first, (the true forlorn of Wit)
Whose favours, like the Sun, warm where you roul,
Yet you like him, have neither heat nor Soul;
So may your Hats your Foretops never press,
Untouch'd your Ribbonds, sacred be your dress;
So may you slowly to Old Age advance,
And have th' excuse of Youth for Ignorance.

———
7 thro'] M; tho' O1–2.

So may Fop corner full of noise remain,
And drive far off the dull attentive train;
So may your Midnight Scowrings happy prove,
20 And Morning Batt'ries force your way to Love;
So may not *France* your Warlike Hands recall,
But leave you by each others Swords to fall:
As you come here to ruffle Vizard Punk,
When sober, rail and roar when you are drunk.
But to the Wits we can some merit plead,
And urge what by themselves has oft been said:
Our House relieves the Ladies from the frights
Of ill pav'd Streets, and long dark Winter Nights;
The *Flanders* Horses from a cold bleak Road,
30 Where Bears in Furs dare scarcely look abroad;
The Audience from worn Plays and Fustian Stuff
Of Rhyme, more nauseous than three Boys in Buff.
Though in their House the Poets Heads appear,
We hope we may presume their Wits are here.
The best which they reserv'd they now will Play, ⎫
For, like kind Cuckolds, tho' w' have not the way ⎬
To please, we'l find you Abler Men who may.   ⎭
If they shou'd fail, for last recruits we breed ⎫
A Troop of frisking Monsieurs to succeed: ⎬
40 (You know the *French* sure cards at time of need.)⎭

*Prologue and Epilogue to the University
of Oxford, 1674*

Poets, your Subjects, have their Parts assign'd
T' unbend, and to divert their Sovereign's mind;
When tyr'd with following Nature, you think fit
To seek repose in the cool shades of Wit,

---

30   abroad;] M; ∼ . O1–2.

And from the sweet Retreat, with Joy survey
What rests, and what is conquer'd, of the way.
Here free your selves, from Envie, Care and Strife,
You view the various turns of humane Life:
Safe in our Scene, through dangerous Courts you go,
10 And Undebauch'd, the Vice of Cities know.
Your Theories are here to Practice brought,
As in Mechanick operations wrought;
And Man the Little world before you set,
As once the Sphere of Chrystal, shew'd the Great:
Blest sure are you above all Mortal kind:
If to your Fortunes you can Suit your Mind.
Content to see, and shun, those Ills we show,
And Crimes, on Theatres alone, to know:
With joy we bring what our dead Authours writ,
20 And beg from you the value of their Wit,
That *Shakespear*'s, *Fletcher*'s, and great *Johnson*'s claim
May be Renew'd from those, who gave them fame.
None of our living Poets dare appear,
For Muses so severe are worship't here;
That conscious of their Faults they shun the Eye, ⎫
And as Prophane, from Sacred places fly, ⎬
Rather than see th' offended God, and dye. ⎭
We bring no Imperfections, but our own,
Such Faults as made, are by the Makers shown.
30 And you have been so kind, that we may boast,
The greatest Judges still can Pardon most.
Poets must stoop, when they would please our Pit,
Debas'd even to the Level of their Wit,
Disdaining that, which yet they know, will Take,
Hating themselves, what their Applause must make:
But when to Praise from you they would Aspire
Though they like Eagles Mount, your *Jove* is Higher.
So far your Knowledge, all their Pow'r transcends,
As what *should* be, beyond what *Is*, extends.

---

20 Wit,] ∼. O1–2.   33 Wit,] ∼. O1–2.

EPILOGUE

OFT has our Poet wisht, this happy Seat
    Might prove his fading Muses last retreat:
    I wonder'd at his wish, but now I find
He sought for quiet, and content of mind;
Which noisfull Towns, and Courts can never know,
And onely in the shades like Laurels grow.
Youth, e'er it sees the World, here studies rest,
And Age returning thence concludes it best.
What wonder if we court that happiness
10 Yearly to share, which hourly you possess,
Teaching ev'n you, (while the vext World we show,)
Your Peace to value more, and better know?
'Tis all we can return for favours past,
Whose holy Memory shall ever last,
For Patronage from him whose care presides
O'er every noble Art, and every Science guides:
Bathurst, a name the learn'd with reverence know,
And scarcely more to his own *Virgil* owe;
Whose Age enjoys but what his Youth deserv'd,
20 To rule those Muses whom before he serv'd:
His Learning, and untainted Manners too
We find (*Athenians*) are deriv'd to you;
Such Ancient hospitality there rests   ⎫
In yours, as dwelt in the first *Grecian* Breasts, ⎬
Whose kindness was Religion to their Guests.⎭
Such Modesty did to our sex appear,   ⎫
As had there been no Laws we need not fear, ⎬
Since each of you was our Protector here. ⎭
Converse so chast, and so strict Vertue shown,
30 As might *Apollo* with the Muses own.

18 owe;] ∼ . O1, O1a, O2.   20 serv'd:] O2; ∼ , O1; ∼ . O1a.

Till our return we must despair to find
Judges so just, so knowing, and so kind.

Epilogue to The Man of Mode

Most Modern Wits, such monstrous Fools have shown,
They seem'd not of heav'ns making but their own.
Those Nauseous Harlequins in Farce may pass,
But there goes more to a substantial Ass!
Something of man must be expos'd to View,
That, Gallants, they may more resemble you:
Sir *Fopling* is a Fool so nicely writ,
The Ladies wou'd mistake him for a Wit:
And when he sings, talks lowd, and cocks; wou'd cry,
10 I vow methinks he's pretty Company,
So brisk, so gay, so travail'd, so refin'd!
As he took pains to graff upon his kind.
True Fops help Natures work, and go to school,
To file and finish god-a'mighty's fool.
Yet none Sir *Fopling* him, or him can call;
He's Knight o' th' Shire, and represents ye all.
From each he meets, he culls what e're he can,
Legion's his name, a people in a Man.
His bulky folly gathers as it goes,
20 And, rolling o're you, like a Snow-ball growes.
His various modes from various Fathers follow,
One taught the Toss, and one the new *French* Wallow.
His Sword-knot, this; his Crevat, this design'd,
And this, the yard long Snake he twirls behind.
From one the sacred Perriwig he gain'd,
Which Wind ne're blew, nor touch of Hat prophan'd.
Anothers diving Bow he did adore,

8 Wit:] ~ . Q1–3, M2; ~∧ M1; ~ , M3.

Which with a shog casts all the hair before:
Till he with full Decorum brings it back,
30 And rises with a Water Spaniel shake.
As for his Songs (the Ladies dear delight)
Those sure he took from most of you who Write.
Yet every man is safe from what he fear'd,
For no one fool is hunted from the herd.

Prologue to the University of Oxford [1676]

THO' Actors cannot much of Learning boast,
Of all who want it, we admire it most.
We love the Praises of a Learned Pit,
As we remotely are ally'd to Wit.
We speak our Poets Wit, and Trade in Ore,
Like those who touch upon the Golden Shore:
Betwixt our Judges can distinction make,
Discern how much, and why, our Poems take.
Mark if the Fools, or Men of Sence, rejoyce,
10 Whether th' Applause be only Sound or Voice.
When our Fop Gallants, or our City Folly
Clap over-loud, it makes us melancholy:
We doubt that Scene which does their wonder raise,
And, for their ignorance contemn their Praise.
Judge then, if We who Act, and They who Write,
Shou'd not be proud of giving You delight.
London likes grossly, but this nicer Pit
Examines, Fathoms all the depths of Wit:
The ready Finger lays on every Blot,
20 Knows what shou'd justly please, and what shou'd not.
Nature her self lies open to your view,
You judge by Her what draught of Her is true,
Where out-lines false, and Colours seem too faint,

Where Bunglers dawb, and where True Poets Paint.
But by the Sacred Genius of this Place,
By every Muse, by each Domestick Grace,
Be kind to Wit, which but endeavours well,
And, where you judge, presumes not to excel.
Our Poets hither for Adoption come,
30   As Nations su'd to be made Free of *Rome;*
Not in the suffragating Tribes to stand,
But in your utmost, last, Provincial Band.
If His Ambition may those Hopes pursue,
Who with Religion loves Your Arts and You,
Oxford to Him a dearer Name shall be,
Than His own Mother University.
Thebes did His Green, unknowing Youth ingage,
He chuses *Athens* in His Riper Age.

Prologue to Circe, *and an Epilogue*

W ERE you but half so wise as you're severe,
         Our youthful Poet shou'd not need to fear;
         To his green years your Censures you wou'd suit,
Not blast the Blossom, but expect the Fruit.
The Sex that best does pleasure understand,
Will always chuse to err on t' other hand.
They check not him that's Aukward in delight,
But clap the young Rogues Cheek, and set him right.
Thus heartn'd well, and flesh't upon his Prey,
10   The youth may prove a man another day;
For your own sakes, instruct him when he's out,
You'l find him mend his work at every bout.
When some young lusty Thief is passing by, ⎤
How many of your tender Kind will cry,   ⎬
A proper Fellow, pity he shou'd dye.   ⎦

---

30 *Rome;*] M; ～ . O1-2.

He might be sav'd, and thank us for our pains,
There's such a stock of Love within his Veins.
These Arguments the Women may perswade,
But move not you, the Brothers of the Trade,
20 Who scattering your Infection through the Pit,
With aking hearts and empty Purses sit,
To take your dear Five Shillings worth of Wit.
The praise you give him in your kindest mood,
Comes dribling from you, just like drops of blood;
And then you clap so civilly, for fear
The loudness might offend your Neighbours ear;
That we suspect your Gloves are lin'd within,
For silence sake, and Cotten'd next the skin.
From these Usurpers we appeal to you,
30 The only knowing, only judging few;
You who in private have this Play allow'd,
Ought to maintain your Suffrage to the Crowd.
The Captive once submitted to your Bands,
You shou'd protect from Death by Vulgar hands.

EPILOGUE

WERE you but half so Wise as y' are Severe,
    Our youthful Poet shou'd not need to fear:
    To his green Years your Censures you would suit,
Not blast the Blossom, but expect the Fruit.
The Sex that best does pleasure understand,
Will always chuse to err on t' other hand.
They check not him that's awkard in delight,
But Clap the young Rogues Cheek, and set him right.
Thus heart'nd well and flesh'd upon his prey,
10 The Youth may prove a Man another day.
Your *Ben* and *Fletcher* in their first young flight

---

34 hands.] Q2; ~ , Q1.   10 Youth] O2; Yonth O1.

Did no *Volpone,* no *Arbaces* write,
But hopp'd about, and short excursions made ⎤
From Bough to Bough, as if they were afraid, ⎬
And each were guilty of some *Slighted Maid.* ⎦
Shakespear's own Muse her *Pericles* first bore,
The Prince of *Tyre* was elder than the *Moore:*
'Tis miracle to see a first good Play,
All Hawthorns do not bloom on *Christmas-day.*
20 A slender Poet must have time to grow,
And spread and burnish as his Brothers do.
Who still looks lean, sure with some Pox is curst,
But no Man can be *Falstaff* fat at first.
Then damn not, but indulge his sterv'd essays,
Encourage him, and bloat him up with praise,
That he may get more bulk before he dyes,
He's not yet fed enough for Sacrifice.
Perhaps if now your Grace you will not grudge,
He may grow up to Write, and you to Judge.

Epilogue to Mithridates

YO'VE seen a Pair of faithful Lovers die: ⎤
    And much you care; for, most of you will cry, ⎬
    'Twas a just Judgment on their Constancy. ⎦
For, Heav'n be thank'd, we live in such an Age
When no man dies for Love, but on the Stage:
And ev'n those Martyrs are but rare in Plays;
A cursed sign how much true Faith decays.
Love is no more a violent desire;
'Tis a meer Metaphor, a painted Fire.
10 In all our Sex, the name examin'd well,

---

12 write,] ∼ . O1–2.   15 *Slighted*] *slighted* O1–2.
24 sterv'd] stew'd O1–2.   25 praise,] ∼ . O1–2.

Is Pride, to gain; and Vanity to tell:
In Woman, 'tis of subtil int'rest made,
Curse on the Punk that made it first a Trade!
She first did Wits Prerogative remove,
And made a Fool presume to prate of Love.
Let Honour and Preferment go for Gold;
But glorious Beauty is not to be sold:
Or, if it be, 'tis at a rate so high,
That nothing but adoring it shou'd buy.
20 Yet the rich Cullies may their boasting spare;
They purchase but sophisticated Ware.
'Tis Prodigality that buys deceit;
Where both the Giver, and the Taker cheat.
Men but refine on the old Half-Crown way:
And Women fight, like *Swizzers,* for their Pay.

Prologue to A True Widow

HEAV'N save ye Gallants, and this hopeful Age,
Y' are welcome to the downfal of the Stage:
The Fools have labour'd long in their Vocation;
And Vice, (the Manufacture of the Nation)
O're-stocks the Town so much, and thrives so well,
That Fopps and Knaves grow Druggs, and will not sell.
In vain our Wares on Theaters are shown,
When each has a Plantation of his own.
His Cruse ne'r fails; for whatsoe're he spends,
10 There's still God's plenty for himself and friends.
Shou'd Men be rated by Poetick Rules,
Lord what a Poll would there be rais'd from Fools!
Mean time poor Wit prohibited must lye,
As if 'twere made some *French* Commodity.
Fools you will have, and rais'd at vast expence,

And yet as soon as seen, they give offence.
Time was, when none would cry, that Oaf was mee,
But now you strive about your Pedigree:
Bawble and Cap no sooner are thrown down,
20   But there's a Muss of more than half the Town.
Each one will challenge a Child's part at least,
A sign the Family is well increas'd.
Of Forreign Cattle! there's no longer need,
When w' are supply'd so fast with *English* Breed.
    Well! Flourish, Countrymen: drink swear and roar,
    Let every free-born Subject keep his Whore;
    And wandring in the Wilderness about,
    At end of 40 years not wear her out.
    But when you see these Pictures, let none dare
30   To own beyond a Limb, or single share:
    For where the Punk is common! he's a Sot,
    Who needs will Father what the Parish got.

Prologue at Oxford, 1680 [1679]

THESPIS, the first Professor of our Art,
    At Country Wakes, Sung Ballads from a Cart.
    To prove this true, if Latin be no Trespass,
Dicitur & Plaustris, vexisse Poemata Thespis.
But *Escalus,* says *Horace* in some Page,
Was the first Mountebank that trod the Stage:
Yet *Athens* never knew your Learned sport,
Of Tossing Poets in a *Tennis-Court;*
But 'tis the Talent of our *English* Nation,
10   Still to be Plotting some New Reformation:
And few years hence, if Anarchy goes on,

---

22   increas'd.] ~ₐ Q1–2.   4   *Plaustris*] Plaustris O1–2, Q1–6.

Jack Presbyter shall here Erect his Throne,
Knock out a Tub with Preaching once a day,
And every Prayer be longer than a Play.
Then all you Heathen Wits shall go to Pot,
For disbelieving of a Popish Plot:
Your Poets shall be us'd like Infidels,
And worst the Author of the *Oxford Bells:*
Nor shou'd we scape the Sentence, to Depart,
20 Ev'n in our first Original, A Cart.
No Zealous Brother there wou'd want a Stone,
To Maul Us Cardinals, and pelt Pope *Joan:*
Religion, Learning, Wit, wou'd be supprest,
Rags of the Whore, and Trappings of the Beast:
Scot, Swarez, Tom of Aquin, must go down,
As chief Supporters of the Triple Crown;
And *Aristotle*'s for destruction ripe,
Some say He call'd the Soul an Organ-Pipe,
Which by some little help of Derivation,
30 Shall then be prov'd a Pipe of Inspiration.

Prologue to Caesar Borgia

Th' unhappy man, who once has trail'd a Pen,
    Lives not to please himself but other men:
    Is always drudging, wasts his Life and Blood,
Yet only eats and drinks what you think good:
What praise soe're the Poetry deserve,
Yet every Fool can bid the Poet starve:
That fumbling Lecher to revenge is bent,
Because he thinks himself or Whore is meant:
Name but a Cuckold, all the City swarms,

12 Throne,] Q1–6; ∼ . O1–2.

10 From *Leaden-hall* to *Ludgate* is in Arms.
   Were there no fear of *Antichrist* or *France,*
   In the best times poor Poets live by chance.
   Either you come not here, or as you grace ⎤
   Some old acquaintance, drop into the place, ⎬
   Careless and qualmish with a yawning Face.⎦
   You sleep o're Wit, and by my troth you may,
   Most of your Talents lye another way.
   You love to hear of some prodigious Tale,
   The Bell that toll'd alone, or *Irish* Whale.
20 News is your Food, and you enough provide,
   Both for your selves and all the World beside.
   One Theatre there is of vast resort,
   Which whilome of Requests was call'd the Court.
   But now the great *Exchange* of News 'tis hight,
   And full of hum and buzz from Noon till Night:
   Up Stairs and down you run as for a Race,
   And each man wears three Nations in his Face.
   So big you look, tho' Claret you retrench,
   That arm'd with bottled Ale, you huff the *French:*
30 But all your Entertainment still is fed
   By Villains, in our own dull Island bred:
   Would you return to us, we dare engage
   To show you better Rogues upon the Stage:
   You know no Poison but plain Rats-bane here,
   Death's more refind, and better bred elsewhere.
   They have a civil way in *Italy* ⎤
   By smelling a perfume to make you dye, ⎬
   A Trick would make you lay your Snuff-box by.⎦
   Murder's a Trade———so known and practis'd there,
40 That 'tis Infallible as is the Chair———
   But mark their Feasts, you shall behold such Pranks,
   The Pope says Grace, but 'tis the Devil gives Thanks.

———

25 and] Q3; aud Q1–2.

Prologue to The Loyal General

IF yet there be a few that take delight
  In that which reasonable Men should write;
  To them Alone we Dedicate this Night.
The Rest may satisfie their curious Itch
With City Gazets or some Factious Speech,
Or what-ere Libel for the Publick Good,
Stirs up the Shrove-tide Crew to Fire and Blood!
Remove your Benches you apostate Pit,
And take Above, twelve penny-worth of Wit;
10 Go back to your dear Dancing on the Rope,
Or see what's worse the Devil and the Pope!
The Plays that take on our Corrupted Stage,
Methinks resemble the distracted Age;
Noise, Madness, all unreasonable Things,
That strike at Sense, as Rebels do at Kings!
The stile of Forty One our Poets write,
And you are grown to judge like Forty Eight.
Such Censures our mistaking Audience make,
That 'tis almost grown Scandalous to Take!
20 They talk of Feavours that infect the Brains,
But Non-sence is the new Disease that reigns.
Weak Stomacks with a long Disease opprest,
Cannot the Cordials of strong Wit digest:
Therfore thin Nourishment of Farce ye choose,
Decoctions of a Barly-water Muse:
A Meal of Tragedy wou'd make ye Sick,
Unless it were a very tender Chick.
Some Scenes in Sippets wou'd be worth our time,
Those wou'd go down; some Love that's poach'd in Rime;
30 If these shou'd fail——
We must lie down, and after all our cost,

Keep Holy-day, like Water-men in Frost,
Whil'st you turn Players on the Worlds great Stage,
And Act your selves the Farce of your own Age.

Prologue to the University of Oxford [1680]

DISCORD, and Plots which have undone our Age
With the same ruine, have o'erwhelm'd the Stage.
Our House has suffer'd in the common Woe,
We have been troubled with *Scotch* Rebels too;
Our Brethren, are from *Thames* to *Tweed* departed,
And of our Sisters, all the kinder hearted,
To *Edenborough* gone, or Coacht, or Carted.
With bonny Blewcap there they act all night
For *Scotch* half Crown, in *English* Three-pence hight.
One Nymph, to whom fat *Sir John Falstaff*'s lean,
There with her single Person fills the Scene.
Another, with long use, and Age decay'd,
Div'd here old Woman, and rose there a Maid.
Our Trusty Door-keepers of former time,
There strutt and swagger in Heroique rhime:
Tack but a Copper-lace to Drugget sute,
And there's a Heroe made without dispute.
And that which was a Capons tayl before,
Becomes a plume for *Indian* Emperour.
But all his Subjects, to express the care
Of Imitation, go, like *Indians*, bare;
Lac'd Linen there wou'd be a dangerous thing,
It might perhaps a new Rebellion bring,
The *Scot* who wore it, wou'd be chosen King.
But why shou'd I these Renegades describe,
When you your selves have seen a lewder Tribe?

10
20

---

26   Tribe?] ~ . O1-2.

Teg has been here, and to this learned Pit,
With *Irish* action slander'd *English* Wit.
You have beheld such barb'rous *Mac's* appear,
30   As merited a second Massacre;
Such as like *Cain* were branded with disgrace,
And had their Country stampt upon their Face:
When Stroulers durst presume to pick your purse,
We humbly thought our broken Troop not worse,
How ill soe'er our action may deserve,
Oxford's a place, where Wit can never sterve.

---

30   Massacre;] ∼ . O1–2.

COMMENTARY

List of Abbreviated References

Absalom: Absalom and Achitophel, Pt. I
Annus: Annus Mirabilis
Bell: *Poetical Works of John Dryden,* ed. Robert Bell, 1854
BH: Johnson's *Lives of the English Poets,* ed. George Birkbeck Hill, Oxford, 1905
Brit. Red.: Britannia Rediviva
Case: Arthur E. Case, *A Bibliography of English Poetical Miscellanies, 1521–1750,* London, 1935
Charleton: To My Honored Friend, Dr. Charleton
Christie: *Poetical Works of John Dryden,* ed. W. D. Christie, 1870
Derrick: *Miscellaneous Works of John Dryden,* ed. Samuel Derrick, 1760
Grierson: *Poems of John Donne,* ed. H. J. C. Grierson, Oxford, 1912, 2 vols.
Hastings: Upon the Death of the Lord Hastings
Her. St.: Heroique Stanzas to the Glorious Memory of Cromwell
Hind: The Hind and the Panther
HLQ: Huntington Library Quarterly
Hoddesdon: To John Hoddesdon, on His Divine Epigrams
Howard: To My Honored Friend, Sir Robert Howard
JEGP: Journal of English and Germanic Philology
Ker: *Essays of John Dryden,* ed. W. P. Ker, Oxford, 1926
Ld. Ch.: To My Lord Chancellor
Macdonald: Hugh Macdonald, *John Dryden: A Bibliography of Early Editions and of Drydeniana,* Oxford, 1939
Malone: *Critical and Miscellaneous Prose Works of John Dryden,* ed. Edmond Malone, 1800
Minor Poets: The Minor Poets: or, The Works of the most Celebrated Authors, 1751
MLN: Modern Language Notes
MLR: Modern Language Review
N&Q: Notes and Queries
Nicoll: Allardyce Nicoll, *A History of Restoration Drama, 1660–1700,* Cambridge, 1923
Noyes: *Poetical Works of Dryden,* ed. George R. Noyes, Cambridge, Mass., 1950
OED: Oxford English Dictionary
Osborn: James M. Osborn, *John Dryden: Some Biographical Facts and Problems,* New York, 1940
PBSA: Publications of the Bibliographical Society of America
PMLA: Publications of the Modern Language Association of America
PQ: Philological Quarterly
Religio: Religio Laici

RES: Review of English Studies

Sac. Maj.: To His Sacred Majesty, A Panegyrick on His Coronation

Scott: *The Works of Dryden,* ed. Sir Walter Scott, 1821

SP: Studies in Philology

Spingarn: *Critical Essays of the Seventeenth Century,* ed. J. E. Spingarn, Oxford, 1908

S-S *or* Saintsbury: *The Works of John Dryden,* ed. Sir Walter Scott and George Saintsbury, 1882–1893

Van Doren: Mark Van Doren, *John Dryden, a Study of his Poetry,* New York, 1946

Verrall: A. W. Verrall, *Lectures on Dryden,* Cambridge, 1914

Ward: *The Letters of John Dryden,* ed. C. E. Ward, Durham, N.C., 1942

Warton: *Poetical Works of John Dryden,* ed. Joseph Warton and John Warton, 1811

W&M: Gertrude L. Woodward and James G. McManaway, *A Checklist of English Plays, 1641–1700,* Chicago, 1945

Upon the Death of the Lord Hastings

Henry, Lord Hastings, eldest son of Ferdinando, sixth Earl of Hunting-don, was born 16 January 1630, and died of smallpox 24 June 1649. His two younger brothers having already died, the death of the young lord left the Earl at this time without a male heir.

A few months later a commemorative volume of the type popular in the seventeenth century was published under the title *Lachrymae Musarum: The Tears of the Muses.* This funereal volume, black with mourning borders, contained the offerings of nearly forty contributors, elegies and mortuary epigrams; most of them were composed in English, but a small group at the end were delivered in Latin and Greek. Among the contributing poets and versifiers whose names may be remembered by students of literature were Robert Herrick, Andrew Marvell, Charles Cotton, Sir John Denham, Alexander Brome, Richard Brome, Mildmay Fane, and Sir Aston Cokayne. And, of course, John Dryden, whose first published poem appeared in this volume.

At the time of Hastings' death Dryden had not yet turned eighteen. One would surmise that his verses were invited, not because they were required to give distinction to the book, but because of his possible friendship with the young Lord Hastings or his family. Actually Dryden's poem was added as a kind of afterthought, along with those of seven other writers, whose verses were not "sent in" until most of the volume was in print (see Textual Notes). Of these eight belated efforts, at least five were composed by Westminster boys.[1] The inclusion of the poems by Westminster boys must have appeared appropriate either because Lord Hastings had attended the school

---

[1] The printed signatures of John Dryden, Cyril Wyche, Edward Campion, and Thomas Adams are followed by the phrase "Scholae Westm. Alumnus." The signature of Radulphus Mountague (Ralph Montagu) is followed by "ex Scholâ Westmonast." Ralph Montagu describes himself as a younger son of Edward, second Baron Montagu of Boughton. One more of the tardy contributors had a Westminster connection: John Harmar (1594?–1670), famed more for learning than for wisdom, served for a time as an undermaster in Westminster School. Ralph Montagu's elder brother, Edward, was also a Westminster boy—and almost certainly the Edward Montagu whose Latin poem made part of the engraving that faced the title page. Because of its position as part of the engraving, it may be conjectured that the offering of Edward Montagu was one of the original contributions and had some special importance attached to it in the mind of the compiler of the collection.

With Thomas Adams, at least, Dryden appears to have maintained connections for many years. Adams contributed preliminary verses to *The Medal,* and contributed a translation to the 1684 volume of *Miscellany Poems* which Dryden and Tonson compiled and edited.

or because he had been intimate with some or all of the little band of Westminster bards.

The collection as a whole represents a very humble level of poetic achievement, and there is no *Lycidas* to brighten its pages. Indeed, the writers seemed to feel no great need for poetic inspiration; as one versifier justified himself, "So he that can't sing Elegies, can groan." As a group the poets lamented the passing of one so young, or so beautiful, or so talented, the last son of a noble house, descended of royal blood; or they offered consolation to the bereaved parents for the loss of a son so virtuous and so worthy; or they bemoaned the misfortune of the girl whom Lord Hastings was about to marry; or they described the effects of the disease; or, remembering the recent execution of Charles I, they bewailed the sinful state of Britain—like the elder Thomas Pestel, who exclaimed:

> O Blood-Royal Fate!
> Great Britains curse, whose sinful, shameful State
> Makes all Heroick Vertue soon decay. . . .

A goodly number of the poems are composed in the strain of what was then taken to be wit.[2] Thus Mildmay Fane, the Earl of Westmorland, breaks into a clench:

> Yet if we'd scan why thus he's Hasting hence,
> His name may give you some intelligence.

And "M. N." (probably Marchamont Needham), describing the effects of smallpox on Lord Hastings' countenance, could write:

> And envious Pimples too dig Graves apace,
> To bury all the Glories of his face. . . .

In the midst of such fancies, it is a relief to come upon the modest virtues of the poems by Herrick and Marvell.

The most touching poem occasioned by the young lord's death was that written by his mother.[3]

---

[2] For examples, cf. l. 4n. and l. 53n.

[3] Lucy, Countess of Huntingdon, wrote her lines in her copy of the 1650 issue of *Lachrymae Musarum*. The copy is now in the Henry E. Huntington Library and Art Gallery. The poem is here printed by permission of the trustees of that institution.

> The Bowells of the Earth my bowells Hide
> Whilst these Dear relicks here interrd abide
> Thus I die Living, thus alass mine Eyes,
> My funerall see, since hee before me Dyes
> Whom I brought forth my Dear Son here he Lies.
> Clear up mine eyes hee Lies not here,
> His Soul is he, which when his Dear
> Redeemer had refin'd to a height
> Of Purity, and Solid Weight,
> No Longer would he let it Stay,
> With in this Crucible of Clay,
> But meaning him a richer Case,
> To raise his Luster, not imbase,
> And knowing the infectious Dust

Of the poems by the six Westminster School writers, Dryden's is the only one in English. While at Westminster, Dryden had translated Latin into English verse, acceptable enough to be preserved by the great Dr. Busby.[4] His Hastings elegy strikes one at first as a profusion of figures and images, but a second glance shows certain principles of organization. The steps that constitute its form are: a lament for the individual who has died, questioning concerning the meaning of life, the expression of grief together with a lament over the sorry state of man, and a consolation.[5] Over and around this framework Dryden strewed his thoughts and conceits with considerable ingenuity. His worst conceits are not worse than those of other poets in the same volume, and his thoughts flow more densely; an occasional line shows a feeling for strength, and an occasional passage, a feeling for compactness. His elegy is far from being the least promising in the collection. In it he followed neither Donne nor Cowley, but the fashion of the times. In no other poem by Dryden are the astronomical and astrological allusions so thickly strewn.

THE VERSE

Dryden's poem belongs to the mid-century in prosody as well as rhetoric. Conceived in a day when smoothness and sweetness had not yet become prime virtues in poetry, it does its share of limping and faltering. Of poems written in heroic couplets by other authors at this time, a considerable proportion exhibit a wild freedom, in which sense and rhetoric roll contemptuously over the limits of the verse form. Another large group, though showing no respect for the integrity of the line, regularly observed the limits of the couplet by setting a well-marked pause, if not a period, at the end of it. To this second group Dryden's elegy belongs; the couplets are generally closed, the only clear instances of enjambment occurring at lines 10–11, 34–35, 44–45, and 102–103. As in other poems of this group, the first lines of Dryden's couplets are likely to run over.

One sort of regularity can be detected in the poem. The syllables are scrupulously counted, ten to a line—so regularly that the hints of a supernumerary syllable in *Heavens* (l. 30), *Heaven* (l. 51), *many a* (l. 56), *Vertuous* (l. 71), *Tempestuous* (l. 90), *heaven* (l. 94), and *Original* (l. 101) con-

---

Might Canker the bright piece with Rust,
Hasted him hence, into his Treasure
Of Blessed Spirits, where till the Measure
Accomplish'd bee of the Elect,
They rest, and Joyfully expect
The image of our Lords perfection,
In the approaching Resurrection.

[4] Cf. Dryden's note at the end of the Argument prefixed to his translation of Persius' Third Satire.

[5] Ruth Wallerstein, "On the Death of Mrs. Killigrew: The Perfecting of a Genre," *SP*, XLIV (1947), 522. Cf. also her *Studies in Seventeenth-Century Poetic* (1950), pp. 115 ff.

vey the impression of oversight due to haste rather than an effect of deliberate intention.

The striving for syllabic regularity infected the elegy with a disease which Saintsbury called apostrophation. Although other contemporary poems were using the same contractions and elisions, Dryden's elegy employs them more profligately than most. There are synaloephas in lines 21, 100, 101, 105, and 106. Words are run together by apostrophation in lines 21, 24, 35, 44, 57, 58, 79, 83, 84, 102, and 103, producing such cumbrous (and then conventional) specimens as *o' th'*, *in 's*, *i' th'*, and *t' hang*. Words are contracted in lines 14, 23, 29, 33, 36, 54, 57, 62, 64, 76, 90, and 96, sometimes in sounds acceptable to the ear (*show'rs*, *heav'n*, *th'row*, *'gainst*, *'bove*), and sometimes in unpleasant consonantal sputtering (*ign'rant*, *filth'ness*) which even the custom of the times hardly excuses. The peculiar form of elision in line 24 (*speak'it*) had been employed in Donne's poems, but could also be found in Cowley's and Davenant's.

In spite of the attempt to maintain syllabic regularity and to observe the limits of the couplet, the peculiar graces and cadences of the neoclassical heroic measure are wanting in this poem. It contains, for Dryden, an unusually large number of internal stops. There are full stops within lines 5, 7, 11, 19, 41, 74, 87, and 102; and slightly less marked stops in lines 10, 23, 34, 35, 51, 52, 71, 89, 91, 99, 101, 103, and 107. Some of these result from an attempt at passionate utterance, the ejaculated rhetorical question (a device that appears often in poems of this time), which may terminate at any point within the line. But some of them are the almost inevitable result of disregarding the integrity of the line.

The most obvious endeavor at moving the passions occurs in lines 81–90, where, significantly enough, the satiric tone is dominant; the passage is marked by juvenile excesses, and lines 83–84 especially by technical inadequacy. On the other hand, there is a suggestion of the later Dryden in the strong couplet (ll. 13–14):

> Our Noble Youth now have pretence to be
> Dunces securely, Ign'rant healthfully.

4 *To bring a Winding* etc. Cf. also ll. 93 ff. Hastings was engaged to be married to Elizabeth Mayerne, daughter of Sir Theodore Turquet de Mayerne (1573–1655), physician to Charles I, and famous in France and England for his medical skill. Hastings died on the eve of his wedding.

The poets of course did not let this sad case of blighted young love go unsung. Herrick and Marvell both referred to it, and Alexander Brome entitled his poem "Upon the unhappie Separation of those united Souls, The Honorable Henry Lord Hastings, And his beloved Parallel." In a plethora of conceits, such as his contemporaries must have admired, Brome addressed the unfortunate girl:

> Poor Hemistick! that but began to be
> Inoculated, when she lost the Tree.

She that had flam'd her soul with Hymens fires,
Who with full Sayls, blown on with strong desires,
In reach of Hav'n, in sight of Safety, sinks;
Up to the lips in Nectar, yet not drinks.
She that had past the Gulf of Love and Wo,
(Which none but we, that taste and feel, can know)
Now must love o'er again, and come to be
New disciplin'd in Cupids A, B, C.
How vast a world has she to range about?
How long a search, ere she can finde one out,
Second to him?

In the Huntingdon family papers, now in the Henry E. Huntington Library and Art Gallery, there are several references to the proposed match. How highly the parents regarded the charms of their son is indicated by a letter from the Countess to her husband, the Earl of Huntingdon, dated 29 January 1649 (HA 5742): "I am confident if the match were once fully agreede upon, that your son by the blessing of God, will so gain upon the old man [Sir Theodore], that hee will bee able to get better conditions for you heereafter then we can with any shew of reason demand for the present."

Elizabeth was soon to have the opportunity of relearning "Cupids A, B, C" with Pierre de Caumont, Marquis de Cugnac. Dorothy Osborne in a letter to Temple, commenting on Elizabeth's "losse of my Lorde Hastings who dyed Just when they should have bin marryed," added critically (*Letters of Dorothy Osborne*, ed. G. C. Moore Smith [1928], p. 67):

> . . . and sure she could not think she had recoverd it all,
> by Marryeng this Buffle headed Marquis. and yet one
> knows not neither what she might think, I remember I
> saw her with him in the Parke a little while after they
> were married and she kist him the kindliest that could
> bee in the middest of all the Company. I shall never wish
> to see a worse sight then twas. . . .

After a very brief married life Elizabeth died at Chelsea 10 July 1653.

7 *death, sins wages.* Cf. Romans, vi, 23.

15 *Rare Linguist.* Several of the elegists commented on Hastings' linguistic gifts. Sir Aston Cokayne wrote that

> his sweet tongue could fall
> Into the ancient Dialects; dispence
> Sacred Judaea's amplest Eloquence,
> The Latine Idiome elegantly true,
> And Greek as rich as Athens ever knew:
> The Italian and the French do both confess
> Him perfect in their Modern Languages.

And Marchamont Needham praised him for

> A Tongue so rarely furnisht, as might boast
> It self of kin to those at Pentecost.

27 *His Body was an Orb.* That is, Hastings' body was the orbit in which his soul moved, revolving on the pole of virtue and learning. Cf. *Her. St.*, l. 18n.

30 *Archimedes Sphere.* Archimedes "invented many fine Machines, and made a Sphere of Glass, whose Circles represented the motions of the Heavens" (*The Great Historical, Geographical and Poetical Dictionary* [1694]).

31–38 The passage is an elaborate and complex compliment based on astronomical lore. Dryden is here apparently employing the astronomical commonplace, derived ultimately from Aristotle, of the two regions of the universe: the supralunary orb of perfection and the sublunary orb of corruption. If so, the passage might be paraphrased thus: Graces, etc. filled up all the parts of his soul. The gifts of the heavens (not Heaven, for the whole passage is astronomical and astrological, not theological) which in others shoot like falling stars from their spheres and are dissipated, in his soul remained fixed and ensphered. Thence they shone throughout his body with sweet influence, letting their glories fall on each limb so that the whole frame was rendered celestial. The body was made celestial in a double sense: (1) it was filled with the specific gifts of the heavens; and (2) unlike the bodies of others, which belong to the sublunary orb of change, corruption, and decay, his acquired the attributes of the celestial or supralunary orb. The *virtues* of his body remained pure, perfect, and unaltered.

This explanation at first seems fantastic when applied to a body that had just undergone the change and corruption of smallpox. It becomes more reasonable when the passage is compared with ll. 63–66, in which Dryden suggests that the ravages of the smallpox were designed to set off the starlike beauty of Hastings' body. Dryden, it appears, conceived of his task as that of transforming imperfections into perfections. In this sense the two passages have an identical purpose.

31–32 Cf. Charles Cotton's elegy:
> 'Twas hard, neither Divine, nor Humane Parts,
> The strength of Goodness, Learning, and of Arts . . .
> Could rescue him from the sad stroke of Fate.

33–35 A possible echo of ll. 34–35 occurs in Henry King's "An Elegy upon my best friend, L. K. C.," written 1657, published 1664 (*Minor Poets of the Caroline Period*, ed. George Saintsbury [1905–1921], III, 245):
> In whose heroic breast, as in their Sphere,
> All graces of your sex concentred were.

Christie noted that Dryden's lines are obviously imitated by John Oldham in his poem "To the Memory of my Dear Friend, Mr. Charles Morwent" (*Remains . . . in Verse and Prose* [1684], p. 55).

35 *conglobate.* Globular, or concentered. John Warton noted that the word was used in the same sense in Lucretius, II, 154. Although Dryden's is the earliest use of the word recorded by the *OED*, it had been employed by Sir Thomas Browne in *Pseudodoxia*, Bk. III, ch. vii (ed. Keynes [1928], II, 202). In Browne's passage it is "seminal matter" which thus *conglobates.*

36 *sweet Influence.* John Warton called attention to Job, xxxviii, 31: "Canst thou bind the sweet influences of Pleiades?"

39–40 Cf. Proem, st. 7.6, to Bk. V of the *Faerie Queene:* "That learned Ptolomaee his hight did take."

39 *learned Ptolemy.* Claudius Ptolemaeus, mathematician, astronomer, and geographer, who flourished at Alexandria in the reigns of Hadrian and Antoninus Pius, A.D. 127 to A.D. 141 or 151. His *Almagest,* developing Hipparchus' geocentric theory of the universe, represents the high point of Greek astronomy.

40 Cf. Carew, "To the Reader of Master William Davenant's Play" [1636], *Poems,* ed. Rhodes Dunlap (1949), p. 97: "Take the just elevation of your Wit."

41–42 Cf. *Eleonora,* ll. 263–265, where after a sketch of Eleonora's virtues Dryden writes:

> This is th' imperfect draught; but short as far ⎤
> As the true height and bigness of a Star   ⎬
> Exceeds the Measures of th' Astronomer.   ⎦

The words after the semicolon might be paraphrased thus: Thrice happy should we all be if we, like Hastings, could attain to perfect, heavenly virtues as far beyond the power of description as the height and bigness of a star are beyond the power of the astronomer to measure.

43 *Liv'd Tycho.* Tycho Brahe (1546–1601), Danish astronomer, who made a famous discovery of a new star in Cassiopeia on 11 November 1572.

49 *The Nations sin.* The idea that catastrophe results from national sin was a commonplace, particularly in the funeral elegy. It is notable that Dryden did not develop this point, but that several of his fellow contributors to *Lachrymae Musarum* did. The royalists could not forget that the king had been beheaded in January and that the House of Peers had been abolished in March of 1649. Samuel Bold apostrophized Hastings:

> Fly then from Babylon up to Sion; there's
> In Heaven both Monarch, and an House of Peers.

Denham developed the same theme:

> What Sin unexpiated in this Land
> Of Groans, hath guided so severe a hand?
> The late Great Victim that your Altars knew,
> You angry gods, might have excus'd this new
> Oblation; and have spar'd one lofty Light
> Of Vertue, to inform our steps aright:
> By whose Example good, condemned we
> Might have run on to kinder Destiny.
> But as the Leader of the Herd fell first,
> A Sacrifice to quench the raging thirst
> Of inflam'd Vengeance for past Crimes: so none
> But this white fatted Youngling could atone,
> By his untimely Fate, that impious Stroke
> That sullied Earth, and did Heaven's pity choke.

And Marchamont Needham opened with the lines:

> It is decreed, we must be drain'd (I see)
> Down to the dregs of a Democracie.

Saintsbury called attention to the fact that Dryden later borrowed the second line of this couplet and, with a slight adaptation, used it twice: *Absalom*, l. 227; and *Hind*, I, 211.

50 *Our dayspring.* Cf. Luke, I, 78–79.

52 *its Ganymede.* Cf. Cowley, "The Second Olympic Ode of Pindar," st. 9, n. 3 (*Poems*, ed. A. R. Waller [1905–1906], p. 168): The poets feigned "that Jupiter falling in love with Ganymedes, the Son of Tros, a most beautiful Boy, carried him up to Heaven upon the back of an Eagle. . . ." It is possible that Dryden meant to suggest something more. According to Alexander Ross in *Mystagogus Poeticus*, 1647 (3d ed. [1653], pp. 131–132), Ganymede "is one that delights in divine counsell or wisedome, and wisedome is the true beauty of the minde wherein God takes pleasure."

53 *Was there no milder* etc. Bell and others since his time have written of the fascination smallpox seemed to have for seventeenth-century poets. By a magical transformation the effects of the disease appeared in poetry as stars or jewels. For example, in his poem "On his Majesties recovery from the small Pox. 1633," William Cartwright wrote that after ages could never conceive that Charles was so frail as to get the smallpox (*Comedies, Tragi-Comedies, with Other Poems* [1651], p. 192):

> Let then the name be alter'd, let us say
> They were small Stars fixt in a Milky-way,
> Or faithfull Turquoises, which Heaven sent
> For a Discovery, not a Punishment;
> To shew the ill, not make it; and to tell
> By their Pale looks the Bearer was not well.

Alexander Brome wrote in a poem entitled "To a Gentleman that fell sick of the small Pox. When he should be married" (*Songs and Other Poems* [1661], p. 107):

> A face that was as clear as day, as bright,
> Should bud with stars like an enamell'd night;
> Your sickness meant to turn Astronomer,
> Your face the Heaven, and every spot a Star.
> Or else would write an Almanack, and raise,
> By those red Letters, nought but holy-dayes.

And in his elaborate Pindaric "To the Memory of my Dear Friend, Mr. Charles Morwent," John Oldham said of his schoolfellow who had died of smallpox (*Remains . . . in Verse and Prose* [1684], pp. 91–92):

> Each Spot does to a Ruby turn;
> What soil'd but now, would now adorn.
> Those Asterisks plac'd in the Margin of thy Skin
> Point out the nobler Soul that dwelt within:
> Thy lesser, like the greater World appears
> All over bright, all over stuck with Stars.
> So Indian Luxury when it would be trim,
>   Hangs Pearls on every Limb.

54 *Pandora's box.* According to the *Historical, Genealogical and Poetical Dictionary* (1703), art. under "Pandora": "Jupiter being angry at Prometheus for stealing Fire from Heaven, sent Pandora [a strange woman of Vulcan's making] with a fatal Box into the Earth, which Epimetheus open'd, and all sorts of Evils flew out of it, only Hope was found at the bottom on't."

55 *Naeves.* From the Latin *naevus*, spot or blemish.

our Venus. A rather odd way of referring to the beauty of Lord Hastings. In the elegy of Phil. Kindar, Hastings is called "the true Story / Of faign'd Adonis."

59–60 Cf. Edward Montagu's elegy:

ut flueret Morbi Dolor aemulus; utque tumebat
pustula, sic tumeat Lachryma mille oculis.

61–62 Dryden seems to have been out of sympathy with the execution of Charles I.

63–64 *Or were these gems* etc. Cf. Thomas Carew, "Epitaph on the Lady S. Wife to Sir W. S." (*Poems*, ed. Rhodes Dunlap [1949], p. 55):

Shee was a Cabinet
Where all the choysest stones of price were set;
Whose native colours, and purest lustre, lent
Her eye, cheek, lip, a dazling ornament:
Whose rare and hidden vertues, did expresse
Her inward beauties, and minds fairer dresse. . . .

In Dryden's poem the gems are corruptions of the flesh. For a conceit of flesh composed of gems, cf. Donne's "Elegie on the Lady Marckham" (Grierson, I, 280):

So at this grave, her limbecke, which refines
The Diamonds, Rubies, Saphires, Pearles, and Mines,
Of which this flesh was. . . .

66 *Constellation.* That is, a lavish arrangement of gems; the word refers back to the metaphor of *gems* in l. 63. Dryden may have had in mind Donne, "Epithalamion, or mariage Song on the Lady Elizabeth, and Count Palatine being married on St. Valentines day," ll. 33–36 (Grierson, I, 128):

. . . and call,
Thy starres, from out their severall boxes, take
Thy Rubies, Pearles, and Diamonds forth, and make
Thy selfe a constellation, of them All. . . .

The word as used here is probably a pun, containing the sense of *a prophecy of his destiny*. The past participle of the verb form, *constellated*, was used to mean *destined*, as in Sir Thomas Browne's "constellated unto knowledge" (*Pseudodoxia Epidemica*, Bk. I, ch. v, ed. Keynes [1928], II, 41).

Christie pointed out Dryden's pronunciation of *-ion* as two syllables, for the sake of rhyme, and referred to *Sac. Maj.*, l. 70; and the epilogue to *Sir Martin Mar-all*, l. 2. Examples of the same pronunciation also occur in *Lachrymae Musarum* in the poems by Westmorland, Millward, and Standish.

68–72 *who from his death* etc. An allusion to the ancient belief that by drawing in the last breath of a dying man we acquire his soul or spirit. One of the other elegists, John Rosse, remarked that Hastings exposed the fallacy of the doctrine of metempsychosis:

> I here dare tell the mad Pythagorist,
> He lyes; his Transmigration now hath mist. . . .

Rosse's argument was that no other body could possibly be found suitable to contain Hastings' great soul.

It will be noted that the adjectives in l. 71 attribute *one* significant virtue to each of the four heroes named in l. 70.

   metempsuchosis. Accented on the third syllable, a pronunciation taught by Busby at Westminster School (cf. John Sargeaunt, *Annals of Westminster School* [1898], p. 119). Percy Simpson observes that educated Englishmen in the sixteenth and seventeenth centuries generally accented the word on the third syllable, and cites instances in poems by Vaughan, T. Pecke, and Alexander Brome ("The Elizabethan Pronunciation of Accented Greek Words," *MLR,* XLV [1950], 509–510).

   80 *this Phoenix.* The aspect of the Phoenix that Dryden here intends to emphasize is its uniqueness. So Cowley, in "The Praise of Pindar," hailing the great Greek lyric poet as inimitable, calls him "the Phoenix Pindar." The Phoenix reappears with a different meaning in Dryden's later work (cf. *Annus,* l. 602n.).

   Cf. Falkland's elegy:

> Farewel, dear Lord and Friend, since thou hast chose
> Rather the Phoenix life, then death of Crows. . . .

The myth of the Phoenix apparently attracted writers of the 1640's, many of whom referred to it; Herrick and Crashaw employed it in several of their poems.

   81–84 Cf. Juvenal, *Satires,* X, 190–200. In his translation of this satire Dryden made his description of old age as repulsive as possible (ll. 305–307, 318–321):

> Mistaken Blessing which Old Age they call,
> 'Tis a long, nasty, darksom Hospital.
> A ropy Chain of Rhumes. . . .
> The Skull and Forehead one Bald Barren plain;
> And Gums unarm'd to Mumble Meat in vain:
> Besides th' Eternal Drivel, that supplies
> The dropping Beard, from Nostrils, Mouth, and Eyes.

   81–82 *three-legg'd graybeards* etc. As Oedipus resolved the Riddle of the Sphinx (Ross, *Mystagogus Poeticus* [3d ed., 1653], p. 393): "The creature with the four feet in the morning is man, who in his infancy, before he is able to walk, crawls upon all four; at noon, that is, in his manhood, makes use onely of his two feet; but in the evening of his age leans on the staffe, which is his third foot."

   82 *Aches.* Christie and others have noted that the word should be pronounced with two syllables.

   84 *Or t' hang* etc. B. C. Clough in *MLN,* XXXV (1920), 116 called

attention to the similarity between this line and Donne's epigram on the antiquary (Grierson, I, 77):

> If in his Studie he hath so much care
> To 'hang all old strange things, let his wife beware.

For another analogue see Earle's character of the Antiquary in *Micro-Cosmographie:* "His chamber is hung commonly with strange Beasts skins, and is a kind of Charnel-house of bones extraordinary. . . ."

90 *And show'rs of tears.* For a strikingly similar line, cf. Davenant, *Gondibert,* Bk. III, canto ii, st. 37:

> Her sighs as show'rs lay windes, are calm'd with tears. . . .

91–92 *overflowing eyes* etc. Cf. the elegy by Sir Aston Cokayne: ". . . and flowing eyes, / Whose yeelding balls dissolve to Delugies. . . ." The image of eyes producing floods may be found in Donne's poems.

95 *Whose skilful Sire.* Sir Theodore Mayerne, who attended Hastings in his last illness.

97 *With greater than Platonic love.* The passage is based on folklore as well as Platonism. It might be paraphrased thus: The generation or propagation of ideas is more glorious than the propagation of bodies; for the generation of bodies is accompanied by diminution and corruption, whereas the propagation of ideas, or souls, occurring like the irradiation of light, forms an incorruptible process, enduring eternally. Dryden could have found this complex of ideas in Browne's *Pseudodoxia,* Bk. III, ch. ix (ed. Keynes, II, 208): "For the generation of bodies is not meerly effected as some conceive, of souls, that is, by Irradiation, or answerably unto the propagation of light, without its proper diminution: but therein a transmission is made materially from some parts, with the Idea of every one: and the propagation of one, is in a strict acception, some minoration of another."

In the back of Dryden's mind there may have been a recollection of the popularity of the theme of Platonic love in the court of Queen Henrietta Maria during the 1630's. The Queen, it will be remembered, had encouraged Davenant to write *The Temple of Love* (1635) and *The Platonic Lovers* (1636).

101–102 *give Hastings o' th' better part.* Cf. Charles Cotton's elegy:

> O could our pious meditations thrive
> So well, to keep his better part alive!

101 A conceit like that in Donne's epistle "To the Countesse of Bedford," ll. 55–57 (Grierson, I, 193):

> If good and lovely were not one, of both
> You were the transcript, and originall,
> The Elements, the Parent, and the Growth. . . .

Cf. also Donne's "To the Countesse of Bedford. Begun in France but never perfected," ll. 23–25 (Grierson, I, 221).

To John Hoddesdon, on His Divine Epigrams

Along with verses signed Henricus Bromley, R. Marsh, and W. James, this, Dryden's second published poem, appeared in commendation of John Hoddesdon's *Sion and Parnassus.* The imprimatur in the volume is dated 7 June 1650; in all probability the book appeared before the middle of August.

About Hoddesdon very little is known. The frontispiece of *Sion and Parnassus* contains a portrait of him as a youth of eighteen. He and Dryden were of about the same age. It is almost certain that Marsh and James, like Dryden, were alumni of Westminster School, and, although there is no record of his attendance, it is probable that Hoddesdon also was a Westminster boy.[1] Dryden matriculated at Cambridge on 6 July 1650. A faint possibility that Hoddesdon too was connected with Cambridge is suggested by the fact that R. Daniel, the printer of *Sion and Parnassus,* had been printer to Cambridge University from 1632 to 1 June 1650.[2] In 1652 Hoddesdon published a second book, entitled *Tho. Mori Vita & Exitus: or The History of Sr Thomas More, sometime Lord High Chancellor of England;* and, in 1654, a third, *The Holy Lives of God's Prophets.* And with that we lose sight of him.

In England during the Renaissance and seventeenth century the epigram was one of the most popular of poetic forms. Ben Jonson called his epigrams "the ripest of my studies"; and many another poet was attracted by the epigram's possibilities, satiric or nonsatiric, secular or sacred. It was nicely suited to be an exercise for schoolboys and novices in poetry. And at a time when poets, like Vaughan and Crashaw, were turning increasingly to religious subjects, it was almost inevitable that a flow of sacred epigrams should occur. In at least three institutions the best students learned perforce to compose divine epigrams, for at the Charterhouse and at Pembroke and Peterhouse in Cambridge they were required at stated intervals to compose Latin and Greek epigrams on scriptural subjects. Catholics and High Anglicans found their subjects largely in the Psalms and the New Testament. The Puritans, though availing themselves of all parts of the Bible, were especially attracted by the Old Testament. Thus in Alexander Rosse's *Three Decades of Divine Meditations* (c. 1630), in John Saltmarsh's *Poemata Sacra* (1636), and in Robert Vilvain's *Enchiridium Epigrammatum* (1654) the majority of the poems are on Old Testament subjects.[3] Judged by this criterion Hoddesdon's work is also in the Puritan tradition, for it contains 238 poems on Old Testament texts and only 75 on New Testament ones. It may be, as Sir Walter Scott observed,

1 Cf. Macdonald, p. 3.

2 Cf. H. R. Plomer, *Dictionary of Booksellers and Printers, 1641–1667,* pp. 60–61.

3 Cf. Austin Warren, "Crashaw's *Epigrammata Sacra,*" *JEGP,* XXXIII (1934), 236.

that Dryden's commendation of such a volume suggests a background of Puritan training. But the point must not be labored, for Hoddesdon was no stereotype Puritan, and his epigrams incline much more to wit and ingenuity than to devoutness.[4]

Dryden's little poem is best read as a tribute of friendship—and friendship warm enough to permit jocularity. It begins with an amiable falsehood (l. 2), which paves the way for a pleasantry (ll. 3–4), and it indulges in a piece of good-natured foolery (ll. 13–14), in which the greybeard of eighteen ripe years remarks—in the manner of Ben Jonson, except for the verb *peep*—upon the youthful promise of the eighteen-year-old bard. There is just a hint of raillery in the double meaning of *enthusiasmes* (l. 18). All this is not to deny the genuineness of Dryden's expressed admiration, but to suggest that owlish solemnity is not the mood in which to approach the poem.

In the compliment to Hoddesdon (ll. 7–16), Dryden combines Greek myth, classical folklore, and Biblical metaphor. This use of seemingly disparate materials is appropriate in view of the mixture in Hoddesdon's own volume of pagan and Christian—or, as the title insists, of Sion and Parnassus. Spenser and Milton, of course, had shown the way.

A more specific relationship to Spenser is suggested by the possible echoes (cf. ll. 7–8n. and 11–16n.) which may indicate that Dryden had been reading Spenser's *Hymnes*.

7–8 Possibly suggested by Spenser, *Hymne of Love*, ll. 183–186:
> His dunghill thoughts, which do themselves enure
> To dirtie drosse, no higher dare aspyre,
> Ne can his feeble earthly eyes endure
> The flaming light of that celestiall fyre. . . .

---

[4] The following examples will illustrate Hoddesdon's addiction to pun and paradox in *Sion and Parnassus:*

Beastes and creeping things
> After the Ayre was filled, and the sea;
> The Earth brought forth her beastly progeny.
> But since Man fell from keeping God's behests
> Hee's turn'd more foule then Fowle, more beast then Beastes.

Noah's Sonnes
> Ham came and saw his Fathers nakednesse.
> But Shem and Japhet cover't: Noy doth blesse
> These two, this curse bequeatheth to their brother
> That he should bow the ham unto the other.

Christ to me is gain
> Crosse others, if you wish there should ensue,
> Crosses, on crosses, multipli'd on you:
> But if you'll needs be crossing, 'tis no losse,
> But rather gain for you to learn Christs X.

The myth of Prometheus, who stole fire from heaven, was intimately connected with the story of Pandora's box, of which Dryden had made use in the elegy on Hastings (cf. *Hastings*, l. 54n.). In Dryden's time the fire, or celestial sparks, stolen by Prometheus, was used to symbolize the artist's quest for, or possession of, inspiration, as in Waller's "To Vandyke" and "Of the Queen" (*Poems*, ed. G. Thorn-Drury [1901], I, 45 and 77). Cf. also John Beaumont's elegy in *Jonsonus Virbius* (1638). Hoddesdon's "sparks divine" (l. 9) mark him as one of a group of writers who were attempting to turn poetry from secular to religious themes. Herbert and Crashaw were especially prominent in this endeavor. Cf. the statement in the preface to *Steps to the Temple* (Crashaw, *Poems*, ed. Waller [1904], p. 67): "Here's Herbert's second, but equall, who hath retriv'd Poetry of late, and return'd it up to its Primitive use; Let it bound back to heaven gates, whence it came."

The association of *fire* and *aspire* with the Prometheus story is almost inevitable. Thirty-five years later Dryden used the same pair of rhyme words in alluding to Prometheus (cf. his translation of Horace, "The Third Ode of the First Book," ll. 38–39).

11–16 Possibly suggested by Spenser, *Hymne of Heavenly Beautie*, ll. 138–139:

> And like the native brood of Eagles kynd,
> On that bright Sunne of glorie fixe thine eyes. . . .

In Dryden, ll. 15–16 seem to echo the *Hymne*, ll. 113–117, in which the rhyme words *grace-face* are also used.

The likening of Hoddesdon to a young eagle is a reference to the popular story of the eagle's method of testing its young. In his account of eagles Pliny wrote, Bk. X, ch. iii (*The Historie of the World. Commonly called, the Naturall Historie of C. Plinius Secundus,* trans. Philemon Holland [1601], I, 272):

> Now as touching the Haliartos, or the Osprey, she onely before that her little ones bee feathered, will beat and strike them with her wings, and thereby force them to looke full against the Sunne beames. Now, if shee see any one of them to winke, or their eies to water at the raies of the Sunne, shee turnes it with the head forward out of the nest, as a bastard and not right, nor none of hers: but bringeth up and cherisheth that, whose eie will abide the light of the Sunne as she looketh directly upon him.

Cf. also Cowley, "The Second Olympique Ode of Pindar," st. 9, n. 4.

13–14 *before the down begin* etc. Cf. Ben Jonson's "To the Immortall Memorie, and Friendship of That Noble Paire, Sir Lucius Cary, and Sir H. Morison": "Who, e're the first downe bloomed on the chin. . . ."

16 *Sun of Righteousness.* A Biblical metaphor. Cf. Malachi, iv, 2: "But unto you that fear my name, shall the sunne of righteousness arise with healing in his wings. . . ." This is an ancient Christian pun, common in seventeenth-century poetry. In John Spencer's ΚΑΙΝΑ ΚΑΙ ΠΑΛΑΙΑ,

Things New and Old (1658), p. 174, the eagle-and-sun metaphor is explained by a citation from Bishop Lake's sermon on Matthew, XXII: Those who can look upon the Sun of Righteousness are the true Christians.

18 *Enthusiasmes.* Here used in the sense of *poetic fervor, divine inspiration;* with perhaps a suggestion of a secondary meaning, the Puritan's rapture issuing from the state of grace or the inner light. The order of ascent, from Scriptures to enthusiasms, may carry a tinge of irony.

20 *Helicon.* "Dryden, with many other persons before and since, confuses Helicon and Hippocrene. Helicon was a mount and not a fount" (Saintsbury). Dryden knew it full well; he pointed out the obvious distinction in the first note on the prologue to the First Satire of Persius. By synecdoche he and his contemporaries referred to the fount as Helicon. Cf. Marchamont Needham's elegy on Hastings (*Lachrymae Musarum,* p. 82): "Suck'd dry the Poets and their Helicon." Also Samuel Sheppard's line (*Epigrams* [1650], sig. A4v): ". . . quaff up all Helicon at one draught." Richard Crashaw, a man of no small learning, several times referred to Helicon as a stream (*Poems,* ed. Waller, pp. 121, 122, 143, 146).

22 *May learn to make* etc. Ambiguous. It ought to mean: The fact that others, learning from Hoddesdon, proceed to write divine epigrams, will redound to his praise. But it might mean: Other poets, learning from Hoddesdon how to write noble, elevated verse, may use their skill to bestow deserved praise upon their master.

Letter to Honor Dryden

This is the earliest extant letter by Dryden. It was first printed in the *Gentleman's Magazine,* LV (1785), pt. i, 337. The Rev. J. B. Blakeway of Shrewsbury, who sent it to Malone, was in all probability the correspondent who contributed it to the magazine.[1] Honor Pigott, whose father "was great-nephew to our author's kinsman, John Driden, of Chesterton," wrote Malone that the Rev. Mr. Blakeway had been a servant in her family and had "monopolised" the manuscript.[2] The autograph letter, on which we have based our text, is now in the William Andrews Clark Memorial Library.

Malone, applying a microscope to the partly defaced date of the letter, concluded that the last digit in the year was a "5"; he therefore dated the letter 23 May 1655. In view of the available evidence about Dryden's departure from Cambridge, it has recently been suggested that the letter should preferably be assigned to 1653.[3] To the unaided eye the figures in the date on the manuscript have now completely disappeared, including

---

1 Malone, I, i, iv; Osborn, p. 46n.
2 Osborn, p. 250.
3 Ward, p. 143.

the day of the month. The ultraviolet light, however, restores most if not all of what Malone probably saw. The third numeral in the year has been completely obliterated. But the fourth is partly recoverable, the lower curve of what seems to have been a "3" being dimly visible—though it could have been a "5." Tentatively we assign the letter to 1653.

Honor Dryden was the daughter of Sir John Dryden, uncle of the poet; and sister to John Dryden of Chesterton, to whom Dryden addressed the fine epistle printed in the *Fables*. She was born about 1637 and died about 1714.[4] According to tradition she was a beauty, although at least one female member of the family did not concur in this opinion. On 15 June 1799 Honor Pigott wrote Malone: "Mrs Honor Dryden I have heard was a very superior Character Both in Goodness & Understanding. I have heard my Aunt Lyster say *she had never been Handsome* But very Attractive to the Men & had several Great Offers but Having been Ill Used by her Cousin Sr Gilbert Pickering she determined never to Marry. . . ."[5] Remaining single, she spent her later years with her brother John Dryden of Chesterton. In his old age the poet found pleasure in visiting his relatives at Chesterton.

Malone pictured the young poet paying "his addresses in vain" to his cousin Honor, and he conjectured that Dryden may have named the character Honoria in *The Rival Ladies* after her. The picture fascinated Bell, who searched through the papers at the family estate of Canons Ashby for further information. There he found two letters of Honor Dryden and one of her sister Ann, all addressed to their father. There was no reference to the poet by name, but in her letter Ann begged her father to let "Mr Conseat come downe this sumer."[6] This, thought Bell, could have been a reference to young Mr. Dryden, and the request could have been made at the suggestion of Honor. A delightful story, but, alas, a tissue of romantic fancy.

The elaborate strain of compliment and flattery, the striving toward wit and ingenuity, the overwrought tropes in the letter and poem were all conventional at the time. Even the figure of the wax and seal, which has been thought to be indelicate, was a commonplace; Dryden could have found it in Spenser, where it does not appear indelicate. The letter is an attempt to say "Thank you" in a witty and entertaining manner. It tells us little beyond the fact that Dryden had received a present of writing materials from his cousin, and that even at this time his pen stole readily into verse.

P. 8: l. 1 *reverend Levite.* The term *Levite* was used, jocularly or contemptuously, for a clergyman or domestic chaplain. Ward suggests (p. 143) that in this instance the reverend Levite may have been one of Dryden's fellow students at Cambridge.

---

4 Malone, I, ii, 3; Bell, I, 19n.
5 Osborn, p. 248.
6 Bell, I, 19n.

8:17 *a longer houre then most persons* etc. That is, most parsons are strictly allotted an hour measured by an hourglass placed at the side of the pulpit. Dryden is maintaining the fiction that he is a preacher, speaking on the text of his cousin's excellencies.

9:9 *retrieve.* That is, pay back.

9:12–19 These lines elaborate a conceit that Dryden may have found in Spenser, *Faerie Queene,* III, viii, 6.7: "And virgin wex, that never yet was seald." The same stanza in Spenser describes the false Florimell as composed of snow and virgin wax mingled with vermilion; in the Letter, Dryden speaks of "that vermillion and snow in your lips and forehead." He employs the same figure of wax and seal in 2 *Conquest of Granada,* V, ii (S-S, IV, 222); and in the *Spanish Fryar,* III, ii (S-S, VI, 455).

Heroique Stanzas to the Glorious Memory of Cromwell

Cromwell died on 3 September, and the funeral ceremonies were held on 23 November 1658. Early in 1659 Dryden's elegy appeared, in company with a very short one by Waller and a very long one by Thomas Sprat, in a little volume called *Three Poems upon the Death of his late Highnesse Oliver Lord Protector of England, Scotland, and Ireland.* The delay in bringing out the volume, the last-minute change of publishers, and the last-minute substitution of the poem by Waller (which had previously been printed as a broadside) for that of Marvell all lead to the suspicion that a change in the political climate was urging caution.[1]

Dryden's elegy leaves no room for doubting his great admiration for Cromwell as an English hero. There is no way of determining, however, to what extent he accepted the theory and principles of government that prevailed under the Commonwealth and Protectorate. Concerning his movements during the decade from 1650 to 1660 we know relatively little, and concerning his opinions and beliefs we know considerably less. He matriculated at Cambridge in July, 1650, and it appears reasonably certain that he left the university by the early part of 1655.[2] His ambitions took him to London, and the available evidence suggests that he took employment in Cromwell's government, possibly as secretary to his cousin Sir Gilbert Pickering, from 1656 until the downfall of Richard Cromwell in May 1659.[3] As a young man of conspicuous ability, of an old, substantial

---

[1] Cf. Macdonald, pp. 3–4.

[2] The probable time of Dryden's departure from Cambridge was fixed by Christie (cf. Osborn, p. 99).

[3] Certain records, though not entirely conclusive, point this way. A payment of £3 for public service between 3 April 1656 and 9 April 1657 was made to one "Dryden." A "John Driden" signed a receipt for £50 from Secretary Thurloe on 19 October 1657. A list of government employees with their allotments of mourning

family, and a cousin of Cromwell's Lord Chamberlain, Dryden had every advantage while he pursued a career in the service of the government. One of his enemies recalled in 1673 that Dryden "was a Poet in Olivers time, and something more subservient to his Principality. . . ." [4] The first part of this assertion must be qualified by the fact that Dryden published nothing between 1650 and the time of Cromwell's death; and the second part of the assertion stands in urgent need of questioning. We know that during the preparations for Cromwell's funeral the requests of Milton

---

cloth for Cromwell's funeral contains the name of "Mr Drayden," and is dated 7 September 1658. (For fuller details concerning the above, cf. Osborn, pp. 168 ff.) Furthermore, there is a list of people who walked in Cromwell's funeral procession, in which list individuals are set down according to official duty and notation is made of the place where each group is to meet to make ready for the procession. One of the groups in the Privy Chamber was the "Secretarys of ye ffrench & Latin Tongs," and listed there along with Milton and Marvell is a "Mr Dradon" (W. Arthur Turner, *PQ*, XXVIII [1949], 320). John Prestwick, in an account of the funeral procession, also lists "Mr Dradon" among the Secretaries of the French and Latin tongues (*Respublica*, in Diary of Thomas Burton [1828], II, 524). The Drydens of these documents cannot with certainty be identified as the poet, but these records taken along with contemporary gossip indicate strongly that our John Dryden did in fact have some employment under Oliver.

The contemporary gossip was set down by Dryden's enemies, whose testimony, though moved by malice, cannot be ignored. A certain R. F., possibly Richard Flecknoe, in *A Letter from a Gentleman to the Honourable Ed. Howard Esq; Occasioned by a Civiliz'd Epistle of Mr. Dryden's, before his Second Edition of his Indian Emperour* (1668), describing Dryden as "the Squire," remarks (p. 8):

> But his Fortune, and that of the Honourable Persons are different; for the Squire mistakenly charges him that the corruption of a Poet, was the generation of a Statesman; but on the contrary the Squire having been imployed as a Puny Statesman under his Father a Zealous Committee-man, and Sir Gilbert Pickering a crafty Privy Councellour in the late times, it may more properly be applied to the Squire, That the corruption of a Statesman is the generation of a Poet Laureat.

And in *The Medal of John Bayes* (1682, p. 8), which in the absence of better evidence is still ascribed to Shadwell, a similar charge is made:

> The next step of Advancement you began,
> Was being Clerk to Nolls Lord Chamberlain,
> A Sequestrator and Committee-man.
> There all your wholesome Morals you suckt in,
> And got your Gentile Gayety and Meen.
> Your Loyalty you learn'd in Cromwels Court,
> Where first your Muse did make her great effort.

Sir Gilbert Pickering, to whom these gossips refer, had been one of Charles I's judges, a member of successive councils of state under the Commonwealth, a member of Cromwell's council and Lord Chamberlain of Cromwell's court. And he continued to act as councillor and Lord Chamberlain to Richard Cromwell. He was Dryden's first cousin, and it is easily credible that he should have secured government employment for his young relative.

[4] *The Friendly Vindication of Mr. Dryden* (1673), p. 15.

and Marvell for a grant of mourning cloth were allowed by the government, but Dryden's request was disallowed.[5] From this evidence we are inclined to believe, in view of his important connections with officials of the Protectorate, that his services to the government were regarded as occasional or unimportant, or that he was not looked upon as a man who had identified himself with the party or the cause.

It is clear, at any rate, that Dryden wrote of Cromwell as an English hero. Patriotic young Englishman that he was, he had reason to speak with awe and pride of Cromwell's achievements, whatever his political sentiments. As the former royalist Waller had exclaimed,[6]

> Ungrateful then! if we no tears allow
> To him, that gave us peace and empire too.

Dryden's praise of Cromwell for establishing order and stability throughout the land is the earliest expression of his profound distaste for unsettled government, a distaste which found expression in several of his later writings; and there were probably few Englishmen who did not breathe a sigh of relief when the bloodshed of the civil wars was ended. And in praising Cromwell for the brilliance of his achievements in foreign policy, Dryden was at one with the nation; for not since the days of Elizabeth had England won such respect abroad. Even those who hated him were forced to admit that Cromwell had made the name of England feared and honored everywhere in Europe.[7]

Although for years after the Restoration Dryden was taunted about his poem to the glory of Cromwell,[8] the *Heroique Stanzas* are far from being

---

[5] "Mr Drayden" requested 9 yards, and was granted none. Cf. Osborn, p. 170.

[6] "Upon the Late Storm, and of the Death of His Highness Ensuing the Same" (*Poems*, ed. Thorn-Drury, II, 35).

[7] Clarendon testified to the respect, or even terror, in which Cromwell was held by France, Spain, the Low Countries, and even the Pope (cf. ll. 113–120n.). The historian Rapin wrote (*History of England*, Bk. XXII, pt. ii [trans. N. Tindal, 1732], II, 600):

> . . . Cromwell, in the space of four or five years carried the glory of his Nation as far as possible, and in that respect was not inferior to Elizabeth. He made himself equally dreaded by France and Spain, and the United-Provinces. These three States courted his alliance and friendship with such ardor, that they may be said to cringe to him beyond what was becoming. Charles Gustavus, King of Sweden, thought himself honoured in being his ally and particular friend. His greatest enemies cannot help praising him on this account.

And Gilbert Burnet reported (*History of His Own Time* [3d ed., 1766], I, 113): "All Italy trembled at the name of Cromwell, and seemed under a pannick, as long as he lived. His fleet scoured the Mediterranean: And the Turks durst not offend him. . . ."

[8] For the obvious purpose of branding him as a turncoat, his enemies kept reminding the public of Dryden's praise of Cromwell. They reprinted the *Her. St.* piratically, changing its title in ways as damaging as possible (cf. Textual Notes). The most malevolent of these reprints appeared in 1681 during the turmoil

a work of partisanship. Compared with Marvell's really personal and moving elegy, Dryden's bears an almost Olympian detachment. It has the solemnity of an historical pronouncement. Cromwell is lauded for great actions and successful policies, the credit for which no reasonable man could have refused him. He is praised for courage, dignity, a commanding air, and an acute understanding of men which enabled him to pick able and trustworthy agents to serve him—all of these, virtues which contemporary observers found in him.[9] Dryden praised his hero without a trace of resentment or ill will toward the royalist party. Sir Walter Scott wisely remarked that in this poem

> Dryden has observed a singular and happy delicacy. The topic of the Civil War is but slightly dwelt on; and, although Cromwell is extolled, his eulogist abstains from any reflections against those, through whom he cut his way to greatness. He considers the Protector when in his meridian height, but passes over the steps by which he attained that elevation. It is also remarkable, that although Sir Gilbert Pickering was one of Richard Crom-

---

over the Popish Plot and Exclusion Bill, and contained the following spurious postscript, designed to appear as the work of Dryden himself:

> The Printing of these Rhimes Afflicts me more
> Than all the Drubs I in Rose-Alley bore.
> This shows my nauseous Mercenary Pen
> Would praise the vilest and the worst of men.
> A Rogue like Hodge am I, the World will know it,
> Hodge was his Fidler, and I John his Poet.
> This may prevent the pay for which I write;
> For I for pay against my Conscience fight.
> I must confess so infamous a Knave
> Can do no Service, though the humblest Slave.
> Villains I praise, and Patriots accuse, ⎫
> My railing and my fawning Talents use; ⎬
> Just as they pay I flatter or abuse. ⎭
> But I to men in Power a Turd am still,
> To rub on any honest Face they will.
> Then on I'le go, for Libels I declare, ⎫
> Best Friends no more than worst of Foes I'le spare, ⎬
> *And all this I can do, because I dare.* ⎭
> *He who writes on, and Cudgels can defie,*
> *And knowing hee'l be beaten still writes on, am I.*
> J. D.

The assault on Dryden was already well under way when the author of *The Censure of the Rota* (1673), p. 10, referred to the *Her. St.* as an elegy on our English Maximin (the tyrant in Dryden's *Tyrannick Love*).

[9] For comments on Cromwell's dignity, majesty, and natural greatness, cf. l. 73n. Burnet reported (*History of his Own Time* [3d ed., 1766], I, 113): "Cromwell shewed his good understanding in nothing more, than in seeking out capable and worthy men for all employments, but most particularly for the Courts of law, which gave a general satisfaction."

well's council, our author abstains from any compliment
to that pageant of authority; when a panegyrick upon the
son was a natural topic of consolation after mourning
over the loss of his father.

Moreover, Dryden in no way espouses the reasons or principles on which
the Independents and Cromwell established their dominion. In fact, he
disregards the controversy. Whatever the right or merit of Cromwell's
claim to power, he had been endued with a natural greatness, circumstances had thrust him into power, and he had conducted himself with
such dignity and success that he appeared to be the choice of providence.
There is nothing of bias, no party prejudice, in Dryden's belief that such
a hero deserves the admiration of his fellow countrymen.

The first sixty-four lines of the *Heroique Stanzas* betray a striking similarity in idea, and occasionally in imagery and phrasing, to Sprat's Pindaric
"To the Happy Memory of the Late Lord Protector," contained in the
Three Poems volume. It would appear that Sprat had completed his offering first, and that Dryden promptly availed himself of it, turning base
metal into gold.[10] Part of Dryden's poem, recounting the extraordinary
successes of Cromwell in foreign affairs, follows the pattern of Waller's
"Panegyric to My Lord Protector" (1655).[11] These are the most obvious

_____

[10] Two considerations make it likely that Dryden borrowed from Sprat rather
than Sprat from Dryden. First, Sprat's poem is loose and Dryden's is tight—an
enormous improvement over the other. Second, we can think of no way by which
Sprat, up in Oxford, could have obtained a copy of Dryden's poem before publication; whereas Herringman the publisher, who entered the *Three Poems* volume
in the *Stationers' Register* early in 1659 and must have had a copy of Sprat's poem,
seems to have had some connection with Dryden at this time (for a discussion of the
contemporary report that Dryden worked for Herringman, cf. Osborn, pp. 170 ff.).
Dryden's borrowing from Sprat on this occasion, without Sprat's knowledge, might
help to explain why Sprat joined in the ridicule of Dryden in the *Rehearsal*.
For the detailed evidence of the striking similarities in imagery and phrasing, cf.
notes on ll. 10–12, 13–14, 17, 22, 23–24, 48, 55–56, and 61–62.

[11] There can be no doubt about Dryden's interest in Waller's "Panegyric"; the
fact that the *Her. St.* are given the form of a panegyric rather than of an elegy, and
are written in quatrains, is almost certainly a sign of Waller's influence. Years
later Dryden recalled a passage in Waller's poem, his own *Threnodia Augustalis*
(1685), ll. 360–361, echoing the "Panegyric," st. 16. But the case for Dryden's indebtedness to Waller in 1659 rests upon similarities in ideas and phrasing, upon
a similarity in the order in which these ideas are expressed, and upon the fact that
at least one perplexity in Dryden can be explained by reference to the parallel
lines in Waller. Beginning with Dryden's allusion to "that bold Greek" in st. 13,
the parallels run as follows:

Heroique Stanzas		Waller's "Panegyric"	
st.	13	st.	18–20
	17		21–25
	18–19		28–31
	21		26
	22		27 and 9
	23		10

of Dryden's sources—though not so obvious as to have called attention
to themselves, for Dryden had already developed his own style, lucid, inci-
sive, and weighty, and had learned how to refine the materials of experience and of other writers' art into a new substance predetermined by his
own will and artistic design. Between his two earliest poems and the
Heroique Stanzas Dryden had read widely and wisely. And although no
poem that we know to be his was printed between 1650 and 1659, we can
be sure that he cultivated the muses—if we can believe the bit of self-
revelation in his letter to Honor Dryden, he could become so impatient
with writing prose that he found his pen "stealing into verse." By 1659
he had discarded most of the juvenile excesses of 1649, and had gained a
goodly measure of strength and certainty.

One important reason for the great differences between the poem on
Hastings and the poem on Cromwell is that the former is purely an elegy
and the latter is essentially a panegyric. There is a special significance in
the fact that Waller's "Panegyric" was one of the sources of the *Heroique
Stanzas*. The difference in genre implied a difference in style: the elegy was
a minor form of poetry, in which ingenuity was expected; but the panegyric
was a species of heroic poetry, in which dignity and elevation were required.
As a suitable verse form for the matter of the *Heroique Stanzas* Dryden
employed quatrains with alternate rhyme, because, as he explained later,
"I have ever judg'd them more noble, and of greater dignity, both for the
sound and number, then any other Verse in use amongst us." [12]

Dr. Johnson remarked of the elegy on Cromwell: "[Dryden's] heroick
stanzas have beauties and defects; the thoughts are vigorous, and, though
not always proper, shew a mind replete with ideas; the numbers are smooth;
and the diction, if not altogether correct, is elegant and easy." [13] Saintsbury
deplored a tendency in the poem toward stately monotony, arising from
disadvantages inherent in the *Gondibert* stanza; but he recognized the
emergence of Dryden's mighty line, especially at the beginning and in
stanzas 13 to 16.[14] In the *Heroique Stanzas* as well as in *Annus Mirabilis,*
said Van Doren, "Dryden wielded with positive assurance a mighty line
which was very much his own"; in elegiac quatrains written before 1659
Van Doren found no verses "more emancipated or more confident" than
stanzas 6, 31, and 37 of the elegy on Cromwell.[15] To these critical comments we should add that the tone of the *Heroique Stanzas* is well sustained,
the whole poem is of a piece. Compared with the offerings of Sprat and
Waller in the *Three Poems* volume, it was sufficient, said Dr. Johnson, "to
raise great expectations of the rising poet." [16]

Lines 66–68 in the *Her. St.* are explained by sts. 23–25 of the "Panegyric." The Waller passages which presumably served Dryden's purposes are given in appropriate
places in the notes below.

[12] "An Account of the Ensuing Poem," prefixed to *Annus;* see p. 51.

[13] Life of Dryden (BH, I, 425).

[14] *History of English Prosody* (1923), II, 362–363.

[15] Pp. 86–87.

[16] BH, I, 334.

THE VERSE

Perhaps the most striking features of the versification are the disappearance of the cacophony which distinguished the elegy on Lord Hastings, and the greatly increased strength of the line in the Cromwell elegy. Dryden's ear had improved almost miraculously since 1649. The vice of apostrophation has been curbed drastically, and the contraction of words follows a normal mode of pronunciation: *Heav'n, int'rest, Count'nance,* and *Sov'raign.* Words are elided in only three instances, and in all three by synaloepha: *t' inflame, th' asserted,* and *th' Isle*—of which only the last seems clumsy.

The gain in strength which can be clearly felt in the *Heroique Stanzas* derives in part from the more frequent use of a verb form at the end of the line. In the Hastings elegy only thirty-five lines in a total of 108 conclude with a verb form, whereas in the *Heroique Stanzas* eighty-four out of 148 are so concluded. Thrusting the verb to the end of the line is frequently achieved by employing within the line a form of the auxiliary verb *do.* In most poems the repeated appearance of the auxiliary verb constitutes a serious weakness, impressing us as mere padding to swell out the line to the required number of syllables. In the *Heroique Stanzas,* however, the auxiliary verb contributes to the effect of emphasis and cool deliberation of statement—quite in keeping with the tone of the poem, which is characterized by strength and dignity, and a cool, impersonal stateliness.

Although other poets had employed the decasyllabic quatrain with alternating rhyme, the form had been given importance in Dryden's time by the publication of Davenant's *Gondibert* in 1651. Dryden undoubtedly learned much from Davenant's stanza. In addition, he probably found advantages in the firmer line of the quatrains which Waller had employed in his "Panegyric" to Cromwell (a work with which, as we have seen, Dryden was almost certainly familiar). Yet the stanza used in the *Heroique Stanzas* bears the clear stamp of Dryden's own genius.

Instead of the usual limpness and flaccidity of Davenant, Dryden's stanza has sinews, it has compression; each line carries more weight, and many of the lines show the pith and marrow that we look for in Dryden's mature work. Whereas Davenant had tended to break down the importance of the line within the stanza, using the run-over line freely, and the internal stop, and the parenthesis containing portions of two lines, Dryden aimed at a tighter structure. There are two important internal stops in the *Heroique Stanzas* (ll. 1 and 58; with partial stops in ll. 71 and 125), and the first of these effects a dramatic abruptness, comparable with the opening of a poem by Donne, without destroying the unity of the line; there are four in the first 148 lines of *Gondibert,* and none of these is utilized for a calculated rhetorical effect. Three clear examples of the run-over line occur in the *Heroique Stanzas* (ll. 71, 125, and 137), together with three instances (ll. 47, 94, and 99) in which a very faint pause may be discerned at the line's end; at least twelve run-over lines are to be found in the opening 148 lines of *Gondibert.* Only one parenthesis occurs in the

Heroique Stanzas (ll. 29–30), as opposed to seven in the first 148 lines of Davenant's epic.

How far toward deliquescence Davenant's stanza tends to slide can be illustrated by one specimen (I, i, st. 21):

> And since fond Lovers (who disciples bee
> To Poets) think in their own loves they find
> More beauty then yet Time did ever see,
> Time's Curtain I will draw o're Rhodalind.

And in this passage the punctuation after *Rhodalind* should be a comma, for the following stanza is part of the same period. Stanzas in *Gondibert* are linked casually (e.g., 19–20, 21–22, and 24–25 of the opening canto), whereas in Dryden's poem the only linked stanzas (2–4) show a deliberate structural development, the first two being adverbial clauses in parallel form, and the third, the suspended conclusion, in a main, independent clause.

Add to these differences the fact that Dryden's syntax is clearer, and his word order much closer to the plain sequences of modern prose—or of Augustan speech.

But it is not enough to point out that Dryden moved away from Davenant in the direction of tightness and regularity and lucidity. Aware of the dangers of a stately monotony in the excessive regularity of the stanza, he deliberately cultivated certain methods of giving flexibility and variety to the form. The most difficult to define with any assurance, because we do not know how scrupulously the printed text follows the author's manuscript, is the presence of apparently hypermetrical lines—lines containing words which, though often contracted, are here, by being spelled out in full, presumably used to give an extra, faintly pronounced syllable to the normal ten syllables of the verse. In the *Heroique Stanzas* the following words appear to be designed for this purpose: *liberall, interest, favorites, Heaven, given, Bolognia's, Treacherous, influence, naturally, Offerings, Feretrian, suppliant, Indian, glorious, watery, Halcyons.* In the first 148 lines of *Gondibert* only three words of this sort occur: *even, Heaven,* and *glorious.* Again, whereas in *Gondibert* the initial trochee, though frequently employed, usually gives the impression of being casually distributed, in the *Heroique Stanzas* (ll. 6, 29, 31, 45, 49, 56, 59, 61, 85, and 125) it appears ordinarily to be deliberate and effective. For example, the initial trochee in line 45, balanced against the word at the other end of the verse, gives a startling emphasis to the antithesis which is at the same time an equation:

> Warre our consumption was their gainfull trade. . . .

And it is notable that stanzas 13 to 16, wherein especially Saintsbury finds evidence of Dryden's "mighty line," contain some of the best examples of the initial trochee, particularly in the verses

> Swift and resistlesse through the Land he past,

and

> Peace was the Prize of all his toyles and care. . . .

Moreover, Dryden achieves flexibility and added force by the adroit man-agement and grouping of unaccented syllables. One of the most brilliantly successful instances can be found in the verse (1. 13)

      Yet 'tis our duty and our interest too,

where the only real accents fall on two words, the only two which by their sense and importance invite emphasis.

And again, although the important stop within the stanza ordinarily happens at the end of the second line, Dryden occasionally introduces an important pause after the first line, as in stanzas 10, 14, 17, and 24. Stanzas 1, 2, 3, 8, 10, 14, 17, 20, 24, 26, and 37 are lacking in an important pause after the second line. Thus Dryden attempts to avoid what Saintsbury calls the " 'rocking-horse' undulation of the quatrain."

It is evident that Dryden went far to refashion the *Gondibert* stanza, that he was engaged in combining tightness and pithiness with flexibility, and that he was solving the problem of making the stresses of rhythm coincide with the stresses of meaning. A sensitive reading of the poem, with an ear to its varied rhythms, will remove part of the onus of Saintsbury's charge against it, the charge of "stately monotony."

For further discussion of the use of the *Gondibert* stanza, see the intro-duction to *Annus Mirabilis*.

1–4 Oliver died during the afternoon of Friday, 3 September 1658. The day of the funeral was to have been 9 November, but the extravagant preparations had not been completed by then and so it was postponed until 23 November. Unfortunately the body could not wait so long because it "purged and wrought through all, so that there was a necessity of in-terring it before the Solemnity of his Funerals" (George Bate, *Elenchus Motuum Nuperorum in Anglia* [1685], Pt. II, 236). Therefore during the night of 10 November the corpse was conveyed through St. James's Park to Westminster Abbey, where it was buried in Henry VII's chapel. Bor-deaux, the French ambassador, mentioned a rumor that the interment at night was due to fear lest the soldiers should seize the corpse as security for their arrears of pay (*Clarke Papers*, ed. C. H. Firth, III [1899], 167–168; F. P. G. Guizot, *History of Richard Cromwell and the Restoration of Charles II*, trans. A. R. Scoble [1856], I, 260).

In speaking of "officious haste" Dryden was not criticizing the govern-ment officials who were responsible for Cromwell's hurried burial, but was reflecting on the indecorous haste of other elegists and panegyrists who apparently released their verse before the official funeral on 23 November.

As Derrick noted, the Roman rites referred to in l. 3 are described by Herodian in Bk. IV of his history, where an account is given of the deifica-tion of an emperor. When fire was touched to the funeral pyre, an eagle was freed from the top of it. The eagle was supposed to carry the soul of the emperor to the skies.

3 Possibly an echo of a line in Henry King's "An Elegy occasioned

by the loss of the most incomparable Lady Stanhope, daughter to the Earl of Northumberland," 1657 (*Caroline Poets*, ed. Saintsbury, III, 242): "And though the ceremonious rites are past."

8 *Authentic.* Used in its original meaning, "authoritative (*properly* as possessing original or inherent authority . . .); entitled to obedience or respect" (*OED*).

9 *Tho' in his praise no arts can liberal be.* The pun is noted by *The Censure of the Rota* (1673), p. 10. Despite all his protests, says the author, Dryden had a great love of "clenching."

10–12 Cf. Sprat, "To the Happy Memory of the late Lord Protector," *Minor Poets*, II, 308: "The Muses are made great by thee, not thou by them."

13–14 Cf. Sprat, *Minor Poets*, II, 308:
'Tis true; but yet our Duty calls our Songs;
　Duty commands our Tongues:
Tho' thou want not our Praises, we
　Are not excus'd for what we owe to thee. . . .

17 Cf. Sprat, *Minor Poets*, II, 308: "What shall I say, or where begin?"

18 *so truly Circular.* Dryden's interest in the perfection of the circular is illustrated elsewhere in *Hastings*, l. 27; *Absalom*, ll. 838–839; and *Eleanora*, ll. 272–273. It was a seventeenth-century commonplace. Cf. Marjorie Nicolson, *The Breaking of the Circle* (1950), pp. 34 ff.

19 *shew'd.* Various editors have called attention to Dryden's shifting use, in both spelling and pronunciation, of *shew* and *show*. Cf. ll. 126 and 146, where the form *show* appears. In Dryden's printed works spelling is not necessarily a guide to pronunciation. The 1660 and 1688 editions of *Astraea* are cases in point. The printer of the 1688 edition used the form *shew* throughout, disregarding rhyme, as the following examples demonstrate:

		1660	1688
ll.	35–36	Gown-shown	Gown-shewn
	83–84	shown-own	shewn-own
	145–146	show-owe	shew-owe
	256–257	show-too	shew-too
	322–323	foreshew-You	foreshew-You

22 Cf. Sprat, *Minor Poets*, II, 309:
Before thy Name was publish'd, and whilst yet
　Thou only to thyself wert great. . . .

23–24 Cf. Sprat, *Minor Poets*, II, 309:
As Bodies in the Dark and Night,
Have the same Colours, the same Red and White.
　As in the open Day and Light;
　The Sun doth only shew
That they are bright, not make them so.

24 A more striking form of the antithesis is found in Donne, *Second Anniversary*, l. 476 (Grierson, I, 265): "By being greater, growne to bee lesse Man."

29–30 In the *Prince,* ch. xxv, Machiavelli points out that Fortune, like a woman, is always favorable to youth because they are bolder and fiercer and they address her with greater audacity than their elders.

31–32 *Him at that age* etc. In 61 B.C., when he had arrived at the age of forty-five, Pompey reached the height of his career with a great triumph at Rome; thereafter his fortunes declined. In 1644, when he was forty-five, Cromwell emerged as the great leader, and his fame and fortune continued to rise until his death.

The author of *The Censure of the Rota* (1673) uses l. 31, together with one from *Tyrannick Love,* to illustrate the (to him) objectionable practice of ending a verse with a preposition.

34 *Sea-mark's.* Sea-mark: "A conspicuous object distinguishable at sea which serves to guide or warn sailors in navigation" (*OED*). G. C. Loane (*N&Q,* CLXXXV [1943], 272) called attention to the use of the term in the *Holy State* (1642), II, vii, 7, where Fuller recounts the profit which one derives from the study of history: "This directs him in his life, so that he makes the shipwracks of others sea-marks to himself. . . ." But *sea-marks* is one of those nautical terms which Davenant liked, and it can be found in the preface to *Gondibert,* 1650 (cf. Spingarn, II, 1, 2, and 14).

37 Whether Cromwell was ambitious has been much disputed. His utterances are consistent with the notion that he was a humble instrument of the Lord and that Providence had shown approval of his career by the series of victories vouchsafed him.

41–44 The simmering quarrel between Cromwell and the parliamentary generals of the Presbyterian persuasion, particularly the Earl of Manchester, burst into flame in November, 1644. It was concerned with both the military conduct and the political purpose of the war. Cromwell felt that the campaign which ended in the second battle of Newbury, 27 October 1644, had been indecisive because of the supine tactics of Manchester, who commanded the army of the association of eastern counties. This supineness he attributed to Manchester's fear of a decisive victory which would imperil a compromise settlement with the King. Manchester hoped that such a settlement would leave Presbyterianism as the national religion. Cromwell, the darling of the sectaries, wanted toleration and a severe restriction of the royal prerogative. He realized that the nation was becoming tired of a war that yielded victories but not victorious campaigns. And he was aware that this unhappy state developed because local levies which fought stubbornly to defend their homes would not continue in the field long enough to reap the fruits of victory. Therefore, to secure a national force the New Model army, with Sir Thomas Fairfax at its head, was formed early in 1645, and to get rid of "our former cheifs" the Self-Denying Ordinance was passed to prevent members of either House of Parliament from holding commissions. But Cromwell was indispensable, and so he was exempted from this condition in time to take a decisive part in the battle of Naseby.

Stickler: "A moderator or umpire at a tournament, a wrestling or fencing match, etc., appointed to see fair play, and to part the combatants when they have fought enough. . . . Hence, one who intervenes as a mediator *between* combatants or disputants" (*OED*).

45–48 The figure in this stanza is drawn from the art of medicine. Hippocrates had effected a cure of consumption "by bleeding in both Hands as long as the Veins would discharge" (Lazarus Riverius, *The Practice of Physick*, trans. Culpepper, Cole, and Rowland [1655], p. 170); and the method of bloodletting and purging was a standard treatment in the days of Dryden (cf. *Dr. Sydenham's Compleat Method of Curing almost All Diseases* [4th ed., 1710], pp. 87–90). If internal hemorrhaging has set in, as Dryden's figure intimates ("We inward bled"), then the opening of the vein becomes an essential part of the treatment (cf. Andrew Broun, *A Vindicatory Schedule, concerning the New Cure of Fevers* [Edinburgh, 1691], p. 147). An understanding of the figure would have prevented much of the controversy that has raged over the meaning of l. 48.

48 Cf. Sprat, *Minor Poets*, II, 316:

> Thy Hand did cure, and close the Scars
> Of our bloody Civil Wars;
> Not only lanc'd but heal'd the Wound,
> Made us again as healthy and as sound. . . .

Dryden's enemies chose to twist the import of his line, especially of the phrase "by breathing of the vein," to mean approval of the execution of Charles I. In the pirated reprint of the poem in folio (1681) the wording was changed slightly and the whole line was emphasized by italics and an initial dagger. In *The Medal of John Bayes* (1682) Dryden is pictured as an enemy of kings:

> On him [Cromwell] you first shew'd your poetick strain,
> * And prais'd his opening the Basilick Vein.

The author of *A Panegyrick On the Author of Absolom and Achitophel, occasioned by his former writing of an Elegy in praise of Oliver Cromwel, lately Reprinted* (1681) used the same tactics; and Robert Gould in his satire *The Laureat* (1687) declared that Dryden would have been pleased to celebrate the death of the son as well as of the father.

John Cleveland had employed the offending phrase in his poem "The Hecatomb to His Mistress," ll. 75–76:

> Now come aloft, come now, and breathe a vein,
> And give some vent unto thy daring strain—

where *breathe a vein* seems to mean *to attain a more rarefied mood by purging away gross and peccant humours*. The phrase was also used in the Restoration period to mean *to purge of vice or folly*. So in Thomas Wood's *Juvenalis Redivivus* (1683), p. 9:

> The Worlds on Fire, it does in madness reign,
> Quench it with Ink, with Satyr breath a Vein.

Christie pointed out that Dryden was fond of the phrase. He used it in *Palamon and Arcite*, III, 755; in the *Spanish Fryar*, V, ii, and in translating Virgil's *ferire venam* (*Georgics*, III, 460) and Juvenal's *mediam pertundite venam* (*Sat.* VI, 46).

Certainly Dryden had no intention of endorsing the execution of Charles I.

He disapproved of it in 1649 (cf. *Hastings,* ll. 61–62n.) and there is no evidence that he changed his mind afterward.

54–56 *Till by new maps* etc. Christie unravels the meaning thus: "till the Island might by new maps be shown thick of conquests, &c., as the galaxy is sown with stars." He observes that the expression *thick of* occurs again in the *Fables,* "Palamon and Arcite," I, 229–230.

55–56 Cf. Sprat, *Minor Poets,* II, 308:

> Others great Actions are
> But thinly scatter'd here and there;
> At best, but all one single Star;
> But thine the Milky-way,
> All one continued Light, of undistinguish'd Day. . . .

Cf. Spenser, *Hymne of Heavenly Beautie,* l. 53: "All sowd with glistring stars more thicke then grasse." Cf. also Cowley, "The First Nemaean Ode of Pindar," st. 3:

> As Heaven with Stars, so let
> The Countrey thick with Towns be set. . . .

57–58 *His Palmes* etc. It was an ancient and widespread notion that the palm tree throve when weighted down. Cf. Cowley, *Davideis,* I, n. 7: ". . . Palm was made the sign and reward of Victory, because it is the nature of that Tree to resist, overcome, and thrive the better for all pressures. . . ." E. S. Parsons (*MLN,* XIX [1904], 47–49) attempted to explain Dryden's reversal of that figure by an allusion to the frontispiece of *Eikon Basilike.* In addition to other objects, the frontispiece contains two palms carrying heavy weights, with the motto: *Crescit sub Pondere Virtus.* Parsons concluded: "It was natural then that, when Dryden was composing his verses in praise of the arch-enemy of Charles, he should call to mind the famous picture, and, recollecting the detail of the palms, he should write antithetically of his hero: '*His* palms, though under weights they *did not* stand, / Still thrived.' "

To understand the lines one must recall two facts. First, the image of the weighted palm did not belong to Charles I but was a fairly common feature of the emblem books, appearing with such mottoes as "Premitur non opprimitur veritas" and "Depressa resurgo." In these emblems the palm represented virtue, or truth, or the righteous man, carried to ultimate victory after hardships or fluctuating fortunes. Second, another group of emblems used the palm tree as a symbol of constancy and unwavering devotion. Thus Alciati presents the picture of a palm tree (*Emblemata* [1621], p. 198) with the commentary: Palma arbor est in Iudea frequens frondibus perpetuo virentibus, quas etiam nunquam amittit. And the motto occurs in the accompanying poem: . . . mentis / Qui constantis erit, praemia digna feret. Dryden is making use of both symbols, saying in effect: Cromwell enjoyed the sign and reward of victory, not after great hardship and misfortune, but with constancy of mind and the unwavering favor of Providence. In this way ll. 57–58 pick up and develop the thought in l. 53: "secure of fortune as of fame."

59–60 *And drew it perfect* etc. This is the first of Dryden's numerous references to painting. Throughout his career he assented to the conventional idea (derived from classical antiquity, especially from Horace's often-quoted phrase *ut pictura poesis*) that, since poetry and painting are sister arts, they are in many respects analogous. Dryden's knowledge of painting, his association with painters, and his use of the parallel between the two arts will be discussed in this edition in the introduction to his translation of Charles du Fresnoy's *De Arte Graphica* (1695). It is sufficient to point out here that his interest in painting was continuous from the publication of *Her. St.* to his last work, the *Fables*.

The art of rounding or modeling by deepening colors rather than by shadows is characteristic of the English school of limning, which derived from Nicholas Hilliard. Normally Dryden esteems shadowing in painting and seems rather proud of his knowledge of this technical subtlety. As a general rule, the manuals on limning and painting which he might have read emphasize the importance of shadows and prescribe methods for handling them effectively. Dryden may have in mind John Bate's rather uncharacteristic statement (*The Mysteries of Nature and Art* [3d ed., 1654], pp. 125–126):

> Shadows best become great pieces, and such as are to be
> viewed afar off. To shadow sweetly, and round withal, is
> a far greater cunning than to shadow hard and dark; for
> to round a work cannot be without some shadows, but to
> shadow as it were not shadowed, is best of all.

Bate is probably paraphrasing a similar passage in Nicholas Hilliard's *Treatise Concerning the Art of Limning* (ed. Philip Norman, Walpole Society, I [1912], 29–30). Dryden may have known Hilliard's work in MS, but it is more likely that he is expressing a traditional view, derived ultimately from Hilliard's practice and studio talk.

61–62 Cf. Sprat, *Minor Poets*, II, 311:

> Thy Country wounded was, and sick, before
> Thy Wars and Arms did her restore. . . .
> Thou didst not draw the Sword, and so
> Away the Scabbard throw . . .
> But that when the great Work was spun,
> War in itself should be undone:
> That Peace might land again upon the Shore,
> Richer and better than before. . . .

63–64 *Bolognia's walls* etc. Scott comments thus:

> This odd simile is borrowed from a very singular, and
> somewhat dubious event, said to have happened during
> the siege of Bologna in 1512. A mine had been run by
> the Spanish besieging army under a part of the wall, on
> which was built a chapel dedicated to the Blessed Virgin.
> Upon the explosion, the chapel and portion of the wall
> which formed its support were heaved into the air, so
> high, that (in spite of all the smoke and dust accompany-
> ing such an eruption) an elegant historian assures us, the

besiegers could see, through the vacant space, the buildings of the town, and the defenders ready to man the
breach. Nevertheless, the chapel and fragment of wall
descended so exactly into the space they had formerly
occupied, that the breach was completely and accurately
repaired. The chapel acquired by this incident a great
reputation for miraculous sanctity.

The "elegant historian" was Guicciardini, who gave an account of the
episode in his *Storia d'Italia*, Bk. X.

65 Dryden is here speaking of what came to be called the English interest in Ireland, not of the Roman Catholic Irish, who had risen in 1641
against the English and Scotch settlers. When Cromwell landed in Ireland
in August 1649, he broke the back of the resistance by storming Drogheda
and Wexford and capturing Kilkenny and Clonmel, the latter after his
only repulse. When he left Ireland in May 1650, the reconquest of Ireland
was certain though it took another two years to complete.

66–68 *And Treacherous Scotland.* After Cromwell's conquest of Scotland, the country was united with England and represented by thirty
members in the Parliament at Westminster, the same number that was
granted Ireland. It was perhaps this generosity in allowing a conquered
nation to be represented in the Government that Dryden had in mind when
he wrote of the Scots as blessing their fate. The corresponding passage in
Waller's "Panegyric" (sts. 23–25) makes this explanation seem plausible:

They, that henceforth must be content to know
No warmer region than their hills of snow,
May blame the sun, but must extol your grace,
Which in our senate has allowed them place.

Preferred by conquest, happily o'erthrown,
Falling they rise, to be with us made one;
So kind dictators made, when they came home,
Their vanquished foes free citizens of Rome.

Like favour find the Irish, with like fate,
Advanced to be a portion of our state;
While by your valour and your courteous mind,
Nations, divided by the sea, are joined.

69–70 Derrick thought this a reference to St. Elmo's lights, but the
phenomenon of these lights on the mast tips traditionally occurred during
or after a storm rather than before it. Dryden's allusion, which is univer-
salized, is rather to the rising and culmination of such star clusters as were
thought to bring storms, the best-known being the Hyades (cf. his translation of Horace, *Odes*, I, iii, 18–21). Cf. also *Faerie Queene*, IV, xi, 13.9:
"And huge Orion, that doth tempests still portend."

71–76 Cf. Waller's "Panegyric," sts. 28–31:
Your never-failing sword made war to cease;
And now you heal us with the arts of peace;

Our minds with bounty and with awe engage,
Invite affection, and restrain our rage.

Less pleasure take brave minds in battles won,
Than in restoring such as are undone;
Tigers have courage, and the rugged bear,
But man alone can, whom he conquers, spare.

To pardon willing, and to punish loath,
You strike with one hand, but you heal with both;
Lifting up all that prostrate lie, you grieve
You cannot make the dead again to live.

When fate, or error, had our age misled,
And o'er these nations such confusion spread,
The only cure, which could from Heaven come down,
Was so much power and clemency in one!

71 *Mine*. A variant spelling of *mien, mein,* and *meen.* "*Mine,* (French) the same as *meen,* the aspect, or garb of any person" (Edward Phillips, *The New World of English Words* [1658]).

73 Even Cromwell's enemies agreed with this judgment. The stern republican Mrs. Hutchinson (*Memoirs of Colonel Hutchinson* [1906], p. 298) thought that Cromwell well became the position he had usurped, having much "natural greatness." Sir Philip Warwick (*Memoirs* [1701], p. 248) said that at Whitehall Cromwell did "appeare of a great and majestick deportment and comely presence." Clarendon (*Rebellion* [1807], XV, 148) wrote that "when he was to act the part of a great man, he did it without any indecency through the want of custom."

75–76 The figure is used in Cowley's Pindaric "To Mr. Hobs" (1656), to which the note is attached:

Virgula Divina; or a Divining Wand is a two-forked
branch of an Hazel-tree, which is used for the finding out
either of Veins, or hidden Treasures of Gold or Silver;
and being carryed about, bends downwards (or rather is
said to do so) when it comes to the place where they lye.

76 For ideas then current about the "growth" of metals, cf. *Annus,* ll. 553–556n.

77–78 That is, having achieved great victories, he turned from the arts of war to the arts of peace.

77 *Feretrian Jove*. The god to whom *spolia opima* were consecrated. *Spolia opima* were the arms torn from an enemy commander by a Roman general in personal combat. The custom of such consecration was supposedly inaugurated by Romulus. Only twice thereafter were *spolia opima* legitimately won. Christie notes that Dryden here writes as if all spoils of war were offered to Jupiter Feretrius, and that in translating Juvenal, X, 133 and *Aeneid,* VI, 855 Dryden introduced the name of the god without warrant from his text.

79–88 *Successfull Councells* etc. Among Cromwell's claims to greatness as a statesman were his promotion of toleration, the union of the three kingdoms into one, his zeal to reform the law and manners, and his use of sea power for colonial expansion and to assert English interests in the Mediterranean. His constitutional experiments were less successful, though parts of them were later adopted. His foreign policy was a strange mixture of religious idealism and worldly wisdom. He ended the war with the United Provinces in 1654 and secured compensation from the Dutch for their massacre of Englishmen at Amboyna in 1623 and recent seizure of ships in the Sound. He also insisted that Dutch ships should strike their flags and lower their topsails when they met men-of-war of the Commonwealth in the "British Main." His hope to form a Protestant alliance in Europe was never fulfilled. Here he was behind the times because he failed to recognize that secular interests rather than religious affinities were the motives of foreign policy. England had complaints against both France and Spain. But France insisted that the Duke of Savoy cease to persecute the Vaudois—Milton's sonnet was a proof of English sympathy—and thus paved the way for an understanding with England. Spain was unable to comply with Cromwell's demands for liberty for English sailors to trade in the West Indies and freedom from molestation in Spanish ports by the Inquisition. This, said the Spanish ambassador, "was to ask his master's two eyes" (speech of 17 September 1656, *The Writings and Speeches,* ed. W. C. Abbott [1937–1947], IV, 262–263). Therefore Cromwell, without a declaration of war, sent a fleet and army to seize San Domingo, which they failed to do, though they did capture Jamaica in 1655. Next year an agreement was reached with France whereby an English expeditionary force was sent to the continent on condition that Dunkirk, when captured, should be handed over to the English. Nothing very striking was accomplished until 1658, but a victory at the battle of the Dunes (4 June) over the Spaniards and their allies, the royalists, led to the surrender of Dunkirk the same month and its delivery to an English garrison. The campaign in Flanders is referred to in ll. 115–116.

    81–84 Cf. Waller's "Panegyric," st. 26:
> Holland, to gain your friendship, is content
> To be our outguard on the continent;
> She from her fellow-provinces would go,
> Rather than hazard to have you her foe.

    85–88 Cf. Waller's "Panegyric," sts. 27 and 9:
> In our late fight, when cannons did diffuse,
> Preventing posts, the terror and the news,
> Our neighbour princes trembled at their roar;
> But our conjunction makes them tremble more.

> Fame, swifter than your winged navy, flies
> Through every land that near the ocean lies,
> Sounding your name, and telling dreadful news
> To all that piracy and rapine use.

    85 *asserted.* To assert is "to declare one's right to, or possession of"

(OED). Cf. also *Annus*, l. 53: "assert the watry ball." In a somewhat different sense the word is used in *Tyrannick Love*, I, i (S-S, III, 394): "And by his fall asserted doubtful fate."

89–92 Cf. Waller's "Panegyric," st. 10:

> With such a chief the meanest nation blessed,
> Might hope to lift her head above the rest;
> What may be thought impossible to do
> For us, embraced by the sea and you?

Thomas Fuller may have borrowed from this stanza of Dryden's in his "Panegyrick on His Majesty's Happy Return" (1660), st. 37 (*Poems and Translations in Verse*, ed. Grosart [1868], p. 103):

> Europ's great arbitrator, in your choice
> Is plac'd of Christendom the casting voice;
> Hold you the scales in your judicious hand
> And when the equal beam shall doubtful stand,
> As you are pleased to dispose one grain,
> So falls or riseth either France or Spain.

90 Dr. Johnson, observing in the Life of Dryden that "It was indeed never in [Dryden's] power to resist the temptation of a jest" (BH, I, 463), illustrated the observation by quoting this line. The jest, of course, depends on the pun in *grave*, which gives point to the antithesis.

94–96 *For though some meaner Artist's* etc. In praising Cromwell in this passage, Dryden uses the technical language of painters. Although in its narrower sense *design* meant "draughtmanship," it frequently connoted also, as it does here, the entire plan of the picture as it is shaped by the imagination of the artist. In this sense it included something of invention as well as of disposition or the proper placing of objects and figures, both in relation to each other and to the whole. Hence it distinguishes between the lesser gifts for color and the skillful distribution of lights (both of which can in some degree be learned from rules) and the more exacting test of the true artist: the ability to invent a subject and to organize it into a harmonious structure.

97–100 The metaphors of the first two lines are drawn from metallurgy, those of the last two lines from the old psychology. Alchemy was an art closely connected with both sciences, but it is unlikely that Dryden intended "the Confident of Nature" to suggest the specific image of the wonder-working alchemist.

For testimony concerning Cromwell's shrewd understanding of men, cf. Burnet, as cited in introduction, footnote 9.

105–108 A conceit based on astrology and politics. The stars balk at, and reluctantly obey, Heaven's decree to create "such Heroick Vertue" because it drains them of their store of good influences; just as the Commons balk at passing an extraordinary tax levy.

It is interesting to note the somewhat imperfect antithesis in this stanza between heroic virtue, the inner force, and the stars, the external force. In st. 6 a similar antithesis exists between native grandeur and fortune; as likewise in st. 32, between the genuine worth of the soul and its imperfect expression in actions. The weaving of antitheses is an important feature in the structure of the poem.

113–120 *He made us Freemen* etc. A rhetorical way of stating that Cromwell's influence on the Continent was very great. Clarendon (*Rebellion,* XV, 152) wrote of the Protector that "his greatness at home was but a shadow of the glory he had abroad," that France, Spain, and the Low Countries "did all sacrifice their honour and their interest to his pleasure," and that he "even terrified the Pope himself" by the threat of sending the English fleet to Rome. Cf. also introduction, footnote 7.

117 *pirate of the land.* The papal power, which had divided and assigned ownership of the lands in the new world. Dryden later expressed himself on the subject through the character of Montezuma in the *Indian Emperour,* I, ii (S-S, II, 337):

> *Mont.* But, by what right pretends your King to be
> This Sovereign Lord of all the World, and me?
> *Piz.* The sovereign Priest———
> Who represents on Earth the pow'r of Heaven,
> Has this your empire to our monarch given.
> *Mont.* Ill does he represent the powers above,
> Who nourishes debate not Preaches love;
> Besides what greater folly can be shown?
> He gives another what is not his own.

120 Pope Alexander VII. Dryden has been sharply criticized for the pun in this line.

121–124 In ll. 121–122 Dryden is probably referring to the attack on San Domingo in 1655 (which failed) and that on Jamaica (which succeeded). Apparently no gold was secured beyond or across the line. As to the "prize," Captain Stayner in 1656 captured part of the Spanish treasure fleet, with bullion valued at perhaps £225,000, and destroyed all but two of the other ships. This happened near Cadiz on 9 September. Cf. C. H. Firth, *Last Years of the Protectorate* (1909), I, 50–52. The charge of bribery in l. 124 echoes a belief long held that Spanish gold had corrupted the councillors of James I. Actually, after the treaty of 1604 with Spain, seven English men and women received pensions, including Cecil later Earl of Salisbury. The number of pensioners was reduced to four by 1613, and then to none (cf. S. R. Gardiner, *History* [1884], I, 214–215; II, 224). About 1636 there was a rumor that Cottington and Windebank had been bribed by Spain (*ibid.,* VIII, 162).

127–128 For a similar figure, cf. *Howard,* ll. 21–22.

129–132 The victorious campaign continued after Cromwell's death, Ypres being taken on 27 September. Also news of the defeat of a Spanish attempt to retake Jamaica found the Protector dead.

134 *As near the center* etc. Cf. Cowley, *Davideis,* III, n. 61:

> As Heavy Bodies are said to move the swifter, the nearer
> they approach to the Centre. Which some deny, and
> others give a reason for it from the Medium through
> which they pass, that still presses them more and more;

but the natural Sympathetical attractive power of the
Centre is much received, and is consonant to many other
experiments in Nature.

135 The image may have been suggested by Spenser's picture of Rome
in *The Ruines of Time,* ll. 76–77:

With her own weight down pressed now shee lies,
And by her heaps her hugenesse testifies.

136 *Like the Vestall.* "Tarpeia, the virgin who betrayed a gate of Rome
to the Sabines, demanded, in recompense, what they wore on their left
arms, meaning their golden bracelets. But the Sabines, detesting her
treachery, or not disposed to gratify her avarice, chose to understand, that
her request related to their bucklers, and flung them upon her in such
numbers as to kill her" (Scott).

138 *That Gyant Prince.* Sir Charles Firth explained the allusion by
citing contemporary references to the capture of a whale in the Thames
on 3 June 1658. Sir Charles cited James Heath's *Flagellum,* and *Mercurius
Politicus,* 3–10 June 1658. Heath, who placed the event on the 2d of June
instead of the 3d, wrote (*Flagellum: Or, the Life and Death, Birth and
Burial, of O. Cromwel, The late usurper* [1679], p. 186):

. . . it pleased God to call him to account of all that Mischief he had perpetrated; ushering his End with a great
Whale some three months before, on the 2 of June, that
came up as far as Greenwich, and was there killed, and
more immediately by a terrible Storm of wind, that prog-
nosticks that the great Leviathan of men, that Tempest
and overthrow of Government, was now going to his own
place.

The event was also taken as a portent concerning the sins of the nation
(though he does not mention Cromwell) by the author of a pamphlet
entitled: *London's Wonder. Being a most true and positive relation of the
taking and killing of a great Whale neer to Greenwich; the said Whale
being fifty eight foot in length, twelve foot high, fourteen foot broad, and
two foot between the Eyes.* Dryden attempts here to turn an unfavourable
portent into a tribute of honor.

139–140 Van Doren noted (p. 2) that st. 35 of the *Her. St.* contains a
faint echo of Milton's "On the Morning of Christ's Nativity." What Van
Doren probably had in mind was l. 186 of the ode: "The parting Genius
is with sighing sent."

The "loud sighs" should probably be taken as the great windstorm, which,
however, did not follow upon Cromwell's death but broke on 30 August,
a few days before the Protector's demise. Cromwell's enemies construed
the storm as a prognostic of the downfall of his government. By a slight
alteration in the facts Dryden managed to suggest a much more sympa-
thetic interpretation.

144 *halcyons.* A symbol of quiet and peace, found in the poems of
Waller, Denham, Marvell, Herrick, Crashaw, Carew, and innumerable
other writers of the age. In Waller's "Puerperium" (1645) the halcyon is

metaphorically the Queen, Henrietta Maria. Likewise in Crashaw's panegyric "To the Queen, upon her numerous Progenie" (1646) the "fair Halcyon" is a member of the royal family. Carew's "In answer of an Elegiacall Letter upon the death of the King of Sweden" contrasts the warlike state of Sweden with the calm security of "Our Halcyon dayes" under the mild Stuart monarchy. During the turbulence of the civil wars and interregnum, royalist writers looked back nostalgically upon the peaceful years of the Stuarts, as did the author of "The Times" (*Rump* [1662], Pt. I, p. 201):

> Such and so sweet were those Halcyon dayes,
> That rose upon us in our Infant rayes;
> Such a composed State we breathed under,
> We only heard of Jove, nere felt his thunder.

In his use of the term, therefore, Dryden is cunningly suggesting that the glory of maintaining the arts of peace, which royalist authors had assigned to the house of Stuart, was really an attribute of Cromwell.

Noyes called attention to Dryden's use of the myth in *Astraea*, 236; and *Ceyx and Alcyone*, 495. Cf. also *Indian Emperour*, IV, iv, and *The Tempest*, V, ii.

To My Honored Friend, Sir Robert Howard

Sir Robert Howard's volume entitled *Poems*, entered in the *Stationers' Register* 16 April 1660 and advertised in *Mercurius Publicus* 21–28 June, was introduced to the public by only one commendatory poem, that of John Dryden. Dryden's poem was probably written before *Astraea Redux* but, if the advertisements are to be trusted, they appeared in print at about the same time.

It is conjectured that Dryden and Howard probably met through Henry Herringman, the publisher of Sir Robert's *Poems*.[1] The brief address "To the Reader," prefixed to the *Poems*, acknowledges the author's sense of obligation to his bookseller's civilities, hinting at amicable relations over a period of time longer than was required to produce the volume of 1660. Dryden's relations with Herringman had begun before the publication of the *Heroique Stanzas;* and, according to contemporary gossip, he was employed by Herringman after the death of Cromwell.[2] However this may

---

[1] Cf. Macdonald, p. 8.

[2] Cf. *The Medal of John Bayes,* pp. 8–9, where the bookseller in the passage quoted below is identified in a note as Herringman:

> But he being dead, who should the slave prefer,
> He [Dryden] turn'd a Journey-man t' a Bookseller;
> Writ Prefaces to Books for Meat and Drink,
> And as he paid, he would both write and think.

have been, the friendship of Howard and Dryden lends special interest to Sir Robert's remark in the prefatory "To the Reader": "I confesse my Interest prevail'd with me though, not wholly to neglect the Reader, since I prevail'd with a worthy Friend to take so much view of my blotted Copies, as to free me from grosse Errors." As the only poet to write commendatory verses for Howard's book, it seems likely that Dryden was the "worthy Friend" who filed and polished Sir Robert's lines.[3] If so, the credit is small, for the lines, even in their polished state, do not altogether belie Scott's judgment of them: "They are productions of a most freezing mediocrity."

To My Honored Friend, Sir Robert Howard, as a commendatory poem, belongs to a variety of poetry that was never tied to the requirements of sober truth. Whatever Dryden's real opinion of Sir Robert's poetic abilities might have been (and an inkling of it may be gathered from the candid remarks he uttered a few years later in the *Defence of an Essay of Dramatique Poesie*), his task in the verses to Howard was to present the subject in the most becoming light possible—even as the painter was expected to represent his subject free of blemishes and deformities. *To My Honored Friend, Sir Robert Howard,* therefore, lacks interest as a critical estimate. But in praising Howard, Dryden reveals certain aspects of the literary values he cherished, and the poem derives added significance from being the earliest expression of his critical principles.

At the outset, in a passage deplorably reminiscent of Milton's praise of Shakespeare, Dryden intimates his preference for native sweetness and the wild notes of unaffected nature, above art and artifice. The bold and swelling metaphor he regards as a dangerous license, liable to ignominious failure. In lines recalling Denham's on the Thames he compares good verse to a mighty river, calm and deep. A strong genius is desirable, but wit and care must accompany it in the poet. Art is best when it conceals art. Two qualities which he singles out for praise in Howard's volume were qualities almost invariably admired in the poetry of Waller and Denham: sweetness and strength. In addition, he accepts the idea of the moral function of poetry (it is, in fact, Queen of moral philosophy); from which it follows that poetry must instruct as well as please. He also shows that he has revolved in his mind the problem of translation. In these ways he anticipates several later developments in his critical theories.

Faced with the task of commending verses which at best were mediocre,

---

Writing a few years later, the author of *A Journal from Parnassus* (ed. Hugh Macdonald [1937], p. 38) also made passing reference to the employment: "Herringam hir'd him by the week to epistolize his Readers."

For Howard's early generosity to Dryden, cf. *The Medal of John Bayes,* p. 9:
> Then by th' assistance of a Noble Knight,
> Th' hadst plenty, ease, and liberty to write.
> First like a Gentleman he made thee live;
> And on his Bounty thou didst amply thrive.

In a note the knight is identified as Howard.

[3] In 1910 some of Howard's unpublished poems were sold at Sotheby's. Corrections in the manuscript were thought to be in Dryden's hand. Cf. Macdonald, p. 8.

Dryden skillfully uses the opportunity to suggest some of the thoughts concerning the excellence of poetry which had engaged his mind, and to celebrate the restoration of the King.

1–8 Cf. *L'Allegro*, ll. 133–134. These lines of Milton's are followed by a passage describing the "melting voice" as it sings "soft Lydian airs, Married to immortal verse"—a passage which Dryden may have had in mind when he wrote ll. 7–8.

16 *Sampson's Riddle*. Cf. Judges, XIV, 5–18.

21–22 Cf. *Her. St.*, ll. 127–128.

26 *Rete Mirabile*. Derrick glossed Dryden's line thus: "A compliment to a poem of Sir Robert Howard's, entitled Rete Mirabile." He was followed in this by several editors until Christie pointed out the error. Sir Robert wrote no poem with this title. Dryden is referring to the Galenic theory that this curious or marvelous network exists in the human brain. "In the Galenic system the *pneuma* of the outer world was supposed to come by the trachea to the heart, where some of it met the *natural spirit* which was thus changed into *vital spirit*. This was then sent to the brain, where in the complex *rete mirabile* it became *animal spirit,* to be distributed to the body via the nerves. Thus the rete was essential to the working of the system." (C. J. Singer and C. B. Rabin, *Prelude to Modern Science: The Tabulae Sex of Vesalius* [1946], p. xliii.) As early as 1522 Berengar of Carpi doubted the existence of the *rete* in the human brain, and in 1543 in his *Fabrica* Vesalius declared categorically that it does not exist (Singer and Rabin, p. xliv). But Galen was not so easily to be downed, and as late as 1661 Robert Lovell placed the *rete* in the human brain, in the third ventricle of it (πανζωορυκτολογια, *sive Panzoologicomineralogia*, p. 323).

31 One of Dryden's many references to the atomic theory of Lucretius. Cf. *Religio*, ll. 18–19; Dryden's Lucretius, "The Latter Part of the Third Book," ll. 19–20. The atomic theory fascinated Dryden and other poets of his time (cf. Van Doren, pp. 16–18).

45–54 This passage, on the restoration of poetry to her rightful kingdom of moral philosophy, ingeniously prepares the way, by an elaborate parallel, to the passage on the restoration of the King.

Dryden had previously expressed approval of an attempt to restore poetry by "Mingling Diviner streams with Helicon" (cf. *Hoddesdon*, l. 20).

55–66 *your art the way has found* etc. Howard's art had grappled with Virgil, the result being a translation of the *Aeneid*, Bk. IV, appearing under the title "Of the Loves of Dido and Aeneas." In the translation Dido becomes Eliza; hence, *Elisa's griefs* (l. 59). The first couplet of Howard's Argument reads:

> In Love's ungentle Flames Eliza fries,
> With her Resolves a guilty Storm complies.

Howard in the prefatory address "To the Reader" confessed of his own translation that he had "rudely gone through" the *Aeneid*. Though short of felicitous, the translation is superior to many of his original poems. It may be that Dryden looked over and smoothed the translation, or it may be simply that Howard was better for having Virgil to follow.

67–82 A reference to Howard's translations of the *Achilleis* of Statius. Dryden's uncomplimentary references to Statius were frequent, usually in comparison with Virgil.

73–76 Despite the clumsy reference to painting in ll. 75–76, the preceding couplet apparently does not refer to figures designed in buff color but in leather. Such figures would be stiff and would lack the grace so highly valued by Renaissance and seventeenth-century painters. Johnson gives no meaning for *buff* except leather, and quotes as an illustration from Dryden's translation of Juvenal, X, 307–308. Dryden uses the word in the same sense in the Epilogue Spoken at the Opening of the New House, ll. 31–32.

77–78 *Perspective* here means an arrangement of mirrors, concave, convex, or cylindrical, by means of which a picture, carefully distorted on geometrical principles and therefore meaningless to the eye, is reflected in its true proportions and relations. Thus the "beauties" may be said to reside in the glass, as the true beauties of nature are discovered in the correcting medium of Howard's art. Gaspar Schott describes a large number of these optical toys (popular in the sixteenth and seventeenth centuries), accompanying his directions for constructing them with theoretical explanations and illustrative plates. Cf. his *Magia Universalis Naturae et Artis* (Bamberg, 1677), Pt. I, bk. iii, pp. 100–169. Joseph Priestley gives a briefer account (also illustrated with diagrams) of "the reformation of the distorted images by convex and other speculums" in his *History and Present State of Discoveries relating to Vision, Light, and Colours* (1772), I, 92–95.

78 *in the Picture be.* Christie notes: "The use of *be* for *are* which occurs twice in this poem (see l. 22) is severely censured by Dryden in Ben Jonson in the part of his 'Defence of the Epilogue to the Conquest of Granada,' where he enumerates several of Ben Jonson's faults of grammar."

83 *Your curious Notes.* The annotations are here accurately described. They do not pretend to be critical observations; they are accounts of the myths found in the poem, full of the antiquarian learning that flourished in the seventeenth century, drawn from such writers as Selden, Mede, and Burton, and they are piled up in enormous detail, like the notes and illustrations to Barton Holyday's Juvenal and Persius.

Malone observed that in 1697 Dryden had written a complimentary statement on Howard's translation of Virgil (cf. Osborn, p. 127). In his notes on the sixth *Aeneid* (not the fifth, as Malone said), Dryden wrote (*Works of Virgil* [1697], p. 631): "Sir Robert Howard in his Translation of this *Aeneid*, which was Printed with his Poems in the Year 1660; has given us the most Learned, and the most Judicious Observations on this Book, which are extant in our Language." Dryden was apparently trusting to his memory, which here was not accurate. Howard translated the fourth *Aeneid*, not the sixth; and he wrote no observations on the book. After thirty-seven years Dryden must have confused the annotations on Statius with observations on Virgil.

89–90 Howard's volume opens with "A Panegyrick to the King." In his prefatory statement "To the Reader," Howard speaks of the circumstances under which he composed the poem:

> Yet I should a little be dissatisfied with my self to appear publick in his praise, just when he was visibly restoring to power, did not the reading of the Panegyrick vindicate the writing of it, and, besides my affirmation, assure the Reader, It was written when the King deserved the Praise as much as now, but separated farther from the Power; which was about three years since, when I was Prisoner in Windsor-Castle, being the best diversion I could then find for my own condition; to think, how great his Vertues were for whom I suffered, though in so small a measure compar'd to his own, that I rather blush at it, than believe it meritorious.

95 *With Monck you end.* Howard's volume concludes with "A Panegyrick to Generall Monck," a poem full of the praise of Monck for his part in the Restoration. The following lines by Howard (p. 285) on Monck's careful and secretive activities might be compared with Dryden's in *Astraea*, ll. 163 ff., though it should be remembered that the topic was common to almost all who wrote of Monck and the Restoration:

> Yet by degrees you mov'd, as after Night
> The Sun begins to shew the World its light.
> At whose approach, darknesse its place resignes,
> And though it seems to move not, yet it shines.
> So softly you began to spread your beams,
> Through all our factions dark in all extreams.
> And though at first, you scarce a motion show'd,
> Yet early glory from your actions flow'd.

96–98 *As Rome recorded* etc. Verginius Rufus, Roman consul A.D. 63. At the revolt of Vindex (68), his soldiers offered to make him emperor, but he refused. After Otho's death, again his soldiers wanted to make him emperor, but again he refused. The epitaph which Dryden quotes in the footnote Rufus composed for himself. It is quoted by Pliny, *Ep.* VI, 10; IX, 19 (Here lies Rufus, who once, having routed Vindex, claimed the sovereignty not for himself but for his country). Several of the poets of the Restoration praised Monck for restoring the King when he might have seized the throne for himself. In his lines on Monck in *Astraea* Dryden makes no mention of this. Cf. *Astraea*, ll. 151–152n.

Astraea Redux. A Poem on the Restoration of Charles the Second

The interim between the death of Oliver Cromwell and the return of Charles II was a period of uncertainty, confusion, and near chaos for all

England. In some verses which he dated 19 February 1660 George Wither
expressed the opinion that

he must be wiser than Apollo,
Who shall inform us, what events will follow.

And then, after describing the hopes and fears of other men in those
troubled days, he added, "But, all these whirlwinds shake no corn of
mine." [1] He was probably the only man in the nation whose corn was
unshaken. Yet at this very time General Monck was taking action to restore
order—and, secretly, making plans to bring in the King. On 21 February
he allowed the excluded members to resume their seats in Parliament. And
this Parliament, after arranging for a free election, dissolved itself on 16
March. Thus far everything favored the desires of the King's party. Nevertheless, though the nation was in no mood for further experimentation,
doubts clouded the prospect, for nobody could be sure how the new
Parliament would respond. On 1 May all doubts were resolved. The King's
messages to the two Houses were received with overwhelming relief and
approval, and only the formalities remained. On 8 May Charles was pro-
claimed rightful king; on the 25th he landed at Dover; and on the 29th,
his thirtieth birthday, he entered London amid wild enthusiasm. All was
joy and hopefulness.[2]

The poets lost no time in raising their voices. Congratulatory, commendatory, and panegyrical verses flowed in a mighty stream from the
presses, one specimen appearing as early as 14 May, and others following
in rapid succession.[3] Some fourscore poems in the learned languages were
contained in a volume issuing from Cambridge, entitled *Academiae
Cantabrigiensis* ΣΩΣΤΡΑ, to which Cudworth, Whichcot, and Isaac Barrow
contributed. The men at Oxford presented their gracious sovereign, in a

---

[1] *Furor-Poeticus*, p. 20.

[2] Contemporary historians bore witness to the general rejoicing. Said Clarendon
at the end of his *History of the Rebellion:* "In a word, the joy was so unexpressible,
and so universal, that his Majesty said smilingly to some about him, 'he doubted
it had been his own fault he had been absent so long; for he saw nobody that did
not protest, he had ever wished for his return.'" Said Samuel Parker (*Bishop
Parker's History* [1730], p. 1): "When Charles the Second returned to the Kingdoms
of his Ancestors, he was received with the Joy of almost all his Subjects, and we
hoped for some thing more than Golden Days. . . ." Said Welwood (*Memoirs*
[4th ed., 1702], p. 125): "The first Years of his Reign were a continued Jubilee."
Said Gilbert Burnet (*History of His Own Time* [3d ed., 1766], I, 127): "With the
Restoration of the King, a spirit of extravagant joy spread over the Nation. . . ."
Said Kennet (*Complete History of England,* III [1719], 241): The King "advanced
toward London with infinite Crowds and incredible Acclamations. . . ." Said
Rapin (*History of England,* trans. Tindal [2d ed., 1732], II, 618): "At the arrival
of the King, the face of England was entirely changed, and joy, pleasures, publick
and private rejoicings succeeded to trouble, fear, and consternation." Pepys's account was written under the date of 31 May.

[3] On 14 May Thomason secured a copy of a poem by one G. S., entitled, *Britains
Triumph for her Imparallel'd Deliverance, and her joyfull celebrating the Proclamation of her most Gracious King, Charles the Second.*

work called *Britannia Rediviva,* no fewer than 137 poems in Latin, Greek, Hebrew, and English. As one of the versifiers remarked,

> Who would not write in such a time as this,
> The King's as well our Subject, as we his.

In less than a month after the King's return Dryden joined the poetic celebrants. *Astraea Redux* was advertised in *Mercurius Publicus* under date of 21–28 June 1660. Thomason dated his copy 19 June.

For his part in the national celebration Dryden was to be damned as a turncoat. Yet he had played but an insignificant part in the government under Oliver. Far more important figures than he deserted to the King's standard. There was General Monck, whose change, after months of excruciating indecision, had made the Restoration possible. And there was Edward Montagu, Pepys's cousin, a devoted follower of Cromwell, and brother-in-law to that powerful Puritan, Sir Gilbert Pickering, Dryden's cousin; the defection of this great parliamentary naval commander to the royal cause was probably second in importance only to Monck's in bringing back the King. Pepys himself had witnessed the execution of Charles I with approval, but by 1660 had become a fervent royalist. Both John Locke and Robert South had written commendatory poems on Cromwell at the conclusion of the peace with the Dutch in 1654; both were contributors to *Britannia Rediviva* in 1660. Waller had celebrated the greatness of the Protector, as he now celebrated the return of the King. The list could be extended indefinitely, but we can rest content with Dr. Johnson's wise observation: if Dryden changed, he changed with the nation.

In his stanzas on Cromwell Dryden had exalted the Protector's firmness in handling domestic and foreign affairs, and had there adumbrated his own lifelong abhorrence of faction, disorder, and the mob, as well as his admiration for strong and stable government. The same fundamental attitude is reflected in *Astraea Redux.* The title means, the Return of Justice. In the course of history, however, Astraea had acquired another meaning. From Virgil through Manilius and Dante she had been associated with imperial authority as well as justice; and in the reign of Elizabeth English poets over and over again identified the monarch with the virgin Astraea, the symbol of justice combined with imperial, secular power.[4]

Dryden, of course, was pleading, not for absolute monarchy, but for a return of constitutional government, in which he apparently felt a strong executive was essential. Indeed, the King himself, acknowledging the authority of Parliament as "most necessary for the government of the kingdom," declared firmly that his return meant "the restoration both of King, and Peers, and people, to their just, ancient, and fundamental rights," as well as the rejection of "arbitrary and tyrannical power."[5] For twenty

---

[4] Cf. Frances A. Yates, "Queen Elizabeth as Astraea," *Journal of the Warburg and Courtald Institutes,* X (1947), 27–82. Miss Yates traces the concept of Astraea from antiquity through the Elizabethan period, and emphasizes particularly the association of the myth with the idea of strong secular government.

[5] Quoted in Clarendon, *History of the Rebellion* (Oxford, 1807), III, ii, 1128, 1132, 1137.

years before the Restoration good royalists took their stand, not upon monarchical absolutism, but upon justice and "the ancient Rights"; and in the struggle of the interregnum they conceived of their enemy, not as parliamentary government, but as arbitrary power.[6] In 1660 an influential section of the King's party, in a public declaration, interpreted the approaching Restoration as "a happy recovery of [the] laws and ancient government."[7] This was the official attitude. In *Astraea Redux* Dryden specifically observes that Charles's power is subordinated to justice and that only his goodness is above the law. The very imagery of the poem, as the following analysis will indicate, underscores the alliance of Charles with justice and order and right and law against arbitrary power and lawlessness. Dryden's insistence upon the King's forgiving nature and his mercy follows the spirit of the King's Declaration at Breda.[8] Amidst all references to faction, madness, and rebellion Dryden does not mention Cromwell or other rebel leaders; he expresses no vindictiveness, demands no punishments. Part of the blame for the nation's past sufferings, he thought, rested on all the people, for whom therefore penitence and a forgiving spirit are prescribed. With the return of law and the ancient rights, along with justice and mercy, he seems to have felt that the injuries of the past had to be forgotten if the nation's wounds were to heal and a new era of glory were to be ushered in. Such a policy the wisdom of the King and his advisers had already adopted. Dryden's poem is both a panegyric and a tract for the times.

Much that is said in the *Astraea* can be found in the other poems written on the same occasion. From reading the effusions one might almost conclude that all drew from a common pool of ideas. Dryden is neither more nor less flattering, is neither more nor less jubilant over the prospect, than his fellow poets. Besides borrowing ideas freely from one another, the poetic tribe helped themselves generously to phrases and lines in the work of their fellow bards. Dryden himself seems to have borrowed from several: most freely from Martin Lluelyn, a bit from Sir Thomas Higgons and Cowley and Waller, and possibly a bit from Brome; striking resemblances

[6] Cf. J. W. Allen, *English Political Thought, 1603–1660* (London, 1938), I, 493 ff.

[7] Cf. Clarendon, *op. cit.*, III, ii, 1140. See also J. W. Allen, *op. cit.*, I, 520. The moderation of the royalist claims may be illustrated by Roger L'Estrange's tract, *A Plea for Limited Monarchy, As it was established in this Nation before the Late War. In an Humble Addresse . . . to General Monck* (1660).

[8] The insistence upon the King's inclination to mercy and forgiveness was a regular feature of the testimonials to the King's character which were published early in 1660. Enemies of the Restoration were careful to point out the danger of a policy of revenge if the King should be recalled. Marchamont Needham in his tract *Newes from Brussels*, which he dated 10 March 1660, followed this strategy. Replies like *The Late News or Message from Brussels Unmasked* emphasized the royal clemency. The King's forgiving nature was praised in other pamphlets as well, such as *A Character of Charles the Second*, attributed to George Morley, later Bishop of Winchester. Royalists in England issued declarations to deny that they had any thought of revenge; these can be traced in the *Catalogue of the Thomason Tracts*, ed. G. K. Fortescue, from 6 March on.

between lines in Dryden's poem and that of Thomas Fuller point to borrowing, but without means of dating Fuller's we cannot determine which
profited by the other's prior appearance.[9] Our poet seldom hesitated to
avail himself of good lines or phrases in other men's works, and seldom
failed to give them additional luster by the use to which he put them.

At the core of the poem we find pagan myth, Christian Revelation, and
an important element that stems from Virgil. The Latin element strikes
us immediately in the title, with its suggestion of the myth of the golden
age. And the motto, or epigraph, taken from Virgil's Pollio (the magnificent
Fourth Eclogue, which for centuries was interpreted as a prophecy of the
coming of Christ) shadows forth the theme of the poem. As the fate-driven
hero, Charles bears some resemblance to Aeneas; the phrase "toss'd by
Fate" (l. 51) almost inevitably recalling Virgil's *fato profugus*. Just as
Aeneas was the prototype of Augustus, so Augustus becomes, in the final
lines of *Astraea*, the prototype of Charles—the final lines which faintly
echo a passage in Bk. VI of the *Aeneid* (cf. Dryden's translation, ll. 1078–
1081); and as Augustus was to carry the Pax Romana to the world, so
Charles's return is to establish justice and peace. The conclusion of *Astraea*,
predicting a golden age, returns us to the thought of the motto, with its
suggestion of the Christian story. Intricately interwoven with the Virgilian
theme we find a crowd of images derived from the Biblical account of the
Atonement and Resurrection. How the Biblical and Virgilian elements
combine and reinforce each other becomes apparent if one pays attention
to the Christian imagery, the main course of which is briefly traced in the
analysis of the verse.

THE VERSE

Van Doren has observed that the first twenty-eight lines of this poem can
be read as a series of seven quatrains.[10] And it is barely possible that Dryden began with the quatrains of Waller's "Panegyric to My Lord Protector"
as a model. The first twenty-eight lines, however, can quite as easily be read
as composed of five units: the first of eight lines; the second, third, and
fourth, of four lines each; and the fifth, of eight lines. Inasmuch as the
remainder of the poem clearly falls into units of two, four, five, six, and
eight lines, irregularly dispersed, it is probable that the opening lines were
not intended to fall into quatrains.

The question has been raised as to why Dryden, who in 1659 and 1666

[9] Using Thomason's dating as our basis, we fix the appearance of Dryden's
poem on 19 June; of Martin Lluelyn's, 24 May; of Higgons', 10 June; of Cowley's,
31 May; of Waller's, 9 June; and of Thomas Mayhew's, 29 May. These Dryden
could have borrowed from, and in some instances undoubtedly did. The dates of
Brome and Fuller not being determined, we cannot be sure who was the victim of
the borrowing. For details concerning Dryden's verbal borrowings, cf. notes, below.
Like Dryden (l. 79) Mayhew referred to Charles as David. Like Dryden (l. 98)
Richard Brathwait referred to the King's Royal Grandsire. But parallels in references and ideas are innumerable, and we have made no attempt to set them down.

[10] P. 87.

believed that the *Gondibert* stanza was "more noble, and of greater dignity, both for sound and number, then any other Verse in use amongst us," should have chosen the heroic couplet for the poem in which he proposed to welcome the newly restored King. It has even been suggested that he rejected the *Gondibert* stanza for *Astraea Redux* because it had taken on the taint of rebellion from its use in his elegy on Cromwell.[11] A more plausible explanation—if an explanation be required—is that the poems welcoming Charles II had to be composed hastily, while the occasion was ripe, and Dryden, as he later acknowledged, wrote couplets more readily than he did stanzas.[12] In addition, his pleasure in technical experiment, and his rapidly developing powers in prosody, made it unlikely that he should cling stubbornly, at this time, to any one form of verse.

Astraea Redux, in fact, conveys the impression that Dryden was trying to combine the advantages of the ease with which he was able to compose couplets, and the increased scope for expanded utterance which he found in the stanza. Most of the couplets are grouped in larger units. There are, in the entire poem, five units of eight lines, thirteen units of six lines, one unit of five lines, thirty-four units of four lines, and only thirty-two couplets which are complete units.

In keeping with the organization of the couplets into larger units, Dryden resorts to various means of avoiding the crisp finality, the brittle and epigrammatic conclusiveness, which the tight couplet possesses, and of giving fluidity to the verse. In addition to a modest number of run-over lines, he employs the enjambed couplet liberally—much more often than in any of his previously published works. One of the devices by which he achieves a grouping larger than the couplet is the placing of an internal stop in the fourth line of a six-line unit (as in ll. 148, 233, and 269), leaving a lightly weighted fragment of a verse which impels the reader swiftly into the following couplet. Though the lines generally are precisely decasyllabic, they have considerably more plasticity than those of the *Heroique Stanzas*. A large number open with two, or even three, unaccented syllables. Moreover, in view of the fact that the use of a verb form to end a verse tends to give the line completeness and make it self-contained, it is interesting to observe that the proportion of verbs concluding verses in *Astraea* is notably smaller than in the *Heroique Stanzas* (44 per cent as against 57 per cent), although greater than in the Hastings elegy (32 per cent). The auxiliary verb *do,* which perhaps contributed to the emphasis and formality in the *Heroique Stanzas* (twenty-three instances in 148 lines), appears much less conspicuously in the *Astraea* (twenty-seven in 323 lines, or 16 per cent as against 9 per cent). In these and in other ways Dryden provides a flexibility of line that made it possible to organize the verse into units larger than the couplet.

By 1659 Dryden had begun to learn to trust his ear, which was becoming

[11] Saintsbury, *History of English Prosody* (1923), II, 363.

[12] In the "Account of the Ensuing Poem," prefacing *Annus Mirabilis*, Dryden says, ". . . I have always found the couplet Verse most easie . . . for there the work is sooner at an end. . . ."

attuned to some of the more subtle harmonies of English verse. A year and a half elapsed between the *Heroique Stanzas* and the *Astraea*, and there are a few indications of small changes in Dryden's sense of harmony. We observe, for example, that only a few words in the *Heroique Stanzas* are contracted, whereas there are more than a score in the *Astraea*. On the other hand, there is a much larger proportion of apparently hypermetrical lines in the *Heroique Stanzas* than in the *Astraea*. In view of the fact that the contractions in *Astraea* are done skillfully (with the exception of *Advent'rers* in l. 305), only such vowels being dropped as can easily be sunk in the pronunciation, it is probable that they are attributable to author rather than to printer. One would gather that Dryden was becoming more sensitive to the regularity of confining the line to ten syllables. Of some interest, too, is his way of dealing with elisions. Theoretically it was considered undesirable that a word ending in a vowel should be followed, without elision (synaloepha), by a word beginning with a vowel. In practice nobody was likely to be bothered by the opening of vowel upon vowel unless, perhaps, when the first word of the pair happened to be *to* or *the*. The *Astraea* has six instances of synaloepha: *Th' Ambitious* (l. 9), *Th' effect* (l. 130), *Th' Attempt* (l. 147), *Th' incensed* (l. 195), *th' approaching* (l. 251), and *th' Almighty* (l. 262). One notices, first, that synaloepha is rejected after the preposition *to*, although such elisions occur in the Hastings elegy and the *Heroique Stanzas*. But elision does not necessarily take place when the definite article is followed by a vowel. In the *Astraea* we find the synaloepha rejected in: *the ear* (l. 7), *the Exil'd* (l. 42), *the Ancient* (l. 93), *the ill* (l. 177), *The agitated* (l. 273), and *the expiring* (l. 285). The principle evidently in operation here is that synaloepha should take place only when the word following *the* begins with an unaccented syllable; the only exception to this rule in *Astraea* is *the expiring*, which seems likely to be due to author's haste or printer's error. In Dryden's management of the elisions in *Astraea* we can detect a finer and more sensitive ear in charge of his verse.

The first triplet employed by Dryden occurs in this poem (ll. 227–229). From this point, and for at least fifty years, the triplet becomes a common, almost an inevitable, feature of poems in heroic couplets.[13]

The vigor that stirs and brims in the *Astraea* was recognized by Saintsbury, who remarked: "There is a sledge-hammer stroke about the verse of *Astraea Redux,* for which, save in casual lines, I do not know where to look before it; and this giant's pulse is kept throughout." [14] Van Doren, however, sees it moving along "with a kind of tepid abandon." "The *Astraea*," he says, "is somewhat more shapeless and profuse than Dryden usually is in his occasional poetry; he has not yet learned his grouping." [15] Yet Van Doren felt a special force, "a new sort of drive," in the conclusion.[16] There is, indeed, a resonant music and a noble eloquence in the

---

[13] Cf. introductory notes to *The Medal*.

[14] *History of English Prosody*, II, 363–364.

[15] P. 117.

[16] P. 87.

peroration; the final paragraph is given a certain unity of sound by the repetition of *you* and *your,* augmented by the swelling crescendo of the long *o* running through lines 318–322.[17] But the poem contains, besides, a surprising number of good things, of unforgettable lines. From the rugged strength of

> Madness the Pulpit, Faction seiz'd the Throne,

and the compact energy of

> Her blowes not shook but riveted his Throne,

and the deft satiric thrust in

> Thus banish'd David spent abroad his time,
> When to be Gods Anointed was his Crime,

and the deadly suavity of

> So these when their black crimes they went about
> First timely charm'd their useless conscience out,

to that line of nicely appropriate sound and rhythm,

> And factious Souls are weary'd into peace;

Dryden shows his easy mastery of pregnant utterance and his command over the varied resources of the couplet.

Astraea Redux lacks the firm structure of the *Heroique Stanzas.* But it is a different sort of poem, with an entirely different organization. Dr. Johnson recognized the presence, to a degree unusual in a poem of Dryden's, of a veritable flood of conceits and images. He quotes, as examples of Dryden's "ambition of forced conceits," the following passages: lines 51–54, 93–96, 151–178, 119–122, 143–144, 207–208, 242–245, and 252–255. And these are but a modest portion of the torrent of figures. At one point Dr. Johnson's extraordinary penetration came close to hitting upon the central imagery of the poem, but he shrank back in horror from what he called Dryden's mention of "one of the most awful passages of Sacred History." [18]

The fact is that much of the meaning of the poem is conveyed by allusions to, symbols of, and images derived from, the cardinal events of Christian faith, the Atonement and triumph over evil and the Resurrection. We are confronted in *Astraea Redux* with a cosmic struggle in which heaven, justice, mercy, order, law, and nature contend with evil, irresponsible power, lawless and savage liberty, base passions, and perpetual dis-

---

17 Saintsbury notes (*op. cit.,* II, 364–365) that Dryden in *Astraea* employs the device of "powdering" the verse with a repetition of a word to provide a sound-accompaniment that helps to weave the passage together into a kind of stanza; his illustration, however, by a curious lapse of memory, is drawn from the poem *Ld. Ch.* The device of powdering by the repetition of "you" or "your" is conspicuous in Davenant's *Poem to the Kings most Sacred Majesty* (1661); and is noticeable, as Saintsbury points out, in Henry King's "Upon the King's happy return from Scotland" (*Minor Poets of the Caroline Period,* III, 190).

18 Life of Dryden (BH, I, 427). A. W. Ward in his chapter on Dryden, *Cambridge History of English Literature,* VIII, calls attention to the "audacious misuse of the classical and Scriptural illustrations in which this poem abounds," especially the comparison of the star which shone at Charles's birth to the star of Bethlehem.

order. The myth of Typhoeus and the blind Cyclops, the earth-born giants, develops the theme of the rebellion against heaven. On the side of evil and rebellion are arrayed madness, faction, despair, designing leaders, power, the vulgar, the rabble, a lawless savage liberty, wild distempered rage, frosts, crude humors, guilt, pollution, Legion, sin, Turks, drunkenness on martyrs' tombs, black crimes, impious wit, wiles, and malicious arts. And with these, in temporary alliance until a greater power breaks their spell, are fate, cross stars, Destiny, Fortune, Fortune's fruitless spite, and the black star. Associated with Charles II are Heaven, miracles, good days, the sacred purple and the scarlet gown, pilgrimage, the sun, virtues, valor, honor, God's anointed, light, wisdom, blessed change, the warmth of lengthening day, Heaven's blessing, Providence, the blessed saints, mildness of temper, a forgiving mind, justice, and goodness. Standing as the central figure in this drama is the newly restored King, the bridegroom of the nation whose absence both Church and state lamented. He is compared with David, who was, of course, a type of Christ. Through sufferings and affliction, innocent though he was, into the death of exile he proceeded. There is a hint of expiation made by one, who paid "that duty . . . we all did owe." And there is the figure of the star that shone at his birth. Clustered together in a brief passage (ll. 241–261) are terms that figure Charles clearly as a type of Christ: miracles, the penitence and sorrow of the land for his unmerited sufferings, his heavenly parentage, and his father's crown. His mind is merciful and forgiving. And his return is a renewal of May and life and flowers (ll. 285–287), it means warmth and thaw and birth after frost (ll. 129–136); and there can be no doubt that the Resurrection thus appears in symbols.

One can say that Dryden was indulging in hyperbolical flattery and toying with sacrilege. But a reading of the other poems written on the same occasion suggests that contemporaries did not find the flattery indecorous, or the comparison of the King with the Saviour shocking and distasteful. We must admit the possibility that Dryden was greatly excited by the King's return, and that to express the depth of his feeling he drew upon the imagery that had touched him most profoundly. A number of the images, as Dr. Johnson observed, are forced conceits, difficult to paraphrase, but conceits through which the thread of intention can be clearly traced. The wild profusion of them gives an intimation of the exuberant joy and breathless excitement which most Englishmen experienced on the King's return.

Title. Astraea, daughter of Themis (Justice) and Zeus, was herself identified as Dike, or Justice. During the iron age she fled the earth. It was fabled that she would return with another golden age. Thus the epigraph of the poem, from Virgil's *Eclogues*, IV, 6: (Now the maiden [Astraea] returns; now Saturn reigns again). That the period before the Restoration was thought of as an "iron age" is indicated by B. Harris' translation of *The Historie of This Iron Age* (2d ed., 1659).

The concept of Justice occupied an important place in Dryden's scheme of things, with implications political and religious. Some of its connotations are revealed in *Brit. Red.*, especially ll. 355–356:

> But justice is heaven's self, so strictly he,
> That could it fail, the godhead could not be.

1 Cf. ll. 9–12n. and ll. 13–18n. The peace of the world was not quite "general," however, for the Portuguese struggle for independence—soon to be aided by an English contingent—went on until Spain formally acknowledged Portugal's independence in 1668. Also the Turks and Venetians were at strife over Candia, and the Turks and Hungarians over Transylvania.

Cf. Cowley, *Ode, upon the Blessed Restoration and Returne of His Sacred Majestie* (1660), p. 1:

> Now Blessings on you all, ye peacefull Starrs,
> Which meet at last so kindly, and dispence
> Your universall gentle Influence,
> To calm the stormy World, and still the rage of Warrs.

2 *a world divided from the rest.* Christie noted this as an imitation of Virgil's *Eclogues*, I, 66: penitus toto divisos orbe Britannos (the Britains, completely sundered from the whole world).

3 *dreadful Quiet.* Christie called attention to Tacitus, *Annals*, I, lxv: ducemque terruit dira quies (A fearful quiet terrified the general).

7 Cf. Cowley, *Davideis*, I, 147: "A dreadful Silence fill'd the hollow place." Seventeenth-century poetry was likely to assign an active role to silence. Under that heading in Joshua Poole's *The English Parnassus* (1657) are found such examples as: "Silence ties up her tongue," and "Now silence lockt the organs of her voice."

This line was much ridiculed by Dryden's enemies. In *A Letter from a Gentleman to the Honourable Ed. Howard Esq* (1668), p. 6, the line is quoted with the comment: "I have not heard of the like Expression unless in a Tale of an Officer, that Commanded a Centinel not to stirr a Foot, but walk up and down, and see what he could hear." The line is also ridiculed by *The Friendly Vindication of Mr. Dryden* (1673), p. 16. Together with the following line it is quoted, inexactly, by Martin Clifford in *Notes upon Mr. Dryden's Poems* (wr. 1672; pub. 1687), pp. 12–13, to show that the poet was sometimes so fascinated by the sound of his verse that he neglected the sense. Alexander Radcliffe in *The Ramble* (1682), p. 4, used the line to burlesque Dryden. Dr. Johnson in the Life of Dryden defended the line thus (BH, I, 334–335):

> Silence is indeed mere privation; and, so considered, cannot invade; but privation likewise certainly is darkness, and probably cold; yet poetry has never been refused the right of ascribing effects or agency to them as to positive powers. No man scruples to say that darkness hinders him from his work; or that cold has killed the plants.

9–12 Charles X of Sweden died in February 1660, at war with all his neighbors. Since his son Charles XI was a minor, he had appointed regents in his will, and recommended to them a general pacification. In the same year by the Treaty of Oliva, peace was made with the King of Poland, the Emperor, and the Elector of Brandenburg; and by the Treaty of Copenhagen, with the King of Denmark. A settlement with the Czar was not reached until the following year.

13–18 The war between France and Spain, having lasted nearly a quarter of a century, was ended in November 1659 by the Treaty of the Pyrenees, when a marriage was arranged between Louis XIV and the Infanta Maria Theresa.

The reference to "the lily's side" in l. 18 is, of course, a play upon the fleur-de-lis, symbol of the French monarchy.

21–28 In these lines Dryden expresses primarily the point of view of the royalists; in many respects, however, he is also voicing the thoughts of all people of affairs, both Parliamentarian and royalist. It would be short of accurate to say that the Presbyterians felt that the nation and Church had long groaned for the return of Charles, but it is true that they considered the activities of the mystic sectaries as madness in the pulpit. Dryden's acid comments on the pretenses to power of the vulgar, or what he was later to call the dregs of a democracy, apparently reflect the scandalized annoyance of all men of substance, of whatever party, toward the democratic movements that had been set in action by the turmoils and struggles of the civil wars. The political and social theories of such groups as the Levellers, the Fifth Monarchists, and the Diggers chilled the blood of men of property throughout the nation. Even Cromwell and his independents were forced to take action against the extremists of the left.

22 Cf. Alexander Brome, *A Congratulatory Poem* (dated 4 June by the Br. Mus. catalogue), p. 9: "This did invade the Pulpit, and the Throne."

29–36 Royalist writers had insisted, and were insisting, that popular rebellion, though ostensibly aimed at the crown, would inevitably sweep on and overwhelm the Church and the nobility as well. "Sacred purple" and "scarlet gown" signify bishops and peers; any symbol of established authority tends to infuriate the enraged multitude. Dryden attributes the violence of the rebellion to leaders hungry for power, who managed to seduce and misguide the masses. But he names no names, and breathes no lust for vengeance. Other celebrants of Charles's restoration, exhibiting much less restraint, poured out their bitterness and contempt toward fanaticism and the mob. Cf. Thomas Pecke, *To the Most High and Mighty Monarch, Charles the II*, pp. 6–8; Henry Oxenden, ΕΙΚΩΝ ΒΑΣΙΛΙΚΗ, *Or an Image Royal*, pp. 3–5; Thomas Mayhew, *Upon the Joyfull and Welcome Return of His Sacred Majestie*, p. 4; Edmund Ellis, *Anglia Rediviva*, p. 5; and Alexander Brome, *A Congratulatory Poem, on the Miraculous, and Glorious Return of . . . Charls the II*, pp. 11–12.

37–42 Typhoeus, or Typhon, was a prodigious, deformed monster, son of Terra, and of the race of Giants. According to *The Great Historical, Geographical, and Poetical Dictionary* (1694):

This Monster came with the other Gyants to Fight and
Dethrone the Gods, who were so frighted at his Presence,

that they fled into Egypt and changed their Forms; but at
last Apollo kill'd him with his Arrows, or according to
others Jupiter struck him dead with a Thunderbolt, and
buried him under Mount Gibel.

Bacon in *De Sapientia Veterum (Philosophical Works,* ed. Robertson [1905],
p. 826) had interpreted the myth of Typhon as meaning that the common
people, if oppressed too long by tyranny, will arise in monstrous fury
against their oppressor. Obviously Dryden could not use this interpretation.
Commenting on the passage in *Astraea,* W. C. Abbott identified Typhoeus
as Oliver Cromwell (*Conflicts with Oblivion* [1935], p. 155). Some support
is given this view by Alexander Ross's interpretation of the myth (*Mystagogus Poeticus* [1653], p. 404): ". . . and surely bloody Tyrants are no
better then the foster-children of Dragons, & the Sons of earth, & of the
race of Gyants, and scourges or plagues sent by God to punish a people,
as they write that Typhon was." But Dryden makes it clear (ll. 43–44) that
the lawless rabble were joined with the "designing leaders" as the rebels
and tyrants; no man is held responsible.

37–38 Cf. *Faerie Queene,* III, vii, 47.3–5, where Spenser describes
Argante, daughter of Typhoeus, and the Titans

which did make
Warre against heaven, and heaped hils on hight,
To scale the skyes, and put Iove from his right. . . .

Cf. also the *Ruines of Rome,* xii, 1–4.

45 *Blind as the Cyclops.* The blind Cyclops, or Polyphemus, was by this
time closely associated with Puritans and the Commonwealth. Cf. Waller,
To the King, upon His Majesties Happy Return (1660), p. 4:

Great Britain, like blind Polipheme, of late
In a wild rage became the scorne and hate
Of her proud Neighbours. . . .

Cf. also John Denham, "The Progress of Learning," (*Poetical Works,* ed.
T. H. Banks [1928], p. 119):

As Joves loud Thunderbolts were forg'd by heat,
The like, our Cyclops, on their Anvils, beat;
All the rich Mines of Learning, ransackt are
To furnish Ammunition for this War. . . .

Alexander Ross in *Mystagogus Poeticus* (1653) explained, p. 87: "A
Common-wealth without a King, is like great Polyphemus without an
eye. . . ." Cyclops he defines as evil spirits, whose delight is in destroying
mankind; they are servants to Vulcan and Mars.

46–48 This picture of primitive life may suggest Hobbes's state of nature,
but it may have been drawn from Virgil's account of primitive society
before the coming of Saturn. Cf. Dryden's *Aeneis,* VIII, 417–424.

51 Cf. Thomas Higgons, *A Panegyrick to the King* (1660), p. 10:

Wander'd at Land, and on the Floods was tost,
And hurried up and down the World by Fate. . . .

52 Cf. Jo. Ailmer, *Brit. Red.* (1660), sig. Bb3: "Heir to thy Fathers Suf-

ferings, and his Crown." There is a paraphrase of this line in Richard Leigh's *The Transproser Rehears'd* (Oxford, 1673), where the author, speaking of Charles II, remarked, p. 75: "For not withstanding that his Majesty, to demonstrate he was Heir no lesse to his Majesties Vertues then his Crown. . . ." In the errata at the end of the volume, "his Majesties Vertues" is corrected to "his Fathers Vertues." In the early 1670's Leigh was engaged in reading Dryden to gather fuel for ridicule.

54 Cf. Martin Lluelyn, *To the Kings most excellent Majesty* (1660), p. 7: "And in Your tempted Pilgrimage, we find."

57–58 John Warton supplies the illustration from Aelian's *Various History* (or *Historical Miscellanies*), XII, xxi:

> The matrons of Lacedaemon, when they received the news that their sons were slain in battle, were accustomed to go forth to inspect their wounds, both before and behind; and when they found the greater number was before, they conducted the bodies of their children to the monuments of their ancestors with great solemnity, and a kind of stern pride in their countenances; but if they perceived any wounds behind, weeping and blushing for shame, they departed with the utmost secrecy, leaving the dead bodies to be interred in the common sepulchre, or carried them away by stealth to be privately buried at home.

58 Scott was pained by the figure, "the confusion of metaphor, where Virtue is said to dress the wounds of Charles with laurels." He found ll. 96 and 244 equally strained or impertinent.

59–60 Compression in this passage has resulted in the omission of a few steps in the argument. Expanded, the thought might be expressed thus: A few rare human beings, by rising above the limitations of their carnal natures, ultimately find their very limitations a source of honor and distinction (like Enoch, who, spurning the flesh in order to walk with God here on earth, was taken to heaven in the flesh). So the King, by rising above the crippling circumstances of his exile, out of the very afflictions of banishment developed the great virtues of patience, steadfastness, courage, and the wisdom that springs from personal experience. Cf. l. 87n.

59 Enoch and Elijah were translated to Heaven in the flesh.

65 *laveering*. "To beat to windward; to tack" (*OED*). Not a common word in the poems of this time, but Davenant uses it in *Gondibert* and in the *Poem to the Earl of Orrery*.

67–70 Marcus Salvius Otho (A.D. 32–69) aided Galba to become emperor of Rome. He apparently hoped to be adopted by the aged Galba as his successor. When Galba instead adopted Piso and declared him to be his heir, Otho revolted and had Galba murdered. His triumph was short, however, for Vitellius soon attacked him and defeated his forces. Otho committed suicide on 15 April 69. Thus did he "hope prevent." He apparently had a good chance to defeat Vitellius eventually, but his nature was such that he did not care to continue the struggle. His effeminacy was described by Suetonius and others. Cf. Dryden's *Juvenal,* VI, 723–724 and note.

74 Charles II was defeated by the parliamentary forces at Worcester, 3 September 1651, and after romantic and exciting adventures managed to escape to France. The second half of the line is a reference to the famous statement of Francis I of France, who wrote to his mother after his defeat at Pavia, 25 February 1525: "Of all things, nothing remains to me save honour and life, which is safe."

77–78 Cf. Waller, *To the King, upon His Majesties Happy Return,* p. 5:
> For, having view'd the persons and the things,
> The Councils, State and strength of Europe's Kings,
> You know your work. . . .

78 *Factor.* That is, agent, representative, or observer. The passage, somewhat obscure, might be paraphrased thus: Charles made all countries which he visited his own by his knowledge and understanding of them; and in observing the secret arts of rule and policy exercised by foreign monarchs, he assumed the role of agent or representative for England in their kingdoms.

79 Cf. II Samuel, xv–xxi. This is Dryden's earliest comparison of Charles II to David.

80 *When to be Gods Anointed* etc. Cf. Martin Lluelyn, *To the Kings most excellent Majesty,* p. 3: "But to be born our Prince, was all Thy Crimes."

86 *purchase.* "Machination; contrivance; management. . . . Hence, the actual bringing about or procurement of any deed or event" (*OED*).

87 *Inur'd to suffer.* The effect of exile upon Charles, in fostering in him patience, restraint, and a power of shrewd observation regarding the strength and weaknesses of other nations, was a theme developed by several of the poets celebrating the restoration. Cf. Davenant, *Upon His Sacred Majesties Most Happy Return,* p. 12; Fuller, *A Panegyrick to His Majesty, on His Happy Return,* pp. 1–2; Sir Robert Howard, "A Panegyrick to the King," *Poems* (1660), p. 5; Waller, *To the King, upon His Majesties Happy Return,* p. 5; Pecke, *To the Most High and Mighty Monarch, Charles the II,* pp. 10–12; Mayhew, *Upon the Joyfull and Welcome Return of His Sacred Majestie,* pp. 5–6.

98–102 *The name of Great* etc. The reference is to Henry IV of France, maternal grandfather of Charles II. Henry had had his troubles with the Catholic or Holy League which was formed in France in protest against the favorable terms granted to the Huguenots by what is generally called "the peace of Monsieur." The league, formed to promote the interests of the powerful family of Guise, established an *imperium in imperio,* and its members exalted obedience to its articles above allegiance to their sovereign, just as the adherents to the Solemn League and Covenant in 1643 were prepared to fight Charles I to secure the predominance of their beloved Presbyterianism.

The parallel between the Holy League and the Solemn League and

Covenant fascinated Dryden. In 1660 he outlined a play about the Holy League and wrote part of it, but put it by on advice of friends. Twenty-two years later he and Nathaniel Lee completed the play as *The Duke of Guise,* in which they satirized Shaftesbury and his adherents. Cf. Dryden's *Vindication of the Duke of Guise.*

106 *Chronicles.* Christie notes: "Similar instances of rhyme occur in Dryden with the word *articles* in the 'Letter to Sir George Etherege,' 37, and with *miracles* in the 'Threnodia Augustalis,' 414. These words were probably pronounced miraclees, chroniclees, &c."

115–118 Actually England during the lifetime of Oliver had been much respected abroad, and France and Spain had been eager solicitors for English aid; but in 1659, a period of weakness and confusion, France and Spain had made peace without much regard for English policies. With the return of the King in 1660 the great body of the English people were confident that their united nation, having done with lacerating itself in civil wars, was ready, like the lion, to pounce upon its foes. Cf. Fuller, *A Panegyrick to His Majesty, on His Happy Return,* p. 5:

> The French, who thought the English mad in mind,
> Now fear too soon they may them Sober find.

Cf. also Waller, *To the King, upon His Majesties Happy Return,* p. 4.

117–118 Cf. Dryden's *Aeneis,* XII, 9–14. The image of the self-flagellating lion is given in Waller's "To My Lord of Falkland" (*Poems,* ed. Thorn-Drury, I, 76):

> A lion so with self-provoking smart,
> (His rebel tail scourging his noble part)
> Calls up his courage; then begins to roar
> And charge his foes, who thought him mad before.

Waller's early editor, Fenton, in a note on this poem points out that this passage has a probable source in Tasso, whose thought Cowley too seems to have copied in his poem to Charles I, "On his Majesties Return out of Scotland" (*Poems,* ed. A. R. Waller, p. 24):

> So a bold Lyon ere he seeks his prey,
> Lashes his sides, and roars, and then away.

See also Cowley, *Davideis,* I, 649–655.

Dryden's sentence would, of course, have called to the minds of his contemporary readers the familiar figure of the lion in the English coat of arms.

121 *Portunus.* A Roman god of shores and harbors. Cf. Dryden's *Aeneis,* V, 314–315.

122 Loane (*N&Q,* CLXXXV [1943], 772) calls attention to *Aeneid,* V, 772: tempestatibus agnam (a lamb to the Tempests).

125–128 From the beginning of his career as a poet, Dryden had a layman's knowledge of the technique of painting. It is not possible to determine how much in his early years he frequented the studios of artists and the collections of connoisseurs, or how much he had read in the available manuals on painting. Directions for "sweetening" or blending colors so that they mingle gradually and harmoniously are frequent in such books.

If there is a specific source for this passage (and it is by no means necessary to postulate one), it could well be William Sanderson's *Graphice* (1658), or one of the several MSS of Edward Norgate's *Miniatura or the Art of Limning*. The fact that later treatises such as the anonymous *The Excellency of the Pen and Pencil* (1668), Alexander Browne's *Ars Pictoria* (1669), William Salmon's *Polygraphice* (1672), and Marshall Smith's *The Art of Painting* (1692) all repeat these directions for "sweetening" indicates that Dryden is referring to a commonplace practice of painters.

The somewhat naïve idea that painting deceives the eye is met frequently in ancient writers (Pliny and Philostratus, for example) and lived on through the Renaissance into Dryden's day. It is discussed at length by Franciscus Junius in his *The Painting of the Ancients* (1638), pp. 54–55.

129–130 Cf. Cowley, *Davideis*, II, 25: "The manner *How* lies hid, th' *effect* we see." Also Fuller, *A Panegyrick to His Majesty, on His Happy Return*, p. 4:

> This silent Turn did make no noise, O strange!
> Few saw the changing, all behold the Change.

Although today it appears that the Restoration was inevitable once Oliver Cromwell was dead, contemporaries could not realize this. In fact, after the defeat of Booth the position of the royalists seemed more desperate than before, and until Monck declared in favor of a new Parliament, men did not perceive how near the Restoration was. Cowley regarded the Restoration as a blessed surprise, observing (*Ode, upon the Blessed Restoration*, p. 7) that the nation appeared to be hastening on

> Even to the last of Ills, Annihilation.
> When in the midst of this confused Night,
> Loe, the blest Spirit mov'd, and there was Light.

144 Cf. Donne, *Second Anniversary*, l. 152 (Grierson, I, 255): "Heaven was content to suffer violence." E. A. Horsman explains (*RES*, n.s., I [1950], 349) the unusual sense of *violence* in Dryden's line, citing Matthew, XI, 12: "And from the days of John the Baptist until now the kingdom of heaven suffereth violence, and the violent take it by force." Also *Brit. Red.*, ll. 35–36, where *holy violence* seems to mean the unremitting energy of devotion and prayer.

145–148 A general uprising throughout England had been planned by the royalists and the "new royalists," as the Presbyterians were styled, for 1 August 1659. Betrayal of plans and the arrest of the leaders paralyzed the movement everywhere except in Cheshire, Lancashire, and North Wales where Sir George Booth got together a force of three or four thousand. He was defeated, however, within three weeks by John Lambert, the leader of the republican forces.

147–148 *but Heav'ns prefixed hour / Not come.* Cf. John, VIII, 20: ". . . for his hour was not yet come."

151–152 On 13 October 1659 the English army leaders, Fleetwood, Lambert, and Disbrowe, turned out the remnant of the Long Parliament (which Oliver Cromwell had expelled in April 1653), commonly known as the Rump, which they had restored the previous May. Monck, commander of the army in Scotland, sided with the Rump. He contrived to spin out time by idle negotiations until pressure of public opinion had disrupted the opposing army under Lambert. The army leaders in London threw in their hands, and the Rump was recalled again in December. At the beginning of January, Monck crossed the border, arriving in London a month later. He was naturally taciturn, and was careful not to reveal his sentiments so that no man knew which side he would take. At first he obeyed the orders of the Rump, but he soon became convinced that its intractability made the continuance of its rule impossible. He withdrew the guard around the Parliament so that the surviving victims of Pride's purge (which had excluded nearly 150 members in 1648) could take their seats on condition that they would vote for dissolution. This compact they loyally carried out. The election of the Convention Parliament returned a huge majority in favor of recalling Charles II, who was speedily invited to return to the throne.

It did not suit Dryden's purposes to mention the long period of uncertainty before Monck's intention was made manifest. In these anxious months neither side was convinced that Monck was the instrument of Providence. Thus George Wither, a republican, writing shortly after Monck's arrival in London, exhorts him to maintain the republic but betrays a sharp anxiety lest the general should lead back the King (*Furor-Poeticus*, pp. 5, 11, and 23). Samuel Pordage, on the other hand, in "A Panegyrick to His Excellency General Monck" which he dated 28 March 1660, although he expresses joy at Monck's coming, yet feels impelled to warn him that, if he usurps the throne, "the sacred powers, / Will blast the first fruits of thy tyranny" (*Poems upon Several Occasions* [1660], sig. B3v).

155–156 Cf. Cowley, *Davideis*, IV, 382–383:

Strange Play of Fate! when might'iest humane things
Hang on such small, Imperceptible Strings!

According to the *OED*, which cites l. 155, *clews* means "threads" or "cords" in a series. This definition leaves l. 156 greatly perplexed. It is more likely that *clew* here is a nautical term, perhaps for clew-line, the tackle by which a sail is drawn up to the upper yard or mast. If so, l. 156 would mean that the *clews* exert strength not by their size but by the arrangement (order) of ropes and pulleys.

159–162 *Mint* means "place of assay"; hence, "test." Line 162 may be paraphrased thus: Our chimaera evades the test of reality, just as the gold does which alchemists make. This by way of saying that Monck could not indulge in wishful thinking, for he faced the test of harsh actuality.

163–168 In the light of the foregoing lines this difficult passage would appear to mean something as follows: Command of an army alone, as Booth's experience had shown, was not enough. Nor could the vague hopes and fancies of sheer good will suffice to restore the King. The hard task of Monck was to sense when the time was ripe and, when he judged that all circumstances concurred, to send through unseen channels the impulses that focused public opinion, established communication between King and Parliament, and set the state in action.

The figure from physiological psychology (ll. 166–168) reflects what was the generally accepted doctrine in 1660. As Descartes explained it in the *Discourse on Method* (*Philosophical Works,* trans. Haldane and Ross [1911–1912], I, 115):

> . . . what in all this is most remarkable of all, is the generation of the animal spirits, which resemble a very subtle wind, or rather a flame which is very pure and very vivid, and which, continually rising up in great abundance from the heart to the brain, thence proceeds through the nerves to the muscles, thereby giving the power of motion to all the members.

Cf. Burton, *Anatomy of Melancholy,* Pt. I, sec. i, subsecs. 2 and 8. Cf. also Denham, "The Progress of Learning" (*Poetical Works,* ed. Banks, p. 116):

> And as in this our Microcosm, the heart
> Heat, Spirit, Motion gives to every part;
> So Rome's Victorious influence did disperse
> All her own Vertues through the Universe.

170 Cf. Martin Lluelyn, *To the Kings most excellent Majesty,* p. 7: "You use no Advocate, but mild Delay."

181 *that polluted nest.* The House of Parliament when occupied by the Rump. Cf. ll. 151–152n.

186 A tomb would make a highly uncomfortable seat. But complaints were common that the Puritans, particularly during the first two years of the Civil War, did defile churches in much the same way as Dryden describes. For example, in *Mercurius Rusticus: or, the countries complaint, of the sacriledges, prophanations, and plundrings, committed by the schismatiques, on the cathedrall churches of this kingdome* (Oxford, 1646), we read that at Westminster Abbey the soldiers "set formes about the Communion Table, there they eat, & there they drink Ale and Tobacco" (sec. iv [p. 237]), and that at Exeter they defiled the cathedral "with tipling and taking Tobacco . . . especially they deface the Bishops Tombs" (sec. iv [p. 241]).

The pronoun *those* in l. 185, however, in contrast to *these* in l. 189, may refer to early Christians given to excessive feasting and drinking at the tombs of martyrs. Several of the Church Fathers condemned the practice (cf. J. A. MacCulloch, *Medieval Faith and Fable* [1932], p. 123). Augustine in particular remarked: ". . . novi multos esse qui luxuriosissime super mortuos bibant . . ." (Migne, *Patrologiae Cursus Completus,* Patrologiae Latinae Tom. XXXII: S. Aurelii Augustini, p. 1342). Augustine's remark was familiar to the seventeenth century; it was quoted by, among others, Jeremy Taylor.

187–188 Cf. *Purchas his Pilgrimage* (1614), p. 294:

> Wine is also forbidden them; but yet they will be drunke with it, if they can get their fill of it. . . . One drinking wine with Busbequius, made great clamors; being asked the cause, he said he did it to warne his soule to flee into

some corner of the bodie, or else be quite gone, lest it
should be polluted with that sinne. Yet in their Fast or
Lent they abstaine very religiously.

190 A reference to the prayer meetings which the army leaders held on
the eve of decisive actions. The most famous of these was held at Windsor
Castle in 1648, when the decision was taken to call "Charles Stuart, that man
of blood, to an account for that blood he had shed, and mischief he had
done to his utmost, against the Lords cause and people of these poor
nations" (William Allen, *A Faithful Memorial of that Remarkable Meeting* [1659], in *Somers Tracts*, VI, 501).

193–194 The first of Dryden's many sardonic comments on members of
the clergy.

194 *in shew*. That is, in appearance only.

195–198 An allusion to the pretentions of the Puritans who thought of
themselves as, and called themselves, Saints engaged in establishing the
Kingdom of God on earth, and who thereupon proceeded, in the immortal
words of Butler, to

> build their Faith upon
> The holy Text of Pike and Gun;
> Decide all Controversies by
> Infallible Artillery;
> And prove their Doctrine Orthodox
> By Apostolick Blows and Knocks. . . .

197–198 In Greek mythology Salmoneus, son of Aeolus, desiring to
be worshiped as a god by his servile subjects, imitated the thunder and
lightning of Zeus by waving torches aloft and driving his chariot over
hollow brazen arches. For his impiety Zeus smote him with a real thunderbolt. His story is told by Virgil; cf. Dryden's *Aeneis*, VI, 788–803.

201–202 Lodovico Sforza (1451–1508), called "the Moor," was famed for
his treachery and scheming as well as his brilliance. He ousted his nephew
from the Duchy of Milan and was accused of poisoning him. Through a
series of alliances and broken alliances, he finally sank to captivity in
France and the ruin of all his fortunes.

203 *Fogue*. "Fury, passion; ardour, impetuosity" (*OED*). Dryden's use
of the word in this line is the earliest cited.

205–206 Scott notes:

> Those persons, who had sat in any illegal high court of
> justice, with a few others, were, at the Restoration, de-
> clared incapable of bearing any public office. . . . Thus
> disqualified, the poet compares these republicans to the
> Spartan slaves, made drunk to excite the contempt of the
> youth for that degrading vice. By the by, Dryden's kins-
> man, Sir Gilbert Pickering, was among the persons so in-
> capacitated.

Dryden's mildness in this passage is in strong contrast with the remarks
of some of his contemporaries. Cf. Thomas Saunderson, *A Royall Loyall*

Poem, pp. 4–5; G. S., *Britains Triumph, for Her Unparallel'd Deliverance,*
p. 15; Fuller, *A Panegyrick,* pp. 9–10.

215–216 When Charles's return became certain, the self-seekers hurried
to Holland to establish themselves in his good opinion. Clarendon wrote
of the group who came in the days just preceding the King's embarkation
for England (*Rebellion* [1807], III, 1162):

> In the mean time Breda swarm'd with English, a multi-
> tude repairing thither from all other places, as well as
> London, with presents, and protestations, "how much
> they had longed and prayed for this blessed change; and
> magnifying their sufferings under the late tyrannical gov-
> ernment;" when some of them had been zealous instru-
> ments and promoters of it.

Thomas Fuller, who like Clarendon was there, recorded the "swarms" of
loyal subjects come to Holland (*A Panegyrick,* p. 7).

218 *our impoverish'd Trade.* During the years previous to 1660 and
especially in 1659, there was what is now called a depression. Contemporaries, opponents of the Protectorate, blamed it on the Cromwellian war
against Spain and to the losses at sea from Spanish privateers. More
general explanations are (1) that the unsettled condition of Great Britain
before the Restoration, and of Europe before the pacifications referred to
in the notes above, produced the decay of trade; and (2) that the century-
and-a-half upward swing of prices, which the influx of precious metals
from the New World started about 1500, had at last come to an end. Cf.
W. R. Scott, *The Constitution and Finances of English, Scottish and Irish
Joint-Stock Companies,* I (1912), 260–262.

219 *Schevelines barren shore.* The King embarked at Sheveling or
Scheveningen, the port of The Hague, on 23 May.

230–231 Cf. Thomas Fuller, *A Panegyrick,* p. 8:

> Not the least loss, onely the Naseby mar'ls
> To see herself now drowned in the Charles.

Under the date of 23 May 1660 Pepys gives an account of the renaming
of certain vessels of the fleet so as to erase unpleasant memories of the
Rebellion:

> After dinner the King and Duke altered the name of
> some of the ships, viz. the Naseby into Charles; the
> Richard, James; the Speaker, Mary; the Dunbar (which
> was not in company with us), the Henry; Winsly, Happy
> Return; Wakefield, Richmond; Lambert, the Henrietta;
> Cheriton, the Speedwell; Bradford, the Success.

The *Naseby,* now the *Charles,* was no longer England's (or, more strictly,
the royalists') shame because it no longer recalled the battle of Naseby
(14 June 1645), in which the parliamentary army had won a complete
victory over the King's forces.

235 *groans beneath Great Gloc'sters weight.* John Warton called attention to *Aeneid,* VI, 412:

                    simul accipit alveo
          ingentem Aeneam. gemuit sub pondere cymba
          sutilis

(At the same time [Charon] welcomes mighty Aeneas in his boat. The patched boat groaned beneath his weight). Cf. Dryden's translation, *Aeneis*, VI, 556–557.

  242–245 Cf. Thomas Fuller, *A Panegyrick*, p. 8:
          Th' officious Wind to serve You did not fail,
          But scour'd from West to East to fill Your Sail,
          And fearing that his Breath might be too rough,
          Prov'd over-civil, and was scarce enough;
          Almost You were becalm'd amidst the Main,
          Prognostick of Your perfect peaceful Reign.

In the Life of Dryden Dr. Johnson quotes Dryden's lines, together with ll. 252–255, to illustrate his comment (BH, I, 427): "How far he was yet from thinking it necessary to found his sentiments on Nature, appears from the extravagance of his fictions and hyperboles. . . ."

  On the subject of the officious wind, cf. James Heath, *A Chronicle of the Late Intestine War* (1676), p. 450:
          No sooner was the Fleet under sail, but the Cannon
          began to roar, giving notice that the Lord of the Sea was
          in his rightful possession; which Thundring continued till
          night: Next day they had little winde, but so much, as on
          Friday-morning they came within sight of Dover. . . .

  249 *submitted Fasces of the Main.* The fasces are a symbol of authority. Christie notes:
          When Publius Valerius, being Consul, called the Roman
          people together to vindicate himself from false accusa-
          tions, he made the lictors who preceded him with the
          fasces, emblems of his consular rank, lower them in recog-
          nition of the people's superior power; and Livy says, 'sub-
          missis fascibus in concionem escendit' (ii.7).

Cf. *Annus*, l. 199.

  252–255 Dr. Johnson observed in the Life of Dryden (BH, I, 428):
          I know not whether this fancy, however little be its value,
          was not borrowed. A French poet read to Malherbe some
          verses, in which he represents France as moving out of its
          place to receive the king. 'Though this,' said Malherbe,
          'was in my time, I do not remember it.'

  260–265 The rules of Policy referred to were those of the cold-blooded Machiavellian school. Machiavelli in *The Prince*, ch. xvii, had argued that a prince, to keep his subjects loyal and united, must not shrink from cruelty, and that it is safer to be feared than to be loved. Dryden's picture of Moses as the prophet of mercy is possibly an answer to Machiavelli's stress on Moses as an armed prophet (ch. vi). For an earlier mention of the principles of the Machiavellian school, cf. *Her. St.*, ll. 29–30n.

261 Before and after the Restoration the King favored an Act of Oblivion for all his enemies except those responsible for his father's execution. After some months of deliberation on the part of Parliament, the King's merciful intentions were incorporated in the Bill of Indemnity, which finally received the royal approval on 29 August 1660.

262–265 Cf. Exodus, xxxiii, 20–23; xxxiv, 6–7.

266–267 Possibly suggested by Cowley's description of Jonathan. Cf. *Davideis,* IV, 489–490:

> To Help seems all his Power, his Wealth to Give;
> To do much Good his sole Prerogative.

268–269 This seems to be a play on words. The surface meaning, that the King's pronunciation turns a hard consonant into a soft, thinly veils the deeper meaning, that the King's mercy softens the rigid or strict interpretation of the laws. The rigid letter that Dryden was thinking of may have been the hard "g" in the Latin *leges.*

273 *Generous.* "Of liquor, esp. wine: Rich and full of strength" (*OED,* which notes that this meaning derives from the Latin, as in Horace's *vinum generosum,* wine of good stock). In Dryden's translation of Virgil we have: "gen'rous Vintage" (*Pastorals,* V, 109); "gen'rous Juice" (*Georgics,* III, 761).

276–278 Under date of 25 May 1660 Samuel Pepys describes the landing at Dover, remarking, "Infinite the crowd of people and the horsemen, citizens, and noblemen of all sorts." And he concludes his account: "The shouting and joy expressed by all is past imagination."

288–291 Cf. Cowley, *Ode, upon the Blessed Restoration,* p. 1:

> No Star amongst ye all did, I believe,
>> Such vigorous assistance give,
>> As that which thirty years ago,
>> At Charls his Birth, did, in despight
>> Of the proud Sun's Meridian Light,
> His future Glories, and this Year foreshow. . . .

Edward Phillips in his continuation of Baker's Chronicle reported this phenomenon (*Chronicle of the Kings of England* [1660], p. 497): "It is observed, that at his Nativity at London, was seen a Star about Noon-time; what it portended, good, or evil, we leave to the Judgment of the Astrologers." What the astrologers made of it depended on their political prejudices. William Lilly, a republican, refused to see anything remarkable in the appearance of the star (*Monarchy or No Monarchy in England* [1651], p. 92): "Many supposed there had appeared a new Starre at his birth, whereas it was the Planet Venus, who is usually seen in the day time." The star took on great symbolic value in the minds of the Court, for the medal struck in honor of Charles's birth featured it prominently; as did the medal struck off in 1660 in honor of Charles's restoration (engraved reproductions of both medals may be found in Fenton's edition of Waller's *Poems,* 1729). This was an open invitation, both in 1630 and in 1660, and royalist poets in droves responded to it, accepting the phenomenon as a miraculous event presaging the exaltation of Charles to honor and greatness.

291 An obvious allusion to the Star of Bethlehem. Cf. Matthew, II, 2 and 9–10. Several other poets celebrating the restoration of Charles chose to parallel the King's return and the birth of Christ: e.g., James Vaughan, in *Brit. Red.* (1660), sig. Bb2; J. Ailmer, *ibid.*, sig. Bb3; Henry Oxenden, *Charls Triumphant*, p. 4.

292 *whiter*. Christie noted that the use of *white* in the sense of "fortunate" is a Latinism. *OED* defines the word in this sense and cites Dryden's line as an example. The adjective occurs several times in the poems of Herrick, in such phrases as "white luck" and "white success." F. E. Hutchinson points out Henry Vaughan's fondness for the word with its Welsh connotations of fair, happy, holy, and blessed (*Henry Vaughan* [1947], p. 162).

Dryden may have been alluding to Charles II not merely as the restorer of the monarchy but as the successor to his father, who had been publicized as the White King, for which see William Lilly, *A Prophecy of the White King* (1644); Christopher Symes, *The Swords Apology* (1644); *N&Q*, ser. 3, II, 351; and Charles Firth, *Oliver Cromwell* (1900), p. 230. Part of the connotation which the adjective possessed in Dryden's mind is made clear by the first note which he attached to his translation of the Second Satire of Persius: "*White Stone*. The Romans were us'd to mark their Fortunate Days, or any thing that luckily befell 'em, with a White Stone. . . ."

Dryden's use of *white* was objected to by some of his contemporaries. The line in *Tyrannick Love*, I, i (S-S, III, 387): "That white one [day], in the crowd, may slip away," was defended as "very elegant Latine" by the author of *Mr. Dreyden Vindicated* (1673), p. 7.

297 An allusion to the doctrine of the balance of power, which Dryden here seems to disapprove of. An earlier reference to the doctrine, or policy, occurs in *Her. St.*, st. 22. The policy had taken shape in the sixteenth century under the Tudor monarchs, becoming a coherent system under Elizabeth. The balance was lost under the first two Stuarts, and not very successfully maintained under Charles II.

300 *Your much lov'd Fleet.* Cf. *Annus*, ll. 53–56n.; *Sac. Maj.*, ll. 97–100n.

301 *the petty monarchs.* That is, even the greatest monarchs who rule only over lands are petty in comparison with him who rules the sea.

306–310 The Dutch had a virtual monopoly of the spice trade with the Far East and kept it, though the East India Company traded with the mainland of India. Spain had lost Jamaica to Cromwell; and Charles declined to surrender it. When Cromwell established regular diplomatic relations with France in 1654, Charles left France in anticipation of his expulsion.

316 In connection with this line, Sir Charles Firth called attention to Charles II's "A Proclamation against vicious, debauched, and prophane persons," which was dated 30 May 1660 (*Dryden: Select Poems*, ed. Christie; rev. Firth [5th ed., 1901], p. 240). After a reproach to those who spend their time in reviling and threatening others (with the idea of showing their own loyalty to the king), the proclamation continues (*Somers Tracts*, VII, 424):

> There are likewise another sort of men, of whom we have
> heard much, and are sufficiently ashamed, who spend

their time in taverns, tipling-houses, and debauches, giving no other evidence of their affection to us but in
drinking our health, and inveighing against all others
who are not of their own dissolute temper, and who, in
truth, have more discredited our cause by the license of
their manners and lives, than they could ever advance
it by their affection or courage. We hope that this extraordinary way of delivering us from all we feared, and
almost bringing us to all we can reasonably hope, hath
and will work upon the hearts even of these men to that
degree that they will cordially renounce all that licen-
tiousness, profaneness, and impiety with which they have
been corrupted, and endeavour to corrupt others, and
that they will hereafter become examples of sobriety and
virtue, and make it appear that what is past was rather
the vice of the time than of the persons, and so the fitter
to be forgotten together.

318–323 There is a resemblance worth noting, especially in the repetition of *happy*, between this passage and the conclusion of Phineas Fletcher's
The Locusts (1627), in which Fletcher addresses Charles I with much the
same fervor as Dryden does Charles II.

319 The line may have been suggested by Donne, "To the Countesse of Bedford," l. 8 (Grierson, I, 195): "Pay all they have, and yet have
all to pay." Cf. also Donne's "Epithalamion, or mariage Song on the Lady
Elizabeth, and Count Palatine being married on St. Valentines day," ll. 93–
96 (Grierson, I, 130).

323 Cf. Martin Lluelyn, *To the Kings most excellent Majesty*, p. 5:
"We still request a King, and that King, Thee."

To His Sacred Majesty, A Panegyrick on His Coronation

Nearly eleven months passed between the return of the King and the time
of his coronation, on St. George's Day, 23 April 1661. According to Von
Ranke, "The coronation of the King had been deliberately postponed to
show that the King of England could govern without having been crowned
and without having taken the solemn pledges attached to the coronation." [1]
An additional motive for the delay is given by Clarendon, who reports
Charles's orders that in preparation for the coronation all the old records
be searched and that all the ancient ceremonies be observed.[2] In this way
the traditional importance of the crown might be impressed upon the

---

[1] *History of England Principally in the Seventeenth Century* (1875), III, 363.
[2] Clarendon, *Life* (1857), I, 455.

people; just as, in May of 1660, the King had desired it to be known that his return meant the restoration of the established laws and the ancient rights of the kingdom.

The festivities began on 22 April with a stately procession, of dazzling magnificence, proceeding from the Tower, through a series of triumphal arches, and so to Whitehall, where the day was concluded by water shows and bonfires. This brings us to lines 41–44 in Dryden's poem. On the following day the King entered Westminster Abbey, where, after the sermon and service, the ceremony took place, and Charles II, amid joyous acclamation and surrounded by bishops and peers, was anointed and crowned with the crown of St. Edward.

For detailed accounts of the splendor of these two days we may turn to Ashmole, Ogilby, John Tatham, Pepys, or John Evelyn, but not to the poets, who were concerned with impressions and interpretations, with the feelings inspired by the occasion. Few of the rhymesters who had celebrated the King's return came forward with a coronation poem; in fact, very few poems on the coronation were published. In effect, the coronation was ceremony without significance, for Charles was an anointed monarch before he returned in 1660. At any rate, the excitement and jubilation which had prevailed in May 1660 had considerably subsided, and the bards seem not to have been stirred. And Charles himself, under the pressure of public affairs and the increasing burdens of kingship, felt no immediate need for the blandishments of the muses. One recalls that His Majesty, informed of John Evelyn's intention to present him with a panegyric on the coronation, remarked wistfully that "he hoped it would not be very long." [3]

At that time the coronation poem had not been methodized into a distinct species of writing. It was occasional verse, often written as a panegyric, sometimes in couplets, sometimes in the irregular lines of the ode. Among the topics likely to be dwelt upon were: propitious circumstances, such as fair weather; the king's private virtues and his royal ancestry; the nation's need for such a king; the joy and hopes of the people; the authority of kingship; the sanction of the Church and of God; and the prospect of peace and unity, sunshine and spring, under the royal sovereignty.

Dryden devotes the greater part of his poem to the praise of Charles's achievements and his great virtues: the King has brought peace and quieted discord; his goodness and wisdom have united the nation; his patience and mercy are healing the wounds of rebellion; his paternal care operates so incessantly that even the pleasure he takes in ships serves the welfare and security of his people. The goodness of the King's actions offers assurance for his subjects' happiness in the future. The King is truly royal by nature. But in addition, he is a sovereign prince, having imperial power derived from the natural patriarchal authority of kingship and from divine sanction as conferred by the Church. It is worth noting that Dryden accepts

[3] Evelyn, *Diary and Correspondence*, ed. Bray (1891), III, 132.

the role of the Church without a murmur, and looks with a coldly critical (though unvindictive) eye upon the "jealous Sects that dare not trust their cause / So farre from their own will as to the Laws."

To His Sacred Majesty is the best of the poems composed for Charles's coronation. It begins splendidly, anticipating the nobility of utterance which graces the opening of Dryden's greatest poems; and it closes (ll. 119–134) in a passage which by the device of assonance achieves sonority and a touch of magnificence. The poem as a whole has a certain inventiveness which is under complete control, and the result is lucidity gained without the sacrifice of color and picturesqueness.[4] Yet there is a certain slackness about *To His Sacred Majesty,* and the poem lacks the excitement and exuberance of the *Astraea,* and falls below the *Heroique Stanzas* in continuous strength.

1–8 Cf. Genesis, VIII. A few of the details may have been suggested by Ovid. Cf. Dryden's translation, *Metamorphoses,* I, 461–472.

5 *that flood in its own depths was drown'd. Drown'd,* perhaps, as rivers or seas may be said to be *drown'd* in the ocean, the depths which they themselves have contributed to. Cf. *Astraea,* l. 303: "Our Ocean in its depths all Seas shall drown." But it is possible that Dryden read the Biblical account of the Deluge as Thomas Burnet later expounded it in the *Sacred Theory,* Bk. I, ch. viii: that the Flood was produced by the collapse of the arches and the crust of the earth, permitting the subterranean waters of the abyss to gush forth; and upon the quieting of the commotion, the Flood waters receded, to be drowned once more in the waters of the abyss. The notion of an abyss of waters was familiar to Dryden's contemporaries (cf. Cowley, *Davideis,* I, n. 10).

13–16 The likening of the king to the sun was a commonplace in poems addressed to James I and Charles I. Sir Francis Fane's *Panegyrick to the Kings most excellent Majesty, upon his Happy Accession to the Crown, and his more Fortunate Marriage* (1662) compares Charles II to the sun and (somewhat clumsily) uses the image of "the dark vapours of Ill Government" drawn up by the heat of prosperity. In Dryden's lines, the damps and vapors signify discord and rebellion.

17–19 The new year, of course, officially began on 25 March. The old year had been tainted by the rebellion of Venner and the Fifth Monarchy men in January 1660–1661, and by small uprisings elsewhere at about the same time; these things had been preceded by, and were accompanied with, inflammatory sermons and quantities of seditious pamphlets.

23 Cf. Exodus, XVI, 13–15.

25–32 The figure of the king "Whose new beames make our Spring, / Men glad, and birdes to sing," was a commonplace in addresses to James I and Charles I. Cf. Drayton, "To the Majestie of King James" (*Works,* ed. Hebel, I [1931], 472): "With thy beginnings, doth the Spring begin." If

---

4 Saintsbury noted in *Sac. Maj.* what he termed a modified form of conceit which escaped the dangers of "Clevelandisms" and yet retained color and picturesqueness (cf. *Dryden* [1881], p. 32).

the spring begins with the king, then he is in a sense the father of spring
—and of succeeding seasons. Thus Ben Jonson's "A Song to Welcome King
Charles" (*Works,* ed. Herford and Simpson, VIII [1947], 416):

> Now, in a garland by the graces knit:
> Upon this obeliske, advanc'd for it,
> We offer as a Circle the most fit
> To Crowne the years, which you begin, great king,
> And you, with them, as Father of our spring.

33 Cf. Spenser, *Hymne in Honour of Beautie,* ll. 71–72:

> Hath white and red in it such wondrous powre,
> That it can pierce through th' eyes unto the hart. . . .

37 Both Pepys and Evelyn took notice of the ladies viewing the procession. Pepys thus describes the scene: "The streets all gravelled, and the houses hung with carpets before them, made brave show, and the ladies out of the windows, one of which over against us I took much notice of, and spoke of her, which made good sport among us." Evelyn thus reports the scene: "This magnificent train on horseback, as rich as embroidery, velvet, cloth of gold and silver, and jewels, could make them and their prancing horses, proceeded through the streets strewed with flowers, houses hung with rich tapestry, windows and balconies full of ladies. . . ."

47–48 The restoration of the Established Church, an important but ticklish subject in 1661, was avoided by most of the panegyrists, but treated at some length with forthright approval by the anonymous *Poem upon His Maiesties Coronation the 23. of April 1661. Being St. Georges Day.* Dryden barely touches upon the subject.

49–58 This passage, in which Dryden associates music, harmony, and the power of creating order out of discord, almost inevitably suggests the power of David's music over the disordered mind of Saul. Possibly Dryden had in mind the passage in Cowley's *Davideis,* I, 456–518, in which the power of David's music is explained by the mystic sympathy existing between music, the soul of man, and the order of nature. The parallel of Charles II and David had occurred to Dryden as he composed the *Astraea,* in which several echoes of the *Davideis* are to be found. By 1661 the parallel between David and Charles had become a commonplace (cf. R. F. Jones, "The Originality of *Absalom and Achitophel,*" *MLN,* XLVI [1931], 214–215).

53–54 Pepys had a less fanciful explanation for the drowning of the music. Under the entry of 23 April 1661 he wrote: "But so great a noise that I could make but little of the musique; and indeed, it was lost to every body."

57 *atone.* That is, bring into harmony.

59 The image recalls the prophet Samuel, who, as God's agent, poured the sacred oil upon the head of Saul and, later, upon the head of David. Cf. *Davideis,* IV, 391 ff.; I, 115 ff.

61 *Dome.* That is, a cathedral church; as in Italian, *duomo.*

64 A figure drawn from the art of distilling. For another example, cf. *Annus,* ll. 51–52; *Ld. Ch.,* ll. 27–30.

70 *fruition.* On this Johnson remarked in the Life of Dryden (BH, I,

428): "Here may be found one particle of that old versification, of which, I believe, in all his works, there is not another. . . ." As several of Dryden's editors have noted, Dr. Johnson was wrong here. For the sake of rhyme Dryden several times used the archaic pronunciation of *-tion* as a dissyllable. Examples are: *constellation* (*Hastings*, l. 66), *execution* (2 *Conquest of Granada*, IV, iii), and *benediction* (epilogue to *Sir Martin Mar-all*, l. 2). Though the pronunciation of *-tion* as a dissyllable was probably archaic, it seems to have been common enough in the poetry of this time. Cf., for examples, Henry Bold's "St. George's Day. Sacred to the Coronation of his most Excellent Majesty Charles the II," printed in his *Poems Lyrique, Macaronique, Heroique, &c.* (1664).

78 A notion possibly stemming from Galen. Dryden could have found it in Dr. Walter Charleton, *Natural History of Nutrition, Life, and Voluntary Motion* (1659), pp. 2–3:

> To nourish, is to substitute such and so much matter, as was decay'd in the parts, namely flesh, nerves, veins, arteries, &c. . . . Nature doth nourish and amplify all parts of an Animal with the same matter, or humour (not with a diverse) out of which she constituted or framed them at the first. Because, whatsoever is superadded to the parts, during their growth, ought to be of the same substance, with what was praeexistent, and so must consist *ex congenere materiâ.* . . .

81–84 The Declaration of Breda had aroused high hopes that the religious contentions in the kingdom might be settled. In the summer of 1660 Parliament considered the religious question, but, unable to agree, adjourned the debate for three months, requesting the King meanwhile to explore possible solutions in conferences with the clergy. As Von Ranke puts it, "The Parliamentary road had thus at last led back to the King. . . ." (*History of England* [1875], III, 351). Late in October of the same year representatives of Anglicans and Presbyterians met with the King at the Lord Chancellor's residence to consider the substance of a declaration, to be issued by the King, which it was hoped might serve as foundation for an accord. At this time the Independents and Anabaptists, resting their hopes in the King, petitioned Charles for freedom of worship. For an account of the petitions and the debate upon them, cf. Baxter, *Reliquiae Baxterianae* (1696), p. 277.

87–88 *Oblivion* here means: "Forgetfulness as resulting from inattention or carelessness; heedlessness, disregard" (*OED*). By a play on words Dryden in l. 88 refers to the Act of Oblivion; the King's will to *forget* was, out of regard to mercy and policy, to overlook certain acts and crimes.

89–90 Cf. the anonymous *Poem upon His Maiesties Coronation the 23. of April 1661:*

> France, Holland, Flanders, Germany you view'd,
> Saluted Spaine; and yet by none subdu'd
> Came purely English home, and from each clime
> You brought their virtues with you, not their crime. . . .

That climate affected the temper and character of men was a theory widely accepted in the seventeenth century. It had been expressed by Bodin (whose views Burton cited), Charron, Du Bartas, and many others. Cf. Marvell, "To His Noble Friend, Mr. Richard Lovelace, upon His Poems": "And as complexions alter with the Climes. . . ." Cf. also Milton, *Paradise Lost*, IX, 45–47; and in the Columbia ed. of his works, III, 237; IV, 296; X, 325. Charron, whose book *Of Wisdom* had many readers in the seventeenth century, examined the effects of the three main climatic regions, Northern, Southern, and Central. As he explained it, Bk. I, ch. xlii (trans. George Stanhope [1697], I, 391–392):

> . . . the Southerly People, being Colder in their Con-
> stitutions, are from hence disposed to Melancholy; and
> this makes them Staid and Solid, Constant, Contempla-
> tive, Ingenious, Wise, Religious, and Devout. . . . From
> the same Superfluity and Predominance of Melancholy
> in their Temper, the Southern People seem to be more
> Lascivious, and Lustful than others. . . . From the same
> sharp, fretting Melancholy, they are Barbarous and Cruel;
> for That Whets the Passions, and urges them to Blood
> and Revenge. Now The Northern People, in whose Con-
> stitution Phlegm is most predominant, and who abound in
> Blood and Spirits; are just opposite to the Former, and
> have the direct contrary Qualities; excepting that they
> agree in that single Point of Cruelty. But This in these
> Parts of the World proceeds chiefly from a very different
> Reason; and that seems to be Want of Judgment; so that,
> like Beasts, They are Strong in their Passions, and Weak
> in those Faculties, that should controul, and keep them
> in. The Countries of the Middle Division . . . are Mod-
> erate in their Passions, Good-Humour'd, Cheerful, Nim-
> ble, and Apt, and Active.

93–94 Dryden appears to subscribe here to the patriarchal theory of the origin of sovereignty, a theory usually associated with Robert Filmer, whose *Patriarcha* was not published until 1680. But Filmer had expounded his views in three works printed before 1660. Moreover, his ideas had for decades been familiar to a rather large circle of friends among whom MS copies of the *Patriarcha* were circulated. But it is not necessary to suppose that Dryden adopted the theory from Filmer; the essential features of the theory had been anticipated by others, at least as early as 1606. Cf. Peter Laslett (ed.), *Patriarcha and Other Political Works of Sir Robert Filmer* (1949), introduction, pp. 7–9, 4, and 28–29.

97–100 Cf. the anonymous *Poem upon His Maiesties Coronation the 23. of April 1661:*

> The Seamans Art, and his great end, Commerce
> Through all the corners of the Universe,
> Are not alone the subject of Your Care,
> But Your delight, and You their Polar-star. . . .

For the King's delight in ships, and his mastery of the arts of navigation and shipbuilding, cf. *Annus,* ll. 53–56n.

102 *fraischeur.* Freshness, or coolness. In the Life of Dryden Dr. Johnson remarked (BH, I, 463–464):

> He had a vanity, unworthy of his abilities, to shew, as may be suspected, the rank of the company with whom he lived, by the use of French words, which had then crept into conversation; such as *fraicheur* for *coolness, fougue* for *turbulence,* and a few more, none of which the language has incorporated or retained. They continue only where they stood first, perpetual warnings to future innovators.

Dr. Johnson misjudged the extent of Dryden's innovations. *OED* records a use of *fraischeur* as early as 1599.

103–104 Allusion to an episode related by Plutarch in his Life of Caesar. Cf. *Plutarch's Lives* (1685), IV, 460–461: [One night the ship carrying Caesar was caught in a heavy wind and rough seas; and the pilot, confounded by darkness and the terrible noise of waves and whirlpools, ordered the sailors to turn about].

> When Caesar saw that, he discover'd himself, and taking the Master of the Vessel by the Hand, who was amazed to see him there, bade him, *Go on boldly, Friend, and fear nothing, thou carriest Caesar and his Fortune along with thee.* The Mariners, when they heard that, forgot the danger of the Storm, and laying all their strength to their Oars, did what they cou'd to force a passage out of the Channel.

111–116 Allusion to the changes and improvements made by Charles in St. James's Park. Lines 111–114 refer to the canal which the King had caused to be built, connecting the park with the Thames. The "mistrustfull foul" are protected in the decoy which Charles built in the park, the decoy coming to be known later as Duck Island (cf. Edgar Sheppard, *Memorials of St. James's Palace* [1894], I, 23–24). Both the canal and the duck refuge are mentioned in Waller's poem "On St. James's Park, as Lately Improved by His Majesty," published in 1661.

117–128 As early as February, London was filled with rumors about the King's marriage. At the time of the coronation negotiations were still going on, Charles moving very deliberately, anxious to carry the approval of his subjects along with him. Spain and Portugal were both eager for an alliance through marriage with Charles. Portugal offered a handsome dowry with Catherine of Braganza, including Tangier and Bombay, and free trading rights with Brazil and the Portuguese East Indies. Spain offered a variety of princesses, together with a dowry to match the magnificence of the Portuguese offer. Thus the Portuguese Indies and the Spanish Indies were rivals for Charles's love. Finally Louis XIV supported the Portuguese match, designing thereby to weaken the power of Spain. When the new Parliament opened on 8 May 1661 Charles announced his intention of marrying Catherine of Braganza. Lines 127–128 refer to the struggle going on between Spain and Portugal. Portugal was still fighting for its independence, and it is likely that, had Charles allied himself with Spain, the Portuguese would have lost their fight.

129–132 A reference to the celebrated oak in which Charles hid after the battle of Worcester. Line 132 is a reference to one of the devices erected for the coronation festivities, on the first triumphal arch through which the cavalcade proceeded on its way from the Tower to Westminster. John Ogilby thus describes it in *The Relation of His Majestie's Entertainment Passing through the City of London, to his coronation: with a description of the triumphal arches, and solemnity* (1661), p. 6:

> Behind the said Figure of Charles II. in a large Table is
> deciphered the Royal Oak bearing Crowns, and Scepters,
> instead of Acorns; amongst the Leaves, in a Label,
> MIRATURQUE NOVAS FRONDES ET NON SUA POMA
> ———'Leaves unknown
> Admiring, and strange Apples not her Own.'
> As designing its Reward for the Shelter afforded His
> Majesty after the Fight at Worcester: an Expression of
> Virgil's, speaking of the Advancement of Fruits by the
> Art of Graffing.

A similar device was planned for the water show on the evening of 22 April. The second "presentment" of the show was a circle, in which three whales chased three ships. From the center of the circle projected a rock out of which sprang the Royal Oak, bearing crowns and scepters instead of acorns. Cf. John Tatham, *Neptune's Address to His Most Sacred Majesty Charls the Second* (1661).

To My Lord Chancellor

Sir Edward Hyde (1609–1674) had been chancellor of the exchequer and a trusted adviser to Charles I until 1646, when he was sent abroad to be with the Prince of Wales. During the years of exile he devoted himself with boundless loyalty and wisdom to the interests of the unfortunate Prince his master. By 1654 he had become probably the most influential member of the little court, working devotedly for the peaceful restoration of the King. When Charles II finally returned to his throne, nobody deserved more credit for the happy event than Edward Hyde. Less than a month after the return Hyde took the oaths as Lord Chancellor, and at the coronation he was created Earl of Clarendon.

Dryden's poem was written to present to the Lord Chancellor on 1 January 1662 (for New Year's Day was celebrated on the first of January, although the year officially began on 25 March). It was a pleasant custom to give presents to the Lord Chancellor on New Year's Day, and Clarendon was not only one of the ablest but also one of the most powerful men in the kingdom. On whom else could Dryden more fittingly have bestowed a copy of verses? A close reading of the poem, however, reveals that Dryden had something more in mind than a graceful tribute to a distinguished man. The passage beginning with line 119 makes it clear that the Lord Chancellor had aroused envy and that a storm had gathered to shatter the calm of his good fortune. To Clarendon's friends the hostility must have appeared formidable, and we know that even as early as 1661 there was sufficient cause for their alarm.[1] Dryden's *To My Lord Chancellor* is a skillful defense of the great minister in a time of trial. The poem suggests that Clarendon's fate has been so closely interwoven with that of the King, that it would be difficult to disentangle the threads; and that Clarendon by his character and his great abilities has become the essential instrument of Charles's aims and policies.

Whether this New Year's gift brought a tangible reward to its author we do not know, for Dryden's relations with the first Earl of Clarendon are obscure. Several years later the poet wrote to Clarendon's second son, Laurence Hyde, Earl of Rochester: [2]

> I never applyd myselfe to any Interest contrary to your
> Lordship's; and, on some occasions, perhaps not known to
> you, have not been unserviceable to the memory & repu-
> tation of My Lord your father.

The nature of the services here referred to has never been discovered. Much more is known of Dryden's relations with Laurence Hyde.[3]

To My Lord Chancellor has far more than its share of conceits and abstruse passages. Scott shrewdly guessed that the involved figures and images were purposely introduced as a kind of subtle compliment to Clarendon's understanding. In his youth the Chancellor had dabbled in verse and had associated with men of letters, including Jonson, Cowley, May, Carew, Waller, and Davenant (cf. l. 5n.). He was himself recognized as a wit and a man of very considerable learning. The ingeniousness of the poem might well remind him of the tastes and pleasures of his earlier years. Some of the more difficult passages of the poem are drawn from the old and new science: the Galenic physiology (ll. 27–30), astrology (ll. 85–86), Copernican astronomy (ll. 109–118), and the old astronomy (ll. 147–156).

---

[1] A strong opposition to the Chancellor had grown up under the leadership of Bristol (cf. Von Ranke, *History* [1875], VI, 27). Pepys under the entry for 27 July 1661 records a conversation with George Montagu, who informed him that Claren-don had aroused a good deal of envy and that several great men, including Buck-ingham and Bristol, were making strenuous efforts to undermine him. Clarendon himself saw the precariousness of his position, and predicted to his friends that a storm of envy and malice would strike him such as he would not be able to endure (cf. *Life* [1761], II, 50).

[2] Ward, p. 21.

[3] To Laurence Hyde, Dryden dedicated two of his plays: *The Duke of Guise* and *Cleomenes*, and in *Absalom* he praised him under the character of Hushai.

As one of the early members of the Royal Society, Clarendon was undoubtedly interested in these subjects and possessed of sufficient knowledge of them to enable him to follow the meaning of the poem without too much trouble.

5 Alfred Harbage in *Sir William Davenant* (1935), p. 35, pointed out that Clarendon had in his youth shared quarters in the Temple with Davenant. In 1629 he contributed a commendatory poem to be printed in Davenant's *Albovine*. Clarendon doubtless wrote other poems, though the present editors have come upon only one. On pp. 39–40 of *Britanniae Natalis* (Oxford, 1630), a collection of verse celebrating the birth of Charles II, is a sixteen-line poem in Latin signed "Ed. Hide ex Ecclesia Chri. Alumnus."

In his *Life* (1857), I, 28, 32–34, 44–45, Clarendon tells us that as a youth he had been the friend of Ben Jonson, who "very much reformed the stage; and indeed the English poetry itself," and of Cowley, who "made a flight beyond all men" but who ascribed much of his success to Jonson's "example and learning." He also enumerated among his friends of the 1630's Thomas May, the author of "one of the best epic [in the MS of the *Life*, *epic* is written over *dramatic*, the word printed] poems in the English language," Thomas Carew, whose poems "were at least equal, if not superior to any of that time," and Edmund Waller, who when near thirty "surprised the town with two or three pieces . . . as if a tenth muse had been newly born, to cherish drooping poetry."

14–16 A reference to the Pope and his election by the cardinals.

19–22 Cf. *Aeneid*, II, 351–352.

23–26 That wit and poetry had been restored along with Charles II was a commonplace of the 1660's. But poetry had not only been restored; it had been restored to the great function which nature ordained for it, to support religion and government. According to the defenders of the muses, the poets were the earliest prophets and lawgivers. Davenant, for example, described the priestly and legislative role of poets thus (*Poem to the Kings most Sacred Majesty*, ll. 1–6):

> Though Poets (Mighty King) such Priests have bin
> As figur'd Virtue and disfigur'd Sin;
> Did in so fair a shape Religion draw,
> As might, like Beauty, both allure and awe:
> Did rigid Rules in cheerful Songs disperse;
> Whilst all were Lai'ty but who dealt in Verse. . . .

Clarendon, as an old lover of the Muses and as a bulwark of religion and law, was thus able to communicate the true spirit of poetry to the Muses' priests, the poets, and so to revive them. In the same way, by the same mysterious sympathy with the royal will, Clarendon was able to communicate the King's purposes and his goodness to the nation (ll. 27–30).

24 Cf. similar phrasing in *Astraea*, ll. 165–166.

25 *Druids.* That is, priests.

27–30 Cf. Clarendon's own statement about his power and influence (*Life,* I, 309):

> The chancellor was generally thought to have most credit
> with his master, and most power in the counsels, because
> the king referred all matters of what kind soever to him.
> And whosoever repaired to him for his direction in any
> business was sent to the chancellor.

Lines 27–30 might be paraphrased thus: The King, the nation's whole soul, dispenses his "vital influence" through Clarendon. Clarendon thus becomes the system of arteries by which these vital spirits are transmitted throughout the body politic and in which simultaneously these spirits are refined into a higher form to constitute the Rational Soul. By so refining, Clarendon creates the nation's Understanding and the nation's Will.

Dryden's figure rests on a fairly complex physiological theory which stems from Galen and which is vividly expressed by Charron (*Of Wisdome* [1651], p. 14):

> This Brain is the seat of the reasonable soul, the source
> of sense and motion, and of the most noble animall
> spirits, composed of the vitall, which being raised from
> the heart by the Arteries unto the brain are concocted
> and reconcocted, elaborated and made subtile by the help
> of the multiplicity of small Arteries, as fillets diversely
> woven and enterlaced, by many turnings and windings,
> like a labyrinth or double net, Rete mirabile; within
> which this vitall spirit being retained and sojourning,
> oftentimes passing and repassing, is refined and perfected,
> and becomes a creature, spirituall in an excellent degree.

38–42 These lines extend the image previously established in ll. 31–36, the joining of the terrestrial and the celestial spheres at the horizon. Charles's and Clarendon's virtues embrace as the celestial sphere embraces the terrestrial. Had any one else occupied Clarendon's position, it would have been as though some smaller body replaced the earth, leaving a gap between it and the sky.

47–48 The same figure is used in *Annus,* st. 253, to suggest the relationship between the King and James, Duke of York.

49–52 Despite the attacks of his enemies, Clarendon's reputation for incorruptibility has remained intact. Burnet wrote of him (*History of His Own Time* [1766], I, 130): "He was a good Chancellour, only a little too rough, but very impartial in the administration of justice."

53–54 Cf. I Samuel, xvii, 38–39. The incident is also used in Cowley, *Davideis,* III, 529–542.

61–64 That is, the King tied Clarendon's legacy of goodness and mercy to the crown by making him Lord Chancellor. It is unlikely that Dryden intended to suggest that Clarendon was tied to the crown by the marriage of his daughter Anne to James, Duke of York, in 1660.

67 *Emp'rique.* Here used in the seventeenth-century sense of quack or

charlatan. It was commonly applied to mountebanks or physicians and their wares. Cf. *Charleton*, l. 7.

72 *As men do nature.* That is, as men unwind the clue of nature (which is the Book of God's Works) by tracing causes in effects until they arrive back at the First Cause, which is God the Creator.

73–76 Cf. *Paradise Lost*, IV, 159 ff. for a description of the odors wafted out from the shores of Araby; on which passage Professor Merritt Y. Hughes notes a parallel in Diodorus Siculus. The imagination of the seventeenth century was still enchanted by the riches of the Indies, and drew some of its most sensuous imagery from the spices, odors, and perfumes of Indian, Arabian, and Eastern lands. A glance at Joshua Poole's *The English Parnassus* (1657) will show what a variety of lines on these topics was available to budding poets. The ideas of wealth, sensuous richness, and the golden age (ll. 135–138) were often associated.

Cf. also Drayton, "To the Virginian Voyage," sts. 8–9. Drayton is here probably following Hakluyt (cf. J. Q. Adams, "Michael Drayton's *To the Virginian Voyage,*" *MLN*, XXXIII [1918], 405 ff.). Amadas and Barlowe in the 1584 voyage had been greeted with odors fragrant and powerful, "as if we had bene in the midst of some delicate garden abounding with all kinde of odoriferous flowers, by which we were assured, that the land could not be farre distant." Dryden probably knew Hakluyt, and may have found his suggestion there.

77–78 For the figure of a rich new world's being discovered in an individual, cf. Davenant, *Poem to the Kings most Sacred Majesty*, ll. 37–42; *Poem to the Earl of Orrery*, ll. 3–6, 21–23.

81–82 *Who* (l. 82) apparently refers to *princes*, not to *subjects*. The couplet might be paraphrased thus: Wise and successful princes, who win the hearts of their subjects, appoint ministers who share some portion of their wisdom and goodness; such princes love to have their ministers praised for the very virtues which they share with their sovereign and because of which their sovereign appointed them.

83–86 In ll. 85–86 Dryden is saying that through Clarendon, Charles as king invisibly transmits his power and inclines his people to obey just as God does through "his bright Ministers the Stars." Apparently Dryden intended *unseen* in l. 85 to modify *convey* in the preceding line and not *pow'r*, which it seems to limit. It would hardly be proper to speak of God's power as unseen, since to men of faith God's power is everywhere evident. The analogy rests upon the fact that the *ways* in which God imposes his power are *unseen*, i.e., not fully perceived and not subject to analysis. No human being can explain exactly how God transmits his power to the stars or how the stars in turn transmit this divine influence to Man. On the human and national level, no citizen can really explain how Charles transmits his power to Clarendon or how Clarendon in turn exercises this ultimately divine influence upon all Englishmen, inclining them to obedience.

The use of *inclines* in l. 86 should be compared with the language of fatalism in ll. 95 ff. Defenses of astrology, to which Dryden would have been led by his interest in the subject, always disclaim fatalistic teaching for the pseudo science and continually cite the aphorism, *Astris agunt* [or *inclinant*], *non cogunt* (we are inclined by the stars, but not compelled).

87–101 Saintsbury pointed out the repetition of *you* and *your* in this passage, which seemed to him to weld the paragraph together and, besides, to provide a substitute for pause variety (*History of Prosody*, II, 364–365). The words *few, true, newborn,* and *new-closing* carry out the assonance.

89–94 Hyde had been the confidential adviser of Charles I from January 1642, and continued so until he accompanied the Prince of Wales abroad four years later. He was therefore not actually present during the King's last sad times (1646–1649). The remarks about his sufferings (ll. 92–94) are somewhat exaggerated.

99–100 Hyde had been the steadfast counsellor of Charles II during the years of exile; his emergence, consequently, could not have been altogether surprising to those who knew the little court of the exiled King. But in England, from which he had been absent for fourteen years, the reappearance of Hyde, now in the fullness of his powers and influence, may well have dazzled the eyes.

105–108 For Dryden's earlier realization of the importance of the arts of peace, cf. *Her. St.,* ll. 77–80. Cf. Milton's sonnet to Cromwell: ". . . peace hath her victories / No less renowned than war."

109–118 The similes are conspicuously based on the new astronomy. Their ultimate source is Copernicus, *De revolutionibus orbis* (1543), Bk. I, ch. 8, which deals with the illusion that the earth is at rest though it is actually in very swift motion. In ll. 113–118 Dryden ascribes to Clarendon a Godlike role. Just as God moves the earth among the planets, so Clarendon moves the sphere of England among those other "flying Orbs," which are the other nations. The phrase "turn and roul" in l. 111 alludes to the diurnal revolution of the earth on its axis and to its annual orbit.

119–126 An allusion to the ancient belief that unalloyed success and greatness invite envy and lead to one's downfall at the hands of fate. Therefore the weak showers of envy and opposition which Clarendon now has to bear, are lesser ills that ward off the greater ill of his fall from power and place (ll. 125–126). There is an ingenious twist in Dryden's argument. Ordinarily the crime that brings about the fall of the great man is the pride inspired in him by his happiness and prosperity. But in this passage *crimes* (l. 119) is used ironically to mean the virtues necessary to the proper and *happy* (i.e., successful) conduct of the Lord Chancellor's office; and *pride* (l. 122) is attributed, not to the great man, but to the opposition, whose arrogance is such that they fancy themselves better qualified than Clarendon.

135–142 Most of this belongs to the conventional scenery of the golden age, which was commonly associated with the mythical paradises of the Greeks, or with the Fortunate Islands (often identified with the Canaries), or with the newly discovered islands of the Caribbean. Cf. *Charleton,* ll. 9–14n.

Thomas Burnet's *Sacred Theory of the Earth* gives expression to the concepts of the golden age which the seventeenth century cherished. Burnet, who quoted Ovid and Virgil to illustrate the tradition, discovered four main features in the earthly paradise: a perpetual spring, an unusually fertile soil which produced food without man's labor, a more or less smooth terrain, and longevity in the human and animal inhabitants.

139–140 As a parallel John Warton cited Virgil, *Eclogues*, IX, 7–8:
. . . qua se subducere colles
incipiunt, mollique jugum demittere clivo
(where the hills begin to slope down gradually and to sink their ridges in soft declivity).

139 *submits.* "To become low or lower" (*OED*, which cites Dryden's line).

147–156 Dr. Johnson remarked (BH, I, 429–430): "Into this poem he seems to have collected all his powers, and after this he did not often bring upon his anvil such stubborn and unmalleable thoughts; but, as a specimen of his abilities to unite the most unsociable matter, he has concluded with lines, of which I think not myself obliged to tell the meaning." Following Dr. Johnson, none of Dryden's editors has felt called upon to explicate ll. 147–156.

The lines bring the poem to a climax in a double sense, in the intricacy of the figure and in the ingenuity—even extravagance—of compliment. They cannot be understood without a grasp of two basic concepts of the old science, both expressed in countless books up to Dryden's time but both conceivably known to Dryden from their classical formulation in Aristotle's *De Caelo*. The first was the view that the heavens were eternal and changeless (*De Caelo*, Bk. I, 269b–270b, 279b–280a; Bk. II, 283b–284b). The second was the view that the four elements had among their attributes either heaviness (Earth being absolutely "heavy," Water relatively so) or lightness (Fire being absolutely "light," Air relatively so). Whereas the heavy elements by their nature moved down toward the center, the light elements moved upward (*De Caelo*, Bk. IV, 307b–313b).

The passage may be paraphrased thus: "Unimpair'd with labours or with time," Clarendon's age seems like an ever renewed youth. In the same way the heavenly bodies, being eternal and changeless, furnish a contrast to our mortal and decaying lives, and measure out time without suffering time's changes. Clarendon's age shall grow without a weight to burden it. ("Weight" means "care" in this line, but its use makes possible not only the paradox of "increase—without weight" but an ambiguity caught up in the different use of "weight" in "weightlesse," l. 155.) His age shall increase like the new years which keep returning always. For since Clarendon's orbit is around Charles, just as the New Year depends on the Sun, Clarendon's age must logically be both weightless and immortal, its center being Charles, who is *above* Clarendon. Dryden may have intended to extend the implication to the full stretch of his royalist position. A life like Clarendon's centered on the King is a life also centered in God, who is above: it is therefore unquestionably immortal.

151 Cf. *Her. St.*, ll. 57–58.

To My Honored Friend, Dr. Charleton

Charleton's *Chorea Gigantum* carried an imprimatur dated 11 September 1662, and it was almost certainly published before the close of the year. The dedication, addressed to the King, was dated 27 April 1662. It is reasonable to assume that Dryden's commendatory poem was composed between the date of the dedication and that of the imprimatur.

Chorea Gigantum; or, the most famous antiquity of Great-Britan, vulgarly called Stone-Heng, standing on Salisbury plain, restored to the Danes was clearly intended as a reply to the theory of Inigo Jones, which had appeared in 1655 under the title of *The Most Notable Antiquity of Great Britain, vulgarly called Stone-Heng on Salisbury plain. Restored by Inigo Jones.* Jones's work, completed and published after his death by his son-in-law John Webb, contended that the ruins had once been part of a Roman temple dedicated to the god Coelus. Charleton argued that the ruins represented the labors of the Danes and were similar to ancient Danish monuments surviving elsewhere; and he considered it highly probable that, far from having been a temple, they were an example of the raised structures where Danish kings or commanders were inaugurated. Contemporary opinion did not follow Charleton's lead. Wood reported that his theory was "exploded by most persons when 'twas published," though Sir William Dugdale accepted it.[1] Charleton's friend John Aubrey, convinced that the great monument was of Druid origin, indulged in a round of facetious mirth at the contentions of *Chorea Gigantum*.[2]

Walter Charleton (1620–1707) was a well-known physician and a writer on a variety of subjects. He had early developed an interest in the new science, some of it as a student of John Wilkins at Magdalen Hall, Oxford. As a very young man he had been appointed physician in ordinary to Charles I, and later held the same appointment under Charles II. A great admirer of Harvey, Charleton was also a friend of Sir George Ent, of Dr. Prujean, and of "our incomparable Mr. Hobbes"; he was one of the first writers to become aware of the importance for psychology of the brilliant work in anatomy carried on by Thomas Willis. On 23 January 1661 he was proposed for membership in the Royal Society, and admitted on 15 May, one of the earliest fellows of the society.[3]

When he met Dryden we do not know. The acquaintance may have come about through Herringman in the late 1650's. Osborn has shown the possibility that Dryden wrote prefaces for two of Charleton's books which Herringman published.[4] It is also possible that they met through the means

---

[1] *Athenae Oxonienses*, ed. Bliss, IV, 754.
[2] Cf. Anthony Powell, *John Aubrey and His Friends* (1948), p. 107n.
[3] Thomas Birch, *History of the Royal Society* (1756–1757), I, 13, 23.
[4] Osborn, pp. 174–175.

of Sir Robert Howard, who like Dryden wrote a commendatory poem for *Chorea Gigantum*. At any rate it was Dr. Charleton who proposed the poet for membership in the Royal Society, on 12 November 1662; on 19 November, Dryden was elected, and on the 26th officially admitted.[5] Since the commendatory poem had been written only a few months previously, it may have played a part in bringing this distinguished honor to its author. A presentation copy of *Chorea Gigantum* now in the Folger Shakespeare Library carries an inscription in Charleton's hand: "For my Learned & obliging Friend, Mr. John Driden." [6]

To interest oneself in Dryden's poem principally because it shows his "early enthusiasm for natural science" is to miss the point, and to blind oneself to its unity. After all, Charleton's book was not a work of natural science but of antiquarian learning and history, an undertaking written in part to celebrate an event in the history of Charles II, to whom the book was dedicated. Inasmuch as an interchange of ideas took place between Dryden and Sir Robert Howard while they were composing their commendatory verses (cf. ll. 43–44n., 47–48n., and 57–58n.) it is pertinent to observe how the significance of the occasion is reflected in Howard's "To My Worthy Friend, Dr. Charleton." According to Howard, Charleton had shown not only the ability, as a physician, to preserve the lives of men but also the power, as a man of learning, to give life to their monuments by discovering the truth of history embodied in the monuments; in the second place, Charleton had restored the ruins of time by sifting out men's errors, which had concealed the wonder of history; and in the third place, by revealing Stonehenge as a coronation throne rather than as a temple, Charleton had not lessened its dignity but had given Englishmen, "so blest with Monarchy," reason for rejoicing in the meaning of the throne as it took form in their own constitutional history.

These ideas were part of Dryden's poem as well. But to see Dryden's meaning more fully one must recall the state of things as loyal Englishmen saw them in the middle of 1662. The King had only recently been restored, and his coronation, an event of awesome splendor, was fresh in memory, removed in time by only a year. The restoration had come about in response to the will of an overwhelming majority in the nation, and it came as the free choice of the people and the Parliament. In the eyes of loyalists it represented an end of tyranny and the restoration of the laws and ancient rights of the kingdom, a recovery from error and a renewal of the legal basis of government in the truth of England's constitutional history. Moreover, the newly restored King had just established himself as the champion of free reason and truth by his chartering of the Royal Society in 1662. Furthermore, the King's interest in ships, navigation, and an expanding navy gave expression to one of the most dynamic currents swaying the country. These were facts fresh in the minds of Dryden's first readers.

---

[5] Birch, *op. cit.*, I, 125, 127.
[6] Osborn, p. 175n.

To My Honored Friend, Dr. Charleton opens splendidly with mention of the tyranny of Aristotle, a tyranny made possible by men's abjuring the use of their own reason, and finally broken down by the facts revealed in discovery and experiment; and the truth transforms a region thought to be harsh and uninhabitable into an earthly paradise. It is left to the reader to make the association between philosophical and political tyranny, and to see in lines 10–14 a suggestion of the better times to come. With line 21 a strongly nationalistic strain is clearly heard, celebrating the English genius and love of free reason, triumphant in the quest of truth—a genius displayed equally in natural science and in the arts of statesmanship. A bare suggestion in lines 25–26 relates the English success in science to their achievements in navigation and their naval supremacy. The ability to sift truth from error is seen equally in natural science and in the historical investigation by which Charleton had restored Stonehenge to the Danes— and to its proper place in English history. From here the poem proceeds in graceful compliment to the newly crowned King, who, as the final line of the poem states, has been restored to his throne even as Stonehenge has been restored *as* a throne.

To My Honored Friend, Dr. Charleton is one of the most successful of Dryden's early poems. Unlike the elegy to Hastings it has no layer of ingenious adornment; and it shows no trace of the opaqueness that characterizes the verses to Clarendon. It has the dignity and the lucidity of the *Heroique Stanzas,* but more ease, more compression, and more unity. The opening statement of the poem is alive with political implications, which are swiftly developed in subsequent lines. As the poem advances, implication, statement, and suggestion are pulled together and merge into a single impelling thought and feeling, pride in the genius of Englishmen—a genius variously expressed but most significantly embodied in the long historical development of the English limited monarchy, the crowning glory of free reason. The import of the poem is brought to a suitable culmination in the compliment to the King, for the dramatic restoration and coronation of Charles II meant not only a restoration of the monarchy, with an end to tyranny and error, but also the leadership of a King whose own genius was admirably constituted to foster those very qualities that made for national strength, glory, and freedom.

A somewhat similar interpretation of the role of Charles II was to appear four years later in *Annus Mirabilis.*

1–4 Cf. Cowley, "To Mr. Hobs" (1656):
>   Long did the mighty Stagirite retain
>   The universal Intellectual reign. . . .

The attack upon the authority of Aristotle had become a commonplace among followers of Bacon. In his *Physiologia-Epicuro-Gassendo-Charltoniana* (1654), p. 2, Dr. Charleton had assailed the "Junior Aristotelians," as he called those who submitted uncritically to the master's rule. In *The Immortality of the Human Soul Demonstrated by the Light of Nature*

(1657), p. 53, Charleton opposed the blind following of authority in terms of moderation that would have appealed to Dryden:

> For my part, truly, I conceive it fitting, that all Schollars should have a reverend esteem of Antiquity, as a good guide of our younger Reason into the waies of Nature; Yet I think it scarce safe for any man to follow it implicitly, and without examination, as if it were impossible for him to erre the whiles, or as if the light of his own understanding were given him to no other use, but to be set in the dark lanthorn of Authority. The Ancients indeed, (thanks be to their bounteous industry) have left us large and noble Foundations; but few compleat Buildings: and who so intends to have his understanding seated commodiously, and in a pleasant Mansion of Science, must advance superstructures of his own; otherwise he wil lie open to the weather of Doubts, and whirlewinds of various Difficulties.

6 *sophisticate*. Refined to the point of uselessness. The subtle speculations of the schoolmen were often likened to cobwebs.

7 *Emp'rique*. In a translation of Lazarus Riverius, *The Practice of Physick* (1655), sig. A1, the empiric is described as "one that gives Physick (Hab Nab, as wee use to say) relying only on Experience, and what he hath seen done before him, not being able to give any reason touching the Disease, its Cause, or Cure."

For the word as applied to politicians, cf. *Ld. Ch.*, l. 67.

9–14 Aristotle, like most of the ancients, had placed the torrid zone between the Tropic of Cancer and the Tropic of Capricorn, and believed that in this region of extreme heat no human being could live (*Meteorologica*, Loeb Library trans., II, 362b). Even before the age of discovery a number of writers disagreed with these conclusions, including Strabo, Albertus Magnus, and Roger Bacon. The discovery by modern travelers of a temperate in a torrid zone is vividly recounted in Burton's *Anatomy*, Pt. II, sec. ii, memb. 3. The significance of the discovery is made sharp and explicit by a quotation from Acosta: ". . . hereupon, saith Acosta, I loudly laughed at the meteorological philosophy of Aristotle. . . ."

In his third voyage, having endured days of intense heat, Columbus finally arrived in a temperate region where the climate was mild and the changes of summer and winter were unknown (cf. *Select Documents Illustrating the Four Voyages of Columbus*, ed. Cecil Jane [1930], II, 26–28). It was a spectacular revelation; and the inhabitants were so fair-skinned, the water in the sounds so fresh, that Columbus was tempted to think he had found the earthly paradise.

In referring to the discovery and the scene of an earthly paradise Dryden was following well-known materials. In Sandys' translation, *Ovid's Metamorphosis*, which Dryden had read as a young man, the translator had written (2d ed., 1632, p. 21) that, although the torrid zone had generally been considered uninhabitable, yet it was

> found now by the Portugals and Spaniards not only pop-
> ulous, but healthfull, pleasant, and abounding with what-
> soever the avarice or voluptuousnesse of man can desire.
> To them under the line the daies and nights are alwaies
> equall; the heat of the one being qualified by the length
> of the other, and coole breises continually blowing from
> nine of the clock untill the evening. . . . Two Summers
> they have, and two harvests: the Trees ever greene, and
> bearing fruit continually.

Such a vision of the earthly paradise, of the golden age in the present, lies behind Marvell's *Bermudas* and the more detailed *Battle of the Summer-Islands* by Waller. Although in 1645 and for a short time thereafter an attempt was made to picture Madagascar as a modern Garden of Eden, the poets were likely to associate the earthly paradise with the islands of the Caribbeans. The attitude survived in the *Sacred Theory of the Earth*, Pt. II, ch. iii, where Burnet, otherwise opposed to the idea of an existing paradise, professed to find a survival of climatic features of the golden age in Bermuda.

For another view of guiltless and happy men in an earthly paradise, cf. the opening scene of Dryden's *Indian Emperour*. That Dryden even at this time was not tempted to idealize the state of savage innocence and ignorance is clear from *Charleton*, ll. 15–20. The testimony of English voyagers who were known to Dryden's contemporaries weighed heavily against any tendency to admire the savage state, which was commonly pictured as brutish.

For an earlier treatment of the earthly paradise or golden age, cf. *Ld. Ch.*, ll. 135–142 and note.

23–24 The Royal Society was fully aware of its indebtedness to Bacon. Cf. Sprat, *History of the Royal-Society* (1667), pp. 35–36. Also Cowley, "To the Royal Society" (1667), st. v:

> Bacon, like Moses, led us forth at last,
>   The barren Wilderness he past,
>   Did on the very Border stand
>   Of the blest promis'd Land,
> And from the Mountains Top of his Exalted Wit,
>   Saw it himself, and shew'd us it.

To some contemporaries, however, Dryden's praise might have seemed excessive. Even Sprat, in the passage cited above, pointed out limitations in Bacon's method and program.

25 *Gilbert*. William Gilbert (1540–1603) was physician to Queen Elizabeth and in 1600 became president of the College of Physicians. In the same year he published his *De Magnete*, which dealt with the properties of magnets as he had experimentally observed them, and which recognized that the earth itself acts as a great magnet.

27 *Boyle*. Robert Boyle (1627–1691), natural philosopher and chemist, who endowed the Boyle Lectures for the defense of Christianity against unbelievers. He was a member of the Wadham College group, and was

instrumental in founding the Royal Society. Although a constant experimenter best known for his work with gases, he was a formidable student of theology and able to read Hebrew, Greek, Chaldee, and Syriac.

28 *his great Brother.* Roger Boyle (1621–1679), Lord Broghill, who was created Earl of Orrery at the Restoration. He was the author of *Parthenissa,* a romance, and of several heroic plays. Dryden dedicated *The Rival Ladies* to him (1664).

31 *Harvey's name.* William Harvey (1578–1657), discoverer of the circulation of the blood. His theory was first offered in 1616 in a lecture and published in 1628 as *Exercitatio Anatomica de Motu Cordis et Sanguinis in Animalibus.* He was at one time physician to Bacon. According to Aubrey, Harvey thought highly of Bacon "for his witt and style, but would not allow him to be a great philosopher."

32 *Ent.* Sir George Ent (1604–1689), one of the original fellows of the Royal Society and a close friend of Harvey. Ent wrote a defense of Harvey's theory, which he published as *Apologia pro Circuitione Sanguinis* (1641), and he persuaded Harvey to publish his *De Generatione Animalium* (1651).

34 *Whose fame* etc. Apparently not an empty compliment. In 1684 Charles Goodall wrote of Charleton (*The Royal College of Physicians of London,* sig. [Uu4v]-[Xx1]):

> Dr. Charlton's very learned and laborious Works (as his *Diatriba de Lithiasi;* His *Oeconomia Animalis;* His *Exercitationes Pathologicae;* His *Inquisitiones Anatomico-Physicae;* His Book *de Scorbuto;* His *Anatomical Prelections* in the College Theatre, with many other ingenious Treatises,) have given him a very high and deserved Reputation in our own as well as foreign Universities. . . . And 'tis very well known how highly he hath been courted to accept of the Professors Chair at Padua.

35–36 It has been suggested that this is a remarkable anticipation of Römer's discovery of the gradual propagation of light, a discovery made some twelve years later (cf. W. T. Lynn, *N&Q,* XII [1903], 504). But Dryden in this instance scarcely deserves the honor of scientific prescience. In 1654 Charleton had written that the motion of light is not instantaneous, "but only Momentary, i.e. that Light is moved in a certain space of time, though imperceptible, yet divisible, and not in one individual point, or Instant" (*Physiologia,* p. 206). Charleton guessed that the speed of light exceeds that of a bullet (*ibid.,* p. 204).

36 *unspent.* Dryden's use of the word echoes a notion found in Aristotle and adhered to by Charleton, that is, that light perpetuates itself in flight. Cf. *Hastings,* ll. 105–106.

37–40 Charleton's enemies failed to take this charitable view of his eclecticism. Charleton himself was conscious of the attacks upon his work, "accusing me of usurping other men's Notions, Maxims, and Experiments for my own, without so much as naming the Authors, to whose bounteous Wit and Industry I was beholding for their discovery and communication" (*The Immortality of the Human Soul Demonstrated* [1657], p. 10). In his classification of philosophers Charleton provided a place for himself as a "renovator" who rescues the good parts of the ancients, and as "an Elector" who selects out of the ancients and moderns alike what can stand the test of reason and experiment (*Physiologia* [1654], pp. 3–4).

43–44 There is an obvious resemblance between this couplet and the second couplet of the following passage of Sir Robert Howard's "To My Worthy Friend, Dr. Charleton":

> How much obliging is Your learned Care!
> Still busie to preserve, or to repair;
> Which unto Men not onely life can give,
> But makes their Monuments themselves to live.

47–48 Cf. the final couplet of Howard's commendatory poem:

> That great Respects not onely have been found
> Where Gods were Worship'd, but where Kings were Crown'd.

53–54 Charles II had viewed Stonehenge during his involved journey of escape after the defeat at Worcester. In the dedication of *Chorea Gigantum,* addressed to Charles II, Charleton remarks upon the King's interest in Stonehenge:

> For, as I have had the Honour to hear from that Oracle
> of Truth and Wisdom, Your Majestie's own Mouth; You
> were pleased to visit that Monument, and, for many
> hours together, entertain Your self with the delightful
> view thereof, when after the defeat of Your Loyal Army,
> at Worcester, Almighty God, in Infinite Mercy to Your
> three Kingdoms, miraculously delivered You out of the
> bloody Jaws of those Monsters of Sin and Cruelty. . . .

It was this story told by the King, according to Charleton, that first prompted him to start an inquiry into the origin of Stonehenge.

57–58 Cf. Howard's commendatory poem:

> Nor is thy Stone-heng a less Wonder grown,
> Though once a Temple thought, now prov'd a Throne. . . .

To the Lady Castlemaine, upon Her Incouraging His First Play

In the first gay years of the Restoration no one was more notorious and no one had more influence with the King than Barbara Villiers, Countess of Castlemaine, who in 1670 was to become Duchess of Cleveland. A young playwright could scarcely have hoped for better fortune than to have her encourage his first play. How Dryden came to enjoy her patronage we do not know, but it was at the Court (and apparently by Lady Castlemaine's prompting) that *The Wild Gallant,* his first play, had what small success it achieved. In the preface to the printed version of this comedy he tells us that "it was receiv'd at Court; and was more than once the Divertisement of His Majesty, by His own Command."[1] When Pepys saw it at Court, 23 February 1663, he thought the play a poor thing but was entranced with the company. If his report can be trusted, Lady Castlemaine must have been among the few who really liked the comedy: "The King did not seem pleased at all, all the whole play, nor any body else, though Mr. Clerke whom we met here did commend it to us. My Lady Castlemaine was all worth seeing to-night and little Steward."

Dryden's poem, then, was in all probability written early in 1663. It was first printed in 1674 (see Textual Notes), very likely without his permission. When in 1693 it was again printed, certain changes had been introduced. By that time, since both Dryden and the Duchess had fallen on evil days, it would have been infelicitous for the poet to say:

> Well may I rest secure in your great Fate,
> And dare my Stars to be unfortunate.

And the compliment in line 58 may well have seemed tired and jaded in 1693. At any rate, these things were part of the six verses omitted from the revised version.

It may be somewhat surprising that Dryden allowed the poem to be published in the 1693 volume, for which he was at least partly responsible. The poem, thin and uninspired, was clearly below his own standards; the revisions, performed in a desultory fashion apart from the purposeful omissions, suggest that he had little interest in it. Perhaps he needed copy to satisfy Tonson, and so passed this little piece along to him.[2]

10 This paraphrases Lucan, *Pharsalia*, I, 128: victrix causa deis placuit, sed victa Catoni (The victorious cause pleased the gods, but the defeated pleased Cato).

19–20 These lines may have been suggested by a passage at the beginning of Bk. II of Lucretius' *De Rerum Natura*, which Creech translated thus:

> But above all 'tis pleasantest to get
> The top of high Philosophy, and sit
> On the calm, peaceful, flourishing head of it;
> Whence we may view, deep, wondrous deep below,
> How poor mistaken Mortals wandring go,
> Seeking the path to Happiness. . . .

24 *Noble Grandison*. The father of Barbara Villiers, William Villiers,

---

[1] Ed. 1669, sig. A2.

[2] The poem is contemptuously referred to in the anonymous "The Session of the Poets, to the Tune of Cock Lawrel," printed in the 1697 *Poems on Affairs of State* but probably written in the 1670's. After bringing Dryden before the court of Apollo and accusing him of stealing *The Wild Gallant* from Sir Robert Howard, the poem continues:

> Dryden, whom one wou'd have thought had more Wit,
> The censure of ev'ry Man did disdain,
> Pleading some pitifull Rhimes he had writ,
> In praise of the Countess of Castlemaine.

2d Viscount Grandison. In the Civil War, Grandison fought for the King and in July 1643 received a mortal wound. He was the uncle of George Villiers, Duke of Buckingham (Dryden's Zimri).

27 *Like them are good.* The stars are "good" because, by perfect obedience to nature's laws (which represent the will of God), they participate in the excellence of God's creation.

33–34 We are not able to determine what incident Dryden here refers to. Perhaps he had in mind a scene from Roman history to which he later alludes (cf. *Annus*, ll. 251–252 and note).

43–44 That is, *waiving* or *disregarding* the artful resolution of the plot, they solved their problem by introducing the *deus ex machina*.

45–50 These lines are vaguely reminiscent of the conceit in Shakespeare's sonnet beginning "When in the chronicle of wasted time."

Annus Mirabilis: The Year of Wonders, 1666

Annus Mirabilis was completed by 10 November 1666, at which time Dryden signed and dated the prefatory "Account." The poem was written at Charlton, Wiltshire, the seat of Dryden's father-in-law, the Earl of Berkshire. Here the poet remained, while the poem was dispatched to London for publication. Twelve days later it had been read and licensed for printing by Roger L'Estrange. The author's address to his brother-in-law, Sir Robert Howard, requesting him to correct the poem and care for it during the printing, suggests a degree of urgency and haste. Unfortunately Sir Robert proved less than diligent in the charge, and a large number of mistakes were made, even though Herringman, Dryden's usual publisher, had the work in hand. By the time Dryden returned to town, in December or early January, the sheets had been run off the press, and, unable to efface the errors, he hastily drew up a statement "To the Readers," followed by a list of errata. After such preparation the poem was published, probably in the latter part of January, 1667.[1] Pepys secured a copy in Westminster Hall on the first of February.

In the prefatory "Account" Dryden describes *Annus Mirabilis* as an historical poem, which, like panegyric, is a branch of epic poesy. The argument, he tells us, was supplied by Sir Robert Howard, who also encouraged him in the writing. There is a good possibility that the original argument consisted of the naval war and the "three glorious victories" resulting from it. The second battle was fought 1–4 June 1666, and the third, 25–26 July, followed by the burning of the Dutch fleet in the Vlie on 9–10 August. If this had been Dryden's subject, the poem could have been started early in August. These events bring the poem through stanza 208. But the fire of London, to the description of which (including a transition, and an account of the King's bounty to the sufferers) Dryden devotes stanzas 209–

---

[1] Entered in *Stationers' Register* on 21 January 1667.

287, lasted from 1 to 4 September; and because accurate details of the catastrophe spread slowly, he could scarcely have made any progress with this section of the poem before the middle of September.

That the account of the Fire may indeed have been added as a kind of afterthought is suggested by a slight change in style, and a somewhat more pronounced change in attitude and tone. Whereas the former part of the poem glorifies English skill, enterprise, and heroism, the latter part reflects rather tartly upon the behavior of the Londoners, the ignoble crowd, the only virtues conceded to them being their obedience and gratitude to the King during and immediately after the Fire. A subtle change in tone commences with stanza 212, containing the image, from Ovid, of the destruction of the world, with an allusion to the myth of regeneration in the figure of the phoenix. Clearly Dryden had heard of the terror and awe inspired by the Great Fire, in which the framework of heaven and earth appeared dissolved in flames, and he drew upon imagery of the supernatural to convey an impression of the disaster. Perhaps his imagination was stimulated by Virgil's account of the burning of Troy; it was certainly stimulated by visions of the *Dies Irae,* the Day of Judgment, and the terrors of night released by evil. Out of the Bible and the legends concerning Doomsday, out of Cowley's Pindaric odes "The 34. Chapter of the Prophet Isaiah," "The Resurrection," and "The Plagues of Egypt," out of Ovid and possibly Davenant and sundry others he drew a portion of the imagery to represent the meaning of the conflagration. And in *Annus Mirabilis* the terror of Doom is heightened by night, bringing the ghosts of traitors and bold specters, who revel, and the dire night hags, who come to dance their round; just as in Cowley the plagues call forth darkness and evil spirits who groan or revel.[2] In the midst of the catastrophe walks the King, righteous leader of his nation, like David or a minor prophet; and his prayers are heard, and the wrath of God is turned away from the people.

But the story of the fire was made to fit admirably into the larger design of the poem. Although the naval battles take up more than half of *Annus Mirabilis,* it is evident from the opening and the conclusion that a larger issue is involved. Trade is the subject of the beginning stanzas, and the wealth and power of London and of the kingdom, secured through trade, is the prophetic vision with which the poem closes. In between, Dryden reflects his theory of kingship, and tries to show the importance of Charles II in the developing mercantile state that was England. His theory of the state, as it may be gathered from the poem, can be summed up as follows: A healthy state seeks power and wealth; wealth flows in from the expansion of foreign trade; trade is the means of enriching the public treasury, and the nation's treasury alone has the resources to wage modern war; a strong king is needed to foster and protect trade, and to lead his people in war; and by victory in war the expansion of wealth and power is guaranteed.[3]

[2] Cf. Cowley, "The Plagues of Egypt," st. 13; "The 34. Chapter of the Prophet Isaiah," st. 6.

[3] In general, this is the pattern of the mercantile state as developed by seventeenth-century English theorists. For a brief summary of the theory, from

Annus Mirabilis attempts to demonstrate that the welfare of the nation, in peace as in war, depended upon "the care, management, and prudence of our King," upon his wisdom, power, and bounty. The incident of the fire enabled Dryden to illustrate the King's heroism, fatherly affection for his people, and bounty, as the naval battles and the repair of the fleet had illustrated his foresight, his genius for the building and supply of ships, and his brilliant leadership in war. As a powerful undercurrent we hear a warning as to the evil of rebelling against such a monarch, whose side is clearly favored by Providence.

Such was the larger design. Yet the title, dedication, and contents hint at a more immediate object, an object that would make the speedy publication of the poem desirable. The dedication displays Dryden's concern, for some reason or other, with trials and judgments of God. Why? The title, which offers a review of the great events of the year 1666, belies the contents, for the poem begins with a naval victory in June 1665, and omits one of the greatest "wonders" of 1666, the plague. Why?

The answer lies in the fact that *Annus Mirabilis* is, in one sense, a piece of inspired journalism, written to sway public opinion in favor of the royal government, which dreaded a revolution—a revolution which, according to republican propaganda, was to be ushered in by omens and portents, by "wonders" signifying the wrath of God against the King and his party. Because of the mystic properties of the figure "666," expectations of revolution had centered around the year 1666; years before, William Lilly had prophesied that "in 1666. there will be no King here, or pretending to the Crowne of England." Fear was widespread. Pepys, recording a conversation with Lord Sandwich on 25 February 1666, reported: "He dreads the issue of this year, and fears there will be some very great revolutions before his coming back again."

The fear had been building up from the beginning of Charles's reign. Bishop Parker related that in the years immediately following the Restoration unrest prevailed in certain quarters, stirred up by the publication of libelous pamphlets full of dire portents. These pamphlets, obviously of republican and dissenting origins, told of monstrous births, wondrous appearances, of crosses and humiliations befalling the King's friends, of signs betokening God's displeasure with the King and threatening to visit His heavy judgments upon the nation if it continued to support the royal government. Three of the pamphlets which Bishop Parker undoubtedly had in mind appeared in 1661–1662. They were entitled: the first, *Mirabilis Annus, the Year of Prodigies;* the second, *Mirabilis Annus Secundus: or, the Second Year of Wonders;* and the third, *Mirabilis Annus Secundus; or, the Second Part of the Second Years Prodigies.*[4]

English and continental sources, cf. Carl Friedrich, *The Age of the Baroque* (1952), pp. 12–14.

[4] The circumstances described in this and the following paragraph are related in greater detail by E. N. Hooker, "The Purpose of Dryden's *Annus Mirabilis,*" *HLQ,* X (1946), 49 ff.

How far these seditious tracts could prevail upon the superstitious and disaffected, nobody knew. But they were clearly dangerous. In *A Discourse concerning Prodigies* (1663) and again in *A Discourse concerning Vulgar Prophecies* (1665) John Spencer, a distinguished scholar of Corpus Christi, Cambridge, speaking both as a scientist and as a friend of the Establishment, attempted to expose the presumptuousness of those enthusiasts who, professing to read the secret will of God in signs and wonders, boldly ventured upon prophecy. A still more significant protest from the royalist side came from Thomas Sprat. As spokesman for the Royal Society, writing at almost exactly the time when Dryden was composing *Annus Mirabilis,* Sprat denounced the seditious practice of "amuzing mens minds, with Prodigies, and conceits of Providences" as a chief cause of the wild distractions into which the nation had been plunged—and "especially this last year," when "this gloomy, and ill-boding humor has prevail'd." [5]

Dryden's immediate object thus becomes apparent, and the urgency of his argument appears from Sprat's words. He was engaged in countering the effects of seditious propaganda represented by a group of pamphlets whose very title he employed against them. He demonstrated that the catastrophes of fire and plague could never be construed as the judgments of an angry God against the King, for in the same period God had blessed the royal government with three great naval victories. With meticulous care Dryden suggested at every point through the poem that heaven and Providence had favored the King's party. As for the interpretation of the catastrophes, Dryden may have recalled the prophetic curse of a royalist poet uttered against the King's enemies in a previous decade: [6]

> May sudden flames their houses melt away,
> And Feavers burn their houses too of Clay. . . .

But Dryden had no intention of insulting the fallen City. Lightly and tactfully he intimates that the disasters might have been punishments inflicted upon the City for its harboring rebellious factions in the past; and then he turns, quickly and thankfully, to the King's bounty and the City's loyalty immediately after the fire.[7] The conclusion of the poem is an appeal at once to the patriotism and the selfish interests of the City. By "passive aptness," by loyalty to the King in his great designs, the majesty of the City would be restored, and it would flourish in the wealth and power of the expanding mercantile state.

In suggesting the argument of *Annus Mirabilis* Sir Robert Howard, who had enjoyed court favor from the beginning of the Restoration, may well have been assured that this poem would give satisfaction to the King's friends. It is difficult to avoid the suspicion that *Annus Mirabilis* was a major factor in Dryden's appointment, little more than a year after the publication of the poem, as poet laureate.

---

[5] *History of the Royal-Society* (1667), p. 362.

[6] "To those who desire no Peace," *Rump,* I (1662), 27.

[7] Sprat likewise emphasized the extraordinary loyalty and resolution of the citizens after the Fire (*History* [1667], pp. 121–122).

What has been said thus far of Dryden's loyalist and patriotic intentions still leaves most of the special qualities of the poem to be explained. What else did he pour into the work? The period from 1664 to 1667 was a busy and productive one: heroic plays, tragicomedies, and a superb critical essay flowed from his pen.[8] In addition, it was a period of reading, speculation, and experiment, in which his eager curiosity, quick apprehension, the range and sensitivity of his critical faculty, and his extraordinary energy combined to lay up those riches of mind which prompted Dr. Johnson to remark: [9]

---

[8] The following are the literary events in Dryden's career from 1664 to 1667. The number of stage-productions and publications in 1667 strongly suggests that a few may have been planned or, in part, written during the long stay at Charlton.

1664
> January: *The Indian Queen* first acted, a little over a month after Dryden's marriage to Lady Elizabeth Howard.
> *c.* May: *The Rival Ladies* first acted.
> 27 June: *The Rival Ladies* entered in *Stationers' Register.*

1665
> 7 March: *Four New Plays,* including *The Indian Queen,* received the imprimatur of L'Estrange.
> Spring: *The Indian Emperour* first acted.
> 5 June: Theaters closed on account of the plague. Dryden probably fled to Charlton shortly afterward.
> Summer: "Verses to the Dutchess" probably written. *Of Dramatick Poesie* begun at about this time.

1666
> Summer: *Of Dramatick Poesie* essentially finished by this time. *Secret Love* probably finished. On 10 November Dryden wrote that he had not long since given Sir Robert Howard a new play to read, almost certainly *Secret Love.* Most of September and October must have been given to composing *Annus Mirabilis.*
> 10 November: *Annus Mirabilis* completed, the prefatory matter signed and dated.
> December: Dryden probably returned to London late this month or early in January.

1667
> 15 January: *The Indian Emperour* revived on the stage.
> 21 January: *Annus Mirabilis* entered in *Stationers' Register,* and probably published within a few days.
> 2 March: *Secret Love* performed. It may have been acted earlier.
> Spring: *The Wild Gallant* revised and acted, following the success of *Secret Love.*
> 7 August: *Secret Love* entered in *Stationers' Register. Of Dramatick Poesie* entered in *Stationers' Register,* with dedication to Buckhurst recently written.
> 15 August: *Sir Martin Mar-all* first acted.
> 12 October: Dedication of *The Indian Emperour* signed and dated. The play printed soon thereafter.
> 7 November: *The Tempest* acted, apparently for the first time.

[9] Life of Dryden, BH, I, 417.

His works abound with knowledge, and sparkle with illustrations. There is scarcely any science or faculty that does not supply him with occasional images and lucky similitudes; every page discovers a mind very widely acquainted both with art and nature, and in full possession of great stores of intellectual wealth.

To this it might be added that his reading in literature was extensive, and probably much less desultory than Dr. Johnson suspected. It would be impossible to trace all, or even most of, the writings that lent a gleam to his imagination as he composed *Annus Mirabilis,* but there are a few which suggest themselves to our notice.

Ovid, the Bible, and three of Cowley's Pindaric odes, as we have observed, helped to furnish Dryden with imagery to represent the Great Fire. Waller's example, perhaps, suggested the opening stanzas, and occasional images or phrases here and there were contributed by various other poets. But among the things which occupied Dryden's mind in the period of *Annus Mirabilis* there are four which seem to have a special relationship to the poem: Lucan, Shakespeare, Virgil, and the investigations and purposes of the Royal Society.

The more elusive of these are Lucan and Shakespeare. That Dryden had Lucan in mind is clear from the prefatory "Account," which recognizes the Latin poet's priority in describing a sea fight. And there is no doubt that Dryden knew more of the *Bellum Civile* (or *Pharsalia*) than the third book. In certain particulars the *Pharsalia* provided hints that Dryden developed for his own purposes, as in his description of the dreams of the Dutch sailors. Beyond this, the Stoic Lucan was, as Dryden points out in the "Account," much addicted to "the morality of a grave sentence"; and in *Annus Mirabilis* the indulgence (though sparing) in sententious utterance, such as in the speech of Stoic courage given to Albemarle (sts. 100–101), together with a preoccupation with fate, carries the suggestion of Lucan along with it. The *Pharsalia,* moreover, besides being a glorification of Stoic virtues, is an illustration of the horrors of rebellion and civil war.

It is not without significance that Dryden's magnificent tribute to Shakespeare was written at about the same time as *Annus Mirabilis,* and that his first adaptation of Shakespeare, *The Tempest,* was produced only a few months after the publication of the poem. This seems to have been the period of Dryden's first great enthusiasm for Shakespeare. We do not know precisely what excited him most, but *Macbeth* seems to have been fresh in his mind, and he apparently read the chronicle histories with attention; the epilogue to *The Tempest* refers to the bloody visions of *Richard III,* and there are faint clues in *Annus Mirabilis* pointing to *2 Henry IV* and *Richard II.* Shakespeare's chronicle histories could have meant various things to Dryden, but not least that they presented an elevated concept of kingship and illustrated the horrors of rebellion.

With Dryden's interest in the work of the Royal Society we follow a much more clearly marked path. His tribute to that august body (sts. 161–166), though it looks at first like a digression, proves to be an essential part in the meaning of the poem. Preceding stanzas describe the genius of the King in naval undertakings, and the natural talents of the English people in commerce and navigation. Then follows the list of discoveries in the art of navigation which the Royal Society would soon bestow upon the nation, enabling English shipping to master the seas. The welfare of the country, then, was best served by following the leadership of the King, whose genius was exactly fitted to develop those talents in his people which led to wealth and power. Thus the section contributes to the larger design of the poem.

The whole poem, in fact, bears remarkable testimony to Dryden's sympathy with the purposes and labors of the Royal Society. The patriotic fervor that we see in *Annus Mirabilis* burns as well in Sprat's *History of the Royal-Society* (1667), where the connections between trade and mechanic arts, and navigation and naval strength, and wealth and power, and submission to the sovereign authority of the King, as necessary features of the expanding mercantile state, are made even more explicit than in Dryden's poem.[10] In *Annus Mirabilis* and the *History of the Royal-Society* we observe the same anxiety to protect the government from the unrest stirred up by the sinister interpretation of prodigies, and the same rejoicing in the courage and loyalty displayed by the City after the plague and fire. Both defend the new philosophy on the grounds that an understanding of the admirable works of God leads to a realization of His power and glory.[11] In both we find the blithe assurance that nature will reveal more of its secrets to the English than to any other nation,[12] and in both the same emphasis on sea power and on the importance of the Royal Society's future contributions to the art of navigation.[13] What is perhaps even more remarkable is that Sprat vigorously argues for the value of the fresh and significant imagery provided by the experimentalists just as Dryden was writing a poem utilizing such imagery.[14]

In *Annus Mirabilis* Dryden draws imagery from both the old and the new science, even as the Royal Society in its early stages collected both old and new, without great rigor in choosing between truth and falsehood.[15] Yet the subjects of natural philosophy from which Dryden selected imagery and allusion were generally those with which the society was currently occupied. The passage on precious stones reflects the discussions then going on among fellows of the society and other scientists.[16] The theory of the tides and their relationship to the moon constituted a major problem in the society.[17] The discovery of the longitude presented the strongest sort of challenge to the society, and the King had offered a reward to the

10 Cf. Sprat, especially pp. 421–425, 78–79.
11 *Annus*, ll. 657–660; Sprat, p. 82.
12 *Annus*, ll. 641–644; Sprat, pp. 114–115.
13 *Annus*, ll. 33–53, 645–664; Sprat, pp. 404, 150.
14 Sprat, pp. 413–419.
15 *Ibid.*, p. 95.
16 Cf. *Annus*, l. 10n.
17 *Ibid.*, ll. 645–648n.

discoverers.[18] The theory of the growth of metals was being examined by the society, and remained current in scientific circles at least as late as 1695.[19] The theories of comets, ranging from poetic fantasy up to the generally accepted view, recall to us that a history of comets, especially of the two recent ones, was one of the society's projects.[20] Even the spicy forests of Ceylon had been a subject of the society's queries.[21] All in all, there can be no doubt that Dryden was deliberately employing the new kind of material drawn from nature, which the Royal Society was earnestly recommending to the attention of English men of letters.

Interestingly enough it was not the scientific imagery but the use of technical terms in describing naval battles, and Latinisms adapted from Virgil, which Dryden underscores in the preface. Latinisms, though by no means all from Virgil, are present in abundance—in much greater abundance than, apparently, even Verrall suspected. But these words retaining their Latin sense were scarcely a startling innovation, for most of them had appeared previously in English, though perhaps less thickly. Along with the words used in their Latin sense, however, we find expressions that render Latin idioms more or less literally (such as "frequent funerals" and "finish all the deaths") and that obtrude upon our attention. These expressions remain curiosities of language, distinguished neither for greatness nor beauty. What appears remarkable is that these experiments in ways of elevating poetic style were made precisely at the time when Milton was about to issue *Paradise Lost.*

Dryden's use of nautical terms was an innovation that met with little or no favor. Actually the technical terms introduced in the description of the naval battles are relatively few and inconspicuous.[22] The passage where they attract attention to themselves is the account of the repairing of the fleet. Here the poet does employ terms that had not before been adapted to the language of poetry. Readers of the passage are not likely to find their understanding impeded by the number of strange words. As a matter of fact, the objection felt by neoclassical critics was not that the terms are technical and particular but that they are low and indecorous, unsuited to the dignity of heroic verse. Whether they are suited to the passage in which they occur is a question that has not been answered.

Whatever the opinion of Dryden's experiments in the language of poetry, his use of nautical terms reveals something of the tastes and attitudes that were shaping his poetry. In the first place, his defense of technical terms in the prefatory "Account" rests upon their accuracy; common terms in poetical descriptions, he says, conceal ignorance, just as general terms in a logical dispute are likely to conceal a fallacy. In this attitude we must discern a reflection of the Royal Society's vigorous disapproval of

---

[18] *Ibid.,* ll. 649–652n.

[19] *Ibid.,* ll. 553–556n.

[20] *Ibid.,* ll. 64–72n.; Sprat, p. 258.

[21] Sprat, p. 169.

[22] As Dr. Johnson remarked (BH, I, 433): "In the battle, his terms seem to have been blown away; but he deals them liberally in the dock. . . ."

general terms.[23] The second point worth noting is that Dryden was somehow encouraged in his use of nautical terms by his model, Virgil. It is
striking that years later, after he had abandoned his defense of technical
terms in poetry, he still thought it no impropriety in translating Virgil to
introduce such nautical terms as *tack to the larboard, veer starboard, stand
to sea, weigh anchor, stand to your tackle, luff to wind, scud amain,* and
slips his haulsers.[24]

The impact of Virgil upon *Annus Mirabilis* is certain, though the manner of it is less than obvious. In the prefatory "Account" Dryden confesses
his obligation to Virgil, "my master in this poem." He points to a few
Virgilian images in the poem, and intimates that the reader may amuse
himself by discovering even more. This is something, but scarcely enough
to justify the sweeping acknowledgment of indebtedness. Dryden's interest
in Virgil, of course, was not new. In 1660 he had written the *Astraea,*
incorporating (as we have observed in the introduction to that poem) a
meaningful Virgilian element in the very structure of the poem. But the
full extent of his debt in *Annus Mirabilis* will not be understood unless
we recall his statement, made years afterward, that he had drawn his con-
ception of poetical wit and imagination from Virgil.[25] In this connection
it is necessary to remember that the preface to *Annus Mirabilis* contains
his first extensive pronouncement (preceded only by a few scattered remarks
in the dedication to *The Rival Ladies*) on wit and imagination. Thus
Virgil was deeply involved in Dryden's thoughts on this matter of prime
importance just at the time when he was planning and writing the poem.

One more train of associations will help to define the nature of Virgil's
influence. Some little time before writing *Annus Mirabilis* Dryden had
become interested in Lucretius to the extent of designing a translation of
portions of *De Rerum Natura.*[26] This interest, though it was not to be
fulfilled for two decades, apparently led Dryden on to a greater work of
the same kind, Virgil's *Georgics,* which he thought of as an imitation of
Lucretius and as a poem more perfect in its type than even the divine
Aeneid.[27] That he had the *Georgics* fresh in mind when he wrote *Annus
Mirabilis* is suggested by the number of borrowed images; it is even possible that he had translated portions, for several expressions in *Annus
Mirabilis* recur in the version of the *Georgics* printed years afterward.

In the *Aeneid* Dryden found a concept of kingship that strongly appealed
to him; and we notice that in his poem he makes Charles II, like Aeneas,
the father of his people, "pious," like Aeneas, in the paternal care which
he exercises over his subjects. Like Aeneas, too, Dryden's king, we are
made to feel, is an instrument of heaven's designs. He has his share of valor

---

[23] Sprat, pp. 16–17.
[24] Cf. Dryden's *Aeneis,* III, 526, 527, 721–722; IV, 602; V, 21–22, 43, and 1011.
The quick eyes of Dr. Johnson had noted a few of these (BH, I, 462).
[25] Preface to *Sylvae* (1685), sig. A6 (Ker, I, 256).
[26] *Ibid.,* sig. a5 (Ker, I, 264).
[27] *Ibid.,* sig. A8v (Ker, I, 259).

as befits the subject of heroic verse, but it is valor, like that of Aeneas, of a most civilized kind, in which wisdom and goodness are generously commingled.

But Dryden stresses his interest in the *Georgics*. In 1666 the *Georgics* struck him as "the divinest part" of all Virgil's writings; and the reason for his great admiration, he intimates, was the excellence of those images of nature in which the *Georgics* abound, and of the poetic style in which they are presented. The reader of *Annus Mirabilis* may well observe the plenty and variety of the images drawn from nature. There are figures and images drawn from the activities of eagles, martins, falcons, and crows, of lions, beavers, hares and hounds, serpents, spiders and flies, bees, and elephants and rhinoceroses, of whales and swordfish. Sun, moon, stars and comets, rivers and ocean, winds and storm, spices and gums, golden sand, gems and metals—these are part of the material woven into the poem. Yet they do little to explain why or how the *Georgics* impressed Dryden at this time.

The answer lies in the fact that in the *Georgics* Dryden found a poem astonishingly adaptable to his needs. It was of the epic variety, for it aroused admiration for virtue, it celebrated the heroic mind, it struck the note of patriotism, and it employed the machinery of gods in the affairs of earth's creatures. More to the purpose, however, is the extraordinary tact with which Virgil gives dignity and significance to ordinary, humdrum things. There is a divine order in nature, in which the least object participates: [28]

> For God the whole created Mass inspires;
> Thro' Heav'n, and Earth, and Oceans depth he throws
> His Influence round, and kindles as he goes.

Moreover, the order in nature is essentially rational, and can be apprehended by human understanding. On this subject Virgil sounds like a member of the Royal Society: [29]

> Happy the Man, who, studying Nature's Laws,
> Thro' known Effects can trace the secret Cause.

Virgil gives dignity and honor to lowly occupations, representing the sire of the gods himself as inventor and patron of the handicrafts and practical arts, under whose auspices ships were built, commerce by sea developed, and observations in astronomy made to facilitate navigation.[30] It is especially interesting that Dryden saw in the little society of the bees the activities of "trading citizens," and in their hive, "the busy shop" where the riches of trade are deposited.[31] The perplexities and worries of statecraft are to be left to the prince. Throughout the *Georgics* we are taught that virtue involves minding our own business diligently, and submitting to fate and the will of heaven.

How ingeniously Dryden adapted the *Georgics* to his own purposes may

---

[28] Dryden's *Georgics*, IV, 324–326.
[29] *Ibid.*, II, 698–699.
[30] *Ibid.*, I, 187–210.
[31] *Ibid.*, IV, 20 and 26.

by this time be discerned. Writing an heroic poem to glorify the mercantile state, he exhibits the dignity of the varied arts necessary to the state, including commerce and shipping, ship repair, and even the art of naval combat essential in trade wars—all of which gain added dignity from the interest and patronage of the monarch. Science, likewise under the patronage of the king, is not only the search into the laws of nature and the mind of God, but also the means by which the secrets of nature are applied to the art of navigation, giving preëminence to English commerce. That Providence favors the king, and that the king has a special genius for ships and naval warfare, indicate that the order of nature is consonant with English mercantile success. For English subjects, virtue consists in "passive aptness"—or diligence in their callings, and submission to the will of heaven and the authority of the king.

How fully the *Georgics* served as a pattern for *Annus Mirabilis* is a matter requiring more detail than can be given here. Enough has been said, however, to suggest with what justice Dryden called Virgil "my master in this poem." And his interest in Virgil's world-soul, manifest in the prefatory "Account," strengthens our belief that his sight flew beyond the scattered words and images which he admits to borrowing.

The imagery of *Annus Mirabilis* is profuse and varied. It exists, according to Dryden himself, not to carry a heavy undertone of passion, but primarily to excite wonder—the proper object of heroic poetry. The image, then, should be bright and vivid. It may merely reflect a commonplace object; in that event it becomes excellent if the words, the sound, the movement of the poetry are so "connatural to the subject" that they bring it to life before us. Or the object may be transmuted, by means of a trope, into something slightly different, something new and delightful. If a poet's imagery is successful, remarks Dryden, "we sit, as in a play, beholding the scenes of what he represents." In *Annus Mirabilis* many of the images give delight because they present, not static objects, but miniature scenes and actions, moving pictures of the near and remote, nature infused with life and motion.

One fact about the images should not be overlooked. Dryden observes that though the same images serve equally for epic and historical poems, those of the historical poem are treated in a somewhat different way, not being subject to the same requirements of severity and elevation. This ought to be sufficient warning. One of the main objections to the imagery of *Annus Mirabilis* has been directed against its occasional lapse from heroic dignity. Why sustained elevation should be demanded of a poem addressed to the metropolis of London is not immediately clear. On the surface the mood of *Annus Mirabilis* is sober. But Dryden's mind was rich and curious, and as a gifted comic poet he was aware of multiple implications in word or image. Even in 1666 he was exploring the unexpected capacity (or, shall we say, ambiguity?) of imagery. For example, the figure in lines 91–92 is accepted by Van Doren as suitably heroic; but Dryden at the same time was using the same figure as a pleasantry in *Secret Love*. Again, the simile in stanza 59 strikes Van Doren as a ridiculous illustration to set against the dignity of the first two lines; but Dryden was using the sober image of the lofty Belgian ships as part of the roisterous comedy of *Secret Love*. Anyone who willfully persists in mistaking the character of Dryden's lucidity will perhaps be best confounded by stanza 61. The naïve reader may find in it a noble and dignified picture of a gnarled old warrior-hero; but even he, prepared by a knowledge of the circumstances (see notes), will discover in the image, besides the portrait of a hero, one of the most delectable pieces of raillery in the literature of the seventeenth century.

Annus Mirabilis is remarkable for the skill by which an urgent, practical problem is raised to a subject of universal meaning. Historically the poem is interesting as one of the most ingenious imitations of Virgil's *Georgics*, and the first notable poem in English in which a significant body of images are deliberately selected from current experiments in natural philosophy or from scientific theories currently exercising reputable scientists. With all this, the poem has variety and life. It moves easily from the realm of the mundane, of trade and shipping and science, to the plane of the heroic and spectacular. The style is plain, but it has strength and nobility when those qualities are needed.

THE VERSE

Annus Mirabilis is the second, and last, of Dryden's poems to be written in the *Gondibert* stanza. During the eight-year interval between this work and the panegyric to Cromwell, he retained an interest in the form, and experimented with it. In *The Rival Ladies*, IV, i (produced *c.* May, 1664), Manuel is given a soliloquy containing two *Gondibert* quatrains. *The Indian Queen*, II, i and III, i (produced January, 1665), presents scenes of heroic love as well as of heroic valor, in which more than a dozen *Gondibert* stanzas are used. Again in *The Indian Emperour* (produced, spring of 1665) near the end of Act I there is an idyllic passage between Cortez and Cydaria in which six *Gondibert* stanzas occur. As a result of this, and perhaps other, experimentation, Dryden in composing *Annus Mirabilis* was more fully aware of the resources of this special form of quatrain than he had been in 1659.

As a long poem with extensive narrative stretches *Annus Mirabilis* required a sort of coherence and continuity that would have been unsuited to the *Heroique Stanzas*. This problem Dryden attempted to meet by grouping his quatrains, tying two or more together by grammatical or rhetorical links, or by linking through rhyme or assonance. The clearest and tightest method of connection is the purely grammatical, as seen in stanzas 16–18, 40–41, 86–87, 107–109, 139–140, 144–145, 172–173, 174–175, 213–215, 219–220, 251–252, 262–263, and 284–285. Besides this, various rhetorical devices of linking stanzas are employed. Thus, parallel and complementary adverbs may open two successive stanzas, as in stanzas 218–219 and 296–297. Or a stanza may begin by picking up a significant word or two from the last line of the preceding stanza, as in stanzas 20–21 and 47–48. Or a pronoun emphasized in one stanza may be repeated in parallel order in the following one, as in stanzas 146–148 and 206–207. Moreover, there are fairly numerous instances of linking through rhyme and assonance (cf. ll. 196–197n.). In addition, a number of simple transition words can be found; *thus* or *so,* for example, will introduce a quatrain that serves to illustrate the thought of the preceding stanza. In these and other ways Dryden attempted to avoid the effect of a string of disjointed stanzas.

In spite of the grouping which we have described, Dryden has yet managed to retain the identity of the stanza in *Annus Mirabilis.* Each stanza is complete, commonly ending in a period; no stanza is concluded in a pause of less than a semicolon in value. The structure within the stanza is firm. Only eight strong internal stops occur within the entire poem. Ordinarily the lines within the stanza are end-stopped, and the movement tends to break after the second line. Yet Dryden perceived that an invariable break in the middle of the stanza, productive of a seesaw monotony, would be intolerable, and he provided for variety. In only 48 per cent of the stanzas is the break sharp and decided; nearly 27 per cent have no pause, or no pause greater than a comma in value, after the second line; and 25 per cent show only a slight break.

Concluding the line with a verb form is calculated to increase the impression of strength and stateliness. It is interesting to note that 48 per cent of the lines in *Annus Mirabilis* are thus ended, as against the 57 per cent in the poem to Cromwell and 32 per cent in the Hastings elegy. As one might expect, lines concluding in a verb form are more frequent in the first two hundred stanzas, which describe the naval scenes, than in the remainder of the poem. One weakness attached to such lines is that they are often achieved at the cost of padding with a form of the auxiliary verb *do.* In the *Heroique Stanzas* 16 per cent of the lines are burdened with such padding; in *Annus Mirabilis* a greater technical skill has reduced the proportion to 7 per cent. And, as with the verb endings, the frequency diminishes after stanza 199.

Sound and cadence are, for the most part, managed with art. Clusters of monosyllables no longer bothered Dryden. He could give them a light and soaring movement, as in stanza 110:

> And first the Martlet meets it in the sky,
> And, with wet wings, joys all the feather'd train. . . .

Or he could give them a massive energy and explosiveness, as in line 478: "And his loud Guns speak thick like angry men. . . ." There are thirty-seven wholly monosyllabic verses in the poem, and one would hesitate to assert that they are consciously designed for specific effects. Yet it is worth noting that in several of them the words are so weighted that the rhythm is slowed down, making for a deliberative, emphatic statement. Perhaps for this reason monosyllabic lines are more likely to occur in the second than in the first half of the stanza.

When *to* or *the* is followed by a word commencing with a vowel, synaloepha commonly, though not always, takes place. There are thirty instances in *Annus Mirabilis,* of which only four (ll. 129, 273, 871, and

932) are somewhat awkward. Contractions are numerous, and often without apparent reason. By synaloepha and contraction the poet may avoid hypermetrical lines, but Dryden seems not to have been anxious to avoid them. There are approximately a hundred hypermetrical lines in *Annus Mirabilis*—so many that it is difficult to think they resulted from the printer's failure to make indicated contractions. And there are certain lines, such as 235–236,

> Such port the Elephant bears, and so defi'd
> By the Rhinocero's her unequal foe,

which a reader can trim down to regularity only by a willful perversity.

Hypermetrical lines are only one device which Dryden used to avoid rigidity in the verse movement. A strongly accented trochee introduces nearly 7 per cent of the lines. And nearly 8 per cent commence with two or three unaccented syllables. A number of lines are effectively introduced by a spondaic foot. How these may combine in varied rhythm and pleasing cadence may be illustrated by stanza 248:

> Thus, to some desart plain, or old wood side,
> Dire night-hags come from far to dance their round:
> And o'r brode Rivers on their fiends they ride,
> Or sweep in clowds above the blasted ground.

Substitutions are, of course, made freely in other parts of the line as well. By these devices and by the artful management of sound Dryden goes far to subdue the pentameter verse to his requirements.

His gift for stately and vigorous lines has been recognized. But he had more subtle effects at his command. A great many illustrations can be found in *Annus Mirabilis,* but two must suffice. First, to suggest the languor of exhaustion after heavy labor (ll. 391–392):

> And weary waves, withdrawing from the fight,
> Lie lull'd and panting on the silent shore.

And second, to suggest, quickly and unemphatically, the grim irony in the peace that descends upon the waters after a disaster (ll. 375–376):

> The wild waves master'd him, and suck'd him in,
> And smiling Eddies dimpled on the Main.

It must be confessed, there are flats, and even depressions, in *Annus Mirabilis,* but in the main they do not spring from any deficiency in Dryden's prosodical resources.

DEDICATION, AND ACCOUNT OF THE POEM

P. 48: l. 8 *by cheaper trials.* Throughout the dedication and in the poem itself, Dryden plays subtly on political and commercial themes, always with the design of strengthening the bonds between the people and the throne. For details, cf. introduction.

49:22 *trouble of perusing a Play for me.* For Dryden's relations with Howard, cf. introductions to *Howard* and *Annus.* The play here referred to was *Secret Love, or The Maiden Queen.*

A connection between Dryden and Howard, hitherto unnoticed, is apparent from a manuscript recently acquired by the Clark Library. It is an indenture, dated 6 September 1661, concerning the privilege granted Howard and his father the Earl of Berkshire to collect Post fines in the Court of Common Pleas. Dryden signed the document as a witness of Howard's signature.

50:8 *Royal Admiral.* James, Duke of York. The "incomparable Generals" were Prince Rupert and the Duke of Albemarle.

50:15–16 *All Gentlemen are almost oblig'd to it.* In the navy of the Restoration the presence of gentlemen volunteers as opposed to "tarpaulin" or professional sailors was much commented on. When the fleet was refitting before the St. James's Fight, which Dryden describes in sts. 178 ff., noblemen flocked to join up.

50:27–28 *But since the Action is not properly one.* Dryden here reflects a commonplace of critical theory which stems ultimately from Petronius (*Satyricon,* c. 118), who warned the poet against following historical fact too closely. In his attack on the mere historical poet, Petronius was generally understood to refer to Lucan and his *Pharsalia.* In the essay *Of Heroique Playes* Dryden referred to Petronius as "the most elegant, and one of the most judicious Authors of the Latine tongue . . ." (1672, sig. a3*v;* Ker, I, 152), quoted with approval his comment on the use of history in the epic, and remarked that Lucan "followed too much the truth of history." It may be, as Ker has suggested, that Dryden's discussion in the preface to *Annus* was prompted by Davenant, who had written in the preface to *Gondibert* (1673, p. 2; Spingarn, II, 3–4):

> Lucan, who chose to write the greatest actions that ever were allowed to be true (which for fear of contemporary witnesses, oblig'd him to a very close attendance upon Fame) did not observe that such an enterprize rather beseem'd an Historian, then a Poet: For wise Poets think it more worthy to seek out truth in the Passions, then to record the truth of Actions; and practise to describe Mankind just as we are perswaded or guided by instinct, not particular persons, as they are lifted, or levell'd by the force of Fate, it being nobler to contemplate the general History of Nature, then a selected Diary of Fortune: And Painters are no more then Historians, when they draw eminent persons (though they term that drawing to the life) but when by assembling divers figures in a larger Volumn they draw Passions (though they term it but Story) then they increase in dignity and become Poets.

Silius Italicus. Titus Silius Italicus (A.D. *c.* 25–101), author of the historical epic *Punica.*

51:6 *tied to the slavery of any Rhyme.* Cf. Dryden's defenses of dramatic rhyme, published at about the same time as this statement, in the dedication of *The Rival Ladies* (1664), *Of Dramatick Poesie* (1668), and the *Defence of An Essay of Dramatique Poesie* (1668). By female rhyme Dryden means double rhyme with feminine ending. He spoke again of female rhymes in the preface to *Albion and Albanius.*

51:25 *Alarique.* Dryden refers to two French heroic poems of the seventeenth century: *Alaric ou Rome sauvée* (1654) by Georges de Scudéry and *La Pucelle* (1656) by Jean Chapelain.

51:27 *old Translation of Homer.* Ker noted that the verse of Chapman's *Iliad* was the septenarian, not the alexandrine.

51:30–31 *much better defended in the Preface to Gondibert.* Davenant wrote (1673, p. 8; Spingarn, II, 19):

> I shall say a little, why I have chosen my interwoven Stanza of four, though I am not oblig'd to excuse the choice; for numbers in Verse must, like distinct kind[s] of Musick, be exposed to the uncertain and different taste of several Ears. Yet I may declare, that I believ'd it would be more pleasant to the Reader, in a Work of length, to give this respite or pause, between every Stanza (having endeavored that each should contain a period) then to run him out of breath with continued Couplets. Nor doth alternate Rime by any lowliness of Cadence make the sound less Heroick, but rather adapt it to a plain and stately composing of Musick; and the brevity of the Stanza renders it less subtle to the Composer, and more easie to the Singer, which in *stilo recitativo,* when the Story is long, is chiefly requisite.

51:33–34 *Naval Fight in the proper terms.* Ker (I, 286) observed that Dryden shared with Ronsard an appreciation of technical words in poetry. Probably his use of nautical language in *Annus* was the result of his enthusiasm for the program of the Royal Society, philological as well as experimental. Cf. introduction to *Annus.* By the time he wrote the preface to his *Aeneis,* toward the end of his career, he had lost his early enthusiasm for technical terms, but even then he did not argue that they should be altogether eliminated from the epic. In his translation of the *Aeneid* he employed nautical phraseology, but not in such profusion as in *Annus.*

When or how Dryden learned his sea language, we have been unable to discover, but it is likely that the library of the Earl of Berkshire at Charlton contained handbooks which served him as a guide.

52:9–10 *Descriptas servare.* Horace, *Ars Poetica,* 86–87: (If I cannot keep the accepted rules and the tone of poetic works, and do not know them, why am I called a poet?)

52:26 *Omnia sponte* etc.: (The most righteous earth returns all of its own free will). Noyes observed that this seems like a schoolboy's exercise, with hints taken from Virgil, *Georgics,* II, 460 and *Eclogues,* IV, 39; and Ovid, *Metamorphoses,* I, 416–417 and *Fasti,* IV, 370. Dryden's line is an hexameter.

53:5–12 *The composition . . . ought to be of wit.* In his account here of wit (including fancy, imagination, and judgment) Dryden considers a subject which fascinated him all his life and to which he returned in many of his essays.

Ker suggested that Dryden was following Davenant's statement on wit in the preface to *Gondibert*. Unquestionably Dryden knew the passage, but the literature on wit, extending from the ancients to the writers of his own day, was so vast that it is highly unlikely that any one writer was the source for his ideas here or elsewhere. The comparison of the imagination to the nimble spaniel evidently pleased him, for he had already used it in the dedication of the *Rival Ladies* (1664), where he had written that "Imagination in a Poet is a faculty so Wild and Lawless, that, like an High-ranging Spaniel, it must have Clogs tied to it, lest it out-run the Judgment (sig. A4; Ker, I, 8). He may have picked up the figure from the *Leviathan* (I, iii), where Hobbes in speaking of the train of imagination had written: "Sometimes a man knows a place determinate, within the compasse whereof he is to seek; and then his thoughts run over all the parts thereof, in the same manner, as one would sweep a room, to find a jewell; or as a Spaniel ranges the field, till he find a scent; or as a man should run over the Alphabet, to start a rime."

For a detailed account of Dryden on wit and the imagination, cf. Commentary on *The Authors Apology for Heroic Poetry and Poetic License* in this edition.

53:17 *jerk or sting of an Epigram.* Since the heroic poem was universally associated with lofty dignity, it is not surprising to find Dryden inveighing against the use of epigram, antithesis, and paronomasia. He was later (*Of Heroique Playes*) to speak of Lucan, who "too often offer'd at somewhat which had more of the sting of an Epigram, than of the dignity and state of an Heroick Poem" (1672, sig. a4; Ker, I, 152); and of Tasso (*Discourse concerning the Original and Progress of Satire*), who is "full of Conceipts, points of Epigram and witticisms; all which are not only below the Dignity of Heroick Verse, but contrary to its Nature . . ." (1693, p. vii; Ker, II, 27).

It will be noted that Dryden does not exclude grave sentences from the heroic poem, though he is doubtful of their value, especially when used often. The propriety of sententiae in the epic was much discussed in French and English criticism of the seventeenth and eighteenth centuries. French critics were wary of them (cf. René Bray, *La Formation de la doctrine classique en France* [1931], pp. 77–78), arguing like Le Bossu that an overabundance of them renders a poem too philosophical. English critics differed in their conclusions, but generally were willing to accept them if they were used sparingly.

53:30–31 *For the two first of these.* In comparing Ovid and Virgil, Dryden was writing of the two Latin poets who above all others appealed to him. In the essay *Of Dramatick Poesie,* written at about the same time as *Annus,* he praised Ovid for his dramatic powers, as well as his writing in the "epic way," and at one time used the same phrasing as here: "movements of a Soul combating betwixt two different Passions" (1668, p. 24;

Ker, I, 53). For an account of Dryden's interest in Ovid, cf. introduction to *Ovid's Epistles*. Virgil he confessed to be his master in *Annus* (cf. introduction and notes).

The vocabulary of the passage on Ovid and Virgil is notable as an example of how easily Dryden (in common with most contemporary critics) turned to terms drawn from painting when he discussed poetry. Ovid's images are pictures, touched with tender strokes; Virgil's pictures are achieved with bold, masterly strokes. Implicit also are two references to historical painting, closely allied in the theory of the day with epic: Virgil's figures have their proper "motions," that is, they display in gesture, posture, and facial expression their passions, their states of mind. Virgil's world, moreover, is a world of ideal beauty, similar to the ideal beauty that the painter depicts in his histories. The *locus classicus* for the treatment of motions and passions (*moti ed affetti*) was Giovanni Paolo Lomasso's *Trattato dell' Arte della Pittura, Scoltura et Architettura* (Milano, 1585), translated in part by Richard Haydock and published at Oxford, 1598. In his second book, Lomasso goes to absurd lengths in cataloguing every possible emotion, illustrating usually from Dante, Ariosto, or Tasso the manner in which poets have expressed these emotions in the actions and postures of their characters. Lomasso's ideas are echoed in most writings on painting during the seventeenth century.

There is ample authority in literary criticism from Aristotle through Scaliger and on into Sidney and even Davenant for the idea that the world of the epic is a heightened and ideally beautiful version of reality. Dryden's criticism of Virgil is consistent on this point. For the development of the theory of ideal beauty in painting, see Erwin Panofsky's *Idea* (*Jahrbuch für Kunstwissenschaft*, VI, 1928) and Rensselaer W. Lee's "Ut Pictura Poesis" (*Art Bulletin*, XXII [1940], 197–210). Dryden developed both of these ideas in his *Parallel of Poetry and Painting*.

The unexpected use of Virgil's world-soul (Dryden's *Aeneis*, VI, 980–992) to illuminate the process of artistic creation is in Dryden's best critical manner.

54:24–25 *Totamque infusa. Aeneid*, VI, 726–727: (Mind, suffused throughout the frame, moves the entire mass, and mingles with the mighty body).

54:28–31 *lumenque juventae. Aeneid*, I, 590–593: ([His mother] had breathed on him the bright light of youth and joyful glory on his eyes: such grace as hands give to ivory, or when silver or Parian marble is encircled by yellow gold).

55:6 *Materiam superabat. Metamorphoses*, II, 5: (The workmanship surpassed the material).

55:13–14 *Dixeris egregie. Ars Poetica*, 47–48: (You will have spoken well, if a skillful method of connecting makes a well-known word new).

55:31–32 *Et nova. Ars Poetica*, 52–53: (New words and words recently coined will gain acceptance, if they come from a Greek source, sparingly changed).

As Verrall noted, there are few linguistic innovations in *Annus*, but

the poem shows frequent use of Latin phrasing. It is probably this sort
of innovation that Dryden had in mind. (Cf. introduction and notes.) His
considered opinion on word coinage, written over twenty-five years later
in the preface to his *Aeneis* (1697, sig. f2v; Ker, II, 234–235), was cautious:

> Upon the whole matter, a Poet must first be certain
> that the Word he wou'd Introduce is Beautiful in the
> Latin; and is to consider, in the next place, whether it
> will agree with the English Idiom: After this, he ought
> to take the Opinion of judicious Friends, such as are
> Learned in both Languages: And lastly, since no Man
> is infallible, let him use this Licence very sparingly; for
> if too many Foreign Words are pour'd in upon us, it
> looks as if they were design'd not to assist the Natives,
> but to Conquer them.

56:13–17 *for the one shows Nature.* In the contrast between the painting of a fair woman and of a lazar, Dryden found a useful image which
could illuminate a number of critical and aesthetic ideas. He returned
to and varied this theme in four other critical essays. In this passage, the
ugly is regarded as a deviation from nature (in the ideal or the normative
sense of that word), a deviation that provokes laughter rather than disgust
and that is the antithesis of the high beauty of heroic poetry and idealized
painting, which evoke admiration, i.e., wonder as well as approbation.
In the *Defence of an Essay* (1668) Dryden argues that, although *Bartholomew Fair* is the "lowest kind of comedy," it is none the less art, since
it differs from the life by having been duly "heightened." Jonson, he says,
"hath made an excellent lazar of it; the copy is of price, though the
original be vile." Something of the same idea is repeated in the preface
to *Tyrannick Love* (1670) when, defending the character of Maximin, he
remarks that "there is as much art, and as near an imitation of nature,
in a lazar as in a Venus." In both these instances *lazar* implies imperfection, deformity, the ugly; but *nature* in the second has lost its normative
meaning and is equivalent to factual reality, to things as they are. In the
dedication of *Aureng-Zebe* (1676) comedy in general is identified with the
imitation of the lower and imperfect aspects of human nature, when
Dryden admits that he is weary of "drawing the deformities of life, the
lazars of the people." Finally, in the *Parallel of Poetry and Painting*
(1695), he associates comedy ("the representation of human life in inferior
persons and low subjects") with genre painting ("clowns, the representation of a Dutch kermis, the brutal sport of snick-or-snee"). Though
admitting that this kind of painting imitates nature, Dryden considers
it low. "Such is a Lazar in comparison to a Venus: both are drawn in
human figures, they have faces alike, though not like faces." Below comedy
and genre painting are farce and the grotesque, which are outside nature
altogether.

It is clear that Dryden habitually thought in terms of the sister arts and
their parallel, and that he held to a hierarchy of the genres, which equated
epic with historic painting, comedy with genre painting, and farce with

grotesque. The existence of these genres depends upon the Aristotelian distinction of imitating the actions of men better than ourselves, like ourselves, or worse than ourselves. What is not so clear is what precisely Dryden meant by *lazar* and what specific painting, if any, he had in mind.

Contemporary theory of painting (but not always contemporary practice) taught the importance of correcting nature's defects and of attaining the ideal beauty in the higher genres. Dürer, of course, had opposed this tendency in Italian renaissance theory, but he had been an exception (*"Der grosse asthetische Exkurs," Von menschlicher Proportion,* III). Caravaggio and his imitators had introduced a new naturalism into even their religious paintings. It is precisely on this ground that Bellori disapproved of Caravaggio, whom he accused of imitating deformity; and it was because of the eclectic beauty of Annibale Carracci's figures that Bellori regarded the Bolognese as a restorer of painting (*Le Vite de' Pittori* [Roma, 1622], pp. 19 ff. and 201 ff.). Dryden's interest in the unbeautiful and the ugly in art derived not only from Aristotle's remarks on comedy, but probably also from actual more or less naturalistic paintings and drawings with which he was familiar. He may, of course, have seen a painting of a leper; Dutch genre painting might have provided his fool.

It is not easy to determine the full significance of the word *lazar* for Dryden. If he meant specifically a leper, the contrast with a fair woman is a violent one, and he has introduced into his aesthetic experience what we should call the grotesque. Blount, Philips, and all writers of dictionaries in the eighteenth century gloss the word only as "leper," and the *OED* records no other meaning. Johnson illustrated his definition ("One deformed and nauseous with filthy and pestilential sores") by quoting from the dedication of *Aureng-Zebe.* But it is possible that Dryden used the word in a more general, and even perhaps in a foreign sense. In Italian *lazzarone* is applied to one of the lowest class in Naples, and hence suggests the proletarian poor of a great city. In Spanish *lazarillo* means a boy who leads the blind beggar. (Hence the name of the hero of *Lazarillo de Tormes,* which had been newly translated by David Rowland in 1653.) St. Lazarus, of course, is the patron saint of beggars. If Dryden used the word *lazar* with these associations in mind, it could have connoted for him not only the general idea of the grotesquely deformed and ugly, the nauseously diseased, but also the blind and maimed beggars of actuality and art.

Elisabeth Sudeck's "Bettlerdarstellungen von Ende des XV. Jahrhunderts bis zu Rembrandt" (*Studien zur Deutsche Kunstgeschichte,* no. 279 [Strassburg, 1931]) discussed the varied and numerous treatments of beggars in European art from Hieronymous Bosch to Rembrandt. She demonstrates the existence of a continuous tradition of beggar art in drawings, engravings, and paintings, some realistic, some grotesque and comic, some sentimental, some picturesque, but almost all well outside the typically renaissance cult of the *beau ideal.* Though in the renaissance chiefly characteristic of German and Dutch art, beggars figure in the work of Annibale Carracci and, in seventeenth-century France, of Jacques Callot. Callot designed a series of street criers and beggars which influenced such Dutch artists as Frederic Bloemaert, Peter Quast, and Saloman Savery, the last of whom lived for a short time in England. It is possible, then, that Dryden saw prints that depicted *lazzaroni* in all their poverty, disease, and ugliness; and that they suggested to him his lazar and such low comedy as *Bartholomew Fair*. The existence of this tradition could hardly have failed to raise critical questions in his inquiring mind. And it is just possible (though the evidence is far from conclusive) that we have here a clue to one of his actual aesthetic experiences.

It is also possible that his interest in the ugly in art was awakened by the well-known third chapter of Plutarch's *De Audiendis Poetis,* in which occurs the famous statement that poetry is a speaking picture and painting a silent poem. Plutarch discusses the paradox that the imitation of ugly objects in a painting can and does give pleasure, and he draws the oversimplified conclusion that our pleasure comes from the recognition of likeness. Turning to poetry he draws a distinction between our responses to a man afflicted with sores in actual life and in tragedy: the one revolts, the other gives pleasure. Dryden treats the idea with much more complexity and sophistication.

Be this as it may, the persistence of the theme in Dryden's criticism suggests that he found it somehow useful in dealing with certain aesthetic concepts and that painting was occasionally helpful to him. Paintings of a fair woman and of a lazar not only helped to illustrate the methods of imitation proper to several genres, but also certain ideas that are constants in his criticism: that art is imitation, whether of the low or of the ideal, the ugly or the beautiful, and that much of its interest derives from its being imitation; that even low subjects must be artfully treated, must be heightened; that *nature* includes not only the conventional ideal norm, but also reality, even in its least attractive aspects; that heroic poetry and heroic painting alike evoke admiration, but that comedy and burlesque, together with their equivalent genre painting, though dealing with the low and the laughably deformed, refer by inference to a normative nature by depicting deviations from the ideal beauty which the higher kinds seek to express. The parallel between the two arts was not always fruitful for Dryden, but here he seems actually to have used it to his own advantage.

56:20–21 *Stantes in curribus. Satires,* VIII, 3: stantes in curribus Aemilianos (Aemilian [ancestors] standing in their chariots).

56:22–23 *Spirantia mollius. Aeneid,* VI, 847: excudent alii spirantia mollius aera ([Others will shape] more smoothly [statues of] breathing bronze).

56:27 *humi serpere.* Cf. Horace, *Ars Poetica,* 28: serpit humi tutus nimium timidusque procellae (He creeps on the ground, too careful and fearful of the gale).

56:29 *Nunc non erat. Ars Poetica,* 19: (Now it were not the place for them).

57:1 *When, for our sakes,* etc. For Dryden's more detailed account of the naval victory here referred to, see stanzas 15 ff. and notes. The Duke of York took command of the fleet in March. On the 23d, the King, the Duke, and the Duchess went down to the *Hope* aboard Sandwich's ship the *Prince*. From there the Duke sailed to the Gunfleet in his yacht (cf. *Journal of Edward Montagu, First Earl of Sandwich,* ed. R. C. Anderson [1929], p. 171). By 7 April the fleet was still "a league and a half thwart off the northern buoy of the Gunfleet sand" within sight of Harwich (*ibid.,* p. 173). It finally weighed anchor on 21 April.

57:18 *when God's people past.* See Exodus, XIV, 21–22.

58:2 *So Moses was upheld.* See Exodus, XVII, 11–13.

58:17 *Leaving our Southern Clime.* After the battle of Lowestoft, Parliament petitioned the King not to allow the Duke to risk his life again in battle. Charles ordered James out of command of the fleet. The plague was raging in London during the summer of 1665, and in late June the court moved first to Hampton Court and then to Salisbury. On 5 August, Charles sent the Duke and Duchess to the north. At this time James was extremely popular and his progress was a triumph. Sir Charles Lyttelton, who was with the party, wrote from York on 7 August (*Hatton Correspondence,* Camden Society [1878], I, 47):

> Last night wee gott hither, having bine mightily feasted and welcomed by the appearance of the nobillity and gentlemen of the contrys with the volunteer troopes as wee passd; but more especially at Sr George Saville's, whose entertainment was indeed very splendid. Hard by his house mett us on the way my Ld of Newcastle and my Lady, whose behavior was very pleasant, but rather to be seene then told. She was dressd in a vest, and, instead of courtesies, made leggs and bows to the ground with her hand and head. The Duke made his entry heere very gloriously, being attended by a greate many nobillity and gentry of theese parts, wth guards of severall regimts and troopes; the Lord Mayor (who presented him, after a very long and courtly speech, to acknowledge his Royal Highss his merrit from the nation for the late victory and other heroick acts, wth a purse of a 100 li in gold, and another to the Duchesse) and all the aldermen and chiefe cittisens going bare before us.

59:1–2 *nec sunt parum.* Pliny, *Ep.,* VII, 28: (There are not a few who call it discernment to disparage their friends).

POEM

1–20 In the Life of Dryden Dr. Johnson remarked that "The initial stanzas have rather too much resemblance to the first lines of Waller's poem on the war with Spain . . ." (BH, I, 431). There is a rough similarity between Dryden's opening stanzas and the first eighteen lines of Waller's "Of a War with Spain, and a Fight at Sea." A few other resemblances exist between subsequent parts of the two poems (cf. notes below).

Dryden opens his poem with a statement of the causes of the second Dutch war, correctly assigning them to commercial rivalry. This conflict, as G. N. Clark points out, is the clearest example of a purely commercial war in English history (cf. *The Later Stuarts* [1949], p. 60). The first Dutch war of 1653–1654 had ended in an advantageous peace, but had left unsettled the commercial rivalry. The extent to which the Dutch engrossed the carrying trade was an old grievance which the Navigation Act of 1651, reinforced at the Restoration, had not ended. One of the most interesting of the economic treatises issued in this decade, Thomas Mun's *England's Treasure by Forraign Trade* (written years before, but not published until 1664, when the time seemed ripe), devotes a portion of its pages to the damages incurred by England through the Dutch shipping and fishing interests. A second war became virtually inevitable. As early as 2 February 1664, as Pepys tells us, men were discussing in coffeehouses the benefits of a war with Holland, saying "that the trade of the world is too little for us two, therefore one must down." Throughout the poem, and especially at the conclusion, Dryden keeps the reader in mind of the economic significance of the Wonderful Year.

2 *cruel when abroad.* Thomas Mun complained of the cruel and unjust violence employed by the Dutch, especially against the English (*England's Treasure by Forraign Trade* [1664], p. 206). In 1665 a treatise had appeared, entitled *His Majesties Propriety, and Dominion on the British Seas Asserted; together with a true account of the Neatherlanders insupportable insolencies . . . As also their prodigious and horrid cruelties in the East and West Indies, and other places.* The instance of cruelty most bitterly remembered, of course, was the massacre at Amboyna in 1619.

4 In the years immediately following the return of Charles II Holland evinced a strong desire for peace and entered into negotiations with England for a trade agreement; the negotiations were carried on from 1660 to 1662, but neither side yielded much. The Dutch seem to have sent lacquered cabinets as gifts to tempt the English ministers, and possibly offered money (cf. Keith Feiling, *British Foreign Policy, 1660–1672* [1930], p. 81). Of their courting the King we have no knowledge. Dryden probably means to say simply that Holland sought peace with England even while her ships and merchants were committing acts of aggression against English merchants.

8 *so base a Coast.* Probably a pun on the French term for the Netherlands, Les Pais-bas.

10 As L. I. Bredvold has shown (*PMLA*, XLVI [1931], 956), during Dryden's time there was still a good deal of speculation about the origin of precious stones. Sir Thomas Browne, discussing one phase of it in refuting the vulgar notion that crystal is concreted ice or snow, remarked (*Pseudodoxia Epidemica*, II, i; *Works*, ed. Keynes, II, 87–88):

> Diodorus in his eleventh Book denieth it, (if Crystal be
> there taken in its proper acception, as Rhodiginus hath
> used it, and not for a Diamond, as Salmasius hath ex-

pounded it) for in that place he affirmeth; *Crystallum esse lapidem ex aqua pura concretum, non tamen frigore sed divini caloris vi.*

At a meeting of the Royal Society on 27 May 1663 the origin of metals and stones was discussed (Birch, *History of the Royal Society* [1756–1757], I, 247). Some present thought

that minerals were produced by certain subterraneous juices, which passing through the veins of the earth, and having mingled therewith, do afterwards precipitate and crystallize into stones, ores and metals of various kinds and figures, according to the various kinds of salts contained in the juices and the earth.

As early as 1660 Robert Boyle had considered the possibility of concretion from liquids, and in 1672 he wrote (*An Essay about the Origine & Virtues of Gems*, p. 5):

Having thus explain'd in what sense my Conjecture about the Virtues of pretious Stones is to be understood; it follows that I propose the Conjecture or Hypothesis it self; the substance of which may be compriz'd in these Two particulars: First, That many of these Gems, and Medical Stones, either were once fluid Bodies, as the Transparent ones; or in part made up of such substances as were once fluid: And secondly, That many of the real Virtues of such Stones may be probably deriv'd from the mixture of Metalline and other Mineral substances, which (though unsuspectedly,) are usually incorporated with them. . . .

We find a somewhat similar image in a speech of Almanzor's (2 *Conquest of Granada*, III, i; S-S, IV, 157): "Bright as young Diamonds in their infant dew."

Christie called attention to the fact that line 10 is part of a passage from which John Oldham seems to have borrowed. Cf. Oldham's "David's Lamentation for the Death of Saul and Jonathan," st. vii.

On the "growth" of metals, cf. ll. 553–556n.

11 Idumaea was a region in southern Palestine, but the odorous juice of the balsam tree was found in Syria, Egypt, and Arabia as well.

Dryden had previously used the figure in the *Rival Ladies*, III, i (S-S, II, 177): ". . . thy Tears / Are sovereign, as those drops the balm-tree sweats." Cf. also Dryden's *Georgics*, I, 86; II, 165–166. Some of the images in sts. 3, 25, and 26 may have been suggested by Virgil's *Georgics*, I, 56–59, in which the *virosa castorea* (cf. *Annus*, l. 97) are mentioned.

12 *And in hot Ceilon* etc. One of the queries sent out by the Royal Society concerned the cinnamon trees in the isle of Ceylon (cf. Sprat, *History of the Royal-Society* [1667], p. 169).

14–16 Dryden's image and authorial note show an acquaintance with recent speculative developments in contemporary physics. (Cf. C. W. Adams' account of Dryden's sources for this passage, *Isis*, XLIV [June,

1953], 100–101.) In 1644 Descartes (*Principia philosophica*, Pt. IV, secs. 49–56) advanced the theory that tides result not from lunar attraction but from lunar pressure. In the same year Giles Persone de Roberval published his *Aristarchi Samii de mundi systemate*, a revised edition of which Marin Mersenne included in his *Novum observationum physico-mathematicarum . . . Tomus III* (1647). In this work Roberval substantially adopted the Cartesian tidal theory, which he further developed by declaring that the pressure of the lunar plenum, being greater along the line of the equator and less at the poles, depresses the equatorial waters and pushes them outward through the temperate to the arctic zones (ed. Mersenne, III, 31–32). At the time Dryden was writing, Roberval's theory seems to have had only limited currency, but it was subsequently popularized in Jacques Rohault's *Traité de physique* (1671), the vade mecum of Cartesian physics.

16 *Belgian.* That is, of the Netherlands. Cf. also ll. 309, 369, 725, 753, 825, 917, etc. In the geographies of the seventeenth century Belgium was synonymous with the Netherlands (cf. Richard Peers, *The English Atlas*, IV [1682]).

17–20 The first war with the Dutch had been waged successfully by Cromwell in 1653–1654. Cf. the epilogue to *Amboyna* for Dryden's later use of the parallel of England to Rome, Holland to Carthage. Noyes called attention to the notoriety which the comparison attained from the speech of Shaftesbury before Parliament 5 February 1673, when, referring to the Dutch, he used Cato's famous phrase, *delenda est Carthago.*

37–56 Dryden correctly represents Charles II as balancing the issues of war and peace. As the King wrote to his sister Henrietta, he had never seen such a lust for war in his people, but he was determined not to be swayed by it. He would be guided only by the honor and good of England, and would be firm in his resolution. But if forced into a war, he would meet it with a navy as fine as men had ever seen. Cf. Arthur Bryant, *King Charles II* (1935), p. 173. Finally, however, the King yielded to the popular outcry for war, being reconciled to it by an unprecedented grant of £2,500,000. He issued a formal declaration of war in March 1665, but fighting had already taken place in West Africa and in New Netherlands.

38 A rendering of a common Latin idiom, as in *consilia eventis ponderare* (Cicero, *pro Rabirio Postumo*, I, i) or *belli consilia expendere* (Tacitus, *Historiae*, I, 87).

40 *Usurpers* refers to Cromwell, who defeated the Dutch in the previous decade. Cf. ll. 17–20n.

49–50 The enormous growth in armies and navies during the seventeenth century made the financing of them a crucial matter. Navies were especially costly. As G. N. Clark points out, a navy, together with facilities for shipbuilding and maintenance, and the large and efficient organization required to support them, were a drain on national resources which only a rich nation could endure (*The Seventeenth Century* [1950], pp. 101, 118–119).

51–52 Cf. Virgil, *Georgics*, II, 325–326:

tum pater omnipotens fecundis imbribus Aether
coniugis in gremium laetae descendit
(Then the almighty father, the Sky, descends in fruitful showers upon the lap of his joyful consort).

Dryden's image is taken from the art of distillation. *Limbecks,* or alembics, were the instruments of distillation, employed in chemistry and alchemy; they were symbols of change or transmutation.

53–56 The King's delight in ships and the sea was already well known. Later John Sheffield wrote of him (*Works* [1723], II, 59–60):

> Besides, the great and almost only pleasure of mind he
> appeared addicted to, was shipping and sea-affairs; which
> seemed to be so much his talent both for knowledge, as
> well as inclination, that a war of that kind was rather an
> entertainment, than any disturbance to his thoughts.

53 *assert the watry Ball.* Perhaps a Latin idiom. The Latin *asserere* regularly means *to claim.*

54 Cf. *Aeneid,* VII, 706–707: magnum / Agmen agens Clausus, magnique ipse agminis instar. . . . Dryden translates thus (*Aeneis,* VII, 975): "And in himself alone, an Army brought."

57–60 In the Life of Dryden Dr. Johnson remarked (BH, I, 431): "It would not be hard to believe that Dryden had written the two first lines seriously, and that some wag had added the two latter in burlesque."

59–60 Christie pointed out that in note *d* Dryden was inaccurate in his quotation. Cf. *Georgics,* IV, 387–389 and 394–395:

> Est in Carpathio Neptuni gurgite vates
> caeruleus Proteus, magnum qui piscibus aequor
> et iuncto bipedum curru metitur equorum.
> quippe ita Neptuno visum est, immania cuius
> armenta et turpis pascit sub gurgite phocas.

For Dryden's translation cf. *Georgics,* IV, 557–560 and 567–568.

62 Cf. Sidney, *Astrophel and Stella,* xiii, 12: "Phoebus drew wide the Curtaine of the skyes."

64–72 The first of the comets appeared to European observers on 17 November 1664, and disappeared after 18 March 1665. The second became visible on 14 December 1664 and remained until the following March or April (Alexandre Pingré, *Cometographia* [1784], II, 10–21). Together they provoked an extensive literature of astrological interpretation and scientific controversy; and both aroused courtly and intellectual interest in England, as may be seen from Pepys's *Diary* during these months (cf. especially the entries for 17 December 1664 and 1 March 1665). Among other works they inspired the royalist astrologer John Gadbury's *De Cometis: or, a Discourse of the Natures and Effects of Comets* (1665), which may have suggested Dryden's use of divergent theories about comets. Gadbury (p. 62) lauds the time of the comets as "not only, ANNUS (sed AETAS) MIRABILIS."

Dryden's first theory, that comets "unctuous exhalations are," was the accepted view (Gadbury, for example, prefers it), stemming ultimately from Aristotle's *Meteorologica*, 341b–344a, as modified by Tycho Brahe's discovery that comets occur above the moon and hence might be "Fir'd by the Sun."

Dryden's second theory, that comets are illusions, was a more daring view advanced in Galileo's *Saggiatore* (1623) and duly summarized by Gadbury (p. 5).

Dryden's third theory is apparently a poetic fantasy of his own analogous to Shakespeare's line (*Midsummer Night's Dream*, II, i, 153): "And certain stars shot madly from their spheres."

Dryden's fourth theory is an ingenious mingling of scientific hypothesis and poetic myth for the purposes of courtly compliment. Newton and Halley were soon to demonstrate the periodicity of comets, but the theory had been immemorially familiar since Pliny the Elder's mention of it as a current speculation in classical times (*Natural History*, II, xxiii, 94). As Gadbury remarks (p. 5), ". . . some there are again, that hold that Comets are Wandering stars of Planets; seldom seen, by reason either of their neerness to the Sun, or their too far distance from the Earth. . . ." Dryden adds to this speculation the mention of Charles's birth star, which he had already celebrated in *Astraea*, l. 288.

Dryden's arrangement of his materials here can hardly be fortuitous. He starts with the familiar notion, moves to the scientific hypothesis, follows with a poetic myth, and ends with a synthesis of hypothesis and myth. He returned to the comets in ll. 1161–1164.

67 *slippery Star*. Probably a Latinism. The verb *labor* means *to slide,* or *slip,* as in *sidera labi* (Propertius, IV, iv, 64). Bell notes that "sliding stars" is an image fairly common in poets before the Elizabethan age, and in some later writers. From Surrey's translation of Virgil he quotes: "And sliding starres provoked unto slepe."

The image may bear an allusion to the popular belief that a fallen star appears as a slippery splotch of jelly. Ker (I, 321) notes Dryden's awareness of this belief in the song of the spirits, *Tyrannick Love*, IV, i. Cf. also Donne, "Epithalamion," ll. 204–205 (Grierson, I, 139):

> As he that sees a starre fall, runs apace,
> And findes a gellie in the place. . . .

71 *round of greater years*. "The rolling year" (*volventem annum*) is a common Latin idiom. Somewhat closer to Dryden's expression is Virgil's *annuus orbis* (*Aeneid*, V, 46).

72 *his walks of light*. A rendering of *solisque vias* (*Aeneid*, VI, 796).

73–76 The Duke of York took command of the fleet on 23 March 1665. In May he put to sea as Admiral of the Fleet, and in command of the Red squadron, with Sir John Lawson as vice-admiral of the Red and Sir William Berkeley as rear-admiral. Prince Rupert, vice-admiral of the entire fleet, commanded the White, with Sir Christopher Myngs as vice-admiral and Robert Sansum as rear-admiral. The Earl of Sandwich commanded the

Blue, with Sir George Ayscure as vice-admiral and Thomas Tiddeman as rear-admiral. On the 2d and 3d of June the battle off Lowestoft took place, here referred to by Dryden—the battle which provided the background for the essay *Of Dramatick Poesie*. The losses on both sides were severe, but the victory was clearly with the English. On 8 June, Pepys recorded his delight in hearing the news of the victory, and a little later set down an account of it. It is vibrant with the excitement which Englishmen felt at the news.

75–76 It was an important phase of Dryden's purpose to keep the reader mindful of the favor which Heaven had shown to the King and the royal family.

75 *fortune did confess*. A Latin idiom, as in *fortunam vultus fassa* (Ovid, *Epistulae*, IX, 126). The Latin *fateri* often means *to bear witness to*.

77–84 More than one English visitor to Venice in the seventeenth century described the "Sposalizio del Mare" on Ascension Day. Venetian dignitaries on the Bucentaur, the state galley, were rowed to the Adriatic where, according to Edmund Warcupp, "after certain Ceremonies, the Duke solemnly marries the Sea, and casts therein a Gold Ring, in real assurance of this Republicks Dominion thereof" (*Italy in its Original Glory, Ruine and Revival* [1660], p. 16).

Never forgetting the maritime destiny of Britain, Dryden here refers to it in terms of the Venetian ceremony. Heaven acts as proxy for Charles, and the precious thing, the gage or pledge which it throws down, is Admiral Lawson. Lawson, one of the most distinguished navy men of the Commonwealth, had declared for Charles and had been vice-admiral of the fleet which went to Holland to return Charles at the Restoration. During the battle with the Dutch he was wounded and died later, on 29 June 1665.

82 Cf. Ovid, *Metamorphoses*, II, 12; *Tristia*, I, ii, 59. Poole gives "green-haired" as a proper poetic adjective to use with "Syrens" (*The English Parnassus* [1657], p. 199). Cf. *All for Love*, IV, i (S-S, V, 404): "sea-green Syrens." Dryden's *Aeneis*, I, 205–206, has "the Sea-green Train / Of beauteous Nymphs"; *Georgics*, IV, 474: "her Sea-green Sisters." Cf. also *King Arthur*, IV, i (S-S, VIII, 183): "our Sea-green Locks."

84 A reference to Protesilaus, the first Greek to leap upon the Trojan shore and the first to be killed. Cf. *Iliad*, II, 695–702.

85 Opdam, commander of the Dutch fleet, was killed in the afternoon of 3 June when his ship engaged the *Royal Charles*, commanded by the Duke of York. After a short encounter, Opdam's ship blew up, killing most of the personnel aboard. Shortly thereafter the Dutch broke off the action and sailed for home. The English gave chase. Dryden tactfully omits any reference to the willfulness of Lord Brouncker, who while York slept countermanded his orders and caused the fleet to slacken sail, thus losing all chance to overtake and destroy the Dutch.

92 Strongly reminiscent of a passage in Dryden's *Secret Love*, III, i (S-S, II, 452):

> . . . as, when it thunders,
> Men reverently quit the open Air,
> Because the angry Gods are then abroad.

Cf. also Dryden's *Fables*, "Of the Pythagorean Philosophy," l. 95: "If Thunder was the Voice of angry Jove. . . ."

93–120 In July 1665 the English fleet under the command of the Earl of Sandwich was cruising about in northern waters in an attempt to intercept the Dutch Admiral De Ruyter on his way home from America, and the Dutch Indiamen, laden with rich cargo. The King of Denmark was in secret negotiation with the English government to aid the British fleet in taking Dutch ships which might be in his harbors, provided he was given half the spoils. Having heard of the Dutch ships which had taken refuge in the harbor of Bergen, Sandwich on the afternoon of 26 July detached eighteen of his ships under the command of Sir Thomas Tiddeman to attempt the capture of the prizes (*Journal of Edward Montagu, First Earl of Sandwich*, ed. Anderson, p. 251). On 1 August, Tiddeman arrived off Bergen "with the 15 sail of men of war and 2 fireships" (*ibid.*, p. 261). The Danish commander of the city had not received orders from his king, and so refused to coöperate with the English, asking that the attack be delayed until he could get orders. Tiddeman refused to wait, and on the morning of the 2d began to fire on the Dutch ships. Dryden was wrong in speaking of seven English ships. Tiddeman wrote to Sandwich (*ibid.*, p. 262): "I got 8 sail in a line, and brought our broadsides on the ships in the harbour, which spread from one side to the other, the other 7 I placed against the Castle as well as they could be placed." The Danes joined with the Dutch in repelling the attack and forced the English to withdraw. Line 120 perhaps refers to the difficulty which Tiddeman reported about anchorage and the use of fire ships (*ibid.*, pp. 262–263):

> The dispute lasted 3 hours and a half, the wind right out of the port, that for my heart I could not get the fireships in, there being so many guns placed on me, that cut to pieces our cables, so that we had like to have drove foul of one another. The wind blew right out, being at South, the worst place that ever men came to; no anchoring without the buoy, so that we were constrained to come to this place to secure our ships, which I bless God brought safe off to Gjelte Fjord, 5 leagues from Bergen.

On stanzas 24–30, Dr. Johnson remarked in the Life of Dryden (BH, I, 432):

> In this manner is the sublime too often mingled with the ridiculous. The Dutch seek a shelter for a wealthy fleet: this surely needed no illustration; yet they must fly, not like all the rest of mankind on the same occasion, but "like hunted castors"; and they might with strict propriety be hunted, for we winded them by our noses—their *Perfumes* betrayed them. The *Husband* and the *Lover*, though of more dignity than the *castor*, are images too

domestick to mingle properly with the horrors of war. The two quatrains that follow are worthy of the author.

96 *fatal.* Fated; or, more likely here, fateful, bearing the threat of disaster. Cf. also l. 866.

97 *Castors.* Beavers, from whose sacs a substance for making perfume was extracted. Cf. Dryden's *Georgics*, I, 87.

101 Cf. *Ld. Ch.*, ll. 73–76.

106 *unequal.* That is, in which the odds are strongly against one side. Note *pugna iniqua* (*Aeneid, X,* 889).

113–116 This passage may have been suggested by the description of a fiery death surrounded by burning spices and gums, found in Waller's "Of a War with Spain, and a Fight at Sea" (*Poems,* ed. Thorn-Drury, II, 26). Lady Winchilsea in her Pindaric "The Spleen," l. 41, may have had the final line of Dryden's passage in mind. Also Pope in the *Essay on Man,* I, 200. The line faintly suggests the description of the Phoenix in Dryden's *Fables,* "Of the Pythagorean Philosophy," l. 599: "He liv'd on Odours, and in Odours dies."

121–124 On 29 August, De Ruyter, convoying some sixty merchant ships, left Bergen for home. A violent gale scattered his force, and in the next two weeks the English fleet under Sandwich was able to capture a number of the Dutch vessels.

123–124 Cf. *Her. St.*, ll. 137–138.

125–140 Christie pointed out that sts. 32–34 are based on the same chapter in Petronius from which the quotation in note *g* is taken. Apparently Waller took the same hint for a passage in his poem "Of a War with Spain, and a Fight at Sea," ll. 51–60 (*Poems,* ed. Thorn-Drury, II, 25).

138–139 note *g. Satyricon*, c. 115: (If you reckon carefully, shipwreck is everywhere).

145–148 In the second Dutch war, England's only ally was Bernhard von Galen, the Bishop of Münster. In June 1665 an agreement between him and England was signed, whereby he in return for a subsidy was to invade Holland. He actually launched an invasion, but was easily driven back; and in April 1666 he "fraudulently" made peace, only some two months after Louis XIV had entered the war on the side of Holland.

146 note *h. Annals*, XIII, liv: nullos mortalium armis aut fide ante Germanos esse exclamant (They shout that no men excel the Germans in arms or in loyalty).

149–152 It is notable here that Dryden treats scornfully the idea that friendship might depend on interest, or that goodness might depend on power. He could scarcely have been a devoted follower of Hobbes at this time. An equally clear indication of his attitude occurs in a speech by Philocles (a noble and righteous man) in *Secret Love*, IV, i (S-S, II, 480):

Int'rest makes all seem reason that leads to it.
Int'rest that does the zeal of Sects create,
To purge a Church, and to reform a State.

155–164 France had threatened by warning the English court that if they persisted in hostility toward the Dutch, France would declare war.

Finally, on 6 January 1666, the declaration was made; England followed with a declaration against France on 10 February. Louis, with his eye on the Spanish Netherlands, took care to participate in the conflict as little as possible. He was not inspired by "secret hate" but by *realpolitik*. He wanted an England weakened by war and subservient to his continental ambitions, not a nation victorious over Holland and able to play her traditional role of protector of the Low Countries.

165–166 Denmark had been courted by both sides. She had found herself in a difficult position after the English attack on Bergen. After much vacillation she took her stand with France and Holland against England in February 1666.

169–176 According to the London *Gazette* for 29 January–1 February 1666 the French proclamation of war subjected Englishmen and their estates in France to immediate hostilities. After protest by the English ambassador, Louis issued a second proclamation, "in which, he allows three moneths time to the English, to transport themselves and their estates out of this Kingdom." The *Gazette* for 8–12 February gave an account of Charles's declaration of war, exhibiting his superior kindliness toward foreigners. It promised

> That if any of the French or Low-Countrey Subjects,
> either out of Affection to His Majesty, or His Government;
> or because of the Oppression they meet with at
> home, shall come into His Majesties Kingdoms, His Majesty
> will protect them in their persons and estates, and
> especially those of the Reformed Religion, whose interest
> His Majesty is pleased most particularly to own. . . .

181 The initial appropriation for the war of two and a half million pounds, an enormous and unprecedented sum at that time, was expected to last for three years. In one year the sum was spent and Parliament, loyally but not gladly, appropriated the additional sum of a million and a quarter.

187–188 The lines are a bit obscure, but they are explained by l. 762 and note.

196–197 This is the first example in *Annus* of a device for linking, by rhyming the last line in a stanza with the opening line of the following stanza. Other examples may be found in ll. 296–297, 1024–1025, and 1116–1117. In two instances the device is used, almost certainly with deliberate intent, to connect stanzas which develop an extended simile: ll. 524–525 and 576–577. There are some examples of linking, perhaps accidental, through rhymes separated by one or two intervening lines: e.g., ll. 167–170, 479–482, 655–658, 799–801, and 819–821. In addition, we find a goodly number of instances in which a kind of linking seems to be effected by assonance: e.g., ll. 68–69 (shown-sun), 88–90 (saw-aw'd), 92–93 (abroad-fraught), 428–429 (away-plain), 508–509 (again-lay), 568–569 (attend-sent), 640–641 (sun-unknown), 696–697 (fought-begot), and 1036–1037 (tear-care). But Dryden's practice of rhyming, and his use of more subtle effects of sound, such as assonance, are subjects too complex for treatment here. They will be discussed in a subsequent volume.

199 *The Fasces of the Main.* Cf. *Astraea,* l. 249; *Threnodia Augustalis,* l. 517. Also "the Fasces of the Sea," in Dryden's *Georgics,* I, 42.

200 Noyes called attention to a story told by Herodotus (*History,* IV, 3–4), in which the Scythians awed their rebellious slaves with whips instead of spears and bows.

201 *the watry Camp. Campus* in Latin means *plain,* of course. The phrase is a rendition of some such Latin expression as *campi natantes* (Lucretius, V, 488), or *camposque liquentis* (*Aeneid,* VI, 724), or *campoque . . . aquae* (Ovid, *Metamorphoses,* I, 41–42).

204 note *h.* Plinius jun., *Panegyr. ad Traianum,* ch. 26: (Swarms of children and future populace).

211–212 The image may be that of the optic glass and the *camera obscura.* Cf. "Epilogue writ by Mr. Dreyden, spoke . . . at Oxford, March 19" [1680/81]:

> As from a darkned Room some Optick Glass
> Transmits the distant Species as they pass,
> The Worlds large Landskip is from far descry'd,
> And men contracted on the Paper glide. . . .

For an earlier instance of Dryden's interest in optic glasses, cf. *Howard,* ll. 77–78n.

213–220 On the day that Rupert and Albemarle took command of the fleet, a rumor reached London that the French fleet was in the channel. Since it was believed that the Dutch had not yet ventured forth, an order was given to divide the English fleet. Rupert was directed to take twenty ships and prevent the French from joining the Dutch. Albemarle with the major part of the fleet was to keep a check on the Dutch. Such division proved to be a major strategic error.

At about the same time that Rupert went off with his command, De Ruyter, the "fam'd Commander" of the Dutch, left port with his fleet. Albemarle had some fifty-six ships to oppose the Dutch fleet of approximately eighty-five (W. L. Clowes, *The Royal Navy* [1897–1903], II, 269).

The two fleets sighted each other about 9 A.M. on 1 June. In a council of war in the English fleet it was determined to attack, in spite of inferiority of numbers. This decision was apparently taken at the insistence of Albemarle, who trusted to the wind to give him the advantage. He also hoped to surprise the Dutch, who were still at anchor. Pepys reported that many of the subordinate officers opposed this plan (cf. entries for 11 June and 4 July 1666).

220 An allusion to the cross of St. George. The same sanguine cross may be referred to in l. 606.

221 Captain John Smith thus described the preparation for a fight at sea (*The Sea-Mans Grammar* [1653], p. 60):

> Thus they use to strip themselves into their short sailes,
> or fighting sailes, which is onely the fore sail, the maine

and fore top sailes, because the rest should not be fired
nor spoiled; besides they would be troublesome to handle,
hinder our sights and the using our armes. . . .

225–226 This war saw the evolution of a type of naval tactics which lasted into the nineteenth century. The normal battle array was that described by Dryden: the ships, drawn up stem to stern in a single close-hauled line, sailed past a similar line of enemy ships, showering them with broadsides. Cf. G. N. Clark, *The Later Stuarts* (1949), p. 62.

228 note k. *Aeneid,* VIII, 691 ff.:

alta petunt; pelago credas innare revulsas
Cycladas aut montis concurrere montibus altos,
tanta mole viri turritis puppibus instant

(They gain the deep; you could believe that the Cyclades, torn from their roots, were floating on the sea and that high mountains were clashing with mountains, so huge are the towered ships on which the heroes stand). Cf. Dryden's *Aeneis,* VIII, 915–918.

229–232 Dryden had evidently taken pains to inform himself of the details of the battle. In the morning Albemarle proceeded in column to engage the rear of the Dutch fleet. Because of the difficulties of the maneuver, by the time he came up with the Dutch admiral he had "but about five-and-thirty ships close up with him and well in hand, the remaining twenty straggling and tailing out so as to afford little support either to him or to one another" (Clowes, *The Royal Navy* [1897–1903], II, 269–270). After a few hours of action Albemarle apparently commanded his ships to put about, the English rear thus becoming the van. And the newly constituted van, says Clowes (*ibid.,* pp. 270–271),

presently got into furious action with De Ruijter and
the comparatively fresh Dutch centre. No doubt the English ships had already suffered severely. This new encounter threw the head of the column into some confusion, of
which De Ruijter knew how to take advantage. . . .

In the confusion, and with the advantage of numbers on the side of the Dutch, Albemarle's ship suffered heavy damage (st. 61).

232 *To finish all the deaths* is based on a Latin idiom, as in Ovid, *Metamorphoses,* XV, 646–647: oravere deum, qui praesens *funera* gentis / finiat Ausoniae.

233–240 In his zeal Dryden exaggerates the difference in size of the Dutch and English ships, though the variation of design did bring about the tactics which he describes in st. 60. The Dutch ships, being relatively flat-bottomed, rose high above the water, and their hulls presented a fine target. The English ships were heavier, and built so low that the bottom tier of guns was useless in heavy seas, their masts and rigging were the obvious targets. And the Dutch were much given to the use of chain-shot, which was especially destructive to masts and rigging. Cf. David Ogg, *England in the Reign of Charles II* (1934), I, 267.

233–234 Reminiscent of Celadon's description of Olinda in Dryden's *Secret Love,* IV, i (S-S, II, 471): "She! hang her, a Dutch-built bottom: She's so tall, there's no boarding her." The same figure is employed in Fuller's *Worthies* (1st ed., 1662), in the famous passage describing the wit contests between Shakespeare and Jonson, where Shakespeare is likened to the light and quick English man-of-war and Jonson is likened to the slow and heavy Spanish galleon.

235–236 G. Loane (*N&Q*, CLXXXV [1943], 273) called attention to Sylvester's handling of the traditional story of the elephant and the rhinoceros ("The Sixth Day of the First Weeke," *Bartas His Devine Weekes* [1605], p. 193):

> But his huge strength, nor subtle witt, can not
> Defend him from the sly Rhinocerot:
> Who never, with blinde furie led, doth venter
> Upon his Foe, but yer the Lists he enter,
> Against a Rock he whetteth round about
> The dangerous Pike upon his armed snout;
> Then buckling close, doth not at random, hack
> On the hard Cuirasse on his Enemies back
> But under's bellie (cunning) findes a skinne,
> Whear (and but thear) his sharpned blade will in.

237 *built*. "Style of construction, build" (*OED*, which cites Dryden's line).

239–240 Cf. Waller, "Of a War with Spain, and a Fight at Sea" (*Poems*, ed. Thorn-Drury, II, 25): "Through yielding planks the angry bullets fly."

241–252 Stanzas 61–66 seem to present a reasonably accurate account of one incident in the battle, in which heroism was mingled with comedy, the comedy delicately suggested in st. 61. A bit of poetic exaggeration appears to have entered into st. 63, if one may judge by Albemarle's own account. According to Albemarle (*Three Sea Journals of Stuart Times,* ed. B. S. Ingram [1936], p. 231):

> The second Passe—standing to the Westward our sayles were all shot to peeces. Having got a little ahead of the Dutch, wee anchored and brought to a chandge of our foresayle, foretopsaile, and maintopsaile. One of our Frigats was disabled having lost his foremast. The *De-fiance* was also much shattered in her sayles and anchored likewise. The Flemings that were to windward standing with us, wee were forced to cut and set sayle to the west of the fleet which did not then anchor.

241–244 The image in ll. 243–244 is suggestive of that which Lucan uses to describe Pompey (*Bellum Civile,* I, 135–143). The more likely source, however, is that noted by John Warton (*Aeneid,* IV, 441–445):

> ac velut annoso validam cum robore quercum
> Alpini Boreae nunc hinc nunc flatibus illinc
> eruere inter se certant; it stridor, et altae
> consternunt terram concusso stipite frondes:
> ipsa haeret scopulis

(And as when Alpine North winds strive with each other to uproot a mighty oak of aged strength, with blasts now on this side, now on that, a creaking ensues, and the lofty leaves strew the ground, as the trunk is shaken; it clings to the rocks).

Woven into this noble Virgilian image and extending through the stanza is a delectable bit of raillery, the point of which is made clear by the account of the incident in the *Gazette*, 4–7 June 1666: "The Duke had all his Tackle taken off by Chain-Shot, and his Breeches to his Skin were Shot off, but he Rigged again with Jewry Masts, and fell into the whole body of the Dutch-Fleet; where he attacqued de Ruiter." The humor of the situation was widely recognized by the coffeehouse wits of the time. Dryden's raillery is admirable by the best standards of his age: it is a gentle thrust, serving to reveal or to heighten certain admirable qualities in the object of raillery—in this instance, the Duke's unshaken courage.

245–248 Part of the imagery in this stanza may have been suggested by *Aeneid*, VIII, 691–693. Cf. *Annus*, l. 228n.

251–252 Christie (citing Livy, V, 41; and Florus, *Epit. Rer. Roman.*, I, 13) notes: "When the Gauls sacked Rome, B.C. 387, the barbarian invaders were struck with awe for a moment by the venerable appearance of the chief Roman citizens sitting in full costume in their chairs of state."

Dryden used the image again in *2 Conquest of Granada*, II, i (S-S, IV, 138):

Here will I sit, and here attend my fate,
With the same hoary majesty and state,
As Rome's old senate for the Gauls did wait.

255 *pious.* That is, exhibiting the tender dutifulness such as children owe to parents, or men owe to their loved comrades. Elsewhere in the poem it may refer to the tender care which parents direct to their offspring, or to the love and worship that men owe to God. Cf. ll. 425, 613, 958, and 1090. Dryden's use of the word recalls the adjective which Virgil applied to his hero. It suggests a resemblance between Aeneas and Charles II in their submission to the will of heaven and in their care of their people.

261–262 Cf. the account in the *Gazette*, 4–7 June 1666, cited in ll. 241–244n.

263–264 Cf. *Aeneid*, I, 393–400; Dryden's *Aeneis*, I, 544–553. Loane (*N&Q*, CLXXXV [1943], 273) notes that *creasts* here apparently refers to the lower part of the swan's neck. *OED* records, as an obsolete meaning, the sense of *dewlap*.

266 *squander.* Scatter. Cf. Dryden's *Aeneis*, II, 571.

267–268 Dryden originally wrote: "Berkley alone, not making equal way." Christie suggested that the original reading was perhaps thought to reflect upon Berkeley, and he pointed out that the revision "deprives the comparison with Creüsa of its appropriateness."

Sir William Berkeley (1639–1666), brother to the Earl of Falmouth, was a favorite of the Duke of York. Falmouth had been killed in the sea battle of 1665, and after that fight there had been talk that Berkeley had acted the part of a coward in the engagement. In the engagement which Dryden is here describing Berkeley fought heroically, some thought desperately, to retrieve his honor. But in the confusion of the tactical maneuvering during the first day Berkeley's ship, the *Swiftsure,* along with two others, was cut off and surrounded. In a furious combat the *Swiftsure* was disabled and then captured, and Berkeley was killed in the action. It is inconceivable that Dryden could have intended a slighting remark. The original reading seems to be an accurate reference to the misfortune of Berkeley's ship, for which he was not to blame—any more than Aeneas' wife, Creüsa, was to blame for her failure to escape. But it is possible that Dryden revised the line to avoid the chance that it might be misconstrued.

272 *deceive.* "To frustrate" (*OED,* which cites Dryden's line).

277–284 This passage, together with the two preceding stanzas, is called by Dr. Johnson (Life of Dryden; BH, I, 432) "one of the fairest flowers of English poetry." The account of the nightmares of the Dutch sailors was probably suggested by Lucan's description of the soldiers' dreams in an interval of the battle of Philippi (*Bellum Civile,* VII, 764–773), though the details of Lucan's picture differ from those of Dryden's.

280 Perhaps an imitation, by ironic reversal, of Virgil, *Georgics,* IV, 83: ingentis animos angusto in pectore. Loane (*N&Q,* CLXXXV [1943], 273) cites *Samson Agonistes,* l. 1238: "bulk without spirit vast." Also *MacFlecknoe,* ll. 195–196.

287 *mould.* Shape, or appearance. Cf. Dryden's *Fables,* "Of the Pythagorean Philosophy," ll. 265 and 663.

291–292 note *l. Aeneid,* I, 209: (He feigns hope with his look and holds his grief pressed deep in his heart).

291 a *Father of the War.* Loane (*N&Q,* CLXXXV [1943], 273) cites Fletcher, *Bonduca,* IV, iii: "Oh only Roman! oh father of the wars." Also Davenant, *Gondibert,* I, v, st. 4: "The Father of those fights we Lombards fought." But Dryden's phrase seems to suggest only the Duke's paternal concern for his men.

303 That is, only cowards count the number of enemy ships.

311 *sheer.* "To cut—as, one's way or passage—through an obstacle" (*OED,* which quotes Dryden's line).

313–320 In the second day's fight the English had forty-four ships and the Dutch about eighty (Clowes, *The Royal Navy* [1897–1903], II, 273). The fight continued all day, during the course of which the Dutch fell into confusion, offering the English an excellent opportunity of doing great damage. But apparently the English were too weakened by their own losses to take advantage of the situation. By evening Albemarle had decided to retreat toward his own coast, and did so.

314 We have not been able to find the story of a swordfish in a whale's belly. That the swordfish attacked ships and whales, however, was an ancient tradition (cf. G. B. Goode, "Materials for a History of the Sword-fish," *Report of the U.S. Commissioner of Fish and Fisheries* [1880], pp. 338–339). Pliny had mentioned the ferocity of the swordfish; and Spenser (*Visions of the Worlds Vanitie,* st. 5) and Donne (*The Progresse of the Soule,* st. 36) both describe its attack upon the whale. The subject was

of current interest when Dryden wrote *Annus Mirabilis,* for in the *Philosophical Transactions* (no. 8, 8 January 1666) we find an account of

> a certain horny Fish . . . who runs its horn into the
> Whale's belly . . . which kind of Fish is known, sometimes to run its horn into Ships (perhaps taking them
> for Whales) and there snapping it asunder; as hapned
> not long since to an English Vessel in the West-Indian
> Seas; the broken piece of that Horn being by the Master
> of that ship presented to the King, and now kept in His
> Majesties Repository.

326 Here the chase-guns are cannon mounted at ports in the bows of the Dutch naval vessels and useful when the enemy is being chased.

327–328 Fire ships, the "grapling Aetna's" of the navy, were greatly favored at this time, more than in later wars (cf. G. N. Clark, *The Later Stuarts* [1949], p. 62).

In a note on *Essay on Man,* I, 213, Pope pointed out that the myth of the lion's needing the assistance of the jackal in hunting probably arose from observations on the lion's defective sense of smell.

330 *fiery Cacus.* Cf. *Aeneid,* VIII, 251–255; Dryden's *Aeneis,* VIII, 335–342.

344 *Check:* "A false stoop, when a hawk forsakes her proper game, and pursues some baser game that crosses her flight." To fly at check means "to pursue such game." *To clip it:* "To move the wings rapidly; to fly rapidly." Cf. *OED,* where Dryden's line is used to illustrate both terms.

345 Possibly an echo of *Macbeth,* III, ii, 50–51.

353–356 Again the insistence on the paternal care which Albemarle exercised over his men—a trait eminently appropriate in the representative of the King, whose fatherly affection for his people Dryden was hoping to demonstrate in this poem.

358 *of conquer'd Nations tell.* Probably an allusion to Monck's success as an admiral in the first Dutch war and to his conquering the royalists among the Scots when he commanded the parliamentary forces in Scotland during the 1650's.

364 *Remote.* In the Latin sense, from *removere: moved back, withdrawn.*

367–368 Cf. Exodus, XIII, 21–22.

373–376 Vaguely suggestive of Lucan's description of the sinking of a ship (*Bellum Civile,* III, 629–633): (And after [the ship] had drunk in the sea through its broken joints, filled to the top of its gangways, it went down into the waves, stirring up the neighboring sea with a whirlpool. The waters drew apart, separated by the sinking ship, and then the sea fell back into the vessel's place).

374 *as he that touch'd the Ark.* Cf. I Chronicles, XIII, 9–10.

384 note *m. Aeneid,* IX, 792–798:

> ceu saevum turba leonem
> cum telis premit infensis: at territus ille,
> asper, acerba tuens, retro redit et neque terga
> ira dare aut virtus patitur, nec tendere contra

ille quidem hoc cupiens potis est per tela virosque.
haud aliter retro dubius vestigia Turnus
improperata refert et mens exaestuat ira.
Cf. Dryden's *Aeneis*, IX, 1072–1079.
For Dryden's previous use of the angry lion in simile or metaphor, cf.
Astraea, ll. 117–118.

Loane (*N&Q*, CLXXXV [1943], 273) noted Horace, *Odes*, I, 6, 6: Pelidae
stomachum cedere nescii (The anger of Achilles, who knew not how to
yield).

391 note *n*. Statius, *Silvae*, V, iv, 5–6: (The boisterous waves roar no
longer; the raging sea is stilled; the sea is pillowed on the shore in slumber).

396 note *o*. June 3 was the anniversary of victories over the Dutch in
1653 and 1665.

397 *happy*. "Favourable, propitious" (*OED*).

402 Loane (*N&Q*, CLXXXV [1943], 273) noted Propertius, III, 7, 12:
nunc tibi pro tumulo Carpathium omne mare est (Now the whole Car-
pathian Sea is your tomb). The Ghost of Almanzor's father in 2 *Conquest
of Granada*, IV, iii (S-S, IV, 189) remarks:

    I dy'd; and for my Winding-sheet, a Wave
    I had; and all the Ocean for my Grave.

415–416 That is, Albemarle was forced to pay a penalty (*ransom*) for an
excess of glory before this time. For the obverse side of the picture of Fortune, cf. *Ld. Ch.*, ll. 119–126 and note.

417–420 The original reading (see text note) was doubtless considered
sacrilegious; hence the revision in this stanza. In the afternoon of 3 June,
which was the third day of the fight (hence Dryden's figure in the first version), Rupert rejoined Albemarle. When it was known in London that a
fight was taking place, orders were prepared for Rupert to rejoin Albemarle at once. But through bungling the orders miscarried. Rupert returned
of his own initiative, having heard the sound of guns (l. 421).

428 *callow*. "Of birds: unfledged, without feathers" (*OED*). Apparently
a favorite word with Dryden. Cf. "callow care" (*Georgics*, I, 562), "callow
young" (*Georgics*, IV, 22), "callow down" (*Aeneis*, VIII, 213; *Pastorals*,
VIII, 57), "callow birds" (*Indian Emperour*, IV, ii; *Tempest*, III, ii).

433 *kind*. "Proper, appropriate, fitting" (*OED*).

435–436 Loane (*N&Q*, CLXXXV [1943], 273) suggests that this may be
adapted from *Aeneid*, II, 726–729. Cf. Dryden's *Aeneis*, II, 988–991.

440 *the feather'd train*. Lest this be noted as a harbinger of what is
thought of as the plague of neoclassical diction, let it be observed that the
device of elegant periphrasis was an inheritance from the golden age of
English poetry, brought to perfection by the middle of the seventeenth century. A glance at Joshua Poole's *The English Parnassus* (1657), under such
a heading as Bird, or Fish, will reveal how fully developed was the technique of translating the simple term into a polite circumlocution, and
how great was the stock of examples ready at hand. In view of this development, it is surprising that Dryden indulged so seldom in the periphrastic
diversion at this time. But his championship of technical terms places him

squarely in opposition to general terms, and his evident sympathy with the aims of the Royal Society would make him averse to vague and inexact terminology.

443 *ken.* "Power or exercise of vision; look, gaze" (*OED,* which cites Dryden's line). Cf. also l. 635.

449–456 Scott notes:

> Betwixt the fleets of Albemarle and Rupert lay some dangerous shoals. . . . On one of these, called the Galloper, Admiral Sir George Ayscue was so unfortunate as to strand his vessel, the Royal Prince, one of the largest in the fleet, and forced by his own seamen to strike his flag. . . . Albemarle observing the cause of this disaster, and that the Dutch had sent a squadron of their fleet to the edge of the sands, as if to provoke the Prince, acquainted him by signal and message, that he should by no means bear up against that squadron, there being a dangerous sand between them; and that the appearance of the Dutch in that place was to tempt him into the toil.

454 The *new Messiah* in this line picks up a conceit contained in the cancelled passage discussed in ll. 417–420n.

455 *braving.* "Daring, defiant, boasting" (*OED*). Cf. *Richard II,* II, iii, 112: "In braving arms against thy sovereign."

465–468 The meeting seems to have taken place, not on the morning of the fourth day, but on the evening of the third day, when Albemarle and Rupert held a council of war, determining at that time to continue the attack the following morning. It was also determined that Rupert, since his ships were fresh, should lead the van. Cf. Thomas Skinner, *Life of Albemarle* (1724), pp. 245–246.

472 Cf. Joshua, x, 12–14.

476 Cf. Waller, "Of a War with Spain, and a Fight at Sea" (*Poems,* ed. Thorn-Drury, II, 24): "And with their smoky cannons banish day." Also Marvell, "On the Victory Obtained by Blake over the Spaniards" (wr. 1657, pub. 1674), *Poems,* ed. H. M. Margoliouth (1927), p. 117:

> The Thund'ring Cannon now begins the Fight,
> And though it be at Noon, creates a Night.

478 *speak thick.* Loane (*N&Q,* CLXXXV [1943], 273) calls attention to 2 *Henry IV,* II, iii, 24, where "speaking thick"—describing the manner of Hotspur—is contrasted with speaking "low and tardily."

479 *breath'd.* That is, given rest, strengthened through rest.

485 *offends.* "To attack, assault, assail" (*OED*).

490 *sullenly.* Slowly.

491 note *p. Georgics,* III, 423–424: (While the central coils and the moving tip of his tail untwine, and his last fold drags its slow coils). John Warton called attention to the same figure in *Aeneid,* V, 273 ff. Cf. Dryden's *Aeneis,* V, 359–366.

492 *volume.* One of Dryden's Latinisms; from *volvere,* to roll or wind. *The Censure of the Rota* (1673), p. 6, cited the word in the phrase "tor-

rents winding in volumes" as an example of Dryden's improper use of foreign words. The *Censure* was referring, somewhat inaccurately, to a passage in *1 Conquest of Granada,* IV, i (S-S, IV, 78).

494 *the throwing nations.* The figure, of course, is taken from the ancient game of chance, the throwing of dice.

500 Cf. Dryden's *Aeneis,* VI, 993: "Blunt not the Beams of Heav'n and edge of Day." *The Censure of the Rota* (1673), pp. 8–9, calls attention, without admiration, to a similar figure in *Tyrannick Love,* IV, i (S-S, III, 425):

> My flaming Sword above 'em to display,
> (All keen and ground upon the edge of day). . . .

There is a play on words involved in *crescents.* In one sense the crescent was a regular battle formation for naval vessels.

513–514 John Warton noted *Aeneid,* VIII, 243–246. Cf. Dryden's *Aeneis,* VIII, 323–328. This is part of the story of "fiery Cacus," to which Dryden refers in *Annus,* l. 330.

520 *offends.* Cf. l. 485n.

521–528 Cf. Ovid's *Metamorphoses,* I, 533–539:

> ut canis in vacuo leporem cum Gallicus arvo
> vidit, et hic praedam pedibus petit, ille salutem
> (alter inhaesuro similis iam iamque tenere
> sperat et extento stringit vestigia rostro;
> alter in ambiguo est, an sit comprensus, et ipsis
> morsibus eripitur tangentiaque ora relinquit);
> sic deus et virgo. . . .

Cf. Dryden's translation, in *Examen Poeticum* (1693), "The First Book of Ovid's Metamorphoses," ll. 718–725.

An example of the unscrupulous criticism from which Dryden suffered in his lifetime is found in *The Friendly Vindication of Mr. Dryden from the Censure of the Rota* (1673). Here the passage is first garbled in misquotation (p. 2):

> Ev'n as the fearful Hare, when cours'd on Plain,
> And longer can't her flight maintain,
> By the fierce Dog, with flix turn'd up does lie,
> Who though not kill'd, yet cannot flie.

Then the critic proceeds purposely to misrepresent the poet's meaning (pp. 2–3).

526 *flix.* "Fur of various quadrupeds" (*OED,* which quotes Dryden's line). Dryden uses the word also in his translation of Ovid cited above.

536 note *q. Odes,* IV, 4, 51–52: ([The wolves] which it is the richest triumph for us to deceive and escape).

549–552 In an entry dated from Whitehall, 10 June, the *Gazette* (7–11 June 1666) reported:

> Letters of yesterday morning from on board the *Royal Charles* tell us our Generals remain on board, using all diligence possible to repair the Fleet, which will in a few days be in a condition to take the Sea again, scarce any

> of the Ships, how sharp soever the late Engagement was
> upon them, needing to put into Dock.

This was overly optimistic. As Dryden indicates in the following stanzas, there was feverish activity in repairing the fleet, and as might be expected, the King took great interest in the proceedings. On 16 June he, the Duke of York, and some ministers of state went down to the fleet to hasten "their speedy putting to Sea."

553–556 The "unripe veins" are deposits of gold or other precious metals still in process of development. The idea that metals "grow" was quite general at this time (cf. F. D. Adams, *The Birth and Development of the Geological Sciences* [1938], pp. 277 ff.). It is clearly expressed by Barba in his *Art of Metals* (1640; English translation, 1670). It is a mistake, Barba argues (pp. 70–71), to

> hold with the vulgar that at the Creation of the world God
> Almighty made the veins of Mettals in the same condi-
> tion, as we now find them at this day; herein doing nature
> a great affront, by denying her (without reason) a pro-
> ductive vertue in this matter, which is allowed unto her
> in all other sublunary things; moreover, that experience
> in divers places hath manifested the contrary: a clear ex-
> ample wherof we have in Ilva, an Island adjoyning Tus-
> cany, full of Iron Mines, which when they have dug as
> hollow, and as deep as they can, the circumjacent Earth
> falls in, and fills them up again; and in the space of ten
> or fifteen years at most, they work those Mines again,
> and thence draw out abundance of Mettal, which that new
> Earth hath been converted into: many do think that the
> same happens in the rich hill of Potosi; at the least all
> of us know, that the Stones, which divers years ago we
> have left behind us, thinking there was not Plate enough
> in them to make it worth our labour, we now bring them
> home, and find abundance of Plate in them, which can
> be attributed to nothing, but to the perpetual generation
> of Silver.

As late as 1695 John Woodward in his important *Natural History of the Earth* wrote (p. 195): "The Metals and Minerals which are lodged in the perpendicular Intervals of the Strata, do still grow (to speak in the Mineralists phrase). . . ."

Out of the same belief springs an image in a speech of Almahide's (2 *Conquest of Granada*, III, i; S-S, IV, 158):

> And in those Clymes which most [the sun's] scorching know,
> He makes the noblest fruits and Metals grow.

On the origin or growth of precious stones, cf. *Annus*, l. 10n.

565–568 The activities described here and in the six following stanzas were among the most lively concerns of the Royal Society, which properly recognized the King's leadership in such matters. Sprat reports (*History of the Royal-Society* [1667], p. 150):

[The fellows] have employ'd much time in examining the
Fabrick of Ships, the forms of their Sails, the shapes of
their Keels, the sorts of Timber, the planting of Firr, the
bettering of Pitch, and Tarr, and Tackling. And in all
Maritime affairs of this Nature, his Majesty is acknowledg'd to be the best Judge amongst Seamen, and Ship-
wrights, as well as the most powerful amongst Princes.

This section of the poem is important to Dryden's purpose. First, it
demonstrates the wisdom and foresight of the King in having provided, at
great cost, the materials with which the speedy repair of the fleet was made
possible; and the speedy repair of the fleet, as it turned out, gave England
command of the seas during the remainder of the year. Second, it demonstrates the economic wisdom of the King. For it was recognized in Dryden's time that, as an alternative to amassing treasure, an admirable method
for making prince and people rich and powerful was to expend, among
the subjects, a great part of the prince's revenue for the building of ships
of war and for the laying up stores of supplies, grain, and other provisions
for their maintenance (cf. Thomas Mun, *England's Treasure by Forraign
Trade* [1664], p. 171).

570 *imps.* That is, repairs; or, more strictly, engrafts feathers (in the
wing) to remedy a deficiency. Cf. also Dryden's *Georgics,* IV, 439: "imp'd
with wings"; where *imp'd* means *provided with.* In the latter sense the
term is found near the beginning of Act IV of the Dryden-Lee *Oedipus:*
"With all the wings with which revenge could imp / My flight."
Cf. *Richard II,* II, i, 292: "Imp out our drooping country's broken wing."
The word is used in this sense by Spenser and Davenant.

571–572 That is, tall fir from Norway restores masts ruined in battle, and
English oak repairs leaks and replaces damaged planks. *Fir* and *Oak* are
the compound subject of the verb *restore.*

573 note *r. Aeneid,* I, 430–436; Dryden's *Aeneis,* I, 598–609. Cf. also
Georgics, IV, 159 ff.; Dryden's *Georgics,* IV, 230–244.

576 Cf. *Aeneid,* VI, 707–709:
> ubi apes aestate serena
floribus insidunt variis, et candida circum
lilia funduntur. . . .

Dryden's *Aeneis,* VI, 961–962 renders the passage:
> In Summer's heat, on tops of Lillies feed,
And creep within their Bells, to suck the balmy Seed.

581–588 Since the poem was written in a place where, as Dryden says in
the prefatory "Account," he had "not so much as the converse of any sea
man," he may have found his technical vocabulary in books. Perhaps the
most likely source is Captain John Smith's *The Sea-Mans Grammar* (1653),
two passages of which will show how careful the poet was in his use of
nautical terminology. The first explains how to make repairs in a damaged
ship under fire (p. 60):
> [During a lull in the battle] fling a man over board to
stop the leakes; that is, . . . trusse him up about the mid-

dle in a peece of canvas, and a rope to keep him from
sinking, and his armes at liberty, with a malet in the one
hand, and a plug lapped in Okum, and well tarred in a
tarpawling clout in the other, which he will quickly beat
into the hole or holes the bullets made.

And the second is a definition of calking (p. 13):

Calking is beating Okum into every seame or betwixt
Planke and Planke and Okum is old Ropes torn in
pieces like a Towze Match, or Hurds of Flax, which being close beat into every seame with a calking Iron and
a Mallet, which is a hammer of wood and an Iron chissell,
being well payed over with hot pitch. . . .

586 *instops.* Dryden's use of this word is the only example recorded
by *OED.*

587 *paid o'r.* A technical expression, rare at this time, but used in
Captain Smith's definition above.

589–592 Dr. Johnson's objections to Dryden's nautical terms are based
on this and the two preceding stanzas, the objections being grounded on
the principle that in poetry "all appropriated terms of art should be sunk
in general expressions, because poetry is to speak an universal language."
In the Life of Dryden (BH, I, 433) he notes Dryden's defense of sea terms,
to which he thus replies:

Let us then appeal to experience; for by experience at
last we learn as well what will please as what will profit.
In the battle, his terms seem to have been blown away;
but he deals them liberally in the dock. . . .

Here he quotes sts. 146–148, on which he remarks, "I suppose there is not
one term which every reader does not wish away."

The appeal to experience might just as easily have revealed that no
reader is baffled by the sense of these stanzas; one does not need to be a
sailor in order to understand. No one has objected to the sea terms in
Dryden's translation of Virgil. The terms in sts. 146–148 probably drew
Dr. Johnson's fire because they are "low" and are clustered too thickly.

589 *dawby Marling.* Cf. *dawby Wax* in Dryden's *Georgics,* IV, 54.
The sense is suggested by the use of *glewy wax* in *Annus,* l. 577.

590 *sear-cloth.* Christie noted that this is a verb, meaning *to cover
with cerecloth.*

595 *big-corn'd powder.* Sprat prints a "History of Making Gun-Powder,"
where the process is described thus (*History of the Royal-Society* [1667],
pp. 282–283):

After the Powder is dried, it is brought again to the
Corning-house, where it is again sifted over the dusting
Bin in other double Sieves, but without any Runners.
These Sieves have both of them smaller holes than the
former: The upper Sieve is called the Separater, and
serves to divide the great corns from the lesser; the great
corns are put by themselves, and serve for Cannon Pow-

der: The lower Sieve is called the dry Duster, and retains
the small corns (which serve for Musquet and Pistol). . . .

601–616 The *London,* under the command of Sir John Lawson, had
blown up in 1665. In its place the City built the *Loyal London* and presented it to Charles in 1666. The ship had a short life, being burned by
the Dutch in the Thames the next year. She seemed ill-fated from the
start. Pepys recorded (26 June 1666) that at the trial of her guns, all of
them exploded.

602 *Phoenix daughter.* The image of the Phoenix, symbol of regeneration, clearly appealed to Dryden; allusions to it appear in ll. 1151
and 1178. Cf. also ll. 113–116n. For earlier allusions, cf. *Hastings*, l. 8on;
Rival Ladies, V, iii; *Verses to the Duchess*, l. 52.

610–611 Details of design favored by the English navy at this time.
For the effect in battle, cf. ll. 233–240.

621–624 Cf. *Georgics*, I, 136: tunc alnos primum fluvii sensere cavatas
(Then for the first time rivers felt the hollowed alders).

This stanza begins an account of the Progress of Navigation, and the
passage is therefore a forerunner of a popular eighteenth-century genre;
concerning which, cf. R. H. Griffith, "The Progress Pieces of the Eighteenth
Century," *Texas Review,* V (1920), 218–233. It will be recalled that Gray's
famous tribute to Dryden occurs in his "Progress of Poesy."

625 *Kern.* "A light-armed Irish foot-soldier; one of the poorer class
among the 'wild Irish,' from whom such soldiers were drawn" (*OED*). Cf.
Richard II, II, i, 156; *Henry V,* III, vii; also *Macbeth,* I, ii, 13.

628 *fin-like Oars.* The analogy of fish and ship as in ll. 619–620, was a
commonplace, especially in the comparison of fin and oar. Cf. *Faerie
Queene,* III, iv, 33.9: "their finny oars." Also Donne, "Progresse of the
Soule," l. 228 (Grierson, I, 304): "finnie oares."

629–632 Saturn, dethroned by his son Jove, fled by sea to Latium, where
he was kindly received. According to the myth, he brought laws and civilized
arts, peace and plenty—the golden age—to Italy. Cf. *Aeneid,* VIII, 319 ff.;
Dryden's *Aeneis,* VIII, 425–432.

639 note *s. Aeneid,* VI, 796: (Beyond the paths of the year and of the
sun).

641–644 Similar optimism prevailed in the Royal Society. Cf. Sprat,
History of the Royal-Society (1667), pp. 114–115:
> And it is a good sign, that Nature will reveal more of its
> secrets to the English, than to others; because it has
> already furnish'd them with a Genius so well propor-
> tion'd, for the receiving, and retaining its mysteries.

Milton's early optimism may be recalled, though Milton had in mind a
different kind of "secret."

645–648 The interest of the ancients in a theory of tides was keenly
renewed by the maritime enterprise of the sixteenth and seventeenth centuries. But whereas the ancients had little data to go on, since they lived
by an inland sea, the moderns, acquainted with both Atlantic and Pacific,
speculated vigorously on this universal phenomenon: in the sixteenth cen-

tury, Patricius, Cardanus, J. C. Scaliger, and the voyagers reported by
Hakluyt and others; in the seventeenth century, Bacon, Gilbert, Kepler,
Galileo, Gassendi, and Descartes. At the time Dryden was writing, the
subject was one of intense interest to the Royal Society, for in 1666 Dr.
John Wallis presented to it his great paper offering a universal theory of
tides. Wallis sent his essay to Boyle on 25 April 1666 (*Philosophical Transactions*, no. 16); on 9 May Oldenburg brought it to the attention of the
society; and at the next meeting, on 16 May, it "was read, and generally
approved of, and thought fit not only to be registered, but also . . . to be
printed" (Birch, *History of the Royal Society* [1760], II, 88–89). It was so
printed in the *Transactions* on 6 August 1666, and the flood of subsequent
observations from members bore out the society's resolution "that Dr.
Wallis should be acquainted with these exceptions" (*ibid.*, p. 89). Wallis'
paper rested on the bold and novel theory, which brought him to the
verge of anticipating Newton's law of universal gravitation, that the earth
and moon have a common center of gravity. Hence Dryden had good reason for feeling that this age-old problem was on the verge of solution.
Cf. *Annus*, ll. 14–16n.

649–652 In Dryden's time there was no practical way of measuring the
longitude at sea. The problem was of vital interest to scientists, and during
the 1660's a great deal of experiment on the subject was undertaken. According to Sprat, the King was "most ready to reward those, that shall discover the Meridian" (*History of the Royal-Society* [1667], p. 150). Of great
importance were the pendulum clocks of the Dutch scientist Christian
Huygens. Huygens completed his first model in 1656 and for many years
afterward continued to experiment and refine successive models. The basic
problem was to develop a timepiece that could withstand the rigors of ship-
board. In 1663 Alexander Bruce, Earl of Kincardine, who had collaborated with Huygens, tried out the clocks in a voyage from Holland to
England. But the weather was rough and the trial unsuccessful. In the
same year the Royal Society had the clocks tested on board a ship commanded by Sir Robert Holmes on a voyage to Lisbon and back. And in 1663
Holmes took the clocks on a voyage to Guinea. The results were considered
encouraging. But further tests in 1668 and 1670 convinced even Huygens
himself that his pendulum clocks were not suitable to ocean travel. During
the 1660's Robert Hook also attacked the problem of longitude with much
vigor. It was not until the late eighteenth century, however, that the
problem was solved in a practical manner.

In the Life of Dryden (BH, I, 434) Dr. Johnson objected to l. 649 because it depended on the prose note attached to it. Said Johnson: "It had
better become Dryden's learning and genius to have laboured science into
poetry, and have shewn, by explaining longitude, that verse did not refuse
the ideas of philosophy." The relevant fact is that Dryden was not engaged
in explaining science, but in observing the enormous importance of science
(as fostered by the King and the Royal Society) to English commerce.

652 It was an accepted principle of mercantilist policy that one

state's gain necessarily meant another state's loss (cf. C. J. Friedrich, *The Age of the Baroque* [1952], p. 13). *Gain* was generally construed to mean gold or silver.

653–656 In this stanza, said Dr. Johnson, the poet was not, perhaps, conscious of the absurdity; the lines, he added, are meaningless (Life of Dryden, BH, I, 460–461). Dr. Johnson judged too hastily. The meaning of the stanza seems to depend upon an idea belonging to the old astronomy, that the terrestrial and the celestial spheres join at the horizon ("our Globes last verge")—an idea which Dryden had used in an earlier poem (cf. *Ld. Ch.*, ll. 31–36 and 38–42n.). Here at the horizon, where the two spheres join, the ocean may be said to lean on the sky; and from here we can with more ease and certainty observe the planets ("our rolling Neighbours") and the moon. Dryden, of course, employs this ancient astronomical theory not because it was scientifically acceptable to him but because it heightened the mystery and remoteness of those undiscovered regions into which British enterprise was soon to penetrate.

653 Somewhat suggestive of *Richard II*, I, i, 93–94:
> Or here or elsewhere to the furthest verge
> That ever was surveyed by English eye. . . .

655 *our rolling Neighbours*. A rendering of concepts familiar in Latin, as in *vicina sidera* (Ovid, *Metamorphoses*, II, 507), and *volvuntur sidera* (*Aeneid*, IV, 524).

657 Concerning the "care" of the fellows of the society, Sprat says (*History of the Royal-Society* [1667], p. 150): "They have principally consulted the advancement of Navigation. . . ."

659–660 In some quarters the members of the Royal Society were suspected of fostering atheism. Dryden here gives the standard defense. It had been outlined by Bacon, who explained that the book of God's works was a necessary complement to the book of God's word (cf. *Advancement*, I, vi, 16). Sprat, writing at the time Dryden was composing *Annus Mirabilis*, developed the same point of view (*History of the Royal-Society* [1667], pp. 132–133). Praising certain great and reverend Anglican churchmen for having taken off the scandal attached to natural philosophy, he remarked:
> . . . they have shewn that in our veneration of Gods
> almighty power, we ought to imitate the manner of our
> respect to Earthly Kings. For as, the greater their Domin-
> ion is, the more observance is wont to be given to their
> neerest Servants and Officers: so the greatness of the Di-
> vine Majesty is best to be worshipp'd, by the due honour-
> ing, and observing of Nature, which is his immediate
> Servant, and the universal Minister of his pleasure.

661–664 It was assumed that the order and harmony of nature were reflections of the Divine Mind, and the laws of nature—since nature was "the universal Minister of his Pleasures"—formed a pattern expressive of God's being and His will. These the natural philosophers could comprehend, but only as abstract formulations or laws, too tenuous for the common or ordinary (*levell'd*) use of mankind until they were transmuted by the philosophers, as substances are by *Limbecks,* into ideas rich in practical value.

663 *Limbecks.* Cf. ll. 51–52n.

669–680 The Dutch, not having suffered so much in the Four Days' Battle, were able to refit and put to sea ahead of the English. For some days before the English fleet put out, the Dutch sailed off the English coast, dating letters and dispatches "From the fleet in the mouth of the river of London." On the evening of 22 July the English fleet assembled and anchored at the Gunfleet. As Dryden says in st. 170, the two fleets were approximately equal in strength.

679 Cf. Donne, "Epithalamion," l. 122 (Grierson, I, 135): "If by that manly courage they be tryed."

681–684 The Plymouth Squadron must have consisted largely of the ships which under command of Sir Jeremy Smyth had been sent to the Straits and the Mediterranean early in 1666 primarily to protect English ships engaged in the Levant trade. In February and March, Smyth's fleet in the Mediterranean managed to awe the French fleet at Toulon under Beaufort and to prevent Beaufort from joining the Atlantic Squadron under Du Quesne and ultimately effecting a junction with the Dutch fleet in the North Sea. By the middle of April, Smyth was recalled, and his ships brought home to be refitted. They were supposed to join with Rupert during the Four Days' Battle, but apparently were not readied in time. Cf. Julian S. Corbett, *England in the Mediterranean* (1904), II, 53–54 and 58.

685–686 Sir Thomas Allin, whose steady adherence to the royalist cause earned the phrase "loyal all along," had been sent late in 1664 to capture the Dutch Smyrna convoy as it came through the Straits. In the middle of December while on a false chase five of his ships ran aground; two were lost and the remainder severely damaged. In this condition he came upon a Dutch fleet of fourteen ships, including three men-of-war. He attacked, sank two merchantmen, and captured two, one of which proved to be rich booty. The expedition, therefore, was only partly successful. Cf. Julian S. Corbett, *England in the Mediterranean* (1904), II, 49. In the St. James's Fight, which Dryden is about to describe, Allin was admiral of the White, and under his command the van had the honors of the day.

687–692 Sir Robert Holmes (1622–1692) had served in the royalist army and later under Rupert in his semipiratical naval forces. Holmes was not particularly friendly with Albemarle. *Gen'rals* therefore is a possessive singular referring to Rupert, to whom Holmes was a "fidus Achates," a faithful and devoted companion.

In the fall of 1663 Holmes had been sent with a squadron to the coast of Africa to protect English traders from the Dutch. There he proceeded to attack the Dutch, and by May 1664 the entire Gold Coast except the Dutch capital, had fallen into English hands (cf. K. Feiling, *British Foreign Policy, 1660–1672* [1930], p. 129). Thus Dryden could say that it was Holmes who first bewitched British eyes with the sight of Guinea gold, as Cato the Censor had urged the Roman Senate to the Third Punic War by displaying

Carthaginian figs, which he said had been picked in Carthage only three days before. Cf. epilogue to *Amboyna,* ll. 19–20.

693–694 Sir Edward Spragge (d. 1673) was vice-admiral of the Blue, under Sir Jeremy (or Jeremiah) Smyth. He was famed as a gallant and able officer.

695–696 Sir John Harman (d. 1673) seems not to have been present in this battle. The encounter referred to, took place during the Four Days' Battle. In a contemporary account, said to be by Harman himself, his activities on board the *Henry* are described in vivid detail (cf. Kennett, *History of England* [2d. ed., 1719], III, 281). Twice the *Henry* was set on flame by fire ships, but through the heroic efforts of Harman and some of his crew the vessel was saved and brought into Harwich.

697–700 Sir Frescheville Holles (1641–1672) was the son of Gervase Holles, a staunch fighter in the King's cause during the civil wars, and Elizabeth Molesworth. Holles's martial endowments are evident enough, but we have found no traces of his, or his mother's, literary talents. During the Four Days' Battle, Holles was in command of the *Antelope.* On the 2d of June his left arm was shot off. Jeremy Roch, who was second-in-command, thus summarized the furious encounter (*Three Sea Journals,* ed. B. S. Ingram [1936], p. 49):

> We received all their broadsides, and would willingly
> have paid them again with double interest, but now, alas!
> our wings were clipped, our ship cruelly shattered, our
> Commander's arm shot off, 55 of our men killed and near
> so many more wounded, our masts, sails and rigging all in
> totters, our deck dyed with blood like a slaughter-house!

699 *fatal.* Destructive; causing grievous harm. Cf. Dryden's *Aeneis,* VIII, 939.

700 *succeeds.* "To cause to take the place of another" (*OED,* which cites Dryden's line). The subject of the verb is *Hollis; hand* is the direct object.

701 John Warton called attention to *Aeneid,* V, 302: multi praeterea, quos fama obscura recondit (Many besides, whom dark report hides).

713–716 The Dutch ships, relatively flat-bottomed, were designed to maneuver in shallow water. In the account of the battle published in the London *Gazette* (30 July–2 August 1666) a few incidents are reported to show how the Dutch took advantage of "their treach'rous shallows." On 26 July: "Our Fleet continued the pursuit, Chasing them over many Flats and Banks, till they came so near the shore, that our great ships could not follow; but left the lesser Fregats to attend them, till they got into the Darlow Channel of Zealand." That same night the squadron of Sir Jeremy Smyth, in pursuit of the Dutch, was forced to lay by "for fear of Shoale ground, the Enemy in the mean time stealing away from him. . . ."

728 *gross.* A military term meaning, *the main body* (of a fleet or army).

731 *blind.* That is, covered or concealed.

735 *officious.* Helpful, obliging, dutiful.

736 note *u. Aeneid,* I, 145–146: levat ipse tridenti / et vastas aperit syrtis

et temperat aequor (With his trident he himself [i.e., Neptune] lifts [the ships from the rocks] and opens the huge quicksands and calms the sea). Cf. Dryden's *Aeneis*, I, 207–210.

739–740 In these lines, as in ll. 989–992, there is a vague suggestion of the atmosphere of terror in *Macbeth,* which Dryden had probably been reading along with Shakespeare's chronicle histories.

740 Loane (*N&Q,* CLXXXV [1943], 273) called attention to 2 *Henry IV,* I, i, 72: "Drew Priam's curtain in the dead of night." *Curtains* here probably has reference to the drapes around a bed.

741–744 The main engagement is thus described in the account of the battle printed in the *Gazette* (30 July–2 August 1666):

> July 25. This Morning it being a fine gale at N.N.E. our Fleet about 11 leagues off of Orfordness, weighed, and in two hours time discovered the Enemy four leagues S.E. by S. with whom they stood, intending to engage them Van to Van: By six of the Clock they got up within two Leagues of them, the wind at N. and by W. the Dutch then drawing up their Fleet into the Form of an Half-Moon, their Ships at equal distance, partly to avoid our Fire-ships; but rather (as supposed) hoping to weather all, or a great part of our Fleet, with either the Van or Rear of theirs.
>
> About half an hour after nine, the Vans on each side came near, the headmost of theirs fired at ours, which returned no shot till near half an hour after they came close up with them, and then the *Anne* began to fire, and presently the whole Squadron of the White was engaged with their Van; within an hour after, the Red Squadron likewise engaged, and after them the Blew; so that by 12 a clock all the whole Fleet was in with them. Between 10 and 11 one of our Fire-ships going on board their headmost Admiral, was put off and burnt down without effect; at 11 the Van of their Fleet . . . bore before the wind from ours.

743 *Sleet.* That is, flakes of metal from the guns, falling like sleet. The *OED* cites Dryden's line as example of the transference of the normal meaning of the word.

750 *Linstocks.* "A staff about three feet long, having a pointed foot to stick in the deck or ground, and a forked head to hold a lighted match" (*OED*).

expires. "To be breathed forth or exhaled; hence of the winds, flame, a projectile: To rush forth" (*OED,* which cites Dryden's line).

752 Loane (*N&Q,* CLXXXV [1943], 273) calls attention to Dryden's translation of Virgil's dant animos plagae, in *Aeneis,* VII, 533: "And lend their little Souls at ev'ry stroke."

759 Cf. *Aeneid,* V, 455: tum pudor incendit viris et conscia virtus (Then shame and awareness of his manhood fire his strength).

760 note *v. Aeneid*, V, 231: (They are able, because they seem [to themselves] to be able).

762 Caesar, of course, is Charles II. The line is an allusion to the well-known story told by Plutarch (cf. *Sac. Maj.*, ll. 103–104n.). Also by Lucan, *Bellum Civile*, V, 577–593.

773–776 The "famous Leader" of the Dutch fleet was Michael Adrianszoon de Ruyter, who through the day of 25 July fought boldly and bravely. The *Gazette* (30 July–2 August 1666) thus described an incident toward the close of this day's battle:

> About four de Ruyter made all the sail he could, and ran
> for it, but made frequent Tacks to fetch off his maymed
> ships, once hazarding himself very much in rescue of his
> second, who at last, was so disabled, that he could not be
> got off. . . .

Dryden compares him to C. Terrentius Varro, one of the two Roman commanders-in-chief at the disastrous battle of Cannae. After the battle he gathered the remnants of his shattered forces and organized what defenses he could. Livy wrote that when he returned to Rome a crowd met him and thanked him "quod de republica non desperasset" (XXII, lxi).

780 *dar'd.* Terrified, motionless with fear. Cf. in a speech of Tiresias (Dryden-Lee, *Oedipus*, I, i; S-S, VI, 149): "the proudest he, / Who leads you now, then cowered, like a dared lark." Cf. *Faerie Queene*, VII, vi, 47.5: "Like darred Larke; not daring up to looke."

Hobbies. A hobby is a species of falcon.

784 Here, as elsewhere, Dryden grossly underestimates the bravery and gallantry and skill of the Dutch navy, and even denies his own countrymen a victory in order to express his contempt for the foe. The Dutch fleet was considerably battered, and to have maintained the battle would have been to invite destruction. The London *Gazette* (30 July–2 August) took a brighter view of the English victory than did Dryden; it concluded its account of the battle thus:

> This is in short the Journal of this glorious Action, which
> in all Senses will pass for a great and happy Victory, when
> we compute the Enemies loss; which besides that of their
> Honor and Reputation, which is indeed irreparable, will
> be found to have been very considerable, even in the
> grosser Notions of spoil and damage.

785–792 The day of St. James, the patron saint of Spain, was 25 July. Preliminary skirmishing took place on 24 July, and the action was concluded on 26 July, but the main engagement occurred on the 25th. In these and in the three following stanzas Dryden deprecates the old policy of aiding the Netherlands against Spain—a policy which, he intimates, had fostered the rise of Holland and France to power.

801–804 "The 'Bourbon foe' of this stanza is Louis XIV, disowned by Henry IV his grandfather, as a foe to the English. William the Silent, the 'first Orange,' detests the fleet of Holland as employed against his benefactors" (Verrall).

805–832 After the defeat of the Dutch, the English fleet continued off the coast of Holland, seizing what shipping ventured by. Rupert and Albemarle, hearing of rich Dutch stores on the islands of Vlieland and Ter Schelling, ordered Sir Robert Holmes with a contingent of troops to destroy them. It was also discovered that some 150 merchant vessels richly laden were anchored in the Vly with only two warships to protect them. Holmes determined to destroy these also. In a surprise attack he was highly successful, burning the stores and most of the ships. The *Gazette* (13–16 August 1666) printed Holmes's own account of the action and then commented on the glory of it, noting particularly the pillaging which Dryden speaks of in ll. 829–832:

> On our side we can onely observe in it a Wise and prudent Counsell seasonably taken, and most vigorously executed; the whole by the blessing of God attended with admirable success, without any considerable loss in the attempt, the several Officers and Commanders in the occasion, bringing home a just reward of Glory and Reputation; and the common Seamen and Soldiers their pockets well lined with Duckets and other rich spoil, which was found in great plenty, as well on board the Merchants ships, as in the Town they burnt, and was freely abandoned to them.

820 *road.* "A sheltered piece of water near the shore where vessels may lie at anchor in safety" (*OED*).

824 *Holland.* That is, Holland linen.

825 *vex'd.* "To disturb by causing physical movement, commotion or alteration" (*OED*, which cites Dryden's line). Cf. Dryden's *Georgics*, I, 278: "vex the thrashing Floor"; *Pastorals*, IV, 40: "vex the fruitful ground."

827 *doom.* Loane (*N&Q*, CLXXXV [1943], 273) construes this to mean "propose to convey." Perhaps, "consign."

829 *rummage.* A nautical term. Cf. Thomas Blount, *Glossographia* (1661): "to remove any Goods or Luggage out of a place. Seamen use it for removing and clearing things in the ships Hold, that Goods and Victuals may be well stowed and placed."

831–832 Another of Dryden's anticlerical sallies.

833 *unsincere.* That is, adulterate, impure; not unmixed. Cf. the speech of Oedipus (Dryden-Lee, *Oedipus*, I, i; S-S, VI, 151):

> Thus pleasure never comes sincere to man,
> But lent by heaven upon hard usury. . . .

Cf. also *Brit. Red.*, l. 181: "Heav'n, to reward him, make his joys sincere."

836 Warton cites *Samson Agonistes*, l. 1538: "For evil news rides post, while good news baits."

847 note z. Ovid, *Metamorphoses*, I, 256 ff.: ([There will come a time] when the sea, when the earth, and the royal palace of heaven will catch fire and burn).

849–852 Perhaps a reference to Cromwell, who came from the country and who was an obscure figure until the 1640's. The passage was probably in Gray's mind when he wrote ll. 57 ff. of the *Elegy*.

857–860 Between one and two in the morning of Sunday, 2 September 1666, the Great Fire of London broke out in Pudding Lane at the establishment of one Farynor, the King's baker. At first it was considered of no particular importance. Pepys, called from his bed by one of his maids who was working late, looked from his window across the city at it and then went back to bed untroubled. Sir Thomas Bludworth, the Lord Mayor of London, was much annoyed at being roused from his sleep. He looked at the fire and remarked contemptuously, in one of the classic understatements of history, "Pish, a woman might piss it out." The flames rapidly got out of control. They were fanned by a strong east wind (Dryden's Belgian wind) and they fed voraciously on the ancient wooden houses huddled together in the slums and on the stores of pitch and other combustibles on the wharves of Thames Street. The fire burned with fury for four days, and when it was finally quenched London was a waste.

While the ruins were still smoldering, the *Gazette* (3–10 September 1666) gave an official account of the origin and progress of the fire. This account, which is printed below, is a succinct and effective statement, but it contains an error in chronology. W. G. Bell (*The Great Fire of London in 1666* [1920], p. vii) pointed out that the narrator was wrong in stating that the second phase of the Fire occurred on Thursday night. Actually this took place on Wednesday night, and by Thursday morning the fire was mostly over. The fire burned four days, not five, as the *Gazette* indicates.

> *Whitehall, Sept. 8.*
>
> The ordinary course of this Paper having been interrupted by a sad and lamentable accident of Fire lately hapned in the City of London: It hath been thought fit for satisfying the minds of so many of His Majesties good Subjects, who must needs be concerned for the Issue of so great an accident, to give this short, but true Accompt of it.
>
> On the second instant at one of the clock in the Morning there hapned to break out a sad & deplorable Fire, in Pudding-lane neer New'Fishstreet, which falling out at that hour of the night, and in a quarter of the Town so close built with wooden pitched houses, spread it self so far before day, and with such distraction to the Inhabitants and Neighbours, that care was not taken for the timely preventing the further diffusion of it by pulling down houses, as ought to have been; so that this lamentable Fire in a short time became too big to be mastered by any Engines or working neer it. It fell out most unhappily too, That a violent Easterly wind fomented it, and kept it burning all that day, and the night following

spreading it self up to Grace-church-street, and downwards from Cannon-street to the Water-side as far as the Three Cranes in the Vintrey.

The people in all parts about it distracted by the vastness of it, and their particular care to carry away their Goods, many attempts were made to prevent the spreading of it, by pulling down Houses, and making great Intervals, but all in vain, the Fire seizing upon the Timber and Rubbish, and so continuing it self, even through those spaces, and raging in a bright Flame all Monday and Tuesday, notwithstanding His Majesties own, and His Royal Highness's indefatigable and personal pains to apply all possible remedies to prevent it, calling upon and helping the people with their Guards; and a great number of Nobility and Gentry unweariedly assisting therein, for which they were requited with a thousand blessings from the poor distressed people. By the favour of God the Wind slackned a little on Tuesday night, and the Flames meeting with Brick-buildings at the Temple, by little and little it was observed to lose its force on that side, so that on Wednesday morning we began to hope well, and his Royal Highness never dispairing or slacking his personal care, wrought so well that day, assisted in some parts by the Lords of the Councel before and behind it, that a stop was put to it at the Temple Church, neer Holborn-Bridge, Pie-corner, Aldersgate, Cripplegate, neer the lower end of Coleman-street, at the end of Basinghall-street, by the Postern, at the upper end of Bishopsgate street, and Leaden-hall-street, at the Standard in Cornhill, at the Church in Fanchurch street, neer Clothworkers-hall in Mincing-lane, at the middle of Mark-lane, and at the Tower dock.

On thursday by the blessing of God it was wholy beat down and extinguished; but so as that Evening it unhappily burst out again afresh at the Temple; by the falling of some sparks (as is supposed) upon a Pile of Wooden buildings, But his Royal Highness, who watched there that whole night in Person, by the great labours and diligence used, and especially by applying Powder to blow up the Houses about it, before day most happily mastered it.

Divers Strangers, Dutch, and French, were, during the fire, apprehended upon suspicion that they contributed mischievously to it, who are all imprisoned, and Informations prepared to make a severe inquisition thereupon by my Lord Chief Justice Keeling, assisted by some of the Lords of the Privy Councel, and some principal Members of the City; notwithstanding which suspicions, the manner of the burning all along in a Train, and so blowen forwards in all its way by strong winds, makes us conclude the whole was an effect of an unhappy chance, or to speak better, the heavy hand of God upon us for our sins, showing us the terrour of his Judgment in thus raising the fire, and immediately after, his miraculous and never enough to be acknowledged Mercy in putting a stop to it when we were in the last despair, and that all the attempts for the quenching it, however industriously pursued, seemed insufficient. His Majesty then sat hourly in Councel, and ever since hath continued making rounds about the City in all parts of it where the danger and mischief was greatest, till this morning that he hath sent his Grace the Duke of Albemarle, whom he hath called for to assist him in this great occasion, to put his happy and successful hand to the finishing this memorable deliverance.

About the Tower the seasonable orders given for plucking down Houses to secure the Magazins of Powder, was more especially successful, that part being up the Wind, notwithstanding which it came almost to the very Gates of it, so as by this early provision, the several stores of War lodged in the Tower were entirely saved: And we have further this infinite cause particularly to give God thanks that the fire did not happen in any of those places where his Majesties Naval stores are kept so as tho it hath pleased God to visit us with his own hand, he hath not, by disfurnishing us with the means of carrying on the War, subjected us to our enemies.

It must be observed, that this fire happened in a part of the Town, where tho the Commodities were not very rich, yet they were so bulky that they could not well be removed, so that the Inhabitants of that part where it first began have sustained very great loss, but by the best enquiry we can make, the other parts of the Town, where the Commodities were of greater value, took the Alarm so early, that they saved most of their Goods of value, which possibly may have diminished the loss, tho some think, that if the whole industry of the Inhabitants had been applyed to the stopping of the fire, and not to the saving of their particular Goods, the success might have been much better, not only to the publick, but to many of them in their own particulars.

Through this sad Accident it is easie to be imagined how many persons were necessitated to remove themselves and Goods into the open fields, where they were forced to continue some time, which could not but work compassion in the beholders; but his Majesties care was most signal in this occasion, who, besides his personal pains, was frequent in consulting all wayes for relieving those distressed persons, which produced so good effect, as well by his Majesties Proclamations, and the Orders issued to the Neighbour Justices of the Peace to encourage the sending in provisions to the Markets, which are publickly known, as by other directions, that when his Majesty, fearing lest other Orders might not yet have been sufficient, had commanded the Victualler of his Navy to send bread into Moore-fields for the relief of the poor, which for the more speedy supply he sent in Bisket out of the Sea stores; it was found that the Markets had been already so well supplyed, that the people, being unaccustomed to that kind of Bread, declined it, and so it was returned in great part to his Majesties Stores again, without any use made of it.

And we cannot but observe, to the confutation of all his Majesties enemies, who endeavor to perswade the world abroad of great parties and disaffection at home against his Majesties Government; That a greater instance of the affections of this City could never be given then hath been now given in this sad and deplorable Accident, when if at any time disorder might have been expected from the losses, distraction, and almost desperation of some persons in their private fortunes, thousands of people not having had habitations to cover them. And yet in all this time it hath been so far from any appearance of designes or attempts against his Majesties Government, that his Majesty and his Royal Brother, out of their care to stop and prevent the fire, frequently exposing their persons with very small attendance in all parts of the Town, sometimes even to be intermixed with those who laboured in the business, yet nevertheless there hath not been observed so much as a murmuring word to fall from any, but on the contrary, even those persons whose losses rendred their conditions most desperate, and to be fit objects of other prayers, beholding those frequent instances of his Majesties care of his people, forgot their own misery, and filled the streets with their prayers for his Majesty, whose trouble they seemed to compassionate before their own.

857 *prodigious.* Ominous; portentous. Like rebellion, the fire begins in the dwellings of the humble people and then sweeps on against Church and state.

859 *aspire.* That is, seek ambitiously to attain.

863 *All was the nights.* Cf. the line of Varro, quoted by the elder Seneca in *Controversiae,* VII, 1 (16), 27: omnia noctis erant, placida composta quiete (All was the night's, lulled to quiet rest).

866 *Those seeds of fire.* Cf. Dryden's *Georgics,* I, 206; *Aeneis,* VII, 472–473: "seeds of envy"; *Aeneis,* VII, 766: "seeds of discord"; also *Fables,* "Of the Pythagorean Philosophy": "seeds of fire" (l. 522). In Dryden's translation of Lucretius (*Sylvae,* 1685) we find: "seeds of things" (Latter Part of the Third Book, l. 35); "seeds of breath" (*ibid.,* l. 112); and "seeds of love" (Beginning of the First Book, l. 27). Cf. *Aeneid,* VI, 730–731: igneus est ollis vigor, et coelestis origo / seminibus. . . .

869–872 The imagery is of pregnancy and birth. Cf. *Fables,* "Of the Pythagorean Philosophy," ll. 331–333:

> The Creature, pent within the narrow Room,
> Breaks his blind Prison, pushing to repair
> His stifled breath, and draw the living Air. . . .

877 *insulting.* Exulting, or leaping wantonly. In the sense of *wanton leaping* the noun is used in Dryden's *Georgics,* III, 99: "The Bull's Insult at Four she may sustain. . . ."

881 note *a.* Terence, *Heauton Timorumenos,* II, iii, 125–126 (366–367). The quotation varies slightly from the standard texts:

> haec arte tractabat virum,
> ut illius animum cupidum inopia incenderet

(She handled the man with skill in order that she might fire his desirous heart by his failure to get her).

888 *nods.* "To incline (the head)." The *OED* cites this line as an example of the meaning, by transference.

889–892 This stanza, together with st. 215, intimates Dryden's belief that the fire served as a penalty for treason and rebellion. Since Dryden was hoping to strengthen the bonds between the King and his subjects, it would have been unwise to emphasize at this time the rebelliousness of the City in the past. Later, in *Brit. Red.,* ll. 152–156, he expressed boldly the belief that both the fire and the plague had been sent to purge rebellion.

Stanza 223 has been generally admired. Dr. Johnson called it "vigorous and animated"; Scott referred to it as "this most beautiful stanza."

The ceremony described is the dance and chant of the witches' Sabbath, in which all participants are ghosts of rebels and traitors. Scott notes:

> The skulls of the regicides, of the fifth-monarchy insur-
> gents, of Philips, Gibb, Tongue, and other fanatics exe-
> cuted for a conspiracy in 1662, were placed on the Bridge,
> Towerhill, Templebar, and other conspicuous places of
> elevation; that of the famous Hugh Peters, in particular,
> was stationed upon the bridge.

890 *Fanatick.* A term applied to the Puritan extremists, many of whom were opposed to the monarchy.

893–896 The idea of guardian angels watching over cities, provinces, kingdoms, and monarchies was later developed as a scheme suitable for furnishing Christian epic machinery (cf. *Satires of Juvenal and Persius* [1693], dedication, pp. xi–xiii).

908 A somewhat similar line occurs in the final speech of Act IV in the Dryden-Lee *Oedipus:* "But gods meet gods, and jostle in the dark." Cf. also a parody of this line in the *Hind,* l. 1898: "But birds met birds, and justled in the dark."

914 Fire buckets were kept in the churches. Cf. *Spanish Fryar,* V, ii (S-S, VI, 514): ". . . my Wife cry'd out Fire, Fire; and you brought out your Church-buckets, and call'd for Engines to play against it."

915 *Some cut the Pipes.* It was a custom formerly to cut the wooden pipes in order to fill the fire buckets. Before the Great Fire, however, cocks had been installed in the New River pipes at the entrance to each ward, so that in the event of fire the pipes would not have to be cut. But in the confusion and disorder of the first day of the Great Fire the pipes conducting the New River waters were severed, with the result that the water escaped and the pipes and cisterns in some parts of the city ran dry. Cf. Bell, *The Great Fire of London,* pp. 35 and 60.

921 *Key.* That is, quay; a wharf or dock in river or harbor. The English-Latin dictionary of Elisha Coles gave as the Latin equivalent of *key:* portus manufactus.

922 note *b. Aeneid,* II, 312: (The straits of Sigeum light up from the blaze far and wide).

925–928 Settle declared (*Notes and Observations on the Empress of Morocco Revised* [1674], p. 83) that this stanza was "stolen" from Cowley's *Davideis* (Poems, ed. Waller, p. 248):

> Swift Jordan started, and straight backward fled,
> Hiding among thick reeds his aged head. . . .

Van Doren noted that the stanza vaguely suggests *Lycidas.* Its ultimate source may have been *Aeneid,* IX, 124–125:

> cunctatur et amnis
> rauca sonans, revocatque pedem Tyberinus ab alto.

Cf. Dryden's translation (ll. 151–152):

> Old Tyber roar'd; and raising up his Head,
> Call'd back his Waters to their Oozy Bed.

926 Scott and Christie note that the river burnt by Vulcan (according to Homer) was the Scamander or Xanthus, not the Simois.

944 The Lombard bankers were the bankers of Lombard Street, near the Royal Exchange; the center of the City's financial activities.

947–948 These lines develop a suggestion contained in st. 215. They are true only in the sense that the flames spread westward along the river, in the direction of the palace of Whitehall; the palace, however, was not too seriously threatened.

949 John Oldmixon (*Essay on Criticism* [1728], pp. 38–39), after commending for its delicacy of thought a verse of Chaucer's which Dryden in the *Fables,* "Palamon and Arcite," III, 190, translated "Up rose the Sun, and up rose Emily"; goes on to say:

Mr. Dryden, in another place,
    Now Day appears, and with the Day the King,
imitates Chaucer, but the Delicacy is lost, for there is
nothing more to be understood by it, as there is in this
Couplet of his to the Dutchess of Ormond upon her going
to Ireland before the late Duke,
    As Ormond's Harbinger, to you they run,
    For Venus is the Promise of the Sun.
Cf. also Cowley, *Davideis*, II, 2: "up rose the Sun and Saul."

955–972 Dryden's praise of the King was not flattery. Contemporaries
recognized Charles's courage and wisdom during the fire, and many of
them, such as Evelyn, were not writing for publication. Sunday Pepys
reported to the King on the extent and danger of the fire and was ordered
to go to the Lord Mayor and offer him any help which he needed from
the crown. By Monday it became evident that the City authorities were
unable to cope with the emergency, and Charles took command. He put
James in control of the city and appointed certain other nobles as his
lieutenants. Charles and James made plans and directed the activities of
the fire fighters, and from time to time they themselves were in the thick
of the fight. Evelyn wrote under date of 6 September:
        It is not indeed imaginable how extraordinary the vigi-
        lance and activity of the King and Duke was, even labour-
        ing in person, and being present to command, order, re-
        ward, or encourage workmen, by which he showed his
        affection to his people and gained theirs.
And a contemporary correspondent wrote to a friend in the country
(HMC, *Le Fleming MSS*, p. 42):
        The King made the round of the fire usually twice a day,
        sometimes on horseback, sometimes on foot, giving orders
        for pursuing the work, by commands, threatenings, de-
        sires, example, and good store of money which he dis-
        tributed to the workers out of bag of 100 l. carried for
        the purpose.

977–984 It was early suggested that the only effective way of fighting
the fire was to blow up houses in its path. In the early stages when this
method would have been successful, the Lord Mayor refused to take action
for fear of financial responsibility for the houses thus destroyed. Later
when some houses were blown up, the gap thus made was not wide enough
to stay the flames, with the result here described by Dryden. Finally toward
the end of the fire the use of gunpowder on a large scale, aided by the
subsidence of the heavy winds, was successful in stopping the flames.

977 The image is used later in a speech of Almahide's in *1 Conquest
of Granada*, V, ii (S-S, IV, 113):
        It was your fault that fire seiz'd all your brest,
        You should have blown up some, to save the rest.
Almanzor's speech that follows strongly suggests that Dryden had the
Great Fire of London in mind.

982 According to Sir Henry Blount, the Turkish military system was designed to produce valor even out of fear. The cavalry, he observed, were wont to bring up the rear of the foot soldiers, in the formation of a half moon; and they were ordered to permit their own forces no retreat, "and in case of Flight, to hold them out to slaughter . . ." (*A Voyage into the Levant* [3d ed., 1638], p. 71).

990 This is the stuff of nightmares. Cf. Antony (*All for Love*, I, i): "The hag that rides my dreams." Also Creon (Dryden-Lee, *Oedipus*, II, i; S-S, VI, 169): "wild horrors of the night / And hags of fancy." The dance may have been suggested by a passage in the third *Georgics,* describing a fury released from subterranean captivity by plague (Dryden's trans., ll. 820–821):

> Tisiphone, let loose from under ground,
> Majestically pale, now treads the round. . . .

995 *retire.* In its French sense *retirer,* to draw back, remove. In ll. 979, 1027, and 1155 the word is used in a common sense.

997–1000 The fire offered an unprecedented opportunity for laboring men to profit, especially porters, watermen, and carters. Thomas Vincent angrily reported the extortion (*God's Terrible Voice in the City* [1667], p. 63):

> Now Carts, and Draies, and Coaches, and Horses, as many
> as could have entrance into the City were loaden, and any
> money is given for help 5 *l.* 10 *l.* 20 *l.* 30 *l.* for a Cart, to
> bear forth into the Fields some choice things, which were
> ready to be consumed; and some of the Countreys had the
> conscience to accept of the highest price, which the Citi-
> zens did then offer in their extremity; I am mistaken if
> such money do not burn worse, than the Fire out of which
> it was rak'd.

999 *th' ignoble crowd.* A translation of Virgil's *ignobile vulgus,* as in Dryden's *Aeneis*, I, 213; IX, 462; XI, 572.

1011–1012 The image was used previously in *Ld. Ch.,* ll. 47–48.

1014–1016 Cf. *Gondibert,* I, vi, sts. 41–42:

> Then it had given your wonder cause to last,
>   To see the vex'd mistakes this summons wrought
> In all my Maim'd Domesticks, by their haste;
>   For some tie on the Limbs which others sought.

> Just such mistakes audatious Ethnicks say
>   Will happen, where the Righteous busie are,
> Through glad and earnest hast in the last day;
>   Whilst others slowly to their doom prepare.

The image in l. 1016 suggests that in Cowley's "The Resurrection":

> Then shall the scatter'd Atoms crowding come . . .
> And where th' attending Soul naked, and shivering stands,
> Meet, salute, and joyn their hands.

Dryden's account of the fire is introduced by an image of the *Dies Irae* (st. 212) drawn from Ovid, and here appropriately reinforced by the imagery of the Judgment Day. Such imagery still exerted a powerful effect upon Dryden's contemporaries; there are numerous examples given in Poole, *The English Parnassus* (1657), pp. 357–359. Dryden introduced similar imagery in *To Mrs. Killigrew*, ll. 178–187.

1014 *dismal.* Suggestive of *Dies Mali* and therefore fitting in this context.

1022 *require.* "To seek after, search after" (*OED*, which cites Dryden's line).

1025 *Vestal fire.* Vesta was the Roman goddess of the household and hearth.

1028 *repeat.* "To encounter or undergo again" (*OED*, which cites Dryden's line). Christie defines it, to *reseek,* which better conveys the Latinate sense.

1029 The fields mentioned in the *Gazette*'s account were Moorfields (cf. ll. 857–86on.), lying to the north of the City.

1030 *obnoxious.* Exposed to, in danger of, susceptible to. Cf. Dryden, *Juvenal,* VI, 674; *Aeneis,* VIII, 521; *Fables,* "Ceyx and Alcyone," l. 491. Cf. also Sprat, *History of the Royal-Society* (1667), p. 243: "I confess many Experiments are obnoxious to failing. . . ."

1057–1064 Dryden does not mean to imply, in this speech of the King's, that any part of the disaster could possibly be attributable to Charles's sins. Rather, he is exhibiting the King as the model of a devout Christian, behaving as the Royal Society thought each good man must conduct himself in time of national afflictions. Sprat wrote on this subject (*History of the Royal-Society* [1667], pp. 363–364):

> Whenever therefore a hevy calamity falls from Heven on our Nation, a universal Repentance is requir'd; but all particular applications of privat men, except to their own hearts, is to be forborn. Every man must bewail his own Transgressions, which have increas'd the Public misery. But he must not be too hasty, in assigning the Causes of Plagues, or Fires, or inundations to the sins of other men.

Cf. ll. 1077–108on.

1064 Loane points out (*N&Q,* CLXXXV [1943], 273) that this line was suggested by a passage in st. 3 of Cowley's paraphrase "The 34. Chapter of the Prophet Isaiah":

> The wide-stretcht Scrowl of Heaven, which we
> Immortal as the Deity think . . .
> Shall crackle, and the parts together shrink
>   Like Parchment in a fire.

Dryden probably had Cowley's lines in mind. But cf. also Shakespeare, *King John,* V, vii, 32–34.

1066 *spotted deaths.* A reference to the plague which had raged during the summer and fall of 1665. Though it was rapidly subsiding in February 1666, Pepys reported on 13 February a temporary (and alarming) increase in the number of cases.

1069 *frequent funerals*. That is, numerous bodies. One of Dryden's Latinisms. Cf. his translation of Virgil, *Aeneis*, II, 493: "The Streets are fill'd with frequent Funerals. . . ." Here *frequent Funerals* translates Virgil's *plurima inertia corpora*.

1077–1080 Scott noted that this stanza, as well as st. 265, resembles David's prayer in I Chronicles, xxi. That portion of the prayer in st. 265 is similar to the prayer of Oedipus in Dryden-Lee, *Oedipus*, II, i (S-S, VI, 160–161).

1081–1088 Cf. Cowley, "The Plagues of Egypt," st. 14:

> Michael, the warlike Prince, does downwards fly
> > Swift as the journeys of the Sight,
> > Swift as the race of Light,
> And with his Winged Will cuts through the yielding sky.
> He past through many a Star, and as he past,
> Shone (like a star in them) more brightly there,
> > Than they did in their Sphere.

1083–1084 The cherub's task was greatly facilitated by the fact that the Tower, where the "magazines of powder" were kept, lay up the wind, and the fact that by royal command the houses close by the Tower had been pulled down to forestall the fire. Even so, the stores of powder narrowly escaped (cf. ll. 945–946). Like Dryden, the London *Gazette* viewed the sparing of the naval magazines as a sign that God was not willing to let foreign foes oppress the land. Cf. ll. 857–860n.

1089–1092 The "pious Structures" were of course pre-Reformation churches and other religious foundations constructed before Luther and Calvin lent support to the doctrine of Justification by Faith "without Works."

1091 Christie noted here *Georgics*, IV, 562: viamque adfectat Olympo (And he aspires to reach Heaven).

1093–1096 Christ's Hospital suffered damage to the extent of £8000 (T. F. Reddaway, *The Rebuilding of London after the Great Fire* [1940], p. 257). The children were not around, however, to watch the destruction, for the Governors had sent them away to safety before the flames reached the institution (W. G. Bell, *The Great Fire of London* [1920], p. 141).

1097–1104 As the fire progressed it had been thought that surely St. Paul's would be spared, and many, particularly the booksellers, had stored their treasures within it for safekeeping. But on Tuesday the great cathedral also yielded to the flames. A contemporary thus described the event (T. Vincent, *God's Terrible Voice* [1667], p. 65):

> Now the Fire gets into Black-fryers, and so continues its
> course by the water, and makes up towards Paul's Church,
> on that side, and Cheap-side Fire besets the great building
> on this side, and the Church though all of stone outward,
> though naked of houses about it, and though so high
> above all buildings in the City, yet within a while, doth
> yield to the violent assaults of the conquering flames, and
> strangely takes Fire at the top; now the lead melts and

runs down, as if it had been snow before the Sun; and the great beames and massy stones, with a great noise fall on the Pavement, and break through into Faith-Church underneath; now great flakes of stone scale, and peel off strangely from the side of the Walls. . . .

1099 As Derrick noted, this is a reference to Waller's "Upon His Majesty's Repairing of Paul's."

1100 The remarkable instance of construction produced by the playing of Amphion's lyre. Cf. Dryden's translation of Virgil's *Pastorals,* II, 29–30.

1103 Dugdale gave the following account of the desecration of St. Paul's by Cromwell's soldiers (*The History of St. Paul's Cathedral in London* [1658], p. 173):

> . . . for the better disposall of the Timber, so imployed for Scaffolds [to support the arched vaults], and otherwise, much of it was sawed up in the Church, Pits being digg'd for that purpose, in severall places thereof; even where some reverend Bishops, and other persons of quality lay interred. Since which time the body of the Church has been frequently converted to a Horse quarter for Souldiers.

The timber, it appears, was sawed up and disposed of in order to pay arrears in wages due to the soldiers.

Details of the desecration of St. Paul's are given in "An Elegy upon the Most Incomparable King Charles the First," a poem attributed to Henry King (cf. Saintsbury, *Minor Poets of the Caroline Period,* III, 259–260).

1119–1120 Far more than half of the old city was destroyed. According to the inscription on the Monument, four hundred streets, eighty-nine churches and numerous other public buildings, and more than thirteen thousand dwelling places were laid waste.

1121–1124 This stanza has found no admirers. It was ridiculed in print as early as 1668 in *A Letter from a Gentleman to the Honourable Ed. Howard.* The anonymous author, after reference to Dryden's principle that "the Poet dresses Truth, and adorns Nature, but does not alter them," proceeds to quote this passage of *Annus;* upon which he comments (pp. 8–9): "Now the Reader may easily judge, whether this be not Moral Truth; if this does not resemble Natural Truth, if it be not Ethical, and if the Squire has not drest Truth, and adorned Nature, but not altered them." Dr. Johnson considered the imagery of the stanza "unexpectedly mean." Scott pointed out the wild mixture of metaphors, from candle-snuffing to falconry. Others have elaborated these objections.

1128 *Lares.* The *Lares Familiares,* of course, who were beneficent spirits exercising care over hearth and household.

1141–1144 On Wednesday, Charles issued two proclamations for the care of the people. He commanded the officers of the counties to send in provisions, especially bread; and he directed that churches, schools, and other public buildings be thrown open for the storage of goods. He also ordered all towns to receive the refugees and to allow them to practice their trades. Clarendon recorded the King's action and the results of it (*Life* [1857], II, 287–288):

> When the night, though far from being a quiet one, had somewhat lessened the consternation, the first care the king took was, that the country might speedily supply markets in all places, that they who had saved themselves from burning might not be in danger of starving; and if there had not been extraordinary care and diligence used, many would have perished that way. The vast destruction of corn, and all other sorts of provisions, in those parts where the fire had prevailed, had not only left all that people destitute of all that was to be eat or drank; but the bakers and brewers, which inhabited the other parts which were unhurt, had forsaken their houses, and carried away all that was portable: insomuch as many days passed, before they were enough in their wits and in their houses to fall to their occupations; and those parts of the town which God had spared and preserved were many hours without any thing to eat, as well as they who were in the fields. And yet it can hardly be conceived, how great a supply of all kinds was brought from all places within four and twenty hours. And which was more miraculous, in four days, in all the fields about the town, which had seemed covered with those whose habitations were burned, and with the goods which they had saved, there was scarce a man to be seen: all found shelter in so short a time, either in those parts which remained of the city and in the suburbs, or in the neighbour villages; all kind of people expressing a marvellous charity towards those who appeared to be undone.

1145–1148 The King's bounty, together with his heroic efforts in fighting the flames, made a deep impression on the city. Like Dryden, the account of the London *Gazette* stressed the gratitude and loyalty of the citizens. Cf. ll. 857–860n.

1150 *auspice.* "Prosperous lead; propitious influence exerted on behalf of any undertaking" (*OED,* which cites Dryden's line).

1151 *hatch.* Loane (*N&Q,* CLXXXV [1943], 274) calls attention to the equally bold use of this word in Dryden's *Georgics,* II, 458: "The World was hatch'd by Heav'ns Imperial King." The boldness of the thought is matched by Milton's in *Paradise Lost,* I, 19–22. But the expression was original with none of these. Cf. George Herbert's "Whitsunday," l. 3. Browne, writing of the Spirit of God, had remarked in *Religio Medici,* Pt. I, sect. 32: "This is that gentle heat that broodeth on the waters, and in six days hatched the World. . . ."

1157–1160 Cf. Ezra, I–III.

1161–1164 The association of comets with plague, fire, and war was well established in poetry by this time. Joshua Poole in *The English Parnassus* (1657) gives as poetic definitions of comet (p. 285), "the dismal star / That threats the world with famine, plague, or war," and "the Star that wears a beard of flame." Cf. Cowley, "The Plagues of Egypt," st. 9:

> From poysonous Stars a mortal Influence came
> (The mingled Malice of their Flame). . . .

Dryden's earlier reference to comets (ll. 64–72) reflects his interest in scientific speculation; this later passage is written in a different key, like several other passages in the last third of the poem.

1165–1167 Planets in a trine aspect to each other (120° apart) were thought astrologically to be in their most perfect, harmonious, and beneficent relationship. Cf. Dryden's ode *To Mrs. Killigrew*, ll. 41–43:

> For sure the Milder Planets did combine
> On thy Auspicious Horoscope to shine,
> And ev'n the most Malicious were in Trine.

Cf. also *Fables*, "Palamon and Arcite," III, 389. The opportunity for a play on words by extending the term to mean the Holy Trinity was too much for Dryden to resist: cf. *Brit. Red.*, l. 33.

1168 *succeed*. Cause to be successful.

1169–1172 The poetical periphrasis for Fire given by Poole (*The English Parnassus* [1657], p. 307) is "the soule of Chymick art." Sprat remarked of the "Chymists" of his day (*History of the Royal-Society* [1667], p. 37): "And without question, they have lighted upon the right Instrument of great productions, and alterations: which must for the most part be perform'd by Fire." According to Sprat (*ibid.*) there were three ranks of Chymists: those given to the pursuit of natural philosophy, those who seek out and prepare medicines, and those who "search after riches, by Transmutations, and the great Elixir." The "Chymick flame" in l. 1169 is probably intended as the "Instrument of great productions, and alterations"; although ll. 1170–1172 suggest the transmutations claimed by alchemy.

1171–1172 The legendary riches of Mexico were still powerful in their effect on the English imagination. Dryden's *Indian Emperour* (produced in 1665) had made liberal use of Montezuma's fabulous wealth.

1185 *Maiden Queen*. Subtitle of *Secret Love*, the play which Dryden wrote at Charlton immediately before commencing *Annus Mirabilis*. *Secret Love* was almost certainly in the stage of rehearsals at the time when *Annus* was published.

1191–1192 Loane (*N&Q*, CLXXXV [1943], 274) notes that the same conceit is employed by Joseph of Exeter, *De Bello Trojano*, I, 516–522, where the Simois is depicted as winding about Troy in admiration.

1193 *The wealthy Tagus*. A river of Spain, once thought to be replete with golden sands. Cf. Dryden's *Juvenal*, III, n. 12. The Tagus was a stock allusion in seventeenth-century poetry (cf. Poole, *The English Parnassus* [1657], p. 200).

1195 An oblique reference to the ambitions of Louis XIV.

1204 *vindicate*. "To defend against encroachment or interference" (*OED*).

1209 Cf. Virgil, *Eclogues,* IX, 59; hinc adeo media est nobis via. This Dryden translated (*Pastorals,* IX, 82): "Already we have half our way o'recome." In 2 *Conquest of Granada,* V, ii (S-S, IV, 215), King Ferdinand is given a line with the same rhythm: "Already more than half the Town is gain'd."

1210 *is left behind.* That is, still remains to be undertaken.

To Mr. Lee, on His Alexander

This poetic epistle appeared late in 1677, printed in Lee's *The Rival Queens, or the Death of Alexander the Great.* Several months earlier, not later than February 1677, Lee's piece of enthusiastic extravagance, "To Mr. Dryden, on his Poem of Paradise," was published in Dryden's *State of Innocence.* Their friendly relations continued for years. In 1678 Dryden contributed an epilogue to *Mithridates;* in 1679, a prologue to *Caesar Borgia;* at Oxford in 1680, a prologue for a special performance of *Sophonisba;* and in 1683, an epilogue to *Constantine the Great.* In addition, he collaborated with Lee in *Oedipus* (acted January 1679) and *The Duke of Guise* (acted by 1 December 1682); and Lee contributed a complimentary poem prefixed to *Absalom* in 1681.

Nathaniel Lee (1649?–1692) seems to have taken a degree at Cambridge, where he was connected with Dryden's college, in 1668/9, thereafter coming down to London. In the decade from 1675 to 1685 he was one of a group of poets who hovered about Dryden and in some measure followed his lead. At least two others were Trinity College men, Richard Duke and Charles Saunders—a fact which suggests that Dryden maintained connections with his college. Tate, Duke, and Otway contributed to *Ovid's Epistles,* and the same trio, late in 1682 and early in 1683, wrote commendatory verses for Creech's Lucretius. Creech wrote a complimentary poem for *Religio Laici,* and dedicated to Dryden his translation of Horace. Lee, Tate, and Duke wrote commendatory verses for *Absalom,* as did Tate for *The Medall.* Duke was a boon companion of Otway's, and a friend to Henry Dickinson, the young man whose translation of Father Simon furnished the immediate occasion for *Religio Laici.* The relationships of the group are much more involved, and the details are not to the purpose here. But out of this group (to which one should probably add Thomas Southerne) came a number of heroic plays and tragedies which made the decade from 1675 to 1685 the most brilliant period for serious drama since the theaters were closed by the Puritans.

Lee, still remembered for his plays of surcharged emotion and his endeavors at an elevated and passionate style, began his dramatic career with a tragedy, *Nero,* in 1675, following it with *Sophonisba* in 1676. His epistle prefixed to *The State of Innocence,* probably written late in 1676, provides the first positive evidence of Lee's discipleship; but Dryden must have known the young man earlier, for Lee's first two plays had been acted by

Dryden's company. The circumstances of Lee's epistle, moreover, hint at something like collusion. In February 1676 Dryden's *Aureng-Zebe* had been published, dedicated to John, Earl of Mulgrave, and in the dedication Dryden revealed his high hopes (hopes encouraged by Mulgrave) that he might be enabled to write an epic poem as the fulfillment of his career. Lee's epistle obligingly picks up the burden, and exhorts Dryden to proceed from his heroic opera to a great epic which would still the clamors of critics. And *The Rival Queens*, in which Dryden's epistle appears, was dedicated to Dryden's patron Mulgrave.

Part of the reason for the bond between the two poets is disclosed by Dryden's *To Mr. Lee*, in which, after deprecating the envy of wits and critics, he commends the young dramatist for daring greatly, writing with perhaps excessive vigor, drawing nature and passion with fire that warms the heart, and soaring in a style that is lofty and full of striking and beautiful images. There is no doubt that Dryden was personally concerned in his praise of those literary qualities which Lee represented. In 1674 or shortly thereafter he had read Boileau's translation of Longinus on the Sublime, and had been enormously impressed. The results are conspicuous in the preface to *The State of Innocence*, where, frequently citing Longinus, Dryden condemns the critics who accept all that is dull, limp, insipid, and flabby as an imitation of nature, and proceeds to justify an heroic style that is rich and impassioned, bold and sublime, full of strong figures and daring imagery. Much of the substance of his epistle *To Mr. Lee* is anticipated here. Returning to the charge again two years later, in the preface to *Troilus and Cressida*, he drew upon Longinus once more to defend a noble boldness of expression and imaginations lofty and heroic. His interest in Longinus, his intense admiration for Shakespeare and Milton, and his desire to write an epic poem that would be sublime, elevated, and vehement—all combine to arouse in him a resentment toward the restrictive tastes of contemporary audiences and readers.

To Mr. Lee is written in the middle style, as befits an epistle. It is several planes removed from the colloquial rhythms and diction, the dash and breeziness, of the prologues and epilogues. The figures, though numerous, are so plain and familiar as to be scarcely noticeable. The poem rises in feeling and dignity as it proceeds.

3–4 The "bribe" was the outrageous flattery of Lee's commendatory poem "To Mr. Dryden, on his Poem of Paradise." In this unhappy effort the young poet had written:

> To the dead Bard, your fame a little owes, ⎤
> For Milton did the Wealthy Mine disclose, ⎬
> And rudely cast what you cou'd well dispose: ⎦
> He roughly drew, on an old fashion'd ground,
> A Chaos, for no perfect World was found,
> Till through the heap, your mighty Genius shin'd;
> His was the Golden Ore which you refin'd.

In the preface to *The State of Innocence* Dryden, with all his tact and grace, commented on Lee's comparison of his poem with Milton's epic (sig. b1; Ker, I, 179):

> And, truly, I should be sorry, for my own sake, that any one should take the pains to compare them together: The Original being undoubtedly, one of the greatest, most noble, and most sublime Poems, which either this Age or Nation has produc'd. And though I could not refuse the partiality of my Friend, who is pleased to commend me in his Verses, I hope they will rather be esteem'd the effect of his love to me, than of his deliberate and sober judgment.

8 *Bessus* is a character in Beaumont and Fletcher's *A King and No King*. In the play Bessus, a cowardly soldier, and two other equally cowardly swordsmen testify to one another's courage and honor.

10 Verrall notes that the suggestion of mutual flattery between states and kings may allude to political overtures to Holland, made in accordance with Danby's policy and exemplified in the marriage of Princess Mary to William of Orange, which occurred in the year Dryden's epistle to Lee was written.

11–12 Another indication of Dryden's lack of sympathy for the Hobbesian account of human nature. *By-ends* are secret aims based on self-interest, concealed designs for one's private advantage. Bunyan's notable character of this name, it might be recalled, did not appear until 1678.

20 *Reversions.* "The right of succession to an office or place of emolument, after the death or retirement of the holder" (*OED*).

31–32 Scott identified this hero as Sir Edward Spragge, who fought gallantly in both the second and third Dutch wars. In 1671 he led a squadron to the Mediterranean for the purpose of punishing the Algerine pirates. The pirates, occupying seven ships, took refuge in the bay of Bugia, where they were protected by a castle and forts and by a boom drawn across the bay. Spragge boldly entered the bay, silenced the forts, broke the boom, and destroyed the pirate fleet. Christie objected to this identification on the grounds that the assault on the Algerine pirates had nothing to do with the Dutch. But, as Saintsbury pointed out, the taking of the Dutchman need not have occurred at the same time as the breaking of the boom.

Dryden had praised Spragge in *Annus*, ll. 693–694.

45–46 R. G. Ham suggested (*Otway and Lee* [1931], p. 109) that Dryden was perhaps referring to the attack on Lee in the satirical "A Session of the Poets"—a poem of doubtful authorship which is still assigned to Rochester. This poem was apparently circulating in manuscript in October 1677 (J. C. Ghosh, *Works of Otway* [1932], I, 18). As printed in the 1680 *Poems on Several Occasions by the Right Honourable, the E. of R—— it contained these lines on Lee (p. 112):

> N—— L——, stept in next, in hopes of a Prize,
> Apollo, remember'd he had hit once in Thrice;
> By the Rubyes in 's Face, he cou'd not deny,

But he had as much Wit, as Wine cou'd supply;
Confest that indeed he had a Musical Note,
But sometimes strain'd so hard, that he rattled ith' Throat;
Yet owning he had Sense, t' encourage him for 't,
He made him his Ovid in Augustus's Court.

It would appear, however, that Dryden was not referring to a particular attack but to a whole school of critics and poets who were so addicted to ease, politeness, and refinement of style that they disdained any sign of boldness or fire, not only in Lee but in Oldham and John Dryden as well.

49–50 A highly interesting compliment, in view of Dryden's virtual obsession with the importance of imagery in poetry. His concern is evident in the "Account" prefixed to *Annus Mirabilis,* but it is stated most vigorously and positively in the preface to *The State of Innocence* (sig. b4v; Ker, I, 186): "Imaging is, in itself, the very height and life of Poetry."

51–52 The infrequency of references to specific painters in Dryden's writings is remarkable in view of his numerous allusions to painting. Even allowing for the exigencies of meter and rhyme, the citing of Titian and Michelangelo as drawers of true beauty suggests that he had not as yet been much influenced by academic taste in painting, which was forming in France and which du Fresnoy expressed in his *De Arte Graphica.* This new taste admired Raphael for his fidelity to the manner of the ancients, his correctness of design, his expression, and his grace. It brought into disrepute colorists such as Titian and Rubens, as well as Michelangelo and his followers, whose violence and distortion seemed a deviation from *la belle nature.* The new taste was reflected in the work of Roland Fréart, Sieur de Chambray, whose attack on Michelangelo in *The Idea of the Perfection of Painting,* translated by John Evelyn in 1668, Dryden in all likelihood had read. That Dryden persisted in his admiration for Michelangelo is not too surprising in view of the appeal which Longinus and the doctrine of the Sublime held for him in the 1670's.

Contributions to Ovid's Epistles

Ovid's Epistles, advertised on 6 February 1680, contains the first of Dryden's translations to appear in print: two epistles of which he was sole translator and one, *Helen to Paris,* written in collaboration with the Earl of Mulgrave. From 1680 to the end of his life the great bulk of his nondramatic poetry was to consist of translations.

In 1693 Dryden recollected that he had translated the Third Satire of Persius "for a Thursday Nights Exercise" while he was a King's Scholar at Westminster School, and that many other exercises of that sort, done at that time, were still, he believed, in the possession of Dr. Busby.[1] In or

---

[1] Dryden, *Satires of Persius* (1693), p. 31.

about 1665 he was planning to translate a portion of Lucretius.[2] And there is some ground for thinking that in the year or two before the publication of *Annus Mirabilis* he may have tried his hand at rendering parts of Virgil and Ovid into English.[3] At any rate, that translations by Dryden began to appear in print by 1680 was probably due in large measure to the fact that in 1679 he had established an enduring business relationship with that extraordinarily shrewd and enterprising publisher, Jacob Tonson, who knew that the public would buy translations. It was Tonson who issued *Ovid's Epistles.*

Precisely what part Dryden played in arranging for the collection known as *Ovid's Epistles* we do not know. He has sometimes been described as the editor of the volume, but there is no evidence that he acted in that capacity. It seems more likely that Tonson collected the pieces, and engaged Dryden, because of his great prestige, to write the preface. There is some support for such a view in the advertisement published by the *True Domestick Intelligence,* no. 76 (23–26 March 1680), which concludes:

> To this Book is prefix'd a Preface, giving some account of
> the Life and Writings of Ovid, and a Discourse of Poetical
> Translations in general; by Mr. Dryden. Sold by Jacob
> Tonson. . . .

Dryden, who almost certainly had tried his hand at translating Ovid long before 1680, may well have suggested the project to Tonson.

Dryden's continuing interest in Ovid may be seen in the fact that in the last two decades of his life his published translations from that poet amount to above seven thousand lines.[4] He was drawn to Ovid partly by a similarity in artistic temperament. Oldmixon remarked in 1728: "Dryden seems to have enter'd as far into the Genius of Ovid as any of his Translators. That Genius has more of Equality with his own than Virgil's; and, consequently, his Versions of Ovid are more perfect than those of Virgil." [5] In the dedication of *Examen Poeticum* (1693) Dryden confessed that his versions of Ovid appeared to him superior to any of his other works of translation, and he added: "Perhaps this Poet, is more easie to be Translated, than some others, whom I have lately attempted: Perhaps too, he was more according to my Genius." [6] When near the close of his life he related, with pardonable satisfaction, that his "Thoughts, such as they are, come crowding in so fast upon me, that my only Difficulty is to chuse or to reject," he may well have compared himself with the Latin poet of incomparable exuberance and fertility.[7]

Ovid would inevitably have attracted an English poet in 1680, for his style represented most of the qualities which the newly formulated ideal

2 Preface to *Sylvae* (1685), sig. a5 (Ker, I, 264).
3 For Virgil, cf. p. 264 above.
4 D. Nichol Smith, *John Dryden* (1950), p. 68.
5 *The Arts of Logick and Rhetorick,* p. 291.
6 Dedication of *Examen Poeticum* (1693), sig. B1v (Ker, II, 9).
7 Preface to the *Fables* (1700), sig. *A2 (Ker, II, 249).

required. In belles-lettres Dryden's contemporaries greatly valued the ease, elegance, politeness, and wit of a gentleman and courtier. For that reason the Court, as Dryden puts it, "is the best and surest judge of writing." [8] Some of the felicities of his own style Dryden attributed to his having enjoyed the conversation of Rochester and other court wits.[9] In an eighteenth-century summary of standard critical opinions, Harwood reported that even Virgil and Horace were deemed inferior to Ovid in courtliness of expression. "The Reason was," said Harwood, "Ovid was a Gentleman, and the others not. . . ." [10] No man, said Joseph Scaliger, could ever successfully imitate Ovid's easiness of style. Commenting specifically on the *Epistles*, Peter Crinitus noted the great elegance of their style; and Joseph Scaliger pointed out that they are the most polite of all Ovid's works, displaying an easy and natural elegance.[11] And Rapin styled them the flower of Roman wit.[12] No wonder that Ovid, as Dryden tells us, had all the Beaux as his professed patrons.[13]

But Dryden's interest in Ovid was of long standing even when the *Epistles* came out in 1680. For seventeen years his talent had been directed mainly to the drama, and he had been aware of much he could learn from Ovid. Of all the ancients, he wrote in 1667, Ovid "had a Genius most proper for the Stage." [14] In particular he noted Ovid's power of showing "the various movements of a Soul combating betwixt two different Passions"—an essential feature of Dryden's technique in his serious plays. Rapin, whom Dryden was reading closely in the 1670's, expressed a preference for Ovid above Tibullus and Propertius because Ovid "is more natural, more moving, and more passionate." [15] At the time when his interest in Shakespeare was at a height, when he was proclaiming Shakespeare's extraordinary genius in depicting and moving the passions, Dryden was using Ovid to illustrate the masterful handling of passion.[16] The indebtedness of Dryden's more serious plays to Ovid must have been considerable.

In still another way Ovid lent himself to Dryden's plans. From 1658 he had been making sundry experiments in the heroic style, and had tried the capacities of the heroic couplet and the *Gondibert* stanza for elevation and nobility of tone. From 1664 he had devoted himself to the writing of heroic plays, a form which he conceived to be closely related to the epic. Precisely when he began to project an epic poem we do not know. It seems

[8] *Of Dramatick Poesie* (1668), sig. A3 (Ker, I, 24).

[9] Dedication of *Marriage A-la-Mode* (1673).

[10] *Biographia Classica* (1778), I, 292.

[11] Scaliger and Crinitus as quoted in Thomas Pope Blount, *De Re Poetica* (1694), pp. 145 and 152.

[12] *Works*, trans. Basil Kennett (2d ed., London, 1716), I, 171.

[13] Preface to the *Fables* (1700), sig. A1*v* (Ker, II, 248).

[14] *Of Dramatick Poesie* (1668), p. 24 (Ker, I, 53).

[15] *Works* (1716), II, 230.

[16] Preface to *Troilus and Cressida* (1679), sig. b2 (Ker, I, 222–223).

clear, however, that during the early 1670's he was exerting himself to secure the patronage needed if he was to embark on such an ambitious and sustained undertaking. In the dedication to *Aureng-Zebe* (1676) he revealed that Mulgrave had known for years of his desire to write an epic and had helped him in an attempt to interest the King and the Duke of York in the projected work. Mulgrave, it will be recalled, was his collaborator in one of *Ovid's Epistles*.

Some portion of the art required by the epic, as he understood it, Dryden certainly acquired from Ovid. At one point in the early 1670's his attention was called to the technique of the "turn"—a feature, he says, of great beauty in heroic verse. And this striking beauty, though he found it in Spenser and Tasso, seemed to have its principal fountain in Latin poetry in the works of Virgil and Ovid.[17] Even before his interest in the "turn," however, he had found in Ovid and Virgil the essentials of heroic verse. Discussing the proper "wit" of an heroic or historical poem, he concluded that there were three necessary qualities: invention, fancy, and elocution. Of these, he said, the first two were displayed most notably in Ovid, the third in Virgil.[18] The revelation of the soul in the violence of its passions—this is an art in which the tender and delicate strokes of Ovid raised him even above Virgil.[19] And some time shortly after 1674 Dryden began to read Longinus attentively, who taught him that "to write pathetically . . . cannot proceed but from a lofty Genius," and that the artful management of the passions makes a discourse sublime.[20] In view of the fact that the epic was then regarded as the sublimest achievement of human art, it is clear how much the ambitious writer of epic could profit by the lessons of Ovid.

To Dryden, nature meant first of all the passions; and part of his motive in translating Ovid was no doubt the delight he took in nature and Ovid. But the publication of *Ovid's Epistles* follows hard upon the printing of Dryden's dramatic version of *Paradise Lost* and upon his adaptation of two tragedies by Shakespeare. There is a good chance that his versions of the *Epistles* should be read not as trifles thrown off in playful moments but as experiments in heroic poetry—and possibly as preparation for the writing of that magnum opus which was never to be penned.

THE VERSE

Dryden describes the style of Ovid in the *Epistles* as "tenderly passionate and Courtly." [21] In 1685 he expatiated on the subject of Ovid's versification: [22]

> Ovid with all his sweetness, has as little variety of Num-
> bers and sound as [Claudian]: He is always as it were

---

[17] Dedication of *The Satires of Juvenal* (1693), pp. l–li (Ker, II, 109).
[18] "An Account of the Ensuing Poem" prefixed to *Annus*, cf. above p. 53 (Ker, I, 15).
[19] Cf. above, p. 54 (Ker, I, 16).
[20] Preface to *Troilus and Cressida*, sig. b1 (Ker, I, 220).
[21] Cf. above, p. 114 (Ker, I, 236).
[22] Preface to *Sylvae*, sig. A5v (Ker, I, 255).

upon the Hand-gallop, and his Verse runs upon Carpet ground. He avoids like the other all Synaloepha's, or cutting off one Vowell when it comes before another, in the following word: So that minding only smoothness, he wants both Variety and Majesty.

On the subject of his translations from Ovid appearing in the *Examen Poeticum,* he said: [23]

> I have . . . attempted to restore Ovid to his Native sweetness, easiness, and smoothness; and to give my Poetry a kind of Cadence, and, as we call it, a run of Verse, as like the Original, as the English can come up to the Latin. As he seldom uses any Synalephas, so I have endeavour'd to avoid them, as often as I cou'd: I have likewise given him his own turns, both on the Words and on the Thought. . . .

This will help to prepare us for the style of Dryden's translation. The strength of line which he had achieved in some of his earlier poems is not here, nor is the variety of his later verse. In spite of the fact that the triplet and alexandrine, which gave variety and fullness, were accepted features of nondramatic poetry by this time and had been used by Dryden himself before 1680, no alexandrine can be found in the three epistles, and the only triplet occurs in the epistle in which Mulgrave collaborated.[24] The sound of Dryden's verse in the *Epistles* is generally sweetened and muted; and even where the sense betokens violence or fierce energy, the verse transforms it to something less immediately threatening. Thus Canace's terrible father is described as he rushes tumultuously from his throne to uncover the fruit of incest, concealed under olive branches:

> With one fierce puff, he blows the leaves away.

And the fearful storm that threatens to delay Aeneas' departure comes to us with all its terror removed:

> But now with Northern Blasts the Billows roar,
> And drive the floating Sea-weed to the Shore.

Dryden's expressed purpose of avoiding the synaloepha was strikingly successful. In *Canace to Macareus* only one instance occurs, *th' unhappy* (l. 83), and in *Dido to Aeneas* there is none. *Helen to Paris*—partly the work of Mulgrave—contains three: *t' other* (l. 117), *th' Essay* (l. 140), and *th' occasion* (l. 172). How sparing Dryden was, may be seen by comparing his translations with others in the same volume.[25]

---

[23] *Examen Poeticum,* sig. B3 (Ker, II, 10).

[24] *Helen to Paris,* ll. 147–149. Most of the other authors represented in *Ovid's Epistles* employed the triplet. There are, for example, two triplets in Tate's "Hero to Leander," four in Otway's "Phaedra to Hippolytus," and eighteen in Aphra Behn's "Oenone to Paris." In the same volume the alexandrine is rather less common, but it may be found in John Caryl's "Briseis to Achilles" and Richard Duke's "Acontius to Cydippe"; and Settle's "Hypsipyle to Jason" concludes with a pair of alexandrines.

[25] For example, in the 116 lines of Tate's "Hero to Leander" there are six synaloephas.

If synaloepha is to be avoided in verse of Ovidian smoothness, how should the poet treat the case of "yawning" vowels for which the synaloepha was devised as a remedy? Dryden does not discuss the question; in fact, he reveals few of his prosodical secrets. In practice the synaloepha was sometimes useful in avoiding a supernumerary syllable, and in Restoration usage it was unlikely to occur except when the definite article or when the preposition *to* of the infinitive, was followed by a vowel. Were "yawning" vowels considered ungainly in other circumstances? No positive answer can be given, but a suggestion may be found in an analysis of the three epistles. The least carefully wrought of the three is the collaborative *Helen to Paris,* and in this there are forty-seven instances of "yawning" vowels in 259 lines, including five in which the definite article or infinitive is involved. In the 212 lines of *Dido to Aeneas* there are thirty instances, including four in which the definite article or infinitive appears. In the 146 lines of *Canace to Macareus* only seventeen instances occur, in none of which we find the infinitive or definite article. One other set of facts should complement these observations. The probable objection to "yawning" vowels was that they introduced a pause in pronunciation which might not coincide with a rhetorical pause. It is interesting, therefore, to note that Dryden sometimes avoids the effect of "yawning" vowels by introducing a rhetorical pause—marked by a comma or semicolon—between them. In the collaborative *Helen to Paris* there are three instances (ll. 204, 220, and 255) in which the objectionable effect is so avoided; in *Dido to Aeneas* there are only two (ll. 1 and 182); and in *Canace to Macareus* there are four (ll. 25, 35, 89, and 95). In these respects, *Canace to Macareus* seems to be the most carefully wrought of the three epistles.

Dryden had two distinct, though not necessarily conflicting, aims in forming the verse of the *Epistles:* the lines were to be smooth and sweet, and they were to be dramatic. The dramatic quality of the style is reflected partly in the plainness of diction and in the sparsity of ornamental adjectives. Other dramatic qualities may perhaps be best viewed in connection with an account of Dryden's handling of the couplet.

In his earlier poetry, conspicuously in *Astraea Redux,* Dryden was accustomed to close his couplets, but also to group them in clusters of four, six, or even eight lines. It is somewhat surprising, therefore, to discover that in *Dido to Aeneas* most of the couplets are not only closed, but are complete grammatical units, concluded with a period or the equivalent. Such independent couplets comprise nearly 72 per cent of the total number of lines in this epistle. In *Canace to Macareus* couplets of this variety comprise only 41 per cent of the total length; in *Helen to Paris,* 47 per cent. Moreover, *Dido to Aeneas* contains the smallest proportion of run-over lines and enjambed couplets. Apparently endeavoring at Ovidian smoothness, Dryden in *Dido to Aeneas* fashioned verse that approached the later Augustan standards of correctness and regularity.

But the epistles, as we have observed, were dramatic. As early as 1666, in the "Account" prefixed to *Annus Mirabilis,* Dryden had commented on the dramatic quality of Ovid. When, in the 1670's, he set about to transform

Paradise Lost into a sort of play, he faced the practical problem of realizing the dramatic possibilities of heroic verse. In the preface to *The State of Innocence,* probably written early in 1677, he reveals part of his discoveries. The mind torn with passion, he observes, is reflected in warm and precipitate utterance, in boldness of figures.[26]

> . . . A man in such an occasion is not cool enough, either to reason rightly, or to talk calmly. Aggravations are then in their proper places, Interrogations, exclamations, Hyperbata, or a disordered connection of discourse, are graceful there, because they are Natural.

How Dryden employed the figures dramatically at this time may be seen at the beginning of Act V of *The State of Innocence.* Lines 17–26 reflect relative serenity; the lines that follow, displaying the conflicting passions of Adam and Eve, have a strikingly different rhythm and cadence, and interrogations, exclamations, and disordered connections of discourse are present in abundance.

Since *Ovid's Epistles* presents a series of soliloquies by love-tormented souls, we are not surprised to find the same figures. *Canace to Macareus* contains nine exclamations and eleven interrogations—a higher proportion than in either of the other two epistles in which Dryden had a hand. The disordered connections of discourse take the form of parentheses, sudden breaks in thought signified by the use of a dash, and internal stops. There are eleven internal stops in *Canace to Macareus,* eleven in *Dido to Aeneas,* and only seven in *Helen to Paris.* Some of these figures, of course, are directly suggested by the Latin original, but the measure and proportion of them are in the control of the translator.[27] It would appear, then, that Dryden was more careful to express dramatic tension in *Canace to Macareus* than in either of the other two epistles.

Yet, conceiving of the style of Ovid in the *Epistles* as "tenderly passionate and Courtly," Dryden had reason to avoid the expression of passion in its utmost violence and turbulence; in the three epistles it is muted and subdued to accord with the ease and smoothness of style which he designed. There is an almost pastoral remoteness about the emotional storms of Canace, Dido, and Helen.

The difference between Dryden's verse in *Ovid's Epistles* and that of his other nondramatic poetry of the 1680's suggests that the three epistles may have been composed some time before they were published. It is tempting to conjecture, because of a rough parallel between the situation of Aeneas and Dido and that of Cleopatra and Antony, that *Dido to Aeneas* served as a kind of preliminary to *All for Love;* and, from a vague resemblance in theme, that *Canace to Macareus* served as a kind of preliminary to *Oedipus.* But there is no real evidence, and such Delilahs must be resisted.

---

[26] *State of Innocence* (1677), sig. b4v (Ker, I, 186).

[27] The figures in Otway's and Tate's epistles, in the same volume, are noticeably fewer and the proportion of internal stops smaller. Tate's "Hero to Leander," for example, contains three internal stops; Otway's "Phaedra to Hippolytus," only one.

One thing more must be said, in view of the fact that Dryden's practice in translation involved the use of previous English translators, from whom on occasion he took rhymes, phrases, and even whole lines.[28] In rendering *Ovid's Epistles* he probably followed Borchard Cnipping's edition of Ovid (1670) as his basic text, and drew for assistance or suggestion upon the following: George Turbervile, *The Heroycall Epistles of the Learned Publius Ovidius Naso* (1567), Wye Saltonstall, *Ovids Heroicall Epistles Englished by W. S.* (1636), and John Sherburne, *Ovids Heroical Epistles* (1639).

In making use of his English predecessors Dryden observed a venerable tradition. His translation of the *Epistles,* however, is not heavily indebted to any previous translator. Most commonly his predecessors served him by suggesting a rhyme word, or occasionally a pair of rhyme words. Now and then he found in them a phrase or a half line which he appropriated; and in two instances he took over a whole line with virtually no change. These borrowings are listed in the notes below. There are, in addition, sundry faint echoes of phrasing in Dryden which may point to further indebtedness, but most of them are so tenuous as not to justify inclusion. Dryden's lines show a neatness, sureness, and harmony of verse and language that could be claimed for none of the earlier translators.

Material for the notes on Dryden's borrowings which follow, is based on a rich and exhaustive study of the translators of Ovid's *Epistles;* this work, still in manuscript, was generously made available by its author, Professor Linda Van Norden.

In the notes which follow we have made no attempt to explain Ovid's subject matter or his art. Texts of Ovid are readily available, and the stories on which the *Epistles* are based are generally familiar. Our primary concern has been with Dryden as a translator, with his method and accuracy, and with his manner of assimilating previous English translations.

Preface

P. 109: ll. 2–4 *I will not presume so far* etc. A remark not to be taken too seriously. In 1693 Dryden confessed that he had not read Sandys' Ovid since he was a boy—probably as a student at Westminster School (*Examen Poeticum,* sig. B2v; Ker, II, 10).

109:18 *or search'd into the nature of it* etc. In the preface to *Sylvae* (1685, sig. a3; Ker, I, 262) Dryden says of Lucretius' treatment of love: "He has given the truest and most Philosophical account both of the Disease and Remedy, which I ever found in any Author. . . ."

109:21 *Authour of a certain Epigram.* See Martial, XI, 20.

28 Cf. J. M. Bottkol, "Dryden's Latin Scholarship," *MP,* XL (1943), 243; Helene M. Hooker, "Dryden's *Georgics* and English Predecessors," *HLQ,* IX (1946), 273–310.

109:23 *fulsome.* "Morally foul, filthy, obscene" (*OED,* which cites this instance).

109:24–25 *naked Familiarity of His Expressions.* See Suetonius, Vita Horati, *De Viris Illustribus:* Praeterea saepe eum inter alios iocos "purissimum penem" et "homuncionem lepidissimum" appellat, unaque et altera liberalitate locupletavit.

110:20 *Cur aliquid vidi* etc. *Tristia,* II, 103: (Why did I see something? Why did I make my eyes guilty?)

111:1 *Nudam sine* etc. *Tristia,* II, 105: inscius Actaeon vidit sine veste Dianam (Unwittingly Actaeon saw Diana unclothed). The word *nudam* does not appear in Ovid's line.

112:16 *Nescivit quod* etc. Seneca, *Controversiae,* IX, 5 (28), 17.

112:28–29 *a secret gracefulness of youth* etc. The concept of the secret grace probably came over into literary criticism from discussions of the art of painting. Generally it had reference to esthetic qualities apart from design or structure. Dryden probably had in mind some such thought as we find in Rapin, *Réflexions sur la Poétique d'Aristote,* II, xv (*Whole Critical Works,* trans. Kennett [2d ed., 1716], II, 200): "Ovid has . . . Youthfulnesses that could hardly be pardon'd, but for the Vivacity of his Wit, and a certain Happiness of Fancy."

112:30 *In the most material part* etc. Rapin, whom Dryden had been reading with care, similarly praised the design of the Elegies: "Ovid did much Violence to himself to unite his *Metamorphoses,* and close them in one Design, in which he was not altogether so happy, as afterwards in his *Elegies,* where well nigh always one may find a certain Turn, which binds the Design, and makes thereof a Work that is just by the dependance and relation of its Parts" (*Whole Critical Works,* trans. Kennett [1716], II, 152). Dryden's preference for Ovid above Tibullus on the grounds that Ovid's elegies show superior design, provoked the dissent of George Sewell. Sewell remarked that to require design in the elegy could be justified rather from the practice of Waller and some of Dryden's contemporaries than from the practice of the ancients, "of whom none but Ovid, and he very seldom, observed that Rule" (quoted in the preface of Dart's *Works of Tibullus* [1720], p. xiii).

113:5–6 *Purpureus late* etc. Horace, *Ars Poetica,* 15–16: (One or two purple patches are sewn on, to shine far and wide).

113:13 *The Title of them* etc. In 1670 Cnipping's edition had the title *Epistolarum Heroidum Liber.*

113:19–20 *this way, which our Poet* etc. The form of the elegiac epistle being a hybrid, there was relatively little discussion of it, and none to dispute Ovid's claims as originator. Neither Boileau's *L'Art Poétique* (1674) nor Mulgrave's *Essay upon Poetry* (1682) takes up the form of elegiac epistle. When Oldmixon in 1703 offered the public his imitations of Ovid's *Epistles,* entitled *Amores Britannici. Epistles Historical and Gallant, in English Heroic Verse,* he could still say (dedication, sig. A8):

There's but little Light to guide a Man in this way of Writing. For, besides the Epistles of Ovid and Sabinus,

> and one of Propertius's, there are no such Letters in any
> of the Ancients; and among the Moderns, none at all,
> except a small Volume in Italian, call'd *Epistole Eroici.*
> . . . The French have nothing in this kind, more than a
> wretched Translation of Ovid.

And the English, added Oldmixon, have Drayton, whose attempts were far
from successful. An account of how the form originated was later given
by Hurd. Ovid took over the substance of the elegy, he observed, and
without the expenditure of much energy or invention contrived a new
sort of poetry. By collecting scattered bits and directing them to one
principal view and superadding a personal address, he became the author
of the elegiac epistle, beautiful examples of which are his *Heroides* and
Epistles from Pontus (*Q. Horatii Flacci Ars Poetica,* ed. Hurd [1749],
pp. xi–xii).

113:20 *vindicated to himself.* To "assert or establish possession of
(something) *for* oneself or another" (*OED,* which cites this passage as its
earliest example).

113:23 *Jupiter ad veteres* etc. *Ars Amatoria,* I, 713: (Jove used to approach the heroines of ancient times as a suppliant).

113:28 *Quam celer e toto* etc. *Amores,* II, xviii, 27: quam cito de toto,
etc. (How quickly my friend Sabinus returned from the ends of the earth).

113:29 *I remember not any* etc. Noyes points out that the observation is
indebted to Heinsius' introductory note to the *Heroides.*

114:15–17 *for his amorous Expressions* etc. This remark is apparently
intended to justify only the *Epistles,* for previously in the preface Dryden
gives up the defense of the *Elegies* and the *Art of Love,* conceding that
they have power to corrupt an empire. In defending the virtue of the
Epistles Dryden is voicing an opinion current in his time, that the warmest
erotic sentiments may be permissible in the poet if his language is chaste.
Mulgrave briefly introduces the theory in his *Essay upon Poetry* (1682,
Spingarn, II, 288):

> Not that warm thoughts of the transporting joy,
> Can shock the Chastest, or the Nicest cloy;
> But obscene words, too gross to move desire,
> Like heaps of Fuel do but choak the Fire.

In the few years preceding *Ovid's Epistles,* during the period of perhaps
his greatest intimacy with Mulgrave, Dryden was evidently reflecting upon
the problem of how obscenity was related to action and expression in
literature. The problem had probably been made acute and personal by
the charges of bawdry made against his comedy *The Kind Keeper* (first
acted on 11 March 1678), but he seems to have reached his conclusions
before this, for in the preface to *All for Love* (advertised in the London
Gazette, 21–25 March 1678), quoting Montaigne to reinforce his judgment,
he wrote (sig. b1v):

> 'Tis true, some actions, though natural, are not fit to be
> represented; and broad obscenities in words, ought in

good manners to be avoided: expressions therefore are
a modest cloathing of our thoughts, as Breeches and Pet-
ticoats are of our bodies. If I have kept my self within
the bounds of modesty, all beyond it is but nicety and
affectation. . . .

In 1685 Dryden applied the theory to his translation of Lucretius (*Sylvae,*
sig. a4; Ker, I, 263): ". . . neither he nor I have us'd the grossest words;
but the cleanliest Metaphors we cou'd find, to palliate the broadness of
the meaning. . . ." This represents a slight modification of his position in
1680, for it recognizes that chaste language can only help to compensate
for unchaste sentiments.

As the age grew more modest, there was less inclination to defend either
lubricity of sentiment or Ovid's erotic poems. Oldmixon remarked of his
own imitation of the *Epistles* (dedication, *Amores Britannici* [1703], sig.
A7v): "I have taken Care, not to offend the Modesty of the Fair, and have
banish'd those Sentiments, which as beautiful as they are in Ovid, wou'd
be as dangerous to Manners, as agreeable for their Tenderness and Passion." The very fact that Ovid's *Epistles* were directed to the passions, even
though the language might be chaste, made against them. As Dryden's
young friend Dennis remarked (*Critical Works,* ed. E. N. Hooker [1939–
1943], I, 284): "For Obscenity cannot be very dangerous, because it is rude
and shocking; but Love is a Passion, which is so agreeable to the movements
of corrupted Nature, that by seeing it livelily touched and often represented, an Amorous disposition insensibly insinuates itself into the chastest
Breast." In 1718, it is true, Dennis observed of a passage in Virgil (*ibid.,*
II, 402–403): "That which makes this one of the beautifullest Passages of
all the Eclogues, is, that there is a very wanton Meaning express'd in very
modest Words, and consequently occasion given to the Reader to shew his
Discernment by piercing the Veil which the Poet has thrown over the
Nudity. . . ." But Dennis was concerned with vindicating playful lubricity
rather than the moving expression of erotic passion. His point of view was
developed by John Bancks, who regarded a poem as inoffensive which,
while skirting lubricity, treated its subject lightly and divertingly. The
real mischief is done, said Bancks, when the piece is aimed at the reader's
passions, as in Ovid (*Miscellaneous Works* [2d ed., 1739], I, x–xi).

After 1680 the objections to Ovid, both on the grounds of his corrupting
the reader's morals and on the grounds of his negligence, "boyisms," and
redundant fancy, tended to lower his reputation. By 1717 Dr. Garth felt
impelled to take up the defense of Ovid, who "I think," he says, "is too
much run down at present by the critical Spirit of this Nation . . ."
(preface to *Ovid's Metamorphoses* [1717], p. xv).

114:24 *All Translation I suppose* etc. Here for the first time Dryden
states his theory of translation. He was to return to the subject several
times in succeeding years. For comment on his theory, see the notes on the
dedication of the *Aeneis.*

115:1 *to run division.* "A florid phrase or piece of melody, a run; *esp.*

as a variation on, or accompaniment to, a theme. . . . *To run division:* to execute such a passage or variation" (*OED*).

115:6–7 *Nec verbum* etc. *Ars Poetica,* 133–134. In 1680 Roscommon published a translation of the *Ars Poetica* into blank verse.

115:11–18 *the Expression of Sir John Denham,* etc. Ker pointed out that Dryden improved his quotation from Denham by omitting four lines which follow the second line as quoted. They are (*Il Pastor Fido . . . Newly Translated out of the Originall* [1647], sigs. (a)-(a)*v.*):

> Those are the labour'd births of slavish brains,
> Not the effects of Poetry, but pains.
> Cheap vulgar arts, whose narrownesse affords
> No flight for thoughts, but poorly sticks at words.

115:25 *Atque ijdem* etc. *Heroides,* VII, 8: (And the same winds bear away your sails and your loyalty).

116:10 *Brevis esse* etc. *Ars Poetica,* 25–26: (I strive to be brief, I become obscure).

116:14–15 *Dic mihi* etc. *Ars Poetica,* 141–142.

116:20 ὃς μάλα etc. *Odyssey,* I, 1: (who was very much tossed [on the sea]).

116:24 *two of our famous Wits* etc. Denham wrote of his method of translation (*The Destruction of Troy, An Essay upon the Second Book of Virgils Aeneis* [1656], sigs. A3–A4):

> . . . Therefore if Virgil must needs speak English, it were fit he should speak not onely as a man of this Nation, but as a man of this age; and if this disguise I have put upon him (I wish I could give it a better name) sit not naturally and easily on so grave a person, yet it may become him better then that Fools-Coat wherein the French and Italian have of late presented him; at least, I hope, it will not make him appear deformed, by making any part enormously bigger or less then the life, (I having made it my principal care to follow him, as he made it his to follow Nature in all his proportions). Neither have I any where offered such violence to his sense, as to make it seem mine, and not his. Where my expressions are not so full as his, either our language, or my Art were defective (but I rather suspect my self;) but where mine are fuller then his, they are but the impressions which the often reading of him, hath left upon my thoughts; so that if they are not his own conceptions, they are at least the results of them; and if (being conscious of making him speak worse then he did almost in every line) I erre in endeavoring sometimes to make him speak better; I hope it will be judged an error on the right hand, and such an one as may deserve pardon, if not imitation.

Cowley in the same year wrote of his imitations of Pindar (*Poems* [1656], sigs. Aaa2–Aaa2*v*):

If a man should undertake to translate Pindar word for
word, it would be thought that one Mad-man had translated another; as may appear, when a person who under-
stands not the Original, reads the verbal Traduction of
him into Latin Prose, then which nothing seems more
Raving. And sure, Rhyme, without the addition of Wit,
and the Spirit of Poetry (quod nequeo monstrare & sentio
tantum) would but make it ten times more Distracted
then it is in Prose. We must consider in Pindar the great
difference of time betwixt his age and ours, which changes,
as in Pictures, at least the Colours of Poetry, the no less
difference betwixt the Religions and Customs of our
Countreys, and a thousand particularities of places, persons, and manners, which do but confusedly appear to our
eyes at so great a distance. . . . And when we have considered all this, we must needs confess, that after all these
losses sustained by Pindar, all we can adde to him by our
wit or invention (not deserting still his subject) is not like
to make him a Richer man then he was in his own Countrey. This is in some measure to be applyed to all Translations; and the not observing of it, is the cause that all
which ever I yet saw, are so much inferior to their Orig-
inals. . . . It does not at all trouble me that the Grammarians perhaps will not suffer this libertine way of
rendring foreign Authors, to be called Translation; for I
am not so much enamoured of the Name Translator, as
not to wish rather to be Something Better, though it want
yet a Name. I speak not so much all this, in defence of my
maner of Translating, or Imitating (or what other Title
they please) the two ensuing Odes of Pindar; for that
would not deserve half these words, as by this occasion
to rectifie the opinion of divers men upon this matter.
. . . Upon this ground, I have in these two Odes of
Pindar taken, left out, and added what I please; nor
make it so much my aim to let the Reader know precisely
what he spoke, as what was his way and manner of speaking; which has not been yet (that I know of) introduced
into English. . . .

117:33 *Poetry is of so subtil* etc. The quotation is from *The Destruction of Troy,* sig. A3.

118:3 *are in my Opinion the two Extremes,* etc. The method of finding
a way between two extremes was a characteristic of Dryden's criticism,
and apparently a reflection of the temper of his mind. Some of the most
illuminating revelations of his taste occur in his comparisons of Shakespeare
and Jonson, Juvenal and Horace, and Homer and Virgil.

F. L. Huntley in *On Dryden's "Essay of Dramatic Poesy"* (Ann Arbor,
1951) has pointed out Dryden's constant use of terms in antithetical pairs,

such as "instruct and delight," "judgment and fancy," and "art and nature." Reviewing Huntley's study, Samuel H. Monk noted (*PQ,* XXXI [1952], 269):

> . . . Dryden's criticism, whether dramatic or non-dramatic, is a world which revolves on an axis of which these apparently antithetical groups of words are the poles. This critical world, however, *includes* both poles, though on occasion Dryden may stand nearer the one or the other. Both, however, are always in view.

Part of the task of reason in criticism, therefore, is to reconcile extremes; but if the reconciliation is to be effected, the antithetical terms must be apparent, rather than real, contradictions. Something of Dryden's mode of thinking is reflected in the conversation between Benzayda and Ozmyn, 2 *Conquest of Granada,* III, ii (S-S, IV, 166):

> *Benz.* My wishes contradictions must imply;
> You must not go; and yet he must not die.
> Your reason may, perhaps, the extremes unite;
> But there's a mist of fate before my sight.
> *Ozm.* The two extremes too distant are, to close;
> And human wit can no mid way propose.

119:1–5 *When a Painter Copies from the Life* etc. Despite the dominant position that portraiture held in the art of Dryden's England, it was generally considered that history painting is a higher genre, since it allows for more invention and for the imitation of *le beau ideal.* Neither Lely nor Kneller was famous for hitting exact likenesses, since flattery was a source of their income. When it suited him, Dryden could always argue against himself. Here he reverses a position which he had taken in 1668 in the *Defence of an Essay* (Ker, I, 114), where he had written:

> There may be too great a likeness; as the most skilful Painters affirm, that there may be too near a resemblance in a Picture: to take every lineament and feature is not to make an excellent piece, but to take so much only as will make a beautiful Resemblance of the whole; and, with an ingenious flattery of Nature, to heighten the beauties of some parts, and hide the deformities of the rest.

This opinion is restated in the *Parallel of Poetry and Painting* (p. 6; Ker, I, 114).

119:9–10 *Et quae* etc. Horace, *Ars Poetica,* 149–150: et quae / desperat . . . relinquit (And those matters which he despairs of making brilliant if he treats of them, he abandons).

119:28 *the Authour who is of the Fair Sex.* Aphra Behn, whose translation of *Oenone to Paris* is labeled "a paraphrase," the only one in the collection so called. In the second edition of the volume a new translation of this epistle, by John Cooper, is added. In his poem "A Satire on the Modern Translators," written in 1685, Prior had some unkind things to say about Mrs. Behn and her translation (*Dialogues of the Dead,* ed. Waller [1907], p. 49):

The Female Wit, who next convicted stands,
Not for abusing Ovid's Verse, but Sands';
She Might have learn'd from the ill-borrow'd Grace,
(Which little helps the Ruin of her Face)
That Wit, like Beauty, triumphs o'er the Heart,
When more of Nature's seen, and less of Art:
Nor strive in Ovid's Letters to have shown
As much of Skill, as Lewdness in her own.
Then let her from the next inconstant Lover,
Take a new Copy for a second Rover:
Describe the Cunning of a Jilting Whore,
From the ill Arts her self has us'd before;
Thus let her write, but Paraphrase no more.

119:31–33 *I have transgress'd the Rules* etc. As Dryden admits, and as the notes below indicate, he has taken a good many liberties. Occasionally he omits a line or a couplet in Ovid, and sometimes he contracts a passage by retrenching the fancy or luxuriance of his original. On the other hand, in one place he adds a couplet with no basis in Ovid, and he frequently expands the sense of his original, developing a meaning that was implicit or latent. Dryden is inclined to translate freely, trying to convey Ovid's meaning but making little effort to hold to his phrasing. Because his interest lies primarily in the dramatic situation, Dryden yields little to the temptation toward diffuseness. In spite of the fact that English requires more words to express a thought than the Latin, Dryden's English versions are not longer by many lines than Ovid's text. Dryden succeeds in catching the spirit of Ovid, and in writing English poetry at the same time. If he seems to depart freely from the words of his original, it must be remembered that the seventeenth-century translator was expected to interpret as well as to translate; his task included the exposition of the text.

119:33–34 *But so many Gentlemen* etc. In the first edition the following gentlemen are identified as translators: Sir Carr Scrope, Mr. Ed. Poley, Mr. Wright, Mr. Pulteney, Mr. Tate, Mr. Tho. Flatman, Mr. Ed. Floyd, Mr. Richard Duke, the Earl of Mulgrave, Mr. Rymer, Mr. Settle, Mr. Otway, John Caryl, Esq., and Mr. Butler. The translators of three of the epistles are not identified. Two of these were apparently done by John Somers, known to posterity as the great Lord Somers. See note to *Dido to Aeneas,* l. 2, below.

Canace to Macareus

Dryden omits the first two lines of the Latin, the genuineness of which was long disputed:

Aeolis Aeolidae, quam non habet ipsa, salutem
    mittit et armata verba notata manu

(The daughter of Aeolus to the son of Aeolus sends the greeting [salvation] which she does not possess herself, and words written by a hand now armed). The obvious reason for the omission of these lines in most MSS was that a space for two verses was left blank in the archetype until the illuminator had put in the initial, and this space was never filled in. Cnipping's edition of Ovid rejects the lines on the authority of Heinsius.

In Dryden's translation lines 35, 52, 54, 86, and 143 have each one a rhyme word identical with that in the corresponding passage of Sherburne. Lines 32 and 53 have each one a rhyme word identical with that in the corresponding passage of Saltonstall. Line 113 uses the same rhyme word as the corresponding passage in Turbervile. Lines 95–96 bear only a faint resemblance to Saltonstall's rendering, but line 60 is taken from Saltonstall with scarcely a change.

4 Cf. Sherburne: "And in my lap the limber paper lies." Cf. also Turbervile: "And in my carefull lap the Paper lyes." Since Ovid's *charta soluta* really means the unrolled scroll or writing material, Dryden is more exact than his predecessors.

5–6 Cf. Sherburne:
> This is my posture whilst to thee I write:
> Thus my obdurate parent I delight.

And Saltonstall:
> Thus Canace doth to her brother write.
> This posture yeelds my father much delight.

19–20 Cf. Saltonstall:
> Now in my fearefull hand I hold a sword,
> That fatall gift, which must my death afford.

24 Cf. Sherburne: "To thee, why more than sister showd I love?"

30 The first half of this line almost inevitably recalls Pope, *Epistle to Arbuthnot*, l. 147: "Soft were my Numbers. . . ."

39–42 Noyes pointed out that these lines have no basis in the Latin text. In the first edition they are inclosed by inverted commas, used apparently to call attention to the lines as additions to the original text.

44 Cf. Turbervile: "And wt his weight my weakened limmes opprest." The "turn" in Dryden's line is faintly anticipated in *Her. St.*, l. 90.

55 *thicker*. More quickly, faster. Cf. *Annus*, ll. 478n. and 497. Cf. also *All for Love*, II, i (S-S, V, 377): "For, all the pleasures I have known, beat thick / On my remembrance."

56 *conscious*. "Having guilty knowledge" (*OED*). For the word in somewhat different senses, cf. *Helen to Paris*, l. 143; *Dido to Aeneas*, l. 112.

59–60 Cf. Saltonstall:
> So that I did suppresse my groanes, and cries,
> And dranke the teares that flow'd downe from my eies.

61–62 Cf. Saltonstall:
> While thus Lucina did deny her aid,
> Fearing my fault in death should be betrai'd.

63–68 These three couplets render three of Ovid's (vv. 57–62) but not exactly. With 67–68, cf. Saltonstall:

> And thou didst put me still in hope of life,
> Saying, deare sister thou shalt be my wife.

69–70 An expansion of Ovid, v. 63.

71–72 An expansion of Ovid, v. 64.

73–78 An expansion of Ovid, vv. 65–66. The sense of ll. 77–78 is implicit in v. 66.

75–76 Cf. *Paradise Lost*, II, 1–5. Also *MacFlecknoe*, l. 107: "High on a Throne of his own Labours rear'd." The rhyme words in *MacFlecknoe*, ll. 108–109, are the same as in the couplet from *Canace*.

85–88 An expansion of Ovid, vv. 73–74.

89–94 An expansion of Ovid, vv. 75–78. Vv. 75–76 are mistranslated. Correctly translated, they read: (As the sea trembles when it is ruffled by a light breeze, / As a branch of an ash-tree is moved by a warm south wind. . . .)

99–100 Cf. Saltonstall:

> He commanded, my son should be straitway
> Cast forth, and made to beasts and birds a prey.

104 Cf. Turbervile: "(You may my case coniecture by your owne)."

111–114 An expansion of Ovid, vv. 95–96.

133–134 A very free rendering of Ovid, v. 115.

135 Translates Ovid, v. 116.

136 A very free rendering of Ovid, vv. 117–118.

146 Cf. Turbervile: "My cruell fathers will. . . ."

Helen to Paris

Dryden omits the initial two lines of the Latin:

> si mihi, quae legi, Pari, non legisse liceret,
> servarem numeros sicut ut ante probae

(If it were within my power not to have read what I have read, I should now be preserving the role of a chaste woman, as I formerly was). The reason for the omission is doubtless the same as for the opening lines of *Canace to Macareus*.

Dryden's rhyme word in line 76 is found in the corresponding passage of Sherburne; that in line 204, in the corresponding passage of Saltonstall and of Turbervile; that in line 209, in the corresponding passages of all three predecessors. The pair of rhyme words in lines 57–58 is found in the corresponding passage of Turbervile.

10 Cf. Sherburne: "Thou that thus cam'st, wert thou a guest, or foe?"

17 Cf. Sherburne: "Yet my fame's cleare, I've liv'd without a staine."

21–22 Cf. Saltonstall:

> Because once Theseus stole me as a prey,
> Shall I the second time be stolne away?

23 Cf. Sherburne: "Had I been wonne, the fault on me might lye."

27–28 Cf. Saltonstall:

> Some kisses only he did striving gaine,
> But no more kindnesse could from me obtaine.

33–36 An expansion of Ovid, vv. 33–34. Cf. l. 34 with Turbervile: "Did Theseus so recant / that Paris should succeede."

41–42 Cf. Saltonstall:

> But because Women should not soone beleeve men,
> For men with flattering words doe oft deceive them.

55–56 A contraction of Ovid, vv. 53–56.

62 Cf. Sherburne: "Yet doe I thinke ours are no lesse." Between ll. 62 and 63 Dryden has omitted vv. 63–64 of Ovid.

63–66 An expansion of Ovid, vv. 65–66.

73–74 Cf. Saltonstall:

> And that thou should'st a painfull voyage take
> Through the rough Seas, and all even for my sake.

Cf. also Turbervile:

> But most of all I weigh
>   thy love that for my sake
> Such paines abodste, whose hope to passe
>   the seas did undertake.

79–82 Translates Ovid, vv. 79–80; but vv. 81–82 are neglected.

87–88 Cf. Sherburne:

> Oft have I read, writ on the boord above
> In wine, my name; and underneath't, I love.

"Within this pleasing grove" is strange for "on the round table." Dryden's predecessors are more accurate in rendering this.

121 Cf. Saltonstall: "Were the first true, the latter part is fain'd."

125–126 Cf. Saltonstall:

> I am content that men may beauty prize,
> That beauty Venus praises, she envies.

136 Following this line, vv. 137–140 in the original are omitted.

143 *conscious.* Sharing in the secret.

154 Cf. Turbervile: "When in a doubt he stood."

164–165 Cf. Sherburne:

> Fame too, annoys us, for the more you praise
> My face, the more his jealous fears you raise.

174 *doubt.* Delay, hesitate. Cf. *All for Love*, II, i (S-S, V, 363): "Yet he but doubts, and parleys. . . ."

177 Cf. Saltonstall: "And you without a wife doe lye alone."

216–217 Cf. Saltonstall:

> Thou that did'st cause my fault, wilt me upbraid,
> O may I first into my grave be laid!

219 Following this line vv. 223–224 in the original are omitted.

225 Following this line vv. 231–232 in the original are omitted.
239 Following this line vv. 247–248 in the original are omitted.
252–253 Cf. Sherburne:
>   That thou dost urge a private conference,
>   I guesse your talke, and what you mean from thence.

Dido to Aeneas

As in the other two epistles, the opening two lines of the Latin are omitted:
>   accipe, Dardanide, moriturae carmen Elissae;
>   quae legis, a nobis ultima verba legis

(Receive, O Trojan, the song of Dido, now about to die; the words which you read are our last).

Immediately following Dryden's translation of *Dido to Aeneas* in the 1680 edition is a second translation of the epistle, identified only as "By Another Hand." This and the translation of "Ariadne to Theseus" were by John—afterward Lord—Somers (cf. *Memoirs of the Life of John Lord Somers* [1716], p. 11). The author of the *Memoirs* of Somers states that Tonson the publisher "had the Honour of being intimate with him, when he was a young Barister." (Cf. also Malone, III, 3; and Henry Maddock, *An Account of the Life and Writings of Lord Chancellor Somers* [1812], p. 94). Somers' version of "Dido to Aeneas" has a few striking resemblances to Dryden's translation (cf. notes on ll. 2, 46, 51, and 79–80). These similarities did not go unnoticed. In the *Wits Paraphras'd: Or, Paraphrase upon Paraphrase. In a Burlesque of the Several late Translations of Ovids Epistles* [1680], a work assigned to Matthew Stevenson, the author, after his version of "Dido to Aeneas," prints the beginning of another translation, purportedly "By Another Hand." The second stops after the first six lines, which are identical with those of the first version; and follows with a note of explanation (p. 140): "And so forward, for it is so like the former Epistle, that one may indifferently serve for both, and I am loath to trouble the Reader with needless Repetition." The implication is unjust to Somers' translation, which is closer to Turbervile, Saltonstall, and Sherburne than it is to Dryden.

2 Identical with the second line of Somers' version.
3–4 Cf. Sherburne: "Not that by words, I hope. . . ."
15–18 A free expansion of Ovid, vv. 15–16. Noyes has observed that in ll. 17–18 Dryden slipped in a reference to the Exclusion Bill. Ovid reads: quis sua non notis arva tenenda dabit? (Who will give over the possession of his fields to strangers?)
24 Cf. Sherburne: "Where wilt thou finde a wife shall love thee so?"
25–28 An expansion of Ovid, vv. 25–26.

29–30 The pair of rhyme words are identical with those in the corresponding passage of Sherburne.

33–34 A very free rendering of Ovid, vv. 31–32. Dryden omits Ovid, vv. 33–34.

39–46 A rather free rendering of Ovid, vv. 39–44.

46 The same rhyme word as in corresponding passages of Sherburne and Saltonstall. Cf. Somers: "Let me owe them, what I would owe to you."

51 Cf. Somers: "Stay only till these raging Tempests cease."

53–54 A free rendering of Ovid, vv. 51–52.

57–58 A free rendering of Ovid, vv. 55–56.

59–60 A free rendering of Ovid, vv. 57–58.

64 Same rhyme word as in the corresponding passages of Sherburne and Turbervile.

65–66 A free rendering of Ovid, vv. 63–64.

72 Same rhyme word as in corresponding passages of Sherburne, Saltonstall, and Turbervile.

73–74 Cf. Turbervile:

> Thy selfe wouldst graunt, thou hadst
> deservde these torments all:
> And thinke the thunder cast on thee
> what so should hap to fall.

76 Same rhyme word as in corresponding passage of Saltonstall.

79–80 Cf. Somers:

> What has your Son, what have your Gods deserv'd?
> For a worse Fate they from flames preserv'd?

Sherburne:

> What hath Ascanius, or thy gods deserv'd?
> Shal waves devoure them, late from flames preserv'd?

Saltonstall:

> What have Ascanius, or those gods deserv'd
> Drowning? which were by thee from fire preserv'd.

Turbervile:

> What poore Ascanius hath
> or Countrie Gods deservde?
> The Sea shall sinck the Saints, which were
> from Phrygian flame preservde.

81 Cf. Saltonstall: "Thy gods and father thou did'st never beare."

97–98 An expansion of Ovid, v. 95.

99–100 An expansion of Ovid, v. 96.

101–102 An expansion of Ovid, v. 97.

102 Same rhyme word as in corresponding passage of Turbervile.

103–104 An expansion of Ovid, v. 98.

105–106 An expansion of Ovid, v. 99.

107–108 An expansion of Ovid, v. 100.

108 This line follows the same rhythm as *MacFlecknoe*, l. 82: "Amidst this Monument of vanisht minds."

109 *dome.* Chapel, or temple. Cf. *All for Love*, I, i (S-S, V, 344).

110 *thrice* is a mistranslation of *quater,* v. 101. Saltonstall and Sherburne render it correctly.

112 *conscious.* Known to herself, felt, sensible. *OED* cites *Paradise Lost,* II, 801: "[The yelling monsters] with conscious terrors vex me round."

121–122 Cf. Sherburne:
> My husband fell, at holy Altar slaine,
> And from that deed, accru'd my brothers gaine.

125–126 Free rendering of Ovid, vv. 117–118.

127–128 Very free rendering of Ovid, v. 118.

131–134 An expansion of Ovid, vv. 121–122.

131–132 Cf. Saltonstall:
> Then sudden warres did me straitway invade,
> Before that I the City gates had made.

133–134 Cf. Somers:
> And force against unfinish'd walls prepare,
> Threatning a helpless Woman with a War.

135–138 An expansion of Ovid, vv. 123–124.

143–146 An expansion of Ovid, vv. 129–130.

161 *deludes.* Evades, eludes (*OED,* which cites Dryden's line).

165–168 A contraction of Ovid, vv. 151–156.

177–178 Same pair of rhyme words as in corresponding passage of Turbervile.

179–182 An expansion of Ovid, vv. 167–168.

181–182 Same pair of rhyme words as in couplet preceding the corresponding passage of Sherburne.

185–186 A free rendering of Ovid, vv. 171–172.

187–188 Cf. Saltonstall:
> When the wind stands faire, thou wilt saile away,
> Now thy ships in the weedy haven stay.

195 Same rhyme word as in corresponding passages of Sherburne and Turbervile.

198 Cf. Sherburne: "Upon my lap the Dardan sword doth lye."

201–202 Cf. Sherburne:
> How well thy gifts doe with my fate agree!
> At easie rate thou'st built a Tombe for me.

211–212 Cf. Turbervile:
> Aeneas gaue the cause
> and sworde wherewith I dyde:
> But desperate Dido on hir selfe
> hir ruthlesse hande hath tryde.

Prologues and Epilogues
edited by John Harrington Smith

Prologue to Albumazar

This prologue must have been spoken in early 1668, for Pepys saw *Albumazar,* "an old play, this the second time of acting," on 22 February of that year at the Duke's Playhouse in Lincoln's Inn Fields. The play, by Thomas Tomkis, was first acted at Trinity College, Cambridge, on 9 March 1615; [1] Jonson's *The Alchemist* was on the stage in 1610. [2] In representing Jonson as the borrower, Dryden may have relied on "an old piece of theatrical gossip"; [3] on the other hand he may have merely assumed that Jonson's play was later in date because it was better than Tomkis'. [4]

The disquisition on plagiarism in this prologue may have been suggested by the play; for *Albumazar* begins with a lecture by the Astrologer in praise of "theevery"; plagiarism is brought into the discussion, and the good repute of theft in Sparta is referred to. [5]

7–8 Subtle is the alchemist in Jonson's play.
9–14 The lines about Jonson and his borrowings repeat parts of *Of Dramatick Poesie:* Jonson was "not onely a professed Imitator of Horace, but a learned Plagiary of all the others . . . you will pardon me therefore if I presume he lov'd their fashion when he wore their cloaths" (1668, p. 14; Ker, I, 43). "He was deeply conversant in the Ancients . . . and he borrow'd boldly from them. . . . But he has done his Robberies so openly, that one may see he fears not to be taxed by any Law. He invades Authours like a Monarch, and what would be theft in other Poets, is onely victory in him" (*ibid.,* pp. 49–50; Ker, I, 82).
19 *Padders.* Highwaymen, riding on "pads"; cf. *Hudibras,* III, i, 1601–

---

[1] Alfred Harbage, *Annals of English Drama* (1940), p. 86.
[2] *Ibid.,* p. 80.
[3] Cf. *Albumazar: A Comedy,* ed. H. G. Dick (1944), p. 50.
[4] In the preface to *Troilus and Cressida* he assumes from what he considers the faults of Shakespeare's play that it was "in all pr[o]bability, one of his first endeavours on the Stage" (1679, sig. A4*v;* Ker, I, 203). And in the epilogue beginning "Were you but half so Wise as Y' are severe" (see p. 158), he similarly reasons, "Shakespear's own Muse her Pericles first bore, / The Prince of Tyre was elder than the Moore."
[5] See *Albumazar,* ed. Dick, p. 75, ll. 37 ff., and the present prologue, l. 35.

1602, "spurr'd, as . . . Padders to secure a Neck" (i.e., their own, from capture and the gallows).

25 *Country Toms.* Highwaymen. "Tom," with a descriptive epithet, would seem to have been a generic term for an anonymous criminal; cf. "peeping Tom," and Narcissus Luttrell, *Brief Relation* (1857), I, 156: "There has been much discourse about the citty of a Whipping Tom, who is used to bestow some pains in chastizeing the posteriors of severall females who have fallen into his hands."

30 *the Aegyptian, way.* George Thorn-Drury, *Covent Garden Drollery*, p. 148, cites Herodotus, II, 89. Dryden's source may have been Montaigne, *Essays*, III, v, or Burton's *Anatomy of Melancholy*, Pt. III, sec. ii, memb. 1, subsec. 2.

35 *Where Theft was prais'd.* Sparta; the corresponding line in the prologue as printed in the second edition of *Covent Garden Drollery* (1672), reads "Such as in Sparta might for Laurels Stand." Dryden was probably reminded of the premium which the Spartans placed on theft by *Albumazar*, I, i: "The Spartans held it lawfull." For accounts of this Spartan doctrine see Xenophon, *Constitution of the Lacadaemonians*, II, 7–9; and (with the classic story of the Spartan boy and the stolen fox) Plutarch, *Life of Lycurgus*, XVIII.

38 *Jack Pudding.* Clown.

39–40 For an anecdote illustrating such a means of endeavoring to insure noninterference with food or drink during the owner's temporary absence see Montague Summers, *Covent Garden Drollery* (1927), p. 122. The story is still current, in a less printable form.

44 *winck.* Close eyes.

47 *Letters of reprizall.* Official warrants "authorizing an aggrieved subject to exact forcible reparation from the subjects of another state" (*OED*); as, the "letters of marque and reprisal" by which privateers were commissioned. *The London Mercury*, no. 20, 8–13 June 1682, has a report of a seventeenth-century Admiralty trial in which were involved such letters "under the Great Seal of England for especial Reprisals against the States-General and their Subjects." Lee uses the figure in the epilogue to *The Rival Queens*, in remonstrating with gallants who make off with the Theatre Royal's actresses as soon as they begin to be valuable to the company: "Pray leave these poaching tricks, if you are wise, / E're we take out our Letters of Reprize": if the poaching continues, the company will revive the custom of having female parts acted by boys.

Prologue to Witt without Money

The date of this revival of Fletcher's play, and consequently of this prologue, is 26 February 1672.[1] The Theatre Royal in Bridges Street, Covent

---

[1] Leslie Hotson, *Commonwealth and Restoration Stage* (1928), p. 254.

Garden, which the King's Company had occupied since May 1663, had been destroyed by fire a month before, on 25 January. The blow to the company was a heavy one. The Duke's Company had moved the preceding fall into a large and lavishly decorated theater, fully equipped with "scenes and machines," in Dorset Garden; and it had Betterton. The King's Company had colorful actors and actresses, and Dryden to write for them; but they were less soundly and honestly led, and might eventually have succumbed to the competition of their rivals even without the additional handicap imposed by this conflagration. As it was, the company had to set up shop temporarily in the small and inadequate playhouse in Lincoln's Inn Fields recently vacated by their rivals. As they had been stripped by the fire of scenes, machines, and costumes, this put them at a great disadvantage; rebuilding their theater cost them nearly £4,000, and even then it could not compete on even terms with the Duke's, which had cost more than twice this sum.[2] The struggles of the King's Company may be traced in the prologues and epilogues following.

Evidently the impoverished company made this selection of a play with a view to dramatizing their situation. A MS copy of the prologue, also, says that it was addressed to the King by Mohun, backed by the other actors "in Melancholick postures." [3]

1–6 The "Beach," "hard Climate," are the inadequate theater in Lincoln's Inn Fields: ll. 5–6 mean, "We must try to make expenses in a location where even the Duke's Company, which had used the place for years, could not succeed."

3 *Dropping*. Dripping. Alexas uses the word in this sense to Cleopatra in *All for Love*, V (S-S, V, 419).

11–12 Charles and his courtiers sometimes gave fine clothes, very little worn, to the actors (see *Roscius Anglicanus*, ed. Montague Summers [1928], p. 21). Evidently this sort of assistance had been given to the burned-out players.

15 *rent-charge*. Pecuniary burden.

17–18 Percy Fitzgerald (*New History of the English Stage* [1882], I, 137) quotes a contemporary ballad "On the Unhappy Conflagration of the Theatre Royal, January 25, 1672":

> Only the zealous hypocrite enjoyed
> To see his scourge thus casually destroyed.
> He cries "Just judgment!"

19 *Temples*. Churches. Cf. *Annus*, l. 860.

20–22 William B. Gardner, *The Prologues and Epilogues of John Dryden* (1951), p. 212, compares *Annus*, st. 212. The lines in this prologue, however, are more clearly anticipated in *1 Conquest of Granada*, V (S-S, IV, 113), where Almahide tells Almanzor that his breast is "at worst, but so consum'd by fire / As Cities are, that by their falls rise high'r."

---

2 See Prologue Spoken at the Opening of the New House, l. 1n.
3 See Textual Notes.

25 An idea developed in *Of Dramatick Poesie* by Neander (1668, p. 46; Ker, I, 78): "For, if you consider the Plots, our own are fuller of variety, if the writing ours are more quick and fuller of spirit. . . ."

Prologue for the Women

This prologue must date between 26 February 1672, when the King's Company began to act at the Old Theatre in Lincoln's Inn Fields after the fire, and 26 March 1674, the date of the "Opening of the New House." The play to which it was spoken is not known.

There were other performances of plays with all-female casts in the period. Killigrew's *The Parson's Wedding* was "acted all by Women" at the first Theatre Royal in October 1664,[1] and there are a prologue and epilogue by Dryden for such a performance of *Secret Love*.[2] Performances with women in men's roles appear to have succeeded on the Restoration stage, doubtless the principal reason for this being suggested in the epilogue to the all-female *Secret Love*, in which Mrs. Reeves is made to say, "Here we presume, our Legs are no ill sight."

In the present prologue Dryden is chiefly concerned to cajole the audience into putting up with the cramped quarters and inadequate accommodations of the Old Theatre, which had been converted from a tennis court—and, as Hotson [3] has shown, one "of the lesser sort," at that.

1–5 The King's Company are still acting at the small Old Theatre; see introduction to Prologue to *Witt without Money*.

13 *And so*. And in like manner. "May," l. 12, appears intended to be understood with "ply," l. 14.

hot Burgundian. Probably, swashbuckling gallant: from John Barrose, "a *Burgonian* by nation, and a Fensor by profession, that lately was come over and had chalenged all the Fencers of England," who was hanged at Ludgate in July 1598 for killing an officer who had arrested him for debt. Cf., in the Herford and Simpson *Jonson*, IX (1950), 383, the note to *Every Man in His Humour*, IV, iv, 17, where Cob calls Bobadill a "fencing Burgullian," and the citations there given, in some of which the spelling "Burgonian" appears. The incident is also noticed in *Jack Drum's Entertainment* (1601) in *The Plays of John Marston*, ed. H. Harvey Wood, III (1939), 200, where M. John fo de King, explaining his decision not to keep his compact to assassinate Pasquill, says, "you see / Mee kill a man, you see mee hang like de *Burgullian*."

---

[1] Pepys, entries for 4 and 11 October. The prologue and epilogue for this production are printed in Thorn-Drury, *Covent Garden Drollery*, pp. 3–5.

[2] First printed in *Covent Garden Drollery* (1672); in the present edition they are printed with the play.

[3] *Commonwealth and Restoration Stage*, p. 123.

14 *o're the Benches stride*. Stand on benches to call attention to themselves. Cf. Dryden's complaint, in the prologue to *Cleomenes*, of ill-bred gallants, "our Bear-Garden Friends,"

> Who to save Coach-hire, trudge along the Street,
> Then print our Matted Seats with dirty Feet;
> Who, while we speak, make Love to Orange Wenches,
> And between Acts stand strutting on the Benches.

15 *upper Boxes*. Nothing appears to be known about the seating arrangements of the Lincoln's Inn Fields theater, and it would seem hazardous to do much guessing on the basis of this prologue. "Good accommodation in the Pit" (l. 10) sounds like humorous irony, and so does "convenient" upper boxes, if ladies and gentlemen had to climb stairs to an upper level to reach them. Hotson (*Commonwealth and Restoration Stage*, p. 123) estimates the dimensions of Lisle's tennis court as 75 feet long by only about 30 feet wide, in contrast to a width of 58 or 59 feet for the burned Theatre Royal (*ibid.*, p. 256). This would make for small seating capacity and few boxes, with consequent overflow into the gallery (or galleries) above, where male and female spectators came to understandings with such regularity as to suggest (l. 20) the paired state of the animals in Noah's Ark.

23 *Gaudy House with Scenes*. The theater in Lincoln's Inn Fields had had scenes when Davenant's company occupied it, from 1661 or 1662 to 1671 (cf. Lily B. Campbell, *Scenes and Machines* [1923], pp. 233–237). The King's Company, however, would have lost its scenery in the fire; for a time it would have had to stage its offerings in very primitive fashion. "Gaudy" refers to the interior decorations of the theater in Dorset Garden occupied by the rival company; see Dryden's Prologue Spoken at the Opening of the New House, l. 6, and note.

Prologue to Arviragus *Reviv'd*

This prologue must date early in 1673, for the troupe of French comedians which it mentions arrived in December 1672 and departed the following May.[1]

Lodowick Carlell's *Arviragus and Philicia* was one of the plays allotted to Killigrew in a division of the repertory pieces dating 12 January 1669.[2] For this revival another prologue was composed and printed in *London Drollery: or, The Wits Academy* (1673), p. 10, under the title "The Prologue to Arviragus and Felicia." It apologized for the production and invited the audience to "take full liberty to day / To Censure lowd the Actors and the Play." Apparently the company found it too abject to be used, and so turned to Dryden.

---

1 Eleanore Boswell, *The Restoration Court Stage* (1932), pp. 117–118.
2 Nicoll, p. 316.

1–2 *sickly Actors*. What members of the troupe were ailing at this time (perhaps with pregnancies—cf. the epilogue to *1 Conquest of Granada*, II, 26–32) is not known.

old House . . . Glorious Theatres and New. The Old Theatre in Lincoln's Inn Fields and the Duke's Theatre in Dorset Garden. See Prologue to *Witt without Money* and notes, and notes to Prologue for the Women.

6 *French Troop*. For visits of French troupes to London during the Restoration see Boswell, *The Restoration Court Stage;* for the one referred to in this line see introduction to the present prologue.

7 *bloody Bills*. Playbills in red ink (Dryden may intend a pun on bill in the sense of weapon). Playbills on posts are referred to in other plays by Dryden, e.g., *Sir Martin Mar-all*, III, and *The Wild Gallant*, II, ii. But the French troupe obviously printed its announcements in larger type than had hitherto been seen in London, and in red. Montague Summers, *Restoration Theatre* (1934), p. 8, p. 27 n. 27, states that in Paris the Hôtel de Bourgogne had the exclusive right to bills in red. They were attention-getting devices which the English companies later adopted: Thorn-Drury (Prologue and Epilogue Notebook, Bodleian MS Thorn-Drury. d. 54, p. 24) cites the prologue to Oldmixon's *The Governour of Cyprus* (1703): "Wide Folio Bills on ev'ry Post we place / And huge RED LETTERS stare you in the Face."

9 *Piece*. Play. In this line and the next, Dryden sarcastically imitates the language of the French bills—"Plume" for pen (and perhaps "incomparable," also); "Messieurs" for gentlemen; "do us grace" for do us the favor.

11–12 The practice of sending a lackey to hold a place would seem to have been introduced by the French troupe, and new at this time; later it became common. Thus Sir Novelty Fashion in *Love's Last Shift* (1696), V, comments that "the women of the town now come down so low that my very footman, while he kept my place t' other day in the playhouse, carried a mask out of the side-box with him."

20 *clap*. The audience would be certain to understand the word in a double sense, especially as it is embedded in sexual imagery. Frenchmen and lust and venereal disease were associated in the popular mind (cf. Dufoy, in Etherege's *The Comical Revenge*). Dryden exploits the association to ridicule the French players in the Epilogue to the University of Oxon. [1673], ll. 8–10. "Clap" as a verb had only recently come into use (cf. *OED*).

21–22 "How polite of us English! We pay the bill, and only the visiting and nonpaying Frenchmen enjoy the play, for only they understand it. We pay for their pleasure."

Prologue and Epilogue to the University of Oxon. [1673]

Since the Italian troupe referred to in the epilogue was that headed by Tiberio Fiorilli or Fiorelli, which Miss Boswell has shown arrived in England on 21 April 1673,[1] these pieces must have been spoken at the Oxford Act in July of that year. Charles Hart was the speaker, and the play was Jonson's *The Silent Woman*.

From 1661 the two principal London companies liked to appear at Oxford for the Act, which began on the Monday following the seventh of July. The town would of course be full at this time and getting permission from the university authorities to come down would mean two or three weeks of profitable business for the players. Of Dryden's prologues and epilogues, eight were written for performances during these July seasons at Oxford. Dons and students would constitute the majority or at least the dominant group in the audience, and in his addresses to them Dryden is always complimentary, as here.

Whether he had an ulterior purpose in being so has been much discussed.[2] In general, there seems to be no reason why the present prologue, or other compliments to the university paid by Dryden in prologues or epilogues spoken before Oxford audiences in the 1670's, need be taken as early moves in a long campaign of his, extending over some fourteen years, to ingratiate himself and so pave the way for some appointment later.

Nor, though of course there is a good deal of elegantly phrased exaggeration in them, do his compliments to Oxford need to be taken as fundamentally insincere. He did write to Rochester, "I have sent Your Lordship a prologue and epilogue which I made for our players when they went down to Oxford. . . . And by the event your Lordship will judge . . . how grosse flattery the learned will endure."[3] But Dryden was well aware that the learned are not unique in their susceptibility to flattery.

The epilogue is wholly given over to sarcastic notices of companies competing (too successfully!) with the King's: a French troupe, the Italians, the Duke's.

1–4 With these lines cf. *Of Dramatick Poesie* (1668, p. 9; Ker, I, 37) where Crites says that the poets in ancient Athens "had Judges ordain'd to decide their Merit, and Prizes to reward it: and Historians have been diligent to record of Eschylus, Euripides, Sophocles . . . and the rest of them, both

---

[1] *The Restoration Court Stage*, p. 118.

[2] See, for example, R. G. Ham in *London Mercury*, XXI (1929–1930), 421–426; Louis Bredvold, *MLN*, XLVI (1931), 218–224; R. G. Ham, *MLN*, XLIX (1934), 324–332; J. A. W. Bennett, *MLN*, LII (1937), 115–117.

[3] Ward, p. 10.

who they were that vanquish'd in these Wars of the Theater, and how often they were crown'd."

14 *Lycaeum.* "The proper name of a garden with covered walks at Athens, in which Aristotle taught his philosophy" (*OED*).

22 *Emperique.* For the contemporary meaning of the term cf. *Charleton,* l. 7n., and the preface to *An Evening's Love* (1671): "In short, there is the same difference betwixt Farce and Comedy, as betwixt an Empirique and a true Physitian: both of them may attain their ends; but what the one performs by hazard, the other does by skill" (sig. A4v; Ker, I, 136).

26 *their.* Antecedent is Vertue, Vice, Passions.

32–35 Dryden's interest in the atomic theory of Lucretius has been noted by Van Doren, pp. 15–17. Cf. *Howard,* l. 31 and note for a previous allusion to Lucretian theory in describing a casual manner of poetic composition.

40 Perhaps the power of the Praetorian Guard to crown or depose the emperor could scarcely be put more strongly than in Maximin's comparison in *Tyrannick Love,* IV, i (S-S, III, 433): "My Loves are like my old Praetorian Bands, / Whose Arbitrary pow'r their Prince commands."

44 *where he took it up.* The thought seems to be: Dryden has always held his title of poet by suffrage of the academic group; he now submits the title to them for revalidation.

45 *Poets.* I.e., poets laureate.

EPILOGUE

7 *French Troop.* See Prologue to *Arviragus* Reviv'd, and notes.

8 *Hot Monsieurs.* Here, a *double-entendre:* impatient, and venereally diseased. Cf. Prologue to *Ariviragus* Reviv'd, l. 20n.

11 *Merry-Andrews.* Clowns; buffoons. The Italians arrived in London in April 1673; see introduction. Fiorilli, who led them, was the greatest scaramouche of his century; for an account of his mastery of facial expression, see E. Gherardi, *Théâtre Italien* (1721), I, 353–354.

14 *Hobby-horses.* "In the morris-dance, and on the stage . . . a figure of a horse, made of wickerwork or other light material . . . and fastened about the waist of one of the performers, who executed various antics in imitation of the movements of a skittish or spirited horse" (*OED*). The hobby-horse was indigenous to England, and that it was popular with English audiences is seen in a prologue to a Restoration performance of *Every Man in His Humour,* ironically apologizing for the preponderance of wit in the play and promising things which the audience will like better, "Have patience but till Easter Term, and then / You shall have Jigg, and Hobby-horse agen" (*A Collection of Poems,* 1672, p. 30).

15–16 That there was in the repertory of the *commedia dell' arte* a mock joust (presumably performed as an *intermède*) is shown by the occurrence of the following in a list of properties from the scenarios reported by Constant Mic, *La Commedia dell' arte* (1927), pp. 206–207: "Two cardboard horses for the tourneying. Rush Lances" (*Deux chevaux en carton pour le tournoi. Des lances en jonc*).

17–18 Dryden may be conjectured to be satirizing either the use of live animals on stage, with the sounds made by players concealed behind the scenes, or animal imitations by the actors using masks. Mic (*loc. cit.*) lists "a live cat" and "an ass's head" as properties.

21–30 These lines attack the Davenant version of *Macbeth,* which was first produced by the Duke's Company in February 1673 and, being plentifully equipped with scenes and machines, was sensationally successful, much to the chagrin of the Theatre Royal. An anonymous author of the time expresses a view of it much like Dryden's (epilogue to *The Ordinary* in *A Collection of Poems* [1673], p. 167):

> Now empty shows must want of sense supply,
> Angels shall dance, and Macbeths Witches fly:
> You shall have storms, thunder & lightning too . . .
> Damn'd Plays shall be adorn'd with mighty Scenes
> And Fustian shall be spoke in huge Machines.

23 *Thunder and Lightning.* For these and how they were made in the period, especially at the Duke's Theatre, see Summers, *Restoration Theatre,* pp. 191 ff. In an epilogue to his burlesque *The Empress of Morocco* (1674) Thomas Duffett alludes to "The Powder Lightning and the Mustard Thunder" used to astound the onlookers in the Davenant *Macbeth.*

24 *Lapland.* A place where witchcraft was thought to flourish. Cf. *Paradise Lost,* II, 665.

26–28 The context indicates a hit at the Davenant *Macbeth.* In the 1674 edition (p. 27) the Second Song of the Witches has, "Sometimes like brinded Cats we shew, / Having no musick but our mew"; and Duffett's burlesque (epilogue to *The Empress of Morocco*) lists "cats" among its dramatis personae. May one conjecture that the weird sisters in Davenant's opera were provided with "familiars" in the form of cats and dogs?

27 Animals were held sacred in Egypt; cf. *Hudibras,* I, i, 773–774, "Th' Aegyptians worship'd Dogs, and for / Their Faith made internecine War." Zachary Grey, who edited Butler's epic in the eighteenth century, points out that the idea occurs in Juvenal, XV, 1 ff.

30 *Simon Magus.* See Acts, VIII, 9: "But there was a certain man, called Simon, which beforetime in the same city used sorcery, and bewitched the people of Samaria, giving out that himself was some great one."

32 *onely Drug.* Only article in no demand. Cf. Prologue to *A True Widow,* l. 6n.

Prologue and Epilogue Spoken at the Opening of the New House

The "New House," the new Theatre Royal in Drury Lane, opened on 26 March 1674. Though new it was by no means so luxurious, well-equipped with scenes and machines, or fit for "operas" as the Duke's Theatre in

Dorset Garden, but was a "Plain Built House." It was the poverty of the company, not their will, that consented to this arrangement, but Dryden puts the best face on the matter that he can.

He is still complaining about the companies of French actors who came to London to compete with the Theatre Royal. Perhaps the troupe he has in mind is one on whose behalf the Treasurer issued a warrant to the Customs Commissioners on 1 June 1674.[1]

1 *A Plain Built House.* Whereas the rival company had been able to spend, as Hotson has shown, £9,000 on the Duke's Theatre in Dorset Garden (*Commonwealth and Restoration Stage,* p. 232), the King's Company had been so hard hit by the fire of 25 January 1672 that it could raise for rebuilding only £3,908. 11*s.* 5*d.* (*ibid.,* p. 255).

5 *Theatres.* The Duke's Theatre.

6 *shining all with Gold.* The most noted feature of the Duke's Theatre was "the great gilded proscenium arch" (Lily B. Campbell, *Scenes and Machines,* p. 241 and n. 2).

9 *Druggets.* Coarse stuffs. Cf. *MacFlecknoe,* l. 33: "coarsely clad in Norwich Drugget."

38 *Troops of famisht Frenchmen.* See Prologue to *Arviragus* Reviv'd, and notes.

46 Dryden is satirizing the attempts of "our fine Fops," l. 45 (that is, Frenchified Englishmen) to use such French words as *bien, cadence.* To "humour the Cadence" presumably means about the same as "keep time"— i.e., wave hand in time to the music. Melantha applies the phrase to the manner of Palamede's singing in *Marriage A-la-Mode,* V, i.

48 *French Machines.* A multiple pun: French operatic "machines," political machinations, and "machine" in the sense of "dildo"—for which word, see *OED.* For "French machines" in this latter sense, in connection with the Earl of Rochester, see Kenneth B. Murdock, *The Sun at Noon* (1939), p. 293 and references supplied in the footnote.

53 Despite W. J. Lawrence's opinion (*Elizabethan Playhouse* [1912], p. 203) that Davenant's *Macbeth* is meant here, the accepted opinion is now that the reference is to an operatic version of *The Tempest* by Shadwell, currently being made ready at the Duke's Theatre for production in April 1674. The matter would seem to have been put beyond a doubt by Helene Hooker, *HLQ,* VI (1943), 228.

EPILOGUE

8 *vallancy.* "Used attributively to designate a form of wig" (*OED*).

11–12 Dryden's image here is based on a theory held by some seventeenth-century writers that the quality of heat was not inherent in fire, but that air, a sort of "nitrious Pabulum or Fewel" produced heat in the process of combustion which a burning body went through: see Walter

---

1 Boswell, *The Restoration Court Stage,* p. 119.

Charleton, *Physiologia* (1654), pp. 309–310; John Ray, *Three Physico-Theological Discourses* (1693), p. 324. Dryden is saying that the would-be wits, judgmentless, but able to "warm" the poet through their favors, are like the sun, who, though soulless and himself lacking heat, is able to warm where he rolls through the intermediary of air.

13 Some beaux went hat in hand so that their periwigs would not be crushed. Cf. Dryden's Epilogue to *The Man of Mode*, ll. 25–26: "From one the sacred Perriwig he gain'd, / Which wind ne're blew, nor touch of Hat prophan'd."

15–16 In rhyme and in ironic condescension these lines forecast Flecknoe's counsel to Shadwell (*MacFlecknoe*, ll. 145–146), "My son, advance / Still in new Impudence, new Ignorance."

17 Fop-corner was a part of the pit where the fops congregated: in *The Plain-Dealer*, II, i, Olivia characterizes one of her acquaintance as "An eternal Babler; and makes no more use of his ears, than a Man that sits at a Play . . . in Fop-corner."

19–20 Nocturnal sports of the bloods of the period are here glanced at. The lines mean something like, "So may you come off well in your midnight battles with the Watch; and when, later, you thunder at the doors of ladies of dubious character, may you gain admittance."

22 Fatal quarrels in the playhouse were not unknown in the period. But this line cannot refer, as Scott thought, to the death of Sir Carr Scroope's younger brother at the hands of Sir Thomas Armstrong, since that brawl did not take place until August 1675 (cf. J. H. Wilson, *The Court Wits of the Restoration* [1948], p. 116).

23 To "ruffle" is to disarray the attire of. In *Sir Martin Mar-all*, Act I, Lady Dupe tells her niece how to lead Lord Dartmouth on by refusals: "You must not suffer him to ruffle you or steal a kiss."

Vizard Punk. Masked prostitute.

27–30 Shadwell, who in a prologue to his operatic *Tempest* answered this epilogue of Dryden's, does not deny that the Duke's Theatre, in comparison with the Theatre Royal, was inconveniently located. He does, however, think the slur about "ill pav'd streets" unfair:

> They scoff at us, & Libell the high wayes.
> Tis fitt we, for our faults, rebukes shou'd meet.
> The Citty ought to mend those of ye street.

See *Works of Shadwell*, ed. Montague Summers (1927), II, 196. This prologue was first printed by W. J. Lawrence, in *Anglia*, XXVII (1904), and then in *The Elizabethan Playhouse* (1912), p. 200.

30 A humorous reminiscence of a line in Orrery's *Mustapha*, II, 1. 230 (*Works*, ed. W. S. Clark [1937], I, 247), in which Solyman recalls his endurance of winter campaigns "where last years Ice was not unthaw'd, / (When in thick Furs, Bears durst not look abroad)." Orrery's play was first performed in the spring of 1665, but Clark (I, 226–228) cites records of revivals down to October 1686: thus it may well be that the audience at the opening of the New House would recognize a hit at what Dryden obviously thinks the inflated language of this Duke's Theatre repertory piece.

32 It has been suggested by other editors that the "three Boys in Buff"

may refer to a droll of the time, *The Three Merry Boyes*. This piece may be consulted in Kirkman's *The Wits*, ed. J. J. Elson (1932), pp. 132 ff.; it has three boys, but no connection appears with "buff" (in any of the meanings listed by the *OED*). Indeed, since the play from which the droll was taken with little change—*The Bloody Brother, or Rollo, Duke of Normandy*—was one in which the King's Company had a proprietary right and which it frequently acted (cf. Arthur Colby Sprague, *Beaumont and Fletcher on the Restoration Stage* [1926], p. 31), it scarcely seems likely that Dryden would cite this droll as "nauseous" theatrical entertainment. The line, thus, remains obscure.

33 *Poets Heads*. A feature of the decorations at the Duke's Theatre was portraits (paintings, no doubt) of the poets. W. J. Lawrence, *Elizabethan Playhouse*, pp. 200–201, cites D'Urfey, *Collin's Walk Through London and Westminster* (1690). The passage (p. 149) reads:

> He saw each Box with Beauty crown'd,
> And Pictures deck the Structure round;
> Ben, Shakespear, and the learned Rout,
> With Noses some, and some without.

Though this last line might appear to suggest that the "heads" were busts, it seems possible that D'Urfey may be recalling and quipping upon Davenant's misfortune. As a poet and the founder of the Duke's Theatre, Davenant would no doubt have been painted side by side with Jonson, Shakespeare, and the rest; and though the painter would presumably have done the best possible for him in the matter of nose, D'Urfey still may have written with tongue in cheek.

34 Dryden's point in this line is that the Theatre Royal had exclusive rights to the best plays of the old dramatists (for a list, dating *c.* 12 January 1669, see Nicoll, pp. 315–316; it is more imposing and longer than the list allotted to the Duke's Company, *ibid.*, pp. 314–315). In the second prologue to his operatic *Tempest* (see above, ll. 27–30n.) Shadwell, the mainstay of the Duke's Company, as Dryden was of the King's, replied to this boast, "Old plays, indeed, the King's Company have, and that's about all. Few good writers of today would take their plays to the Theatre Royal." ("Too much of the old witt They have, Tis true: / But they must look for little of ye new.")

35 "The best wit (plays) from the older period, their exclusive property, and hitherto unproduced in these times, the management at this theatre will now proceed to revive for your delectation, as a more than sufficient offset to the empty magnificence which is the best the other house has to offer."

Play, taken in conjunction with *cards* (l. 40), suggests that Dryden is thinking of the competition between the theaters in terms of a card game.

38–39 Pierre Perrin's *Ariane, ou le mariage de Bacchus* was acted at the Theatre Royal 30 March 1674. It is to this forthcoming attraction, to be sung in French by French players imported for the occasion, that Dryden alludes in these lines.

40 Probably a *double-entendre,* the line meaning, "You know that French players are always certain to draw customers when the Company

is at low ebb," and "You know that the French mark cards to ensure winning when they need it most." *OED* does not give the meaning "to mark cards" for "to ensure cards," but an insinuation at the expense of the French seems intended by the line.

Prologue and Epilogue to the University of Oxford, 1674

This pair of poems must have been spoken at the Act in July, presumably near the end of the company's stay, if one can judge from the retrospective tone of the epilogue, for example in lines 26–28. But in framing it Dryden expected that relations between the players and the town would be better than—apparently—proved to be the case, for when the company left late in July it did so under a cloud, and was not permitted to return the following summer.[1]

12 *in Mechanick operations wrought.* Given technological application.

13 *Man the Little world.* I.e., the microcosm, corresponding point by point to the "great" world (l. 14), the macrocosm. See E. M. W. Tillyard, *The Elizabethan World Picture* (1948), pp. 84–93.

14 *Sphere of Chrystal.* Scott finds here an allusion to "the glassie globe that Merlin made" (*Faerie Queene,* III, ii, 21) which was "round and hollow shaped . . . Like to the world it selfe, and seem'd a world of glas" (st. 19).

19–23 This emphasis on "our dead Authours" and the great names of past dramatists in the repertory of the King's Company may be because the company was miserably short on new plays. It had scored in May with Lee's first play, *Nero,* but Dryden, upon whom it was accustomed to rely, had nothing at the moment. On the other hand, the Duke's Company had Shadwell, whose operatic *Tempest* had been a great success in April; in the fall it would produce a new tragedy by Settle, the author of *The Empress of Morocco;* and Crowne and Ravenscroft were on its string. See Shadwell's taunt, quoted in note to l. 34 of Dryden's Epilogue Spoken at the Opening of the New House.

24 See Martial, IX, xi, 16–17:

> nobis non licet esse tam disertis,
> qui Musas colimus severiores

---

[1] Cf. Summers, *Playhouse of Pepys* (1928), p. 128. Summers quotes from the *Letters of Humphrey Prideaux,* where it is reported that the players, having indulged in such forms of outrageous conduct as prowling about the town by night and breaking windows, departed from Oxford with small profits—and with no encouragement to return.

(To us who cultivate more severe muses it is not permitted to be so elegant in phrase). Noyes points out that Dryden quotes the Martial passage in the dedications to *Examen Poeticum* and the *Aeneis*.

26 Possibly an echo of Virgil, *Aeneid*, VI, 258: procul, o procul este profani.

27 Possibly an echo of Exodus, xxxiii, 20: "Thou canst not see my face: for there shall no man see me, and live."

32 *stoop*. See below, l. 37n.

34 *Take*. Succeed with the audience.

35 *Hating themselves*. The pronoun is intensive, not reflexive, the line being a precise repetition, in meaning, of l. 34.

37 Here Dryden has the Oxford audience out-Joving Jove himself, for at Athens in the fifth century B.C. Zeus was, it appears, regularly "represented as standing with an eagle on his head as a symbol of his royalty" (Aristophanes, *The Birds, The Complete Greek Drama*, ed. Oates and O'Neill [1938], II, 756). Pithetaerus offers this to the Chorus as a proof that the birds were the original masters and kings over men and should think of themselves as superior even to the Olympians.

In *stoop* (l. 32) and *Mount* (l. 37) the imagery is drawn from falconry: the poets, thought of as noble birds of prey, must come near the earth to please the London pit, but must soar if they hope to approach the standards of the Oxford audience.

EPILOGUE

1–2 For how literally these lines are to be taken, cf. introduction to Dryden's Prologue to the University of Oxon. [1673].

9–10 A delicate way of saying, "We of the King's Company hope that you will permit us to come down every year for the Act in July."

13 *favours past*. Previously given permissions to put on plays at Oxford.

17 *Bathurst*. Ralph Bathurst, Vice-Chancellor of the University. Presumably it was Bathurst who had given the King's Company permission to come to Oxford for the Act.

18 A puzzling line. Probably "his own Virgil" means "Bathurst's favorite author, Virgil." The line would then mean, "And to whom learned men owe almost as much as they owe to Virgil himself, the author whom Bathurst so admires."

23–25 Line 25 should perhaps be paraphrased, "with whom hospitality was so highly regarded as to be given the status of a religious observance."

Epilogue to The Man of Mode

The play, Sir George Etherege's last of three and his finest, was acted before the King on 11 March 1676,[1] at the Duke's Theatre. Dryden and Etherege

---

[1] Nicoll, p. 310.

were, of course, friends; cf. the tribute to "gentle George" in *MacFlecknoe,* ll. 151–154, and in the *Letter to Etherege.*

3 Harlequin was the comic servant in the *commedia dell' arte.*

9 *cocks.* To "swagger, strut" (*OED*), like a barnyard cock. Or, to set the hat, with a flourish, at a jaunty angle.

12 *graff.* Graft. The form in "t" is "possibly due to the use of *graft* as past tense and past participle of *graff*" (*OED*). Dryden uses both forms of the word, as suits his convenience; both appear, for instance, in 2 *Conquest of Granada,* II (S-S, IV, 147):

> Love is a tender Amity, refin'd:
> Grafted on friendship it exalts the kind.
> But when the Graff no longer does remain
> The dull Stock lives; but never bears again.

16 *Knight o' th' Shire.* Member of Parliament for a county. Cf. the Franklin in Chaucer's *Prologue,* l. 356.

18 Legion's his name. See Mark, v, 9.

22 *Wallow.* "A rolling walk or gait" (*OED*).

24 *Snake.* "A long curl or tail attached to a wig" (*OED,* which cites, from Swift, an illustrative passage, "We who wear our Wigs with . . . Snake").

26 For the hatless mode, see Epilogue Spoken at the Opening of the New House, l. 13n.

28 *Shog.* A shake or jerk.

33–34 The usual disclaimer that specific persons are aimed at. Contemporaries thought, with some reason, that at least Dorimant and Medley could be identified with real persons. But it is probably true that Sir Fopling himself was a generalized caricature of social follies; Dryden's assertion, therefore, seems justified.

Prologue to the University of Oxford [1676]

This was not printed until the 1684 *Miscellany* but can be dated on the basis of a MS version in the Bodleian Library headed "A Prologue to the University of Oxford at the Act 1676; by his Majesties Servants."[1] The contemporary copyist would have been in a position to know the date and, it would seem, could have no reason for misstating it. However, W. J. Lawrence, who first called attention to the Bodleian MS version,[2] was willing only to say that the dating was "not improbable," and pointed out that a visit of the King's Company in 1676 is not corroborated by other evidence.

---

[1] See Textual Notes.
[2] *TLS,* 16 January 1930, p. 43.

The prologue has sometimes been assigned to 1681, on the ground that in the 1684 collection it follows a prologue beginning "Discord, and Plots which have undone our Age" which can confidently be dated 1680. But sequence in the *Miscellany* can scarcely be taken as reliable evidence of date.

For remarks on the Oxford prologues generally, and how far Dryden may be considered to be wooing the university in them, see introduction to Prologue and Epilogue to the University of Oxon. [1673].

20 *justly please*. Please according to the known rules of art.

22–24 An illustration of Dryden's known fondness for drawing a parallel between the arts of poetry and painting.

30–32 "To be made Free of Rome" means "to be admitted to rights as Romans." There were varying degrees of Roman rights; a tribe or city could have the civil rights without the political rights, as in Livy, VIII, xiv: "To the Campanians . . . was given citizenship without voting rights" (*civitas sine suffragio*).

33–38 Dryden's "own Mother University" was of course Cambridge, but these lines need not amount to a hint that Dryden would like an appointment at Oxford.

Prologue to Circe, *and an Epilogue*

Charles Davenant was the oldest of the many sons of Sir William, the founder of the Duke's Company. *Circe* was produced at Dorset Garden on 12 May 1677 [1] when its author was only nineteen. It succeeded, partly because it was heavy with operatic elements (which, as Dryden so frequently laments, were wont to bring the playgoers of the day flocking to the Duke's Theatre) and partly, perhaps, through the influence of a clique of wits.[2]

Dryden on another occasion used the first ten lines verbatim but followed them with new matter, to serve some other young author of a first play, identity unknown. This alternate version of "Were you but half so wise as you're severe," its date not being known, is in this edition printed immediately following the present prologue.

7 *check*. "Rebuke, reprove, reprimand" (*OED*).

8 *Rogues*. "Rogue" was frequently used as a term of amorous endearment in the period.

---

[1] Nicoll, p. 310.
[2] See ll. 30 ff.

9 *flesh't.* Incited by having been given a taste of the meat of the quarry; cf. Sir Toby's metaphor to Sebastian in *Twelfth Night,* IV, i, "You are well flesh'd. Come on." Dryden may also intend a pun on *flèche,* arrow, in a phallic sense.

13–15 Cf. Mrs. Peachum in *Beggar's Opera,* I, iv: "Women . . . are so partial to the brave that they think every man handsome who is going to the camp or the gallows."

19–25 The "Brothers of the Trade," in the more obvious sense, are Charles Davenant's fellow poets. Their hearts are aching, partly from envy of this author who is having a play produced and partly because (though they would normally be admitted without charge) for this play—*Circe* being an "opera" produced with scenes and machines—the free list has been suspended and they have been forced to pay five shillings, double the normal price of admission to the pit.

The prologue is an exercise in *double-entendre,* even more than commonly laden with sexual imagery. In this system of meaning the "Brothers of the Trade" are thieves and diseased gallants, the male consorts of those charmers who instruct the fumbling youth.

29 "These Usurpers" are the malcontent fellow dramatists; "you" are the "great Dons of Wit" (as Dryden calls them in the epilogue to *The Indian Emperour*), Rochester, Sedley, and the rest, whose choice of the pit as their place in the theater had given distinction to it, and who (l. 31) have taken *Circe* under their patronage and thus are obligated to insure its success. Rochester wrote the epilogue for the play.

EPILOGUE

1–10 For notes to these lines cf. Prologue to *Circe,* notes to ll. 7, 8, and 9.

12 Arbaces is the principal character in Beaumont and Fletcher's *A King and No King.*

15 *The Slighted Maid* was a feeble tragicomedy by Sir Robert Stapylton. In his critical essays Dryden twice refers to it as lacking progression in the plot (Ker, I, 209; II, 145).

16–17 Dryden appears to be conjecturing from the comparative merit of the two plays. Actually, *Othello* preceded *Pericles.*

21 *burnish.* "To grow plump, or stout, to spread out" (*OED*).

24 *sterv'd.* Starved.

Epilogue to Mithridates

Nathaniel Lee's *Mithridates, King of Pontus,* was first acted *c.* March 1678, at the Theatre Royal.[1] For Dryden's relations with Lee, see introduction to his *To Mr. Lee, on His* Alexander, above.

---

[1] Nicoll, p. 367.

10–11 The prologue is spoken by a man.

20 A "cully" is a dupe. The word is in this period most frequently used to mean a man deceived by a woman, e.g., a kept mistress.

21 *sophisticated.* "Adulterated; not pure or genuine" (*OED*).

24 *the old Half-Crown way.* Cf. Dryden's prologue to Harris' *The Mistakes,* l. 33: "A Common Harlot's price—just half a Crown."

25 The reference is to Swiss mercenaries; cf. *Hind,* l. 1471.

Prologue to A True Widow

Shadwell's play was printed early in 1679 (his epistle dedicatory, to Sedley, is dated 16 February 1678/9). Since in that day a play would normally be printed as soon as feasible after its initial run, it would seem that *A True Widow* must have been acted first in early 1679 or late 1678; Summers' guess of December 1678 seems a reasonable one.[1] The play has sometimes been dated earlier, in March 1678, on the basis of a passage in Act I in which a character named Lump declares, "I think not any one wise, who does not know what he shall do this day fifty years, if he lives; I for my part do. . . . Upon the one and twentieth of March, I shall fifty years hence, dine with Mr. Ananias Felt." But it would seem, for many reasons, scarcely possible to fix the première of the play at 21 March 1678, solely on the basis of this passage.

The present prologue, with a few inconsequential variants, was printed with Mrs. Behn's *The Widdow Ranter* (1690), but this would seem to have been done upon the initiative of Knapton, who printed the play—not Dryden,[2] who wrote for the Behn play a different prologue and an epilogue; these will be printed subsequently in this edition.

2 Subsequent lines explain why the stage is in process of being ruined: fools are becoming so plentiful in life that people need not come to the theater to see them in plays.

6 *grow Druggs, and will not sell.* Cf. Epilogue to the University of Oxon. [1673], l. 32: "And Wit the onely Drug in all the Nation." The notion of "drugs on the market" (unsalable commodities) developed in the seventeenth century, when so many new "panaceas" and the like came into existence that public demand could not absorb them all—especially as many were fashioned from common herbs, and almost any landowner could have "a Plantation of his own" (l. 8).

1 *Playhouse of Pepys,* p. 141 n. 165.

2 See the discussion of the case in Autrey Nell Wiley, *Rare Prologues and Epilogues* (1940), pp. 280–282, and W. B. Gardner, *The Prologues and Epilogues of John Dryden* (1951), pp. 309–311.

Osborn suggests, in a work now being prepared for publication, that ll. 6–8 and, especially, 17 and 30 contain references to the rough treatment accorded Dryden's *Limberham* when it was produced in March 1678, hostile critics accusing the poet of having therein represented prominent men and women of the town.

9 *His Cruse ne'r fails.* Cf. 1 Kings, XVII, 12–16.

10 *God's plenty.* An anticipation of the language of Dryden's famous appreciation of Chaucer, in the *Preface to The Fables.*

11 *rated.* Assessed for taxation.

13–14 Dryden has a specific act of Parliament in mind: 29–30 Car. II, cap. I, 1676, "An act for raising money by a poll and otherwise, to enable his Majesty to enter into an actual war against the French King, and for prohibiting several French commodities." The ban on French imports was in effect several years later. Cf. Luttrell, *Brief Relation*, I, 53, August 1680: "Great quantities of French goods have been destroyed by the officers of the Custome house in severall parts of the kingdome, pursuant to the late act."

20 *Muss.* "A game in which small objects are thrown down to be scrambled for; a scramble" (*OED*).

25 *drink swear and roar.* Cf. the advice to Og (Shadwell) in 2 *Absalom and Achitophel*, l. 478: "Drink, swear, and roar, forbear no lewd delight / Fit for thy bulk."

31 *Sot.* Fool.

Prologue at Oxford, 1680 [1679]

The prologue as printed here is the version entitled "The Prologue at Oxford, 1680" in the 1684 *Miscellany Poems.* The year 1680, however, can scarcely be the date for the poem in this form. It would seem that it was the other version of the prologue, differing from this one in a number of respects, which was spoken during the 1680 summer season at Oxford, and the play with which it was used that year was evidently Lee's *Sophonisba*: for when Lee's play was printed, in the second edition, in the spring of 1681,[1] this other version was printed with it, with the heading, "Prologue to the University of Oxford. Written by J. Driden, Esquire." For variants between this version and the one here printed, see Textual Notes.

One difference helps to date the present text. The allusion to "us Cardinals" and "Pope Joan" in line 22 identifies the play for which it must have been spoken as Settle's *The Female Prelate: Being the History of the Life and Death of Pope Joan.* Settle's play was first introduced to the London audience about September 1679.[2] If one tries to accept the date given in the *Miscellany* and have it that Oxford did not see the Settle play and hear the

1 *Term Catalogues* for May, ed. Arber, I, 446.
2 Nicoll, p. 372.

Pope Joan version of the prologue until July 1680, the difficulty is that the Oxford season for that year is already occupied by Lee's play and the prologue in the other version. Two speakings to two different plays in such short space would, on various considerations, seem rather improbable. The alternative, which seems more likely, is to assume that Settle's play was tried at Oxford in July of 1679, before its London première, the prologue in the version here printed being used on that occasion; and that when the company returned the following summer it used the prologue again, for *Sophonisba*, but in so doing had to refurbish it, lines 21–22, for instance, having to be dropped as entirely inappropriate to Lee's play.

4 As noted by Noyes, in this line Dryden is quoting Horace's *Ars Poetica,* l. 276: (Thespis is said to have conveyed his poems in wagons).

5–6 A humorous mistranslation of what Horace says in ll. 278–280:

post hunc personae pallaeque repertor honestae
Aeschylus et modicis instravit pulpita tignis
et docuit magnumque loqui nitique cothurno

(After his [Thespis'] time, Aeschylus, the inventor of the mask and the dignified tragic robe, built a stage of boards of moderate size and taught speaking in a lofty style, and how to tread in the buskin).

8 A tennis court was used for this production, as frequently for performances at Oxford in this period; see Sybil Rosenfeld in *RES,* XIX (1943), 366–371.

12 *Jack Presbyter.* Label for a dissenter in the period, "Jack" being from John Calvin.

13 From early times dissenting ministers, compelled by the laws against them to improvise, appear sometimes literally to have preached from tubs or barrels. Thus Horton Davies, *The Worship of the English Puritans* (1948), p. 93, quotes from a description of a dissenting service in 1568, "their preacher used a half of a tub for a pulpit." The conformists never let the nonconformists forget the lowly origin of their rostra, and "tubthumper" became the term for a pulpit-pounding dissenting preacher.

18 *Oxford Bells.* "Probably some pasquinade against the Whigs, then current in the University" (Scott).

19–20 A cart was not only Thespis' vehicle (ll. 2, 4) but also what malefactors were carried in, e.g., to Tyburn.

21–22 The lines show that the prologue was spoken by an actor who played one of the cardinals in Settle's play.

24 The "Whore" (Revelations, XVII) and the "Beast" (*ibid.,* XIII, XVII) were in this period taken as referring to the Romish Church.

25–26 *Scot.* Duns Scotus, 1265?–?1308; *Swarez.* Francisco Suarez, 1548–1617; *Tom of Acquin.* St. Thomas Aquinas, 1225–1274. If the dissenters should gain control of the university, these renowned theologians (being Catholics—the Triple Crown of course standing for the Papacy) could no longer be studied there.

28–30 Some obscure academic joke seems adumbrated here. However, if Aristotle was said (facetiously) to have called the soul an organ pipe, one can understand why the dissenters would have had to reinterpret him in order to claim him, for their hostility to organs was well known; cf. *Rump* (1662), I, 8, 15, 100. Conversely, if his dictum could be interpreted into "Pipe of Inspiration," the dissenters could accept him, for they made much of inspiration, "new light," or "inward light," the soul being merely the passive instrument through which the Spirit spoke. Cf. *Hudibras*, I, i, 515–518:

> This Light inspires and plays upon
> The Nose of Saint, like Bag-pipe Drone,
> And speaks through hollow empty Soul,
> As through a Trunk, or whisp'ring Hole.

That Dryden disliked the doctrine may be seen in his prologue to *Oedipus*, ll. 29–31.

There may be in the last line of the present prologue an unsavory *double-entendre* forecasting Swift's satire on the Aeolists in *A Tale of a Tub*, sec. viii; for "pipe" can mean "clyster-pipe," as in the "Dedication to Prince Posterity" of Swift's satire: "Who has annihilated them? Were they drowned by Purges or martyred by Pipes?"

Prologue to Caesar Borgia

Lee's play was first acted at Dorset Garden *c.* September 1679.[1] For Dryden's relations with Lee, see introduction to his *To Mr. Lee, on His* Alexander, above.

7–10 Since Saintsbury there has been general agreement that Dryden in these lines is expressing his resentment at the failure of *The Kind Keeper*.

18–19 The specific broadsides referred to (if indeed Dryden has specific ones in mind) have not been identified.

22–31 For the Court of Requests, cf. introduction to I. S. Leadam, *Select Cases in the Court of Requests* (1898). When the Court of Requests was reactivated after the Restoration and its Masters were in 1662 assigned a place in the Chapel Royal for hearing petitions, its former quarters, the White Hall (on the second floor of Westminster Hall) seems to have been taken over by the Court of Wards and Liveries; the Court of Requests, however, retained title to a smaller room adjacent to it. By 1669 this smaller room was left vacant by the demise of the court, and the crowd moved in. Wine (l. 28) and ale (l. 29) were apparently sold there, and Londoners used it like a coffeehouse or tavern for meeting friends and associates (cf. *Diary*

---

[1] Nicoll, p. 367.

of *Robert Hooke,* ed. H. W. Robinson [1935], entries for 3, 8, and 10 May 1679), and the newsmongers gathered there to spread rumor and excitement.

31 *Villains* perhaps refers to Titus Oates and other informers, who were feeding the mob's fear and hatred by inventing details of a "Popish Plot." Or it could refer to malicious newsmongers who were spreading the excitement provided by the "Plot."

34 For some reason Dryden seems to have been interested in the subject of poisoning and ratsbane at this time. Cf. also his prologue to *The Spanish Fryar,* ll. 46–47. A similar interest is displayed in Oldham's "Satyr, in Imitation of the Third of Juvenal" (*Poems and Translations* [1683], p. 185), a work written in May, 1682.

36–37 In Lee's play (IV, i) Machiavel does away with a henchwoman of his by getting her to smell a pair of perfumed (poisoned) gloves.

40 *the Chair.* In the play, Borgia has his brother bound in a chair and tortured to death. Lee apologizes to the squeamish, in his epilogue: "Yet more, the horrid Chair the Mid-night show— / He [the author] says 'twas done two hundred years ago."

41 *But.* Only.

42 The Devil and the Pope would be readily associated in the minds of nonconformists at this period, and Lee's play depicts Machiavellism and devilry in a Catholic country.

Prologue to The Loyal General

The play, by Nahum Tate, was first acted at Dorset Garden *c.* December 1679.[1]

It is plain from this prologue that Dryden is becoming progressively less able to hold his mind to the sort of theme which had been enough for him in the early seventies; the virus of politico-religious controversy is beginning to have its way with him. Here his ostensible theme, however, is of the former sort: the bad taste of the town, which had rejected *The Kind Keeper* the year before (thus showing itself unable to "digest the Cordials of strong wit," l. 23) and was currently patronizing "farce" (l. 24).

"Farce" as a method opposed to the method of comedy was clearly recognized early in the Restoration period. In the epilogue to *The Wild Gallant* revived, printed in 1669, Dryden speaks of the difficulty of writing true comedy, which holds the mirror up to nature, and admits that to suit the taste of the audience he has garnished his play with "Fool and Farce." In the preface to *An Evening's Love* he distinguishes between the two methods in an extended and brilliant passage. See also his *A Parallel of Poetry and Painting.*

"Farce" as the name for a dramatic genre was applied in the period to

---

[1] Nicoll, p. 374.

various kinds of stage-piece emphasizing ridiculous action rather than nature and probability. It was first used as a label for performances of the *commedia dell' arte,* with their stress on mimicry and pantomime.[2] Shortly thereafter it was applied to the short pieces in which Thomas Duffett, in the service of the King's Company, burlesqued such successes by the Duke's Company as Settle's *Empress of Morocco* and Shadwell's *Psyche.* By the date of this prologue of Dryden's a new meaning for "a farce" had developed. The term was now being applied to short pieces made by cutting down full-length plays (at this time, generally of the pre-Commonwealth period), preserving and stressing their broadly comic features; three such "farces" are printed in *The Muse of Newmarket* (1680). From farces manufactured from old plays it would be only a step to original pieces so called, similarly brief and neglectful of probability in action and character. But these at least do not become plentiful before the eighteenth century.

Dryden here aims his satire at farce as a method practiced by his competitors in their full-length comedies. Shadwell took the same view: in the dedication of *A True Widow* he speaks of "little Poetasters of the fourth rate" who "hold, that Wit signifies nothing in a Comedy" and rely on action—"the putting out of Candles, kicking down of Tables, falling over Joyntstools, impossible accidents, and unnatural mistakes (which they most absurdly call Plot)."

5–7 *some Factious Speech . . . Shrove-tide Crew.* As to the "speech," Dryden may have in mind *An Account of the Proceedings at the Guild-Hall . . . on Saturday, September 12, 1679. With the Substance of Sir Thomas Player's Speech, and the Lord Mayor's Answer Thereunto* (1679). In this the crowd attending on Player is said to have been composed of "several Hundreds of the Principal Citizens of London," but according to *A Vindication of Sir Thomas Player* (n.d.), a Tory critic said it "lookt like a tumultuous Number of Apprentices doing Execution upon Bawdy-houses." This comes very close to Dryden's lines 6–7, for the "Shrove-tide Crew" are London prentices celebrating the Tuesday before Ash Wednesday in their traditional fashion. That they had been at it this year is proved by Luttrell, *Brief Relation,* I, 9: "In the Easter holidays the prentices were up, and proceeded to pulling down the bawdy-houses . . . but were opposed by some souldiers and the watch, between whom were frequent scuffles, in which severall were hurt." Player's speech, it seems, was of an inflammatory nature, and Dryden, in addition, may have been irritated by a broadside, *Protestants Congratulation to the City for their Excellent Choice of Members to serve in Parliament, October 7, 1679,* Sir Thomas Player being one.

5 *City Gazets.* News sheets issued by printers in the "Protestant" (i.e., antipapist) interest.

8 Dryden calls the pit apostate because it has neglected its duty to encourage good drama, and instead has encouraged farce (l. 24).

2 Cf. the prologues and preface to Edward Howard's *The Womens Conquest* (1671), and the preface to his *The Six days Adventure* (1671) and the commendatory verse to this play by Ravenscroft.

9 "You are not fit to sit below, but, to accord with your taste, should sit in the upper gallery"—price, 12*d*. Summers, *Restoration Theatre*, p. 41, aptly cites, from Swift's *Tale of a Tub*, the snubs suffered by the plain-coated brothers: "If they went to the Play-house, the Door-keeper showed them into the Twelvepeny Gallery."

10–11 These lines mean, "Go to Bartholomew Fair; there you will find entertainment fit for you." Cf. "Bartholomew-Fayr" in *A Choice Compendium, or, An Exact Collection of . . . Songs* (1681):

Here's the Whore of Babylon, the Devil and the Pope,
The Girl is just a going on the Rope.

16–17 The lines mean that the poets write, and the pit occupants judge, with the same frenzy and unreason that were displayed by the enemies of Charles I.

16 *Forty One*. The year 1641 marked the beginning of the rebellion against Charles I. The success of that rebellion provided inspiration for the disaffected at the time of the Popish Plot. Narcissus Luttrell records (*Brief Relation*, I, 76): "About this time the presse abounds with all sorts of pamphlets and libells; one side running down the papists and upholding the dissenters; the other side cryeing down both . . . and sounding nothing but 41."

17 *Forty Eight*. Charles I was executed in January 1648/9.

20 *They*. The indefinite pronoun.

25 *Barly-water*. "A drink, made by the decoction of pearl barley, used as a demulcent" (*OED*).

28 *Sippets*. Sippet, "a small piece of toasted or fried bread, usually served in soup or broth" (*OED*).

31 *after all our cost*. I.e., cost of mounting the production.

32 *in Frost*. When because of ice on the Thames or because of severe cold the watermen could not ply their trade.

Prologue to the University of Oxford [1680]

This racy piece can be assigned to the Act of 1680 from the allusions to the "rebels" who had deserted the King's Company and were playing in Edinburgh.

4 *Scotch Rebels*. The rebels to the company were the decamping actors, but political rebels also were still active in Scotland. English troops under the Duke of Monmouth won a victory over them at Bothwell Bridge, 22 June 1679, but trouble was still going on in the summer of 1680, as is shown by Luttrell (I, 51–52) under date of July: "We have information from Scotland of another defeat of a party of rebels there by the kings forces." Whether this latest affray would have come to Dryden's attention early

enough to have inspired the comparison in l. 4 it is impossible to say. The "rebels" were Covenanters, left-wing Protestants.

5 Dissatisfied with the continuing regime of the older actors at the Theatre Royal—Mohun and Hart—some of the company, led by Cardell Goodman and Thomas Clarke (Hotson, p. 262) at some time in 1679 went to Edinburgh and began to act there. In February 1680 Goodman and Clarke returned (Hotson, p. 262; their return is noticed in the prologue to Crowne's *Thyestes,* produced in March). Some of the rebels, however, remained in Scotland, and they are the group satirized here. Joe Haines led them, at least in the spring of 1680. Summers (*Playhouse of Pepys,* p. 95) points out that the second prologue to Ravenscroft's *Titus Andronicus,* not printed until 1687, but capable of being plausibly dated before the Long Vacation of 1680, reads:

> Come all and pay your Foyes before you go,
> Else we must troop to Scotland after Joh—
> We by the last advice for Certain hear
> That Haynes does head the Rebell-Players there.

What performers were with the rebels in the summer of 1680 can only be conjectured. Summers (*Playhouse,* p. 95) says that Mrs. Corey was one, but he cites no evidence, nor does he indicate whether he identifies her with the lady in ll. 10–11, or her in ll. 12–13. Perhaps she might be equated with the fat nymph, for as Mrs. Corey could play such parts as Mrs. Joyner in *Love in a Wood,* the Widow Blackacre in *The Plain-Dealer,* and Strega in Duffett's *The Amorous Old-woman,* she may well have been of ample habit.

6 *kinder hearted.* I.e., more "susceptible."

7 *Carted.* The jest is that carts were vehicles in which bawds and whores were ridden. In Dekker's 2 *Honest Whore,* V, ii, the Bridewell master says of his charges that "to calm their pride, / Instead of coaches they in carts do ride."

8 Act in a company with Scotch actors? The blue bonnet was of course the traditional headgear worn by the Scot—for instance, by Tam O'Shanter.

16 *Drugget.* Coarse cloth. Cf. Prologue Spoken at the Opening of the New House, l. 9n.

19 *Indian Emperour.* A reference to Dryden's play.

20–24 The Scots were jeered at for their alleged lack of linen; thus John Cleveland's *The Rebel Scot,* l. 101 (*Caroline Poets,* ed. Saintsbury, III, 59): "Lord! what a godly thing is want of shirts!"

25–28 *Teg.* Generic term for Irishman in the period, like Taffy for a Welshman, Jockie for a Scot: see *Rump,* I, 257. The most famous Teg of the period was of course the Irish servant so named in Sir Robert Howard's popular and long-lived comedy *The Committee.*

Irish players were at Oxford for the Act in 1677, as shown by an "Epilogue to the University of Oxford 1677—by Mr. Jo: Haynes" which begins, "From Ireland, led by Fame, we came to see / An Oxford Act, Englands Epitome" (Thorn-Drury, Notebook, p. 62a). In 1680 the Dublin Company, whose patron was the Duke of Ormond, Chancellor of the University, almost got the invitation again—the King's Company had to get the King himself to intercede in their favor (see Hotson, pp. 263–264, and S. Rosenfeld in *RES*, XIX [1943], 370).

29 *Mac's.* A plural: Irish. Cf. Captain Macmorris in *Henry V*.

30 *second Massacre.* In the late summer of 1641, afraid of the consequences of a Puritan victory in England, the Irish had rebelled and put to death many English Protestants who during the regime of James had settled in the north of Ireland. Besides the religious persecution of Irish Catholics under Lord Strafford's governorship, economic abuses and confiscation of Catholic estates had combined to arouse bitter anti-English feeling. When the war began to go against Charles I, he negotiated with the Irish rebels for an army to use against the Puritans, offering toleration of Catholicism and a parliament free from the restrictions of Poynings' Act. The Irish, both Protestant and Catholic, rebelled later against the Puritan government in 1648, proclaiming Charles II king. Cromwell put down the uprising mercilessly, the massacre of the town of Drogheda typifying his savage reprisals.

32 Equivalent to the modern expression "has the map of Ireland in his face."

33 *pick your purse.* Metaphorically, by taking your money for a poor performance.

TEXTUAL NOTES

Introduction

CHOICE OF THE COPY TEXT

The copy text chosen is normally the first printing, on the theory that its accidentals are likely to be closest to the author's practice; but a manuscript or a subsequent printing may be chosen where there is reasonable evidence either that it represents more accurately the original manuscript as finally revised by the author or that the author revised the accidentals.

REPRODUCTION OF THE COPY TEXT

The copy text is normally reprinted *literatim,* but there are certain classes of exceptions. In the first place, apparently authoritative variants found in other texts are introduced as they occur, except that their purely accidental features are made to conform to the style of the copy text. These substitutions, but not their minor adjustments in accidentals, are recorded in footnotes as they occur. In the second place, accidentals are introduced or altered where it seems helpful to the reader and (1) there is no doubt that the ambiguity is unintentional and (2) there is a single resolution of the difficulty. Normally, but not necessarily, there is precedent in the seventeenth-century editions for these helps to the sense. All such changes also are recorded in footnotes as they occur. In the third place, turned b, q, d, p, n, and u are accepted as q, b, p, d, u, and n, respectively, and if they result in spelling errors are corrected in the text and listed in the footnotes.

Certain purely mechanical details, however, have been normalized without special mention. Long "s" has been changed to round "s," "VV" to "W"; swash italics have been represented by plain italics; head titles, section titles, display initials, the position of footnotes and stanza numbers, and so on, have been made uniform with the style of the present edition; stanza numbers have been corrected; wrong font, and turned letters other than q, b, p, d, u, and n, have been adjusted; medial apostrophes that failed to print have been restored; italicized plurals in -'s have been distinguished (by italic final "s") from possessives (roman final "s"); quotations have been marked with inverted commas at the beginning and end only and always; spacing between words and before and after punctuation has been normalized when no change in meaning results; the common contractions have been counted as single words, but otherwise words abbreviated by elision have been separated from those before and after if the apostrophe is present; if the elided syllable is written out as well as marked by an apostrophe, the words have been run together (*"speak'it"*).

TEXTUAL NOTES

The textual notes list the relevant manuscripts and printings, assign them sigla, and give references to the bibliographies where they are more fully described. The full titles in the seventeenth-century editions are noted here. Normally only the seventeenth-century editions are cited, but the eighteenth-century editions have always been examined for possible authoritative readings before they have been eliminated from notice. The textual notes also outline the descent of the text through its various manuscripts and printings, indicate which are the authorized texts, and explain how the copy text was selected in each instance. A list of copies collated follows.

The sigla indicate the format of printed books (F = folio, Q = quarto, O = octavo, etc.) and the order of printing, if this is determinable, within the format group (F may have been printed after Q1 and before Q2). If order of printing is in doubt, the numbers are arbitrary, and they are normally arbitrary for the manuscripts (represented by M).

Finally the variants in the copies collated are given, normally in a single list. This list is not exhaustive, but it records what seemed material, viz.:

All variants of the present edition from the copy text except in the mechanical details listed above.

All other substantive variants and variants in accidentals markedly affecting the sense.

All errors of any kind repeated from one edition to another, except the use of -'s instead of -s for a plural.

Spelling variants where the new reading makes a new word (e.g., *then* and *than* being in Dryden's day alternate spellings of the conjunction, a change from *than* to *then* would be recorded, since the spelling *then* is now confined to the adverb, but a change from *then* to *than* would be ignored as a simple modernization).

In passages of verse, variants in elision of syllables normally pronounced (except that purely mechanical details, as *wrack'd, wrackt,* are ignored). Thus *heaven, heav'n* is recorded, but not *denied, deny'd.*

In variant states where variants in the settings of individual forms are numerous, they are listed again, form by form. There are no instances of this practice in the first volume.

When variants in punctuation alone are recorded, the wavy dash is used in place of the identifying word before the variant punctuation. A caret indicates that the variant is the omission of any punctuation.

The texts of the plays have been arrived at on similar principles, but the textual notes thereto, and the textual notes to subsequent volumes of the poems, will be governed by the problems encountered. The introduction to the textual notes in each volume will indicate any changes in method.

Upon the Death of the Lord Hastings

The poem was printed only once in the seventeenth century, in *Lachrymæ Musarum; The Tears of the Muses: Exprest in Elegies ... Upon the death of ... Henry Lord Hastings.* Two issues of *Lachrymæ* have been recorded, the first dated 1649, the second, with cancel title page, dated 1650 (Macd 1a, 1b); there are other cancels in the second issue, but the leaves on which Dryden's poem appears were retained unaltered. Dryden's poem arrived late: on sig. E8*v* appears a note, "Here was the end of the Book intended to have been; and so was it Printed, before these following Papers were written or sent in." Then follow six poems; Dryden's appears on sig. F6*v*–F8*v*, pp. 88–92, and is signed "Johannes Dryden, Scholæ Westm. Alumnus."

The text of the poem in the present edition is taken without emendation from the Clark copy of Macd 1b (*PR2439.B5L2.1650), which has been collated with the following additional copies: Macd 1a: Huntington (102353); Macd 1b: Huntington (102355 [with the 1649 t.p.], 102354, 102837), Folger (B4877).

To John Hoddesdon, on His Divine Epigrams

These commendatory verses first appeared on ¶4r–*v* of a volume by John Hoddesdon entitled *Sion and Parnassus, or Epigrams On severall texts of the Old and New Testament. To which are added, A Poem on the Passion. A Hymn on the Resurrection, Ascension, And feast of Pentecost,* London, 1650 (O; Macd 2). Dryden's poem is there titled, "To his friend the Authour, on his divine Epigrams," and signed "J. Dryden of Trin. C." After this first printing the poem was lost sight of for over a century. Malone is usually given credit for recovering it and adding it to the Dryden canon, but whatever credit is due to the discoverer should go to John Nichols, who in 1780 reprinted the lines with the rather proud note: "Neither these verses, nor the prologue and two epilogues to 'The Duke of Guise,' having yet found admittance among the Works of this great Poet; I am happy in being thus able to supply the deficiency" (*A Select Collection of Poems: With Notes, Biographical and Historical,* I, 181).

The text of the poem in the present edition is taken from the Clark copy of *Sion and Parnassus* (*PR3515.H18S6), with one emendation, in line 18, and romans and italics reversed. The following copies have also been collated: Huntington (80585), Folger (H2295).

18 Enthusiasmes] Euthusiasmes O.

Letter to Honor Dryden

The original of this letter is now in the William Andrews Clark Memorial Library.

9:18 ow[n]] *a hole in the paper.* Date] *the figures not bracketed are visible under ultraviolet light.*

Heroique Stanzas to the Glorious Memory of Cromwell

Dryden's poem first appeared in *Three Poems Upon the Death of his late Highnesse Oliver Lord Protector of England, Scotland, and Ireland. Written by Mʳ Edm. Waller. Mʳ Jo. Dryden. Mʳ Sprat, of Oxford,* dated 1659. (Q1; Macd 3a). It appears on pages 1–9, with the title, "Heroique Stanza's, Consecrated to the Glorious Memory of his most Serene and Renowned Highnesse Oliver Late Lord Protector of this Common-Wealth, &c. Written after the Celebration of his Funerall." It was reprinted separately as *An Elegy on the Usurper O. C. by the Author of Absalom and Achitophel, published to shew the Loyalty and Integrity of the Poet,* dated 1681 (F; Macd 3b), and again, with the same title, dated 1682 (Q2; Macd 3c). In Q1 and Q2 line 48 (with a dagger prefixed) and the first four words of line 125 are emphasized by being set in italics. Both editions include a spurious "Postscript" signed "J. D." The three poems were reprinted as *Three Poems Upon the Death of the Late Usurper Oliver Cromwel. Written by Mr. Jo. Drydon. Mr. Sprat, of Oxford. Mr. Edm. Waller,* dated 1682. Two states of this edition have been recorded, for the second of which Dryden's poem was completely reset (Q3; Macd 3dii; Q4; Macd 3di; as may be seen from the collations below, Macdonald has the states in reverse order). Here Dryden's poem appears on pages 1–7, with the title "Heroiqe Stanza's, On the Late Usurper Oliver Cromwel. Written after his Funeral." It was again reprinted separately as *A Poem Upon the Death of the Late Usurper, Oliver Cromwel. By the Author of the H——d and the P———r,* dated 1687 (Q5; Macd 3e).

The three poems by Dryden, Sprat, and Waller were reprinted in *A Collection of Poems on Affairs of State; viz.* [9 titles, and] *Poems on Oliver, by Mr. Driden, Mr. Sprat, and Mr. Waller,* dated 1689 (Q6; Case 188(1)(a)). Dryden's poem appears on pages 20–24, and is entitled "Heroick Stanza's, on the late Usurper Oliver Cromwell, Written after his Funeral, by Mr. Drydon." Another edition of this volume, with the poet's name spelled "Dryden" on the title page and in the head title of the poem, is also dated 1689 (Q7; Case 188(1)(b)). Here the poem appears on pages 23, 22, 20, 21, 19 (i.e., 18–22).

Dryden's poem was again printed separately sometime between 1691 and 1693 as *A Poem Upon the Death of His Late Highness, Oliver, Lord Protector of England, Scotland, & Ireland. Written by Mr. Dryden* (Q8; Macd 3f). This edition is dated 1659, and for a long time was supposed to be either the second or the first. Percy J. Dobell (*John Dryden: Bibliographical Memoranda,* London, 1922, pp. 1–4) first pointed out that the type, paper, spelling, capitalization, italics, and, it might be added, the punctuation, mark it as a production of much later date. The probability is that Jacob Tonson had it reprinted specifically for binding up with remainder copies and reprints of others of Dryden's poems in the fourth volume of his works. It is listed on the volume title pages of 1693 and later (Macd 106b–e); it is not listed on the general title page of 1691 (Macd 106a). Separate copies of the reprint are not uncommon: some may have been sold separately to owners of sets purchased before the reprint was available, and others doubtless come from volumes subsequently broken up. Whether Dryden authorized the reprint we do not know; Dobell thought he probably did not; but Tonson was Dryden's usual publisher at this date, and it seems unlikely that he would reprint the poem against Dryden's wishes.

Dryden's poem was again reprinted, with Sprat's and Waller's, in *Poems on Affairs of State: From the Time of Oliver Cromwell, to the Abdication of K. James the Second*, dated 1697 (O1). Two states of this edition are recorded (Case 211(1)(a) and (b)), the second state having some cancelations and insertions, but preserving unaltered the leaves on which Dryden's poem appears (pages 7–12). The poem is here entitled, "Heroick Stanza's, on the late Usurper Oliver Cromwell: Written after his Funeral, by Mr. Dryden." The second edition of this volume is also dated 1697 (O2; Case 211(1)(c)), and the third edition 1699 (O3; Case 211(1)(d)). In these editions Dryden's poem appears on pages 6–11.

The evidence in the textual notes as to the genealogy of the various editions can best be summarized in diagram:

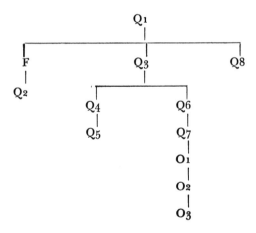

Dryden very probably had nothing to do with any but Q1 and Q8. F, Q2, and Q5 were, as their title pages make clear, published by Dryden's enemies to discredit his loyalty to King Charles and his conversion to Catholicism. None of the variants in these editions can be authoritative. It is unlikely, also, that Dryden authorized any of the other reprints in which Cromwell is called "the late Usurper"; presumably he would have objected to placing the derogatory title at the head of his poem of praise: in Q8, which Dryden may have authorized, Cromwell is called "His Late Highness." Here, how-

ever, the text exhibits no variants that can be identified as author's alterations. The text of the present edition, therefore, is taken from the Clark
copy of Q1 (*PR3419.T31), emended in lines 12, 60, 63, 65, 66, 81, 90, 117,
and 138. The following copies of the several editions have also been collated:

Q1: Folger (W526), Harvard (15435.27.2*), Huntington (79301); F: Clark
(*fPR3419.T31a.1681 [2 cop.], *PR3419.T31.1681 [cop. 2], *PR3419.T31.
1682 [cop. 2]), Harvard (15435.27.4F*); Q2: Yale (Rare Book Room Ij.D848.
+659c), Texas (Wj.D848.659tc); Q3: Clark (*PR3419.T31.1682a); Q4: Clark
(*PR3419.T31.1682 [2 cop.]), Folger (D2382); Q5: Clark (*PR3419.T31a.
1687), Harvard (15435.26*), Yale (Rare Book Room Ij.D848.659xx); Q6:
Harvard (Gay 10.9*); Q7: Clark (*PR1195.H5C65.1689 [2 cop.]), Yale
(Ij.M368.689), Folger (C5176); Q8: Clark (*PR3419.T31a.1691; *PR3413.
A1.1683; *PR3410.C93, v. 4; *PR3410.C94, v. 4; *PR3410.C95a, v. 4); O1:
Clark (*PR1195.H5P7; *PR1195.H5P7.1697), Folger (P2719), Yale (Ib68.
697 [cop. 1]); O2: Clark (*PR1195.H5P7.1697a); O3: Clark (*PR1195.H5P7.
1699), Yale (Ib68.697c).

1 time;] Q1, Q3, Q6–8, O1–3; ~ₐ F, Q2, Q4–5.   3 ere] Q1, Q6; e're
F, Q2–5, Q7–8, O1–3.   4 too] Q1, F, Q2–6, Q8, O1–3; to Q7.   7
Heav'n] Q1, Q3–5; Heaven F, Q2, Q6–8, O1–3.   7 what] Q1, Q3–8,
O1–3; the F, Q2.   8 choice:] Q1, Q3–5; ~ . F, Q2, Q8, O1–3; ~ ; Q6–7.
9 liberall] Q1, Q3–8, O1–3; lib'ral F, Q2.   12 own:] Q6–7; ~ . Q1, F,
Q2–5, Q8, O1–3.   13 interest] Q1, F, Q2–8, O3; int'rest O1–2.   15
Lest] Q1, Q2–8, O1–3; Least F.   18 *Fame*] Q1, Q3–8, O1–3; Frame F,
Q2.   20 *equall perfect*] Q1, F, Q2–3, Q7–8, O1–3; *equalperfect* Q4; *equal-
perfect* Q5; equal, perfect Q6.   21 Heav'n] Q1, Q3, Q8; Heaven F, Q2,
Q4–7, O1–3.   24 not] Q1, F, Q2–8, O2–3; nor O1.   28 too] Q1, F,
Q2, Q5–8, O1–3; two Q3–4.   29 of] Q1, F, Q2–5, Q8; to Q6–7, O1–3.
31 rank'd] Q1, F, Q2–8, O1–2; rank O3.   33 He, private,] Q1, Q3–4,
Q8; He private, F, Q6–7, O1–3; He private Q2; He, private Q5.   38
Heaven] Q1, F, Q2–7, O1–3; Heav'n Q8.   39 unsought rewards] Q1,
Q3–8, O1–3; rewards unsought F, Q2.   40 that] Q1, Q3–8, O1–3; which
F, Q2.   40 given] Q1, F, Q2–7, O1–3; giv'n Q8.   41 Cheifs] Q1, F,
Q2–6, Q8, O3; Chief Q7, O1–2.   41 of] Q1, Q3–8, O1–3; in F, Q2.
42 sought] Q1, F, Q2–8; fought O1–3.   44 make] Q1, F, Q2–8, O1–2;
made O3.   46 We] Q1, F, Q2–5, Q8; He Q6–7, O1–3.   47 end our]
Q1, F, Q2–8; hinder O1–3.   47 fighting] Q1, Q3–8, O1–3; Fightings F,
Q2.   48 stanch] Q1, F, Q2–7, O1–3; stench Q8.   48 of the] Q1,
Q3–8, O1–3; *of a* F, Q2.   50 subdue;] Q1, Q3–5, Q8; ~ . F; ~ , Q2,
Q6–7, O1–3.   51 battails] Q1, Q3–8, O1–3; Battle F, Q2.   52 on]
Q1, F, Q2, Q4–8, O1–3; one Q3.   54 Till] Q1, F, Q2–5, Q8; Still Q6–7,
O1–3.   55 where e're] Q1, F, Q2–8, O3; were e're O1–2.   56 is] Q1,
F, Q2–7, O1–3; are Q8.   59 Heav'n] Q1, Q3–5; Heaven F, Q2, Q6–8,
O1–3.   59 his] Q1, F, Q2–8, O1–2; its O3.   60 drew] F, Q2–8, O1–3;
dtew Q1.   61 Prize] Q1, Q3–8, O1; Price F, Q2, O2–3.   61 his] Q1,
F, Q2–8, O1–2; its O3.   61 toyles] Q1, F, Q2–6; toil Q7–8, O1–3.   63
walls] Q6–8, O1–3; wall Q1, F, Q2–5.   65 owes;] Q8; ~ₐ Q1; ~ , F,

Q2–7, O1–3.   66 *Scotland*] F, Q2–8, O1–3; *Seotland* Q1.   66 in-t'rest] Q1, F, Q3–8, O1–3; Interest Q2.   70 pale] Q1, Q2–8, O1–3; pail F.   71 influence] Q1, F, Q2–5, Q8, O1–3; influences Q6–7.   71 Mine] Q1, Q3–6; Mein F, O2–3; Main Q2; Mien Q7–8, O1.   73 Coun-t'nance] Q1, F, Q2–6, Q8; Countenance Q7, O1–3.   74 naturally] Q1, Q3–8, O1–3; nat'rally F, Q2.   76 Sov'raign . . . doth] Q1, Q3–8, O1–3; sovereign . . . does F, Q2.   77 Offerings] Q1, F, Q2–7, O1–3; Off'rings Q8.   78 depos'd] Q1, F, Q2–3, Q5–8, O1–3; despos'd Q4.   79 Coun-cells] Q1, F, Q2–4, Q6–8, O1–2; Councils Q5, O3.   81 suppliant] Q1, F, Q3–8, O1–3; supplicant Q2.   81 peace,] F, Q5–8, O1–3; ~∧ Q1, Q3–4; ~ . Q2.   82 in] Q1, F, Q2–8, O1–2; of O3.   84 buy] Q1, F, Q2–8, O1–2; by O3.   85 th'] Q1, F, Q2–5, Q8, O1–2; the Q6–7, O3.   90 Than] Q1, Q3–8, O1–3; Then F, Q2.   90 light] F, Q2–8, O1–3; leight Q1.   91 where it was] Q1, F, Q2–7, O1–3; where-e're 'twas Q8.   92 were in] Q1, F, Q2–6, Q8, O3; where in Q7, O1; wherein O2.   94 some meaner] Q1, F, Q2–5, Q8; that some mean Q6–7, O1–3.   96 still] Q1, Q3–8, O1–3; all F, Q2.   98 alloy] Q1, Q8; allay F, Q2–7, O1–3.   100 she] Q1, Q3–8, O1–3; the F, Q2.   104 to] Q1, F, Q3–8, O1–3; of Q2.   105 Heav'n] Q1; Heaven F, Q3–8, O1–3.   105 sets] Q1, F, Q2–5, Q8; set Q6–7, O1–3.   110 portend] Q1, F, Q2–5, Q7–8, O1–3; pretend Q6.   117 Land,] F, Q2–8, O1–3; ~∧ Q1.   125 above] Q1, Q3–8, O1–3; ~ , F, Q2.   126 to] Q1, F, Q2–5, Q8, O2–3; or Q6–7, O1.   130 when] Q1, F, Q2–6, Q8, O1–3; when the Q7.   132 could] Q1, F, Q2, Q8; can Q3–7, O1–3.   134 does] Q1, Q3–5, Q8; doth F, Q2, Q6–7, O1–3.   135 by] Q1, Q3–8, O1–3; with F, Q2.   136 decease] Q1, Q3–8, O1–3; de-crease F, Q2.   137 sent] Q1, F, Q2–8; ~ . O1–3.   138 That] Q1, Q3–8, O1–3; The F, Q2.   138 watery] Q1, Q3–5; Watry F, Q2, Q6–8, O1–3.   138 Heard,] F, Q2; ~∧ Q1, Q3–5; ~ ; Q6–8, O1–3.   146 a . . . stands] Q1, Q3–8, O1–3; and . . . stand F, Q2.

To My Honored Friend, Sir Robert Howard

"To my Honored Friend, Sr Robert Howard, On his Excellent Poems" was first printed in Howard's *Poems*, 1660, on A6r–A8r (O1; Macd 4a), and signed "John Driden." The sheets of this edition were subsequently reis-sued with a cancel title page, *Poems on Several Occasions*, dated 1696 (O2; Macd 4b). Dryden's verses were reprinted in *A Collection of Poems by Sev-eral Hands*, dated 1693, on O1r–O4r, pp. 191–197 (O3; Case 151(c)). The sheets of this edition were subsequently reissued with a cancel title page, *The Temple of Death . . . The Second Edition*, dated 1695 (O4; Case 151(d)).

The Clark copy of O1 has a press variant, "Pannegyrick" in the ninth line of the title page, that is not recorded by Macdonald, but has no variants from other copies in the text.

There is no evidence that Dryden had anything to do with O3–4. The text of the present edition is therefore taken from the Clark copy of O1 (*PR3517.H3A17), with the punctuation of lines 28, 58, and 64 emended, and italics and romans reversed. The following copies of the several editions have also been collated: O1: Huntington (124100-01), Newberry (Case Y.185.H835); O2: Folger (H3004); Clark (*PR3517.H3A17.1696); O3: Clark (*PR1213.C7.1693), Folger (C5174); O4: Harvard (15476.153*).

21 souls,] O1–2; ~∧ O3–4.   28 caught?] ~ . O1–4.   58 wore.] ~∧ O1–4.   64 those,] ~ . O1–4.

Astraea Redux. A Poem on the Restoration of Charles the Second

The first, separate edition of *Astræa Redux* is dated 1660. In this edition two states of the inner form of sheet C have been recorded, the first (F1; Macd 5ai) differing from the second (F2; Macd 5aii) in lines 151, 166, 195, 208, and 210. The poem was reprinted, together with *To His Sacred Majesty* and *To My Lord Chancellor,* in the 1688 edition of *Annus Mirabilis* (Q; Macd 9c), pages [79]–96. In the 1690's remainders of the 1688 edition of *Annus Mirabilis* were bound up with other pieces as the fourth volume of Dryden's works (Macd 106a–e).

The type for Q was set from a copy of F2. That F2 is the corrected state of the first edition is proved by the resetting of line 151, where F1 reads "lose" and F2 "loose": in both states the line runs from margin to margin, but in F1 "*MONCK*" is spelled with a swash "*M*"; clearly the compositor replaced the swash with a plain italic letter to make room for the extra "o" in "loose"; had the change been from "loose" to "lose," he would have justified the line by inserting a space at the end. The resetting of line 151 and the correction of "behold" to "beheld" in line 195 may have been ordered by the press corrector. There seems to be no reason, however, why anyone but the author should have wished to substitute "And glass-like" for "Like glass we" in line 208. The erroneous substitution of a period for a colon at the end of line 210, the last line of verse in the inner form of sheet C, doubtless resulted when the compositor, without referring to the outer form, repaired an accidental disturbance of the type that occurred while the chase was unlocked for the other changes. The substitution of a semi-colon for a comma at the end of line 166 may have resulted from a similar accident, but it is here accepted as being the better reading, and so likely to be authoritative.

Dryden seems not to have revised the poem again. Q differs from F2 only in elisions and accidentals, most significantly in lines 164 and 167. Lines 163–168 are admittedly difficult, but the punctuation of the passage found in F2 seems (*contra* Noyes, p. 943) to be more satisfactory than that in Q. Therefore the text of the present edition is taken from the Clark copy of F2 (*PR3419.A81), emended in the punctuation of lines 11, 79, 80, 85, 121,

182, 201, 208, 210, 225, and 279. The following copies of these editions have also been collated: F1: Folger (D2386(ai)); F2: Harvard (15431.12*), Folger (D2386(aii)), Huntington (125990); Q: Clark (*PR3410.C95a, *PR3413.A1.1682, *PR3419.A61.1688 [2 cop.]), Folger (D2210).

11 breath'd,] Q; ~∧ F1–2.   79 time,] Q; ~. F1–2.   80 Crime,] Q; ~∧ F1–2.   85 before,] Q; ~∧ F1–2.   120 Off'ring] F1–2; Offering Q.   121 slain,] Q; ~∧ F1–2.   151 loose] F2, Q; lose F1.   164 see] F1–2; ~; Q.   166 Brain;] F2; ~, F1, Q.   167 dispense,] F1–2; ~∧ Q.   182 dispossest,] ~. F1–2, Q.   195 beheld] F2, Q; behold F1.   201 *Sforza,* . . . brain,] Q; ~∧ . . . ~∧ F1–2.   208 And, glass-like,] ~∧ ~∧ F2, Q; Like glass we F1.   210 bliss:] F1; ~. F2, Q.   225 out,] Q; ~∧ F1–2.   265 *Long-Suff'ring*] F1–2; *Long-suffering* Q.   279 shore,] ~. F1–2, Q.   286 Intrest] F1–2; Interest Q.

To His Sacred Majesty, A Panegyrick on His Coronation

The first, separate edition of *To His Sacred Majesty* was published in 1661. Two states of the outer form of sheet A are recorded, one having in line 32 the reading "Not only King of us" (F1; Macd 6ai), the other "Not King of us alone" (F2; Macd 6aii). Errors in the outer form of sheet B, "Your your" in line 122, and "ovn" in line 136 were allowed to stand, "ovn" perhaps being accepted as a variant spelling, and the second "your" normally being blocked out with ink by the printer.

Two states of the second printing, in Pierre de Cardonnel's *Complementum Fortunatarum Insularum,* 1662, have also been recorded. In the first (O1; Macd 6b), the full text is found on pages 34–39, F1*v*–F4*r*. In the second (O2; James M. Osborn, "Macdonald's Bibliography of Dryden," *MP,* XXXIX [1941], 71–72), F3 and F4 are cancels, and the poem is cut off after line 78. The reprinted lines, on F3*r*, page 37, show only one variant from the text of the first state: "Ang" has been corrected to "And" in line 76. In both states, Dryden's poem is followed by a French translation of the full text.

The poem was again reprinted together with *Astræa Redux* and *To My Lord Chancellor,* in the 1688 edition of *Annus Mirabilis* (Q; Macd 9c), pages [97]–105. In the 1690's, remainders of the 1688 edition of *Annus Mirabilis* were bound up with other pieces as the fourth volume of Dryden's works (Macd 106a–e).

There seems to be no clear evidence as to which state of the first edition is the corrected one. The 1662 printing was set from a copy reading "Not only King of us," the 1688 printing from one reading "Not King of us alone." Macdonald accepts the latter as the revised reading, presumably because Dryden may have supplied the copy for the 1688 edition, and no plausible argument may be advanced for the authority of the reading "Not only King of us." Dryden does not appear to have revised the text for either the second or the third printing. Therefore the text of the present edition has been taken from one of the Clark copies of F2 (*fPR3419.T81. 1661 [cop. 1]), emended in the punctuation of line 45. The following copies of the several editions have also been collated: F1: Folger (D2386(ai)), Huntington (123082); F2: Clark (*fPR3419.T81.1661 [cop. 2]), Folger (D2386(aii)); O1: Clark (*PR3419.T81.1662); Folger (C498); O2: Yale (Z66.64n.Lon.1662); Q: Clark (*PR3413.A1.1683; *PR3410.C94, v. 4; *PR3419.A61.1688 [2 cop.]), Folger (D2210).

32 Not King of us alone] F2, Q; Not only King of us F1, O1–2.   45 Next,] Q; ~∧ F1–2, O1–2.   78 *O2 ends with this line.*   79 seditions] F1–2, O1; seditious Q.   111 th'] F1–2, O1; the Q.   122 Your love] O1, Q; Your your love F1–2 (*in most copies the second "your" is blocked out with ink*).   136 own] O1, Q; ovn F1–2.

To My Lord Chancellor

The poem was printed only twice in the seventeenth century, separately, with the date 1662 (F; Macd 7), and with *Astræa Redux* and *To His Sacred Majesty* in the 1688 edition of *Annus Mirabilis* (Q; Macd 9c), pages [107]– 116. In the 1690's, remainders of the 1688 edition of *Annus Mirabilis* were bound up with other pieces as the fourth volume of Dryden's works (Macd 106a–e). There is no certainty that Dryden corrected the poem for the second printing: the substantive variant in line 81 may well have originated in the printing house; that in line 148, an error, certainly did so. Therefore the text of the poem in the present edition has been taken from the Clark copy of the separate edition (*fPR3419.T91), without emendation. The following copies of the several editions have also been collated: F: Huntington (123083), Harvard (15435.27.2.5F*), Folger (D2387); Q: Clark (*PR3413.A1. 1683a; *PR3410.C93, v. 4; *PR3419.A61.1688 [2 cop.]), Folger (D2210).

55 Heav'n] F; Heaven Q.   81 the] F; their Q.   145 th'] F; the Q.   148 Your] F; Yours Q.

To My Honored Friend, Dr. Charleton

These commendatory verses were printed only once in the seventeenth century, on b2r–v of Walter Charleton's *Chorea Gigantum*, 1663, entitled "To my Honour'd Friend, Dʳ Charleton, on his learned and useful works; and more particularly this of Stone-Heng, by him Restored to the true Founders," and signed "John Driden." Dryden's poem was corrected while the sheet was being run off. Macdonald refers to several variant states, but only examples of the first (Q1; Macd 8ai) and last (Q2; Macd 8aii) of these have been examined for the present edition. In the Folger Shakespeare Library is a copy of Q1 presented to Dryden which has five additional manuscript corrections to the poem. (This is the copy referred to by Mac-donald, p. 12.) Since the ink appears to be the same as that in the inscription and in a deletion on page 14 of the volume, the corrections may be Charleton's; the evidence of the handwriting is inconclusive. The corrections are as follows:

> 10 in a] in y^e   10 Zone:] ∼ ;   11 fevrish] fev'rish
> 11 breez:] ∼ ;   35 Fl es (*so in this and some other copies*)] Flie's

The first of these corrections is found, again in manuscript, in the other Folger copy of Q1, which is printed on large paper. It is, however, the sort of change that might occur to any literal-minded reader. It might be thought that Charleton would take care to present Dryden with the corrected text of his poem, but the readings in lines 13, 22, and 50 make it fairly certain that he did not. The reading of Q2 in line 13 is a grammatical improvement, that in line 22 is a metrical improvement, and that in line 50 brings Dryden's remarks into closer parallel with Charleton's arguments, which do not specify the grounds on which the Danish kings were chosen but emphasize the applause accorded the elected monarchs by their people.

The variant readings of the reprint of Dryden's poem in *Poetical Miscellanies: The Fifth Part,* 1704, do not appear to be authoritative. Therefore the text in the present edition is taken from the Clark copy of Q2 (*DA142.C47), emended in the punctuation of lines 6, 26, and 48. The following additional copies have also been examined: Q1: Folger (C3666(ai) [2 cop.]); Q2: Huntington (114340), Folger (C3666(aii)).

> 6 sophisticate,] ∼ . Q1–2.   13 who] Q2; that Q1.   22 Th' . . . not the] Q2; The . . . not Q1.   26 awe;] ∼ . Q1–2.   39 of Ore] Q2; in Ore Q1.   48 Crown'd,] ∼ . Q1–2.   50 Joy'd with] Q2; Chose by Q1.   52 rule] Q2; sway Q1.   55 Royal] Q2; Kingly Q1.

To the Lady Castlemaine, upon Her Incouraging His First Play

The poem was first published in *A New Collection of Poems and Songs,* edited by John Bulteel, on pages 71–74 (O1). There are at least four issues: the first has Bulteel's name on the title page, which is dated 1674 (Macd 55); the second has a cancel title page, from which Bulteel's name has been omitted, dated 1674 (Case 157(b)); the third has a cancel title page, *A New Collection of New Songs and Poems,* dated 1674; the fourth has a cancel title page, *Melpomene: or, The Muses Delight,* dated 1678 (Case 157(c)). The only other difference among the four issues is in the cancelation of the half title in the last three and its replacement in the third issue with a cancel half title. In this edition Dryden's poem has the title, "To the Dutchess of Cleaveland." A somewhat shortened and revised version, entitled "To the Lady Castlemaine, upon her incouraging his first Play," was published in Dryden's *Examen Poeticum*, 1693, on pages 295–298 (O2). Macdonald records two states of this edition, the second differing from the first only in having the text of Tate's poem "Syphilis" reset (Macd 45ai–ii).

W. J. Lawrence records the existence of a manuscript version in the Bodleian Library (M; MS Eng. Poet. e. 4, pp. 173–174) in "a neatly penned quarto manuscript volume of miscellaneous late seventeenth century verse . . . evidently compiled by some Oxford graduate" ("Restoration Dramatic Prologues," *TLS*, 16 January 1930). Here the poem is entitled, "To the Countess of Castlemaine, for procuring a Play of his might be printed." While M gives the fuller text of O1, it has a striking number of the individual readings of O2, as well as unique readings of its own.

It follows that O1, O2, and M are connected through a common intermediary. There is no way to date M relative to O1 and O2, so that we are not required to take it as the ancestor. On the other hand, it seems to be generally agreed that a compositor worked from printed copy when he could, and there is nothing in O2 to prevent the assumption that its printer was supplied with a copy of O1 corrected by the author. We may therefore take O1 as our copy text. It is possible that M preserves some authoritative readings overlooked or rejected when the copy for O2 was prepared, but none of its peculiar variants seems markedly characteristic of Dryden.

Therefore the text of the present edition has been taken from the Harvard copy of the second issue of O1 (15476.20*), emended from O2 in lines 3, 6, 9, 10, 17, 18, 29, 34, 35, 40, 41, 47, 48, 50, 51, and 52. The six lines omitted from O2 have been retained in square brackets. The following copies of the several editions have also been collated: O1 *second issue:* Folger (B5457); O1 *third issue:* Folger (B5458a), Chicago (Rare Book Room PR3328.B8.1674 Carpenter); O2 *first state:* Clark (*PR3413.Z4M1e); O2 *second state:* Clark (*PR3413.Z4M1e.1693).

3 And] O1–2; For M. 3 long] O2, M; for O1. 4 By their misfortunes] O1–2; They by misfortune M. 5 So my much-envy'd] O1–2; Just so my envyed M. 6 thrown] O2; cast O1, M. 9 Virtue] O2, M; Virtues O1. 9 oppose;] O2; ~ , O1, M. 10 While] O2; When O1, M. 17 Fame and Praise] O2, M; Praise and Fame O1. 18 Smile] O2, M; Smiles O1. 26 born . . . Heav'n, and] O1–2; sun . . . Heaven M. 29 pow'r] O1–2; Power M. 29 never use but for] O2, M; use but for your own O1. 32 though] O1–2; but M. 34 would] O2, M; did O1. 34 wait] O1–2; ward M. 35 such] O2; that O1, M. 37–38 *Omitted from O2.* 39 be?] O1, M; ~ , O2. 40 which] O2; that O1, M. 40 captives] O2, M; castives O1. 40 free.] O1, M; ~ ? O2. 41 will] O2, M; would O1. 43 Who] O1–2; Which M. 47 the] O2; her O1; their M. 48 them] O2, M; her O1. 50 to age] O2, M; of age O1. 51 this long growing] O2; this vast growing O1; your vast wondrous M. 51 to Poetry] O2, M; of Poesie O1. 52

You justly (Madam)] O2; You, Madam, justly O1, M.   54   Muse;] O1;
~. O2; ~: M.   55–58 *Omitted from O2.*   56 your] O1; their M.
57 this] O1; the M.   58   One soveraign] O1; I had a M.

Annus Mirabilis: The Year of Wonders, 1666

The first edition of *Annus Mirabilis* bears the date 1667 on the title page;
the imprimatur, signed by Roger L'Estrange, is dated November 22, 1666.
In this edition, four states of sheet C have been recorded: in the first state
(O1; Macd 9ai) the sheet appears as it came off the press; in the second
state (O2; Macd 9aii) C6 has been canceled and replaced by a leaf having a
revised version of stanza 105 of the poem; in what may be called the third
state (O3; Percy J. Dobell, *John Dryden: Bibliographical Memoranda*, London, 1922, p. 6), C1 has also been canceled and replaced with a leaf having
a revised version of stanza 67; in what may be called the fourth state (O4;
Macd 9aiii) C6 and C1 have been canceled as before, but the cancel C1 is
printed from a different setting of type than the corresponding cancel in
the third state, having, for instance, no comma after "alone" in line 267.
The two cancels for C1 were probably printed simultaneously. The collations made for the present edition have also turned up two states in the
outer form of sheet A in the first edition, one reading "ezcellent" in the
sixth line from the bottom of A8*v* and found in O1–3, the other reading
"excellent" and found in O4.

On the recto of the last preliminary leaf is a list of sixteen corrections,
with a prefatory note "To the Readers": "*Notwithstanding the diligence
which has been used in my absence, some faults have escap'd the Press: and
I have so many of my own to answer for, that I am not willing to be charg'd
with those of the Printer. I have onely noted the grossest of them, not such
as by false stops have confounded the sense, but such as by mistaken words
have corrupted it.*" This errata list is itself not without error. It seems likely,
also, that one additional error has been omitted from the series "page 53.
line 5. . . . *ibid.* line 11. . . . *ibid.* line 7. . . . *ibid.* in the note,"
where the last two errors occur on page 56. Presumably the first error noted
on page 56, to which the page number was attached, has dropped out; perhaps it was "To" instead of "Too" in line 874. Since Dryden does not list
errata in punctuation, it is impossible to prove that the accidental variants
in the cancel leaves, C1 and C6, come from his pen.

The second edition (O5; Macd 9b) is dated 1668. It was printed from O1,
the uncorrected state of the first edition. Dobell (*op. cit.*, p. 5) argues that
it is a piracy, from the fact that its imprint bears the name of the publisher
of the first edition, who would presumably have sent a corrected copy to
the printer. Certainly there is no evidence that Dryden had anything to do
with correcting its text.

The third edition (Q; Macd 9c) is dated 1688. Here *Annus Mirabilis* is
followed by reprints of *Astræa Redux, To His Sacred Majesty,* and *To My*

Lord Chancellor, which have special title pages but continuous paging and signatures with the first poem. The four constitute the first collected edition of Dryden's poetry. In the 1690's, remainders of this edition were bound up with other pieces as the fourth volume of Dryden's works (Macd 106a–e). Copy for Q was O3 or O4, more probably the latter as Q is normally more heavily punctuated than the other editions but does not have a comma after "alone" in line 267.

The variants in Q are strikingly numerous and include a number of corrections not noted in the list of errata in the first edition. Earlier editors have supposed from this that Dryden revised the copy for Q, and have consequently chosen to reprint it, but as a matter of fact there is no certainty that any of the variants is authoritative.

One hesitates, for example, to attribute to Dryden transpositions and deletions of insignificant words in the preliminaries, or such variants as "steer" for "sheer" in line 311 of the poem, "doth" for "does" in line 460, "Foundations" for "foundation" in line 577, "hastning" for "'hasting" in line 742, "a" for "the" in line 922, or "give" for "drive" in line 1120, where the variants amount to no more than a letter or two, or the meaning is not altered. In line 778 of the poem, the reading "close to" for "to the" is probably a compositor's error, taken in from the line below. The readings "from the noise" for "are from noise" in line 364 of the poem, and "measure of Longitude" for "knowledge of Longitudes" in the note to line 649 may have been dictated by Dryden, but they may equally well, it would seem, have originated in the printing house.

Therefore the text in the present edition has been taken from the Folger copy of O1 (D2238(ai)), corrected from the errata and the substantive variants in O2–4. Additional emendations have been introduced in "An Account of the ensuing Poem" at page 50:17, 50:33, 51:3, 53:25, 54:19, 54:25, 54:31, 55:5, 57:14, 57:22, and 58:22, and in the poem itself at line 59, Note g, lines 190, 191, 197, Note k, lines 344, 348, Note n, lines 428, 432, 440, 495, Note p, lines 518, 556, Note q, lines 655, 790, 799, 856, 865, 874, 876, 896, 903, 1004, 1015, 1048, 1054, 1067, and 1115. Italics and romans in the "Account of the ensuing Poem" (except for the inserted "Verses to her Highness") have been reversed. The following copies of the several editions have also been collated: O2: Clark (*PR3419.A61.1667a), Folger (D2238(aii)); O3: Clark (*PR3419.A61.1667b), Folger (D2238(aiii)), Huntington (122997), Harvard (15435.23.5(A)*), Newberry (Case Y.185.D8571; C6 not canceled); O4: Clark (*PR3419.A61.1667c); O5: Clark (*PR3419. A61.1668), Folger (D2239), Harvard (15435.23.7*); Q: Folger (D2210), Clark (*PR3419.A61.1688 [2 cop.]; *PR3410.C93, v. 4; *PR3410.C94, v. 4).

"To the Metropolis": *head title* ɪᴛs] O1–4, Q; it's O5. 48:2 is it] O1–5; it is Q.

"An Account of the ensuing Poem": 50:17 formost] Q; *for most* O1–5. 50:21 latter] O1–5; *later* Q. 50:33 Historians] O5, Q; *Historiaus* O1–4. 51:3 for] Q; *fro* O1–5; *from* O5. 51:25 latter] O1–5; *later* Q. 52:2 Arts] O1–5; *Art* Q. 52:33 so is it] O1–5; *so it is* Q.

53:13 of that] O1–5; *of* Q. 53:25 deriving] Q; *driving* O1–5. 53:31 latter] O1–5; *later* Q. 54:19 be set] O5, Q; *beset* O1–4. 54:21 we so] O1–5; *so we* Q. 54:25 *molem*] Q; motem O1–5. 54:31 *Pariusve*] Q; pariusve O1–5. 55:5 excellent] O4–5, Q; *exellent* O1–3. 56:8 well the] O1–5; *well* Q. 56:24 will] *the "w" failed to print in some copies of O1–4 (type broken).* 56:27 have said] O1–5; *said* Q. 56:29 *erat*] O1–4, Q; erit O5. 57:7 ere] O1–5; *e'er* Q. 57:14 Law,] ~ . O1–5, Q. 57:15 he] O1–4, Q; she O5. 57:22 obey,] Q; ~ . O1–5. 58:22 Envoy] O5, Q; Envoy' O1–4. 58:28 train's] O1–4, Q; trains O5.

Poem: 3 own.] O1–5; ~ ; Q. 13 of their] O1–5; of the Q. 26 seav'n] O1–5; seven Q. 39 Land . . . freed] O1–4, Q; ~ , . . . ~ , O5. 43 on] O1–4 *errata*, O5, Q; an O1–4 *text.* 59 hear] here O1–5, Q. Note *d* ponti armenta & magnas pascit] O1–4 *errata*, O5; . . . poscit Q; pouti armenta, & magnas poscit O1–4 *text.* 87 Heav'n] O1–5; Heaven Q. 106 undertake] O1–4 *errata*, O5, Q; undertook O1–4 *text.* 142 Heav'n] O1–5; Heaven Q. 150 interest] O1–4, Q; int'rest O5. Note *f* fit naufragium] O1–4 *errata*, O5, Q; naufragiunt est O1–4 *text.* Note *g* them,] O5; ~ . O1–4, Q. 184+ DUKE] O1–4, Q; *Duke of* O5. 190 praise;] Q; ~ . O1–5. 191 same,] O5, Q; ~ . O1–4. 197 Duke] Q; ~ , O1–5. 219 a loud] O1–4 *errata*, O5, Q; aloud O1–4 *text.* 226 dreadful] O1–4 *errata*, O5, Q; distant O1–4 *text.* Note *k* *revulsas*] Q; revultas O1–5. 267 who neerest Danger lay] O3–4, Q; not making equal way O1–2, O5. 279 mighty] O1–5; might Q. 311 sheer] O1–5; steer Q. 324 rise.] *failed to print in some copies of Q.* 326 send:] *colon failed to print in some copies of Q.* 344 wind,] ~ . O1–5, Q. 348 Bird?] ~ . O1–5, Q. 364 are from] O1–5; from the Q. 366 foll'wing] O1–5; following Q. Note *n* ac terris] ac tenis O1–5; antennis Q. 417–420] O2–4, Q; O1 *and* O5 *read:*

  For now brave *Rupert*'s Navy did appear,
    Whose waving streamers from afar he knows:
  As in his fate something divine there were,
    Who dead and buried the third day arose.

428 away;] ~ . O1–5, Q. 432 cries:] ~ . O1–5, Q. 435 were] O1–5; where Q. 440 train,] ~ . O1–5, Q. 460 does] O1–5; doth Q. 462 th'] O1–5; the Q. 494 fear.] O1–5; ~ : Q. 495 passions] passion, O1–5, Q. Note *p* Virgil.] *the period failed to print in the copies of O3 and O4 examined.* Note *p* extremæque] O5; extremœque O1–4, Q. 507 one] O1–4 *errata*, O5, Q; own O1–4 *text.* 518 board] Q; boar'd O1–5. 546 ev'n] O1–4, Q; even O5. 556 day:] ~ . O1–5, Q. Note *q* opimus] opinius O1–5, Q. 568 Surgeons] O1–4 *errata*, O5, Q; Chyrurg'ons O1–4 *text.* 577 foundation] O1–5; Foundations Q. 600 into the] O1–5; into Q. 655 know,] O5, Q; ~ . O1–4. Note *s* vias] O1–4 *errata*, O5, Q; vicis O1–4 *text.* Note *t* knowledge of Longitudes] O1–5; measure of Longitude Q. 681 new] O1–5; now Q. 710 Heav'n] O1–5; Heaven Q. 719 off] O1–4, Q; of O5. 731 flats] O1–4 *errata*, O5, Q; flots O1–4 *text.* 734 host] O1–5; hosts Q. 742

hasting] O1–5; hastning Q.   775   *Varro*] O1–4 *errata*, O5, Q; *Verro*
O1–4 *text*.   778   to the] O1–5; close to Q.   790   *Philip's*] O1–5;
Philips's Q.   790   bring:] Q; ~ . O1–5.   Note *y* Philip's] O1–5;
Philips's Q.   799   know,] O5; ~ . O1–4; ~ ; Q.   830   Smile] O1–4
errata, O5, Q; Smiles O1–4 *text*.   832+   TRANSITUM] O1–5; Transit Q.
835   palling] O1–4 *errata*, O5, Q; falling O1–4 *text*.   856   known:] ~ .
O1–5, Q.   865   source] scource O1–5, Q.   874   Too] O5, Q; To
O1–4.   876   old:] ~ . O1–5, Q.   879   tender] O1–4 *errata*, O5, Q;
open O1–4 *text*.   896   lookt] Q; look O1–5.   903   Mothers] Q;
Mother O1–5.   Note *a* accenderet] O1–4 *errata*, O5, Q; accruderet
O1–4 *text*. 922   with the] O1–5; with a Q.   923   waken'd] O1–4, Q;
weaken'd O5.   939   straggle] O1–5; struggle Q.   990   night-hags]
O1–4 *errata*, O5, Q; night has O1–4 *text*.   1004   Tempest] O1–5; Tempests Q.   1004   flie:] ~ . O1–5, Q.   1015   blows,] O5, Q; ~ . O1–4.
1044+   KING'S] O1–5; *Kings's* Q.   1048   possess:] ~ . O1–5, Q.   1054
friends, the good] Q; friends the good, O1–5.   1067   shun,] Q; ~ . O1–5.
1077   threatnings] O1–5; Threatings Q.   1092   Ere] O1–5; E're Q.
1094   in] O1–5; in the Q.   1115   Not] Nor O1–5, Q.   1120   give]
O1–5; drive Q.   1136   grain:] O1–4; ~ . O5, Q.   1168   work] O1–5;
Works Q.

To Mr. Lee, on His Alexander

These commendatory verses, signed "John Dryden," were first printed in
Lee's *The Rival Queens, or The Death of Alexander the Great,* 1677, on
a1r–v (Q1; Macd 10a). The catchword on the verso of the preceding leaf in
this edition, [A4], is "PROLOGUE," which may indicate that the original
plan for the work did not include Dryden's poem. The prologue is found
on a2.

  The Rival Queens was reprinted in the seventeenth century as follows:
1684 (Q2; Macd 10b); 1690 (Q3; W&M 744); 1694 with imprint reading
"Bentley" (Q4; Fredson Bowers, "Nathaniel Lee: Three Probable Seventeenth-Century Piracies," *PBSA,* XLIV [1950], 62–63); 1694 with imprint
reading "Bently" (Q5; Bowers, *loc. cit.*); and 1699 (Q6; Macd 10d). The
"1691" edition (W&M 745) is a "ghost" (Bowers, p. 62, n. 2). Q2 was set
from a copy of Q1, Q3 from a copy of Q2, and so on, except that Q6 was
set from a copy of Q4. There is no evidence that Dryden was concerned
with any edition after the first.   Therefore the text of the present edition is
taken from the Clark copy of Q1 (*PR3540.R61), without emendation but
with italics and romans reversed. The following copies of the several editions have also been collated: Q1: Huntington (146637), Harvard (*EC65.
L5145.677r), Folger (L865 [2 cop.]); Q2: Clark (*PR3540.A19.1687), Harvard (*EC65.L5145.677rb), Folger (L866); Q3: Clark (*PR3540.R61.1690),
Texas (Aj.L514.677rc), Folger (L867); Q4: Clark (*PR3540.R61.1694), Har-

vard (*EC65.L5145.677rc), Folger (L868); Q5: Northwestern (822.4.L47r), Harvard (*EC65.L5145.B694wa); Q6: Folger (L869).

2 not] Q1–3, Q6; not not Q4–5.   4 Bribe] Q1–4, Q6; Bride Q5.
17 there] Q1–4, Q6; their Q5.   20 ev'n] Q1–4, Q6; even Q5.   30
opprest] Q1; exprest Q2–6.   46 your] Q1, Q4–6; you Q2–3.

Contributions to Ovid's Epistles

The first edition of *Ovid's Epistles* is dated 1680 (O1; Macd 11a), the second, 1681 (O2; Macd 11b), the third, 1683 (O3; two issues with variant imprints but otherwise printed from the same setting of type, Case 165(c)–(d)), the fourth, 1688 (O4; Case 165(e)), and the fifth, 1693 (O5). The preface is signed "J. Dryden" in O1, unsigned in O2–5. O2 was set from a copy of O1, O3 was set from a copy of O2, and so on. There is no evidence that Dryden ever revised his contributions to the collection. Therefore the text of the present edition is taken from the Clark copy of O1 (*PR3421.O96E6), emended at page 109:23, 110:1, 112:8, 113:4, 114:24, 115:10, 115:11, 115:12, 115:22, 115:26, 116:11, 116:20, 116:24, 117:6, 117:25–26, 118:19, 118:32, and 119:9 of the preface, lines 47 and 88 of *Canace,* lines 37, 40, 83, 86, 88, 104, 107, 117, 147, and 247 of *Helen,* and lines 18, 75, 85, 126, and 156 of *Dido.* In the preface italics and romans have been reversed. The following copies of the several editions have also been collated: O1: Folger (O659), Huntington (81888); Harvard (Lo10.544 [2 cop.]); O2: Clark (*PR3421.O96E6.1681), Folger (O660), Harvard (Lo10.544.3); O3 *Case 165(c)*: Folger (O661): O3 *Case 165(d)*: Harvard (Lo10.544.4); O4: Clark (*PR3421.O96E6.1688), Folger (O663), Harvard (Lo10.544.5); O5: Claremont (DR.PR3418.Ov4e(1693)), Folger (O664).

Preface: 109:23 passage] O2–5; *paslage* O1.   110:1 some] O2–5; *ome* O1.   111:1 *Nudam sine*] O1; Sine O2–5.   112:8 *Metamorphoses*] O4–5; Metamorphosis O1–3.   112:16 *relinquere:*] O1–3; ~ . O4–5.   113:4 somewhat] O2–5; *some what* O1.   113:5 *Purpureus*] O1–3; Purpuerus O4–5.   113:23 ad] O1–4; at O5.   113:27 Letters,] O1–3; ~ . O4–5.   114:24 heads:] O3–5; ~ . O1–2.   115:10 *translate, as*] translate. *As* O1–5.   115:11 Rich.] O2–5; ~ₐ O1.   115:12 *Pastor*] *italics of copy text not changed to romans.*   115:22 in] O2–5; *it* O1.   115:26 What] O3–5; *what* O1–2.   116:11 Either] *either* O1–5.   116:20 °Os] O2–4; °Os O1, O5.   116:24 *Imitation.*] O2–5; ~ₐ O1.   117:6 undertaking. To] O2; *undertaking, to* O1; *undertaking; to* O3–5.   117:25–26 disappointed] O2–5; *disapointed* O1.   118:19 unreasonable] O2–5; *unreasonahle* O1.   118:32 Original.] O2–5; ~ , O1.   119: 9 ——*Et quæ*] O2–5; Et quæ—— O1.
  Canace: 9 his] O1–2; the O3–5.   17 Gods] O1–3, O5; God's O4.   38 follow'd] O1–2; ~ ! O3–5.   46 pow'rful] O1–2; powerful

O_3-$_5$.　47 not,] O_3-$_5$; ∼$_\wedge$ O_1-$_2$.　62 ev'n] O_1-$_3$; even O_4-$_5$.　63 Count'nance] O_1-$_3$; Countenance O_4-$_5$.　79 Swath'd,] O_1-$_2$; ∼$_\wedge$ O_3-$_5$. 85 as a] O_1-$_4$; as the O_5.　88 Expos'd,] O_3-$_5$; ∼$_\wedge$ O_1-$_2$.　111 To] O_1-$_3$, O_5; Too O_4.　113 *lets*] O_1-$_4$; *let's* O_5.　115 Too] O_1-$_3$, O_5; To O_4.

Helen: 37 who's] O_2-$_5$; whose's O_1.　40 face,] O_2-$_5$; ∼? O_1. 42 willing] O_1-$_3$, O_5; wiling O_4.　64 or] O_1-$_2$; and O_3-$_5$.　83 fear'd] ∼, O_1-$_5$.　86 thing;] O_3-$_5$; ∼, O_1-$_2$.　88 I] O_2-$_5$; I O_1. 104 Love] ∼, O_1-$_5$.　107 too] O_2-$_5$; to O_1.　117 t'other] O_2-$_5$; to'ther O_1.　147 'em] O_2-$_5$; e'm O_1.　167 possest.] O_1-$_2$; ∼, O_3-$_5$. 190 *Minoian*] O_1-$_3$; *Minonian* O_4-$_5$.　191 Were] O_1-$_2$, O_5; Where O_3-$_4$.　203 Court.] O_1-$_2$; ∼, O_3-$_5$.　247 sweeter] O_2-$_5$; sweter O_1.

Dido: 4 affection] O_1-$_2$; affections O_3-$_5$.　5 what ere] O_1; what e're O_2-$_5$.　6 loose] O_1; lose O_2-$_5$.　7 left,] O_1-$_2$; ∼$_\wedge$ O_3-$_5$.　18 Prince?] O_2-$_5$; ∼. O_1.　47 Heav'ns] O_1-$_4$; Heaven's O_5.　61 There] O_1-$_4$; Their O_5.　72 hair.] O_1; ∼, O_2-$_5$.　73 fall,] O_1-$_3$; ∼; O_4-$_5$.　75 away:] ∼. O_1-$_3$; ∼, O_4-$_5$.　85 *Creüsa*] *Crëusa* O_1; *Creusa* O_2-$_5$.　105 gloomy] O_1-$_2$, O_5; glomy O_3-$_4$.　126 stands,] ∼. O_1-$_5$.　137 one] O_1-$_2$, O_4-$_5$; on O_3.　156 years,] ∼. O_1-$_5$. 164 Conqu'ring] O_1-$_4$; conquering O_5.　178 combine.] O_1-$_2$; ∼, O_3-$_5$.

Prologue to Albumazar

The "Prologue to *Albumazar*" was first published anonymously in 1672, appearing on pages 87–88 of both the first edition (O1) and second edition (O2) of *Covent Garden Drollery* (Macd 54a–b [two issues, the differences not affecting this poem], and Macd 54c). The subsequent printings recorded in the seventeenth century are on pages 279–281 of the first edition (O3) and pages 273–276 of the second edition (O4) of Dryden's *Miscellany Poems*. Macdonald records four issues of the first edition of *Miscellany Poems:* the first is dated 1684 (Macd 42ai); the second, with the first edition of *Sylvæ* appended, and a general title page, *Miscellany Poems, in Two Parts,* is dated 1685 (Macd 43aii); the third, separate, has a new imprint, dated 1688, on a slip pasted over the old (Macd 42aii); the fourth, with *Sylvæ* appended as before, has the 1688 imprint slip pasted on the general title page (see Macd 43aii). Macdonald also records two states of these issues, the second having a cancel quarter sheet in place of 2E2,3 to revise Chetwood's translation of Virgil's eighth Eclogue. None of the variants thus recorded affect our poem. The second edition of *Miscellany Poems* is dated 1692. Macdonald records two issues, differing only in the setting of the imprint (Macd 42bi–ii).

Lawrence (*op. cit.*) records the existence of a manuscript version in Bodleian MS Eng. Poet. e.4, pages 172–173 (M); for a description of the volume in which it occurs, see the textual notes to *To the Lady Castlemaine*, p. 384 above.

The variant readings indicate that O2 is derived from O1, and cannot be the ancestor of the other texts; that O4, undoubtedly printed from O3, is textually identical with it; and that O1, O3–4, and M have a common intermediary. Since we cannot date M within narrow limits, we are not required to take it as the ancestor, and as a matter of fact it may well be a copy of O3–4 that agrees with O1 only by chance. On the other hand, it seems to be generally agreed that a compositor worked from printed copy when he could, and there is nothing in O3 to prevent the assumption that its printer was supplied with a copy of O1 corrected by the author.

Therefore the text of the present edition is taken from the Clark copy of the second issue of O1 (*PR1213.C87), emended in lines 4, 5, 6, 9, 10, 12, 16, 18, 21, 22, 28, 29, 30, 33, 34, 35, 37, 38, 39, 40, 42, 43, 45–46, and 47. The following copies of the several editions have also been collated: O1, *first issue:* Harvard (11445.1*); O2: Folger (C6624B); O3, *first issue, first state:* Folger (D2314, Dobell copy); O3, *first issue, second state:* Clark (*PR3413.Z4M1b [2 cop.]); O3, *third issue, second state:* Clark (*PR3413. Z4M1b.1688); O4, *first issue:* Folger (D2316), Harvard (15437.2.9*); O4, *second issue:* Clark (*PR3413.Z4M1a.1692).

2   pass] O1, O3–4, M; please O2.   4   and when] O3–4, M; and O1–2. 5   *Iohnson* (of those few the best)] O3–4; Johnson of those few the best, M; *Iohnson,* of those few, the best O1; *Iohnson* of those few, the best O2. 6   As . . . master-piece] O3–4, M; And . . . master piece O1–2.   9   we may] O3–4, M; I should O1–2.   10   lik'd the . . . who wore the] O3–4, M; likes my . . . that wears my O1–2.   12   becomes] O3–4, M; became O1–2.   15   does] O1–4; doth M.   16   one] O3–4, M; a O1–2.   18 call;] ~ . O1–4, M.   21   Nay] O3–4, M; Who O1–2.   21   Ceremony] O1–4; Ceremonies M.   22   Muse;] O3–4, M; ~ . O1–2.   26   that] O1–4; the M.   28   strip . . . these] O3–4, M; stript . . . they O1–2. 29   Dare . . . mummeys] O3–4, M; 'Twill . . . mummey O1–2.   30 way:] O3–4; ~ . O1–2; ~ ; M.   33   Such men] O3–4, M; Yet such O1–2. 34   Art,] M; ~ . O1–4.   35   And might, where Theft was prais'd, for Laureats] O3–4, M; Such as in *Sparta* weight for Laurels O1; . . . might for Laurels O2.   37   the] O3–4, M; their O1–2.   37   benefits] O3–4; benefit O1–2, M.   38   *Jack Pudding*] O3–4; *Jack* Pudding O1–2; Jack Pudding M.   39   Whose Dish to challenge, no man] O3–4, M; Where Broth to claim, there's no one O1–2.   39   has] O1–4; hath M.   40 when once h'] O3–4, M; after he O1–2.   42   amiss] O3–4, M; a miss O1–2.   43   thefts] O1–4; Theft M.   43   still] O3–4, M; will O1–2. 45–46   *These lines are not in O1–2.*   47   For . . . you] O3–4, M; Now . . . we O1–2.   48   These] O1–4; Those M.

Prologue to Witt without Money

The Prologue to *Witt without Money* was first published anonymously in 1672. It appeared on pages 8–9 of the first edition of *Westminster Drollery,*

The Second Part (O1; Macd 52 [two issues with variant title pages are recorded, Case 150(2)(a)–(b)]); on pages 9–10 of the second edition, entitled *The Last, and now Only Compleat Collection, of the Newest and Choisest Songs and Poems, that are now Extant both at Courts Theatres and elsewhere* (O2; W. C. Hazlitt, *Hand-book of the Literature of Great Britain,* London, 1867, p. 168); on page 11 of the first edition of *Covent Garden Drollery* (O3; Macd 54a–b [two issues, the differences not affecting this poem]); and on pages 10–11 of the second edition (O4; Macd 54c). Only lines 1–22 appear in O3. The full title in all these printings of 1672 is "The Prologue to Witt without money: being the first Play acted after the Fire."

The other recorded seventeenth-century printings are on pages 283–284 of the first edition (O5), and on pages 277–279 of the second edition (O6) of Dryden's *Miscellany Poems;* for the various issues and states of these editions, see the textual notes to the Prologue to *Albumazar,* above. Here the lines are entitled, "Prologue Spoken the first day of the King's House Acting after the Fire. Writ by Mr. Dryden."

Macdonald also records the existence of two manuscript versions of the prologue, one in British Museum MS Sloane 4455, folio 26*v* (M1) and one in Bodleian MS Eng. Poet. e.4., page 175 (M2). For a description of the Bodelian volume see the textual notes to *To the Lady Castlemaine,* p. 384 above. The British Museum volume is made up "probably of several 17th and early 18th century commonplace books, which have been broken up and the leaves guarded. . . . The Dryden Prologue occurs among material written in a late 17th century hand" (letter from C. E. Wright, Assistant Keeper of the Manuscripts, British Museum). In M1 the lines have the title: "The Prologue of ye Play entitled Witt with out money—Spoken at the Dukes old Theatre (after the Kings was burnt) by the King's players. Feb. 26. 1671. The Curtaine being drawne up all the Acto^{r}s were discover'd on the stage in Melancholick postures & Moone [i.e., Michael Mohun, the actor] advancing before the rest speaks as follows, addressing himself chiefly to ye King then p^{r}sent." In M2 the lines are followed by "John Dryden," and have to the left of the last couplet the notation, "To the King."

The variant readings indicate that O2, certainly printed from O1, is textually identical with it except for the correction of one obvious error; that O3 derives from O1–2, and that O4 derives partly from O3, which lacks the last eight lines, and partly from some other source; that O6, certainly printed from O5, is textually identical with it; that M1 and M2 have a common intermediary; and that this intermediary has a common intermediary between it and O1–2 and O5–6. Since we cannot date the manuscripts accurately with relation to the printed texts, we are not required to take one of them as the copy text; on the other hand, there is nothing to prevent the assumption that O5 was printed from a copy of O1 or O2 corrected by the author. It is possible that M1 or M2 preserves authoritative readings that were overlooked or rejected in preparing the copy for O5, but the present text is taken simply from the Clark copy of the first issue of O1 (*PR1209.W532.1674), emended from O5 in lines 2, 4, 9, 10, 12, 18, 23, 24, and 25.

The following additional copies of the several editions have also been collated: O1, *second issue:* Harvard (*EC65.A100.671w); O2: Folger (L472); O3, *first issue:* Harvard (11445.1*); O3, *second issue:* Clark (*PR1213.C87); O4: Folger (C6624B); O5, *first issue, first state:* Folger (D2314, Dobell copy); O5, *first issue, second state:* Clark (*PR3413.Z4M1b [2 cop.]); O5, *third issue, second state:* Clark (*PR3413.Z4M1b.1688); O6, *first issue:* Folger (D2316), Harvard (15437.2.9*); O6, *second issue:* Clark (*PR3413.Z4M1a. 1692).

1 escape] O1–6, M1; escape't M2. 2 on the] O5–6, M1–2; on O1–4. 2 Beach] O1–6, M2; breach M1. 3 o're] O1–6, M1; ore M2. 4 on] O5–6, M1–2; from O1–4. 5 From that . . . must wait for] O1–6, M1; In this . . . expect our M2. 6 Whence even . . . forc't by] O1–4; Whence ev'n . . . O5–6, M1; From which . . . ev'n for M2. 7 does] O1–6, M1; doth M2. 8 But . . . before] O1–6, M1; What . . . till now M2. 9 are chang'd too] O4–6; are chang'd to O1–3; too are changed M1–2. 10 for] O5–6, M1–2; of O1–4. 11 furnish] O1–6, M1; furnisht M2. 12 While] O5–6, Whilst O1–4, M1–2. 12 the guests] O5–6, M1–2; our guests O1–4. 13 *Of*] O1–6, M1; For M2. 13 *besides*] O1–4, M2; *beside* O5–6, M1. 13 had] O1–6; took M1–2. 15 '*Tis*] O1–6; That's M1; It's M2. 16 You cherisht it, & now its fall] O1–2, O5–6, M1; . . . cherish . . . O3–4; Heroick souls! With pity that M2. 18 that fire] O4–6, M1–2; the fire O1–3. 19 furious] O1–6; publick M1–2. 22 *Fate contrives*] O1–6, M2; fates contrive M1. 23–30 *These lines omitted from O3.* 23 great] O1–2, O4–6, M1; fam'd M2. 23 does farr] O5–6, M1; does so O4; doth farr O1–2, M2. 24 equals] O2, O4–6, M1–2; equald O1. 25 does] O4–6, M1; doth O1–2, M2.

Prologue for the Women

The "Prologue for the Women, when they Acted at the Old Theatre in Lincoln's-Inn-Fields" was first printed on pages 285–286 of the first edition (O1) and reprinted on pages 279–280 of the second edition (O2) of Dryden's *Miscellany Poems;* for the various issues and states of these editions see the textual notes to the Prologue to *Albumazar,* p. 390 above. There is no evidence that Dryden corrected the text for the second edition. Therefore the text of the present edition is taken from one of the Clark copies of the second state of the first issue of O1 (*PR3413.Z4M1b [cop. 1]), emended in lines 1 and 6. The following additional copies of the several editions have been collated: O1, *first issue, first state:* Folger (D2314, Dobell copy); O1, *first issue, second state:* Clark (*PR3413.Z4M1b [cop. 2]); O1, *third issue, second state:* Clark (*PR3413.Z4M1b.1688); O2, *first issue:* Folger (D2316), Harvard (15437.2.9*); O2, *second issue:* Clark (*PR3413.Z4M1a.1692).

1 Were] Where O1–2. 6 wonted] wanted O1–2.

Prologue to Arviragus *Reviv'd*

The "Prologue to *Arviragus* Reviv'd: Spoken by Mr. Hart" was first printed on pages 281–283 of the first edition (O1) and reprinted on pages 276–277 of the second edition (O2) of Dryden's *Miscellany Poems;* for the various issues and states of these editions see the textual notes to the Prologue to *Albumazar,* p. 390 above. There is no evidence that Dryden corrected the text for the second edition. Therefore the text in the present edition has been taken from one of the Clark copies of the second state of the first issue of O1 (*PR3413.Z4M1b [cop. 1]), emended in lines 6, 8, and 16. For the additional copies of the several editions collated, see the textual notes to the Prologue for the Women, above.

6 delight,] ~ . O1–2.   8 ˙Play,] ~ . O1–2.   16 Breeding,] ~ . O1–2.

Prologue and Epilogue to the University of Oxon. [1673]

The "Prologue, to the University of Oxon. Spoken by Mr. Hart, at the Acting of the *Silent Woman,*" and the "Epilogue, Spoken by the same," were first printed respectively on pages 263–265 and 265–267 of the first edition of Dryden's *Miscellany Poems* (O1) and were reprinted on pages 260–262 and 262–264 of the second edition of the same collection (O2); for the various issues and states of these editions see the textual notes to the Prologue to *Albumazar,* p. 390 above. There is no evidence that Dryden revised the text for the second edition. Lawrence (*op. cit.*) records the existence of a manuscript version of each piece in Bodleian MS Rawl. Poet. 19, "a manuscript volume of seventeenth century miscellanea in more than one hand," on folios 149r–v and 152r–v, respectively (M). M may derive from O1 or independently from the lost original; there is nothing to prove that it embodies any authoritative variants. Therefore the text of the present edition has been taken from one of the Clark copies of the second state of the first issue of O1 (*PR3413.Z4M1b [cop. 1]), emended in line 40 of the prologue. For the additional copies of the several editions collated see the textual notes to the Prologue for the Women, p. 393 above.

Prologue: 7 is this of] O1–2; it is at M.   13 the] O1–2; that M. 20 Follies and Faults] O1–2; Follyes M.   22 Th'] O1–2; The M.   24 where] O1–2; whence M.   25 th' Anatomy] O1–2; ye Anatomies M. 28 Poetry] O1–2; Poesy M.   34 And] O1–2; Which M.   39 wish it rather] O1–2; rather wish it M.   40 *Prætorian*] O2, M; *Prætorian* O1. 41 this] O1, M; the O2.

Epilogue: 2 haste . . . draw] O1–2; speed . . . are M. 4 th']
O1–2; yᵉ M. 8 those . . . too] O1–2; these . . . to M. 9 Cost]
O1–2; costs M. 11 Th'] O1–2; The M. 13 Humours] O1–2; Humour M. 14 two] O1–2; to M. 15 *Scaramoucha*] O1–2; Skara-
mouch M. 21 But when all] O1–2; When all this M. 23 Light-
ning] O1–2; lightening M. 31 *Johnson*] O1–2; Johnsons M. 32
Wit] O1–2; Wit's M. 34 By] O1–2; To M. 36 their] O1–2; the M.

Prologue and Epilogue Spoken at the Opening of the New House

"A Prologue spoken at the Opening of the New House, Mar. 26. 1674,"
and the corresponding "Epilogue," were first printed respectively on pages
286–289 and 289–291 of the first edition of Dryden's *Miscellany Poems* (O1)
and were reprinted on pages 281–284 and 284–286 of the second edition of
the same collection (O2); for the various issues and states of these editions
see the textual notes to the Prologue to *Albumazar*, p. 390 above. There is
no evidence that Dryden corrected the text for the second edition. There
is a manuscript version of each piece in the Huntington Library (Ellesmere
MS vol. 129, items 8923 and 8925 respectively; cited below as M) bound in a
miscellaneous collection of seventeenth-century manuscripts. They may
derive from O1 or independently from the lost original; there is no evidence
that any of the numerous variants in them is authoritative, although some
of the readings are more correct than those in O1 and O2. Therefore
the text of the present edition is taken from one of the Clark copies of the
second state of the first issue of O1 (*PR3413.Z4M1b [cop. 1]), emended in
lines 18 and 35 of the prologue and 7 and 30 of the epilogue. For the additional copies of the several editions collated see the textual notes to the
Prologue for the Women, p. 393 above.

Prologue: 3 fal'n] O1–2; fallen M. 8 the . . . Room] O1–2; our
. . . roofe M. 11 than] O1–2; then M. 18 Live:] M; ~ . O1–2.
21 th'] O1–2; yᵉ M. 26 Th'] O1–2; the M. 35 To] O1–2; or M.
35 Plays,] M; ~ . O1–2. 36 Whilst] O1–2; While M. 41 these
. . . Conqu'rors] O1–2; those . . . Conquerers M. 42 than] O1–2;
then M. 43 in your] O1–2; in their M. 46 *Ben*] O1–2; bon M.
49 prophesie] O1–2; prophecy M. 50 over-rate] O1–2; venerate M.
53 Machines and Tempests] O1–2; Tempests and Operas M.
Epilogue: 1 was] O1–2; were M. 3 that] O1–2; wᶜʰ M. 7
thro'] M; tho' O1–2. 8 white] O1–2; shock M. 11 like the] O1,
M; like O2. 16 th'] O1–2; yᵉ M. 18 train] O1–2; braine M. 20
Batt'ries] O1–2; batteries M. 24 rail] O1–2; ~ , M. 30 abroad;]
M; ~ . O1–2. 32 Rhyme] O1–2; ryhmes M. 32 than] O1–2; then
M. 34 their] O1–2; yᵉ M. 36 w' have] O1–2; wee'v' M. 37

we'l . . . who] O1–2; wee . . . that M.   39 frisking] O1–2; dancing M.
40 at] O1–2; in M.

Prologue and Epilogue to the University of Oxford, 1674

The "Prologue, to the University of Oxford, 1674. Spoken by Mr. Hart," and the corresponding epilogue, were first printed respectively on pages 267–269 and 269–271 of the first edition of Dryden's *Miscellany Poems* (O1), in which the epilogue appears a second time on pages 275–277 (O1a); they were reprinted on pages 264–265 and 265–268 of the second edition of the same collection (O2). For the various issues and states of these editions see the textual notes to the Prologue to *Albumazar*, p. 390 above. There is no evidence that Dryden ever revised the text of the prologue. The text of the epilogue on pages 269–271 of the first edition and the title as given on page 275 are presumably the more correct in each instance, for the version in the second edition combines the two. The title on page 269 of the first edition reads, "Epilogue, Spoken by Mrs. Boutell. Written by Mr. Dryden," that on page 275, "Epilogue to Oxford: Spoken by Mrs. Marshall, Writ by Mr. Dryden." Therefore the text of the present edition is taken from pages 267–271 of one of the Clark copies of the second state of the first issue of O1 (*PR3413.Z4M1b [cop. 1]), emended in the punctuation of lines 20 and 33 of the prologue and 18 and 20 of the epilogue. Possibly line 16 of the prologue should end with a comma or semicolon. For the additional copies of the several editions collated see the textual notes to the Prologue for the Women, p. 393 above.

Prologue: 20 Wit,] ∼. O1–2.   33 Wit,] ∼. O1–2.
Epilogue: 4 sought for] O1, O2; here sought O1a.   10 possess,] O1, O2; ∼? O1a.   12 know?] O1, O2; ∼. O1a.   14 last,] O1, O2; ∼. O1a.   17 reverence] O1, O2; Rev'rence O1a.   18 owe;] ∼. O1, O1a, O2.   20 serv'd:] O2; ∼, O1 ∼. O1a.   25 Whose] O1, O2; Where O1a.

Epilogue to The Man of Mode

The Epilogue to *The Man of Mode* was first printed in the first edition of the play, 1676 (Q1; Macd 110a), and reprinted in the editions of 1684 (Q2; W&M 552–553 [two issues, the differences not affecting the epilogue]) and 1693 (Q3; Macd 110c). The type for Q2 was set from a copy of Q1, the type for Q3 from a copy of Q2. There is no evidence that Dryden revised the text after its first printing.

Macdonald records three manuscript versions of the epilogue, British Museum MSS Sloane 203, folio 95*r* (M1), and Sloane 1458, folio 23*r* (M2), and Bodleian MS Don. b. 8, pages 558–559 (M3). M1 is in a volume of "medical and other collections ranging in date from 1640–1690, of Dr. John Downes, M.D., Physician to St. Bartholomew's and Christ's Hospitals" (letter from C. E. Wright). Willard Thorp has described the volume in which M2 occurs as follows: "The manuscript consists of poetical pieces and extracts collected by Richard Enock . . . [and] bears the date 1677, with his signature, on the first page" (*RES*, IX [1933], 199). George Thorn-Drury has described the volume in which M3 occurs as "a large folio MS. book, containing some seven hundred pages, . . . compiled by Sir William Haward" (*RES*, I [1925], 325). In M2, the lines are headed, "The Epilogue written by Mr Dryden and spoken by Smith or S^r ffopling."

The variant readings indicate that Q1–3 are textually identical, and that there is an intermediary between Q1–3, M1, and M2–3, the connection to the two latter being through another intermediary. Considering the nature of the collections in which the manuscript versions are found, it is most unlikely that any is an ancestor of the printed text: M1 may well be a descendant; M2 and M3 give some evidence of being collaterals, and it has been argued that they preserve authoritative readings that were rejected or overlooked when Q1 came to be printed. Thorp argued that the order of lines in M2 is nearer than any other version "to what its author originally intended" (*op. cit.*, p. 198). Thorn-Drury (*op. cit.*, p. 325) urged "serious consideration" of the readings of M3 in lines 6 and 10, and H. F. B. Brett-Smith took them into his text in *The Dramatic Works of Sir George Etherege* (Oxford, 1927, II, 288). They have not been taken into the present text. Brett-Smith said of the additional couplet found in M3 (and M2), "This hit at Buckingham is obviously authentic, but as it was suppressed in the editions I have not replaced it in the text" (*op. cit.*, II, 294). Thorp and Thorn-Drury took the couplet to be a humorous reference by Dryden to himself. The couplet has been omitted from the present text.

The text of the present edition has been taken from the Clark copy of Q1 (*PR3432.M21), emended in the punctuation of line 8 and with the use of italics and romans reversed. The following additional copies of the several editions have also been collated: Q1: Folger (E3374), Texas (Wj. Et36.676m), Harvard (*EC65.Et363.676m); Q2, *W&M* 552: Clark (*PR3432. M21.1684); Q2, *W&M* 553: Folger (E3375), Harvard (*EC65.Et363. 676mb(A)); Q3: Clark (*PR3432.M21.1693), Folger (E3376), Harvard (*EC65.Et363.676mc).

1 shown,] Q1–3, M3; ~∧ M1; ~ . M2.   2 seem'd] Q1–3, M2–3; seem M1.   2 heav'ns] Q1–3; heavens M1–3.   3 Those] Q1–3; Such M2; These M1, M3.   6 they] Q1–3, M1; hee M2; it M3.   8 Wit:] ~ . Q1–3, M2; ~∧ M1; ~ , M3.   10 I vow] Q1–3, M1–2; I, now M3.   12 *After this line M2 has two others:* Labouring to putt in more as Mr Bayes / Thrums in Additions to his ten yeares playes.   14 file] Q1–3, M1, M3; fill M2.   14 God-a'mighty's] Q1–3, M1, M3; God Almighty, M2.   14

fool] Q1–3, M1–2; Toole M3. 14 *After this line M3 has two others:* Labour, to put in more, as Master Bayes / Thrumms in Additions to his ten-yeares playes. 15–16 *In M2 these lines follow the line here numbered 20.* 22 taught the] Q1–3, M2–3; taught a M1. 23–24 *In M2 these lines follow the line here numbered 30.* 24 he] Q1–3, M2–3; that M1. 25–26 *Omitted from M2.* 26 nor touch of Hat] Q1–3, M1; nor Hatt M3. 28 a shog] Q1–3, M1; the shog M2; one shogg M3. 30 a] Q1–3, M1; his M2–3. 32 took . . . who] Q1–3, M1; takes . . . that M2–3. 33 man] Q1–3, M1, M3; one M2. 34 For] Q1–3, M1, M3; And M2.

Prologue to the University of Oxford [1676]

This "Prologue to the University of Oxford" was first printed on pages 273–275 of the first edition of Dryden's *Miscellany Poems* (O1) and reprinted on pages 270–272 of the second edition of the same collection (O2); for the various issues and states of these editions see the textual notes to the Prologue to *Albumazar*, p. 390 above. There is no evidence that Dryden corrected the text for the second edition. A manuscript version of the prologue in Bodleian MS Eng. Poet. e.4, pages 178–179 (M), is titled "A Prologue to the University of Oxford at the Act 1676; by his Majesties Servants"; for a description of the volume in which it occurs, see the textual notes to *To the Lady Castlemaine*, p. 384 above. M may derive from O1 or from O2, or independently from the lost original; there is no evidence that the numerous variant readings in it are authoritative. Therefore the text of the present edition is taken from one of the Clark copies of the second state of the first issue of O1 (*PR3413.Z4M1b [cop. 1]), emended in the punctuation of line 30. It is possible that line 8 should also end with a comma. For the additional copies of the several editions collated see the textual notes to the Prologue for the Women, p. 393 above.

2 we] O1–2; they M. 10 th' Applause] O1–2; applause M. 13 that . . . does] O1–2; the . . . doth M. 15 and] O1–2; or M. 23 too] O1–2; to M. 25 But] O1–2; Now M. 26 by each] O1–2; and each M. 27 Wit, which] O1–2; him, who M. 29 Adoption] O1–2; Adoptions M. 30 *Rome;*] M; ∼. O1–2. 32 your] O1–2; the M. 33 those Hopes] O1–2; his hopes M.

Prologue to Circe, *and an Epilogue*

The Prologue to *Circe* was first printed in the first edition of the play, 1677 (Q1; Macd 111a), and reprinted in the second edition, 1685 (Q2; Macd 111b). The first ten lines appeared as the first ten lines of "An Epilogue. Written by Mr. Dryden" on pages 291–293 of the first edition of Dryden's

Miscellany Poems, 1684 (O1) and on pages 286–287 of the second edition of the same collection, 1692 (O2). For the various issues and states of these editions of *Miscellany Poems,* see the textual notes to the Prologue to *Albumazar,* p. 390 above. Dryden seems not to have revised either the prologue or the epilogue after their first printings. Therefore, in the present edition, the prologue has been printed from the Clark copy of Q1 (*PR3397.D2C5), emended in line 34 and with the use of italics and romans reversed, and the epilogue from one of the Clark copies of the second state of the first issue of O1 (*PR3413.Z4M1b [cop. 1]), emended in lines 10, 12, 15, 24, and 25. The emendation adopted in line 24 was suggested by W. A. Wright to W. D. Christie (Dryden, *Poetical Works,* ed. Christie, London, 1911, p. xiii). The following additional copies of *Circe* have been collated: Q1: Folger (D 302 [3 cop.]); Q2: Folger (D 303 [2 cop.]), Texas (Aj.D272. 677cb). For the additional copies of *Miscellany Poems* collated see the textual notes to the Prologue for the Women, p. 393 above.

Prologue: 29 you,] Q1; ~ . Q2. 34 hands.] Q2; ~ , Q1.
Epilogue: 10 Youth] O2; Yonth O1. 12 write,] ~ . O1–2. 15
Slighted] slighted O1–2. 24 sterv'd] stew'd O1–2. 25 praise,] ~ .
O1–2.

Epilogue to Mithridates

The Epilogue to *Mithridates* was first printed in the first edition of the play, 1678 (Q1; Macd 112a), and reprinted in the second and third editions, 1685 (Q2; W&M 736–737 [two issues with variant imprint]) and 1693 (Q3; Macd 112c). The 1697 edition recorded by Macdonald appears to be a bibliographical ghost. The type for Q2 was set from a copy of Q1, the type for Q3 from a copy of Q2. Dryden does not seem to have revised the text after its first printing. Therefore the text of the present edition is taken from the Clark copy of Q1 (*PR3540.M61), without emendation but with the use of italics and romans reversed. The following additional copies of the several editions have been collated: Q1: Folger (L854 [2 cop.]), Harvard (*EC65. L5145.678m); Q2, *W&M 736:* Clark (*PR3540.A19.1687), Folger (L855 [2 cop.]); Q2, *W&M 737:* Huntington (146633); Q3: Folger (L856 [3 cop.], Harvard (15484.12.3*).

11 Is] Q1; *'Tis* Q2–3. 21 but] Q1–2; *hut* Q3.

Prologue to A True Widow

The Prologue to *A True Widow* was first printed in the first edition of the play, 1679, which was subsequently reissued with a cancel title page dated 1689 (Q1; Macd 113a–b). The publisher of the second issue, James Knapton, transferred the prologue to another of his publications, Aphra Behn's *The Widdow Ranter,* 1690 (Q2; Macd 122). Dryden had written a different prologue and an epilogue for *The Widdow Ranter,* but these were the property of Jacob Tonson, who had published them separately in 1689. The text of the Prologue to *A True Widow* in the present edition is taken from the Clark copy of the first issue of Q1 (*PR3671.S8A1, v. 2), emended in line 22 (the exclamation points in lines 23 and 31 seem intended to mark emphatic expression) and with the use of romans and italics reversed. The following additional copies of the several plays have been collated: Q1, *first issue:* Folger (S2881 [2 cop.]); Q1, *second issue:* Folger (S2882); Q2: Clark (*PR3317.W61), Folger (B1774).

9 Cruse] Q1; *Cause* Q2.   12 Poll] Q1; *Pole* Q2.   20 than] Q1; *then* Q2.   22 increas'd.] ~ₐ Q1–2.

Prologue at Oxford, 1680 [1679]

The later form of this prologue was the first to be printed, in the 1681 edition of Nathaniel Lee's *Sophonisba,* at the end of the play, and with the title "Prologue to the University of Oxford" (Q1; Macd 117a). Subsequent editions of *Sophonisba,* in which the prologue continued to be printed at the end of the play, are dated 1685 (Q2; Macd 117b); 1691 (Q3; W&M 752–753 [two issues with variant imprints]); 1693 (Q4; [two issues with variant imprints, "For Tho. Chapman" (Macd 117d) and "For R. Bentley"]); 1697, with "Theatre-Royal" (hyphen) on the title page (Q5); and 1697, with "Theatre Royal" (no hyphen) on the title page (Q6; Bowers, "Nathaniel Lee: Three Probable Seventeenth-Century Piracies," *PBSA,* XLIV [1950], 64). The text of Q2 was set from a copy of Q1, the text of Q3 from a copy of Q2, and so on.

The earlier form was first printed on pages 277–278 of the first edition of Dryden's *Miscellany Poems* (O1) and reprinted therefrom on pages 272–273 of the second edition of the same collection (O2). For the various editions, issues and states of *Miscellany Poems* see the textual notes to the Prologue to *Albumazar,* p. 390 above. Here the prologue is entitled "The Prologue at Oxford, 1680." In the present edition, the text is taken from one of the Clark copies of the second state of the first issue of O1 (*PR3413. Z4M1b [cop. 1]), emended in lines 4 and 12. The following copies of the various issues and editions of *Sophonisba* have been collated: Q1: Clark (*PR3540.S71.1681), Folger (L871), Harvard (*EC65.L5145.676sb); Q2: Clark (*PR3540.A19.1687); Q3, W&M 752: Clark (*PR3540.S71.1691); Q3, W&M 753: Clark (*PR3540.S71.1691a); Folger (L873); Q4, *Chapman:* Folger (L875); Q4, *Bentley:* Folger (L875A); Q5: Folger (L880), Harvard (15484.6*); Q6: Clark (*PR3540.S71.1697), Cornell (2711.L46.so). For the additional copies of *Miscellany Poems* collated see the textual notes to the Prologue for the Women, p. 393 above.

2 from] O1–2; *in* Q1–6.   4 *Plaustris*] Plaustris O1–2, Q1–6.   6
that] O1–2; *e're* Q1–6.   11 few] O1–2; *some* Q1–6.   11 goes] O1–2,
Q6; *go* Q1–5.   12 shall] O1–2; *will* Q1–6.   12 Throne,] Q1–6; ~ .
O1–2.   17–18 *omitted from Q1–6.*   19 scape] O1–2; *want* Q1–6.
20 Ev'n] O1–2; *Even* Q1–6.   21–24 *omitted from Q1–6.*   25 *Scot,
Swarez, Tom of Aquin, must*] O1–2; Occam, Dun, Scotus [*sic*] *must, though
learn'd,* Q1–6.   27 *Aristotle's*] O1–2; Aristotle Q1–6.   30 then be
prov'd] O1–2; *thence be call'd* Q1–6.   30 Inspiration.] *Q1–6 continue
with the following lines:*

> Your wiser Judgments farther penetrate,
> Who late found out one Tare amongst the Wheat.
> This is our comfort, none e're cry'd us down,
> But who dislik'd both Bishop and a Crown.

Prologue to Caesar Borgia

The Prologue to *Caesar Borgia* was first printed anonymously in the first
edition of the play, dated 1680 but advertised in the *Term Catalogue* for
November 1679 (Arber ed., I, 370). There are two issues of this edition, the
former with a longer dedication than the latter; in the first (Q1), Dryden's
prologue is anonymous and a word is missing in line 33; in the second (Q2),
Dryden's name appears in the caption and line 33 is corrected, but the type
is otherwise undisturbed. The second edition of *Caesar Borgia* is dated 1696
(Q3; Macd 114b). No copy of a 1679 edition (W&M 727) has been found
(Fredson Bowers, *A Supplement to the Woodward & McManaway Check
List*, Charlottesville, Virginia, 1949, p. 7).

The type for Q3 was set from a copy of Q2. There is no evidence that
Dryden corrected the text for Q3. Therefore the text of the present edi-
tion is taken from one of the Clark copies of Q2 (*PR3540.C11), emended
in the spelling of line 25 and with the use of italics and romans reversed.
The following additional copies of the several editions and issues have also
been collated: Q1: Folger (L846A); Q2: Clark (*PR3540.A19.1687), Folger
(L846), Harvard (*EC65.L5145.680c(A)); Q3: Clark (*PR3540.C11.1696),
Folger (L847), Harvard (15484.6*).

9 swarms,] Q1–2; ~∧ Q3.   25 hum and] Q3; hum aud Q1–2.   33
show you] Q2–3; show Q1.

Prologue to The Loyal General

The Prologue to *The Loyal General* was printed only once in the seventeenth century, in the first edition of the play, 1680 (Macd 115). Dryden
seems never to have revised the text, which was first reprinted in the 1702

edition of *Miscellany Poems*. The text in the present edition is taken from the Clark copy of the 1680 edition (*PR3729.T1L9), without emendation but with the use of romans and italics reversed. The following copies of this edition have also been collated: Folger (T193), Texas (Wj.T188.68ol), Harvard (*EC65.T1878.68ol).

Prologue to the University of Oxford [1680]

This "Prologue to the University of Oxford" was first printed in the first edition of Dryden's *Miscellany Poems* (O1) on pages 271–272, and reprinted on pages 268–269 of the second edition of the same collection (O2); for the various issues and states of these editions see the textual notes to the Prologue to *Albumazar*, p. 390 above. There is no evidence that Dryden revised the text after the first edition. The text of the present edition is taken from one of the Clark copies of the second state of the first issue of O1 (*PR3413.Z4M1b [cop. 1]), emended in lines 26 and 30. For the additional copies of the several editions collated see the textual notes to the Prologue for the Women, p. 393 above.

26 Tribe?] ~ . O1–2.　　30 Massacre;] ~ . O1–2.

INDEX TO THE COMMENTARY

Names

Topics